More More France Please

Please

Helena Frith Powell

www.helenafrithpowell.com

GIBSON SQUARE
LONDON

For Julia

Other books by Helena Frith Powell

Ciao Bella, 2007
Two Lipsticks & a Lover, 2006

This edition first published in 2007 by

Gibson Square
47 Lonsdale Square
London N1 1EW
UK

UK Tel: ++44 (0)20 7096 1100
Fax: ++44 (0)20 7993 2214

US Tel: ++1 646 216 9813
Fax: ++1 646 216 9488

Eire Tel: ++353 (0)1 657 1057

info@gibsonsquare.com
www.gibsonsquare.com

ISBN 9 7 8 1 9 0 3 9 3 3 7 7 0 (1 9 0 3 9 3 3 7 3 3)
Previously published in 2005 (printed four times)

Printed by Clays Ltd

Index

Acknowledgements

A huge thank you to John Witherow and Carey Scott at the *Sunday Times* for giving the go-ahead for the French Mistress column, which was the catalyst for this book, as well as to Peter Conradi. Also to Karen Robinson for coming up with the name. Masses of thanks to all the people that feature in the book. I have been hugely impressed and touched by the amount of time people have been prepared to give to me and how open they have been with their stories. Thank you to Jaqcues Kuhnlé for reading through it all and correcting both my French and my English. Thanks to my friend Jonathan Miller for his brilliant editing and ceaseless enthusiasm. Also many thanks to the witty and wonderful Carla McKay for coming up with hundreds of titles and listening to me drone on for hours, something that is unlikely to change. I am eternally indebted to Peter and Dominique Glynn-Smith for bringing us to France in the first place. I dread to think how dull our lives might have been if it hadn't been for that chance meeting with you. Thanks also to Martin Rynja, my publisher, for coming up with the idea for the book and his exceptional support throughout the process. I am indebted to Dawn Alderson at Russell-Cooke Solicitors, Bill Blevins at Blevins Franks International and John Siddall Financial Services for all their invaluable professional help. Finally a huge thank you to my lovely husband Rupert who always was, and always will be, my favourite editor.

Foreword

Since I wrote the first edition of this book, I still can't believe how lucky I am to be living in France with my family of seven. It is paradise here and I would advise anyone to pack their bags and move over immediately!

But just a word of caution. Think very carefully about how you're going to survive once here. When we moved we were pursuing our dream without having given it much thought. In fact, we were not prepared in the slightest. We didn't have to be. Property prices were negligible compared to England and we could (just about) ride out the bad patches on the mortgage payments thanks to skilful acrobatics with credit cards. But even for us, it remains not at all *simple comme bonjour.*

Although they still have a long way to go, property prices all over France are now catching up with those in the UK. It is no longer possible to sell a two-up two-down in Birmingham, buy a château in the Dordogne and still have enough left over to live off for ten years. You can still pursue your dream, but it is more difficult than ever to come to France with no preparation except the vague idea that you'll figure that one out once your settled.

I know of one family who moved to Limousin just over a year ago. They have four children, two boys and two girls. The mother is French and was fed up with life in Kent. They sold up on a whim and bought a larger house than they could afford in Kent, thinking they would fine because it would be easy for her to find work right away. They tried various things such as work for a British-run estate agent that allows people to set up franchises. It didn't work out. Nine months later the husband started commuting back to Kent to work. Three months later they realised the family would fall apart if they were separated all week and his wife and children are now also back in Tunbridge Wells. They haven't given up hope, though, and are hanging on to their house in France in the hope that one day they can come return to their idyllic life.

Another couple I know came here with a lot of money in the bank, having sold a very successful retail business in the UK. They bought a vineyard in the South of France and started to make wine. This was five years ago. Now they, too, are back in the UK and their beloved vineyard is on the market. They were quite successful but just didn't make enough money from selling the wine to service the overheads. The original fortune was quickly spent renovating their house and building the winery.

So the lesson is simple. By all means go for it, but be thoroughly prepared! I hope this new updated edition will help you to be just that. With some armchair emigration and time to think about your plans before you leave you will hopefully be able to avoid a few costly mistakes on your way to an ideal life in France.

Helena Frith Powell
Sainte Cécile
France
April 2007

Bon Voyage!

This is the book I wish I could have read before I moved to France. I hardly knew the country at all, and knew nothing of how to live there. I was carried away by the whole adventure of it. Going to a new place, a strange language, a different culture. I was fed up with living in a small village in Sussex where the pub was the focal point of life. I was tired of getting on smelly trains up to London most mornings and horrified at the prospect of spending everything I ever earned on school fees. Even if France wasn't the answer, it had to be better than where we were.

But why did we pick France? France is the country that has everything: the most romantic city in the world, great food, fine wines, two skiing areas, great beaches, endless countryside, trains that run and roads that let you drive. But above all, it is as far south as you can go before things get strange. I would not dream of living full-time in Italy. I remember too vividly the hassle my aunt endured when she owned a house on the Amalfi coast. And even though the weather is better in the south of Spain, I just don't feel comfortable there; neither in the British enclaves, nor in the parts reserved for the Spanish. Spain has the air of having been half-built by a Moroccan in a hurry. France feels solid. British buyers are considering buying houses in more exotic locations—Morocco,

Croatia, Thailand. Yet what would I do if anything went wrong? How happy would I feel with this culture? How would I understand the language, laws and customs?

Britain has had a relationship with France for more than a thousand years, even if most of the time we have been enemies. But we are more like members of a family who always argue at Christmas. When I lived in Germany, *that* felt really strange. People would stop me when I was driving and tell me to turn on my lights. At street crossings, nobody moves until the little green man tells them to. All this felt very alien. In contrast, France feels familiar. Many of the words are similar; the people are courteous, even if sometimes difficult. There is a bad bureaucracy, but it is a bureaucracy that works. France is both familiar and foreign, I thought.

In retrospect I was naïve. We showed up in an isolated house, with a water system supplied by a spring, an electricity current that kept going off, all the while speaking only a few words of the language. In addition, I was about to give birth to our second child. It is only through good luck that things didn't go horribly wrong for us.

What I have tried to do here is to cover the topics that are essential if you are to make a success of living in France. I have had the help of many others who have been very kind in sharing their success and failure with me. Things that I wish I had known before we moved and things I found out through (sometimes) bitter experience.

If a second house or new life in France isn't yet an option for you, I hope this book will give an idea of the exhilaration and challenges that are involved in moving abroad. There is nothing wrong with a bit of armchair emigration—there are certainly fewer forms to fill in!

Helena Frith Powell
Sainte Cécile
Languedoc

1
Languewhat?

I had never thought about living in France until my husband came back from a press trip to Thailand. Before he had unpacked the suitcases, he told me we were moving there. I ignored him.

'I met a couple on a boat,' he said. 'I want to go there and write a book.'

'Don't be ridiculous,' I said. 'Things aren't that bad.'

'They live in the Languedoc. It's in the south.'

'The what-e-doc?' I said. 'Never heard of it.'

To me the south of France was Cap d'Antibes, Juan-les-Pins, Monte Carlo. Beautiful people, vast yachts and rocky beaches. Good for a holiday, but not a place to live and bring up children.

At the time we were living in Sussex in a converted printing press. We had just finished doing it up, a job that had taken almost two years. Rupert, my husband, worked for a newspaper. I was working freelance as a journalist, as well as headhunting for media companies. I had been living in England almost all my life and felt at home there. I couldn't imagine a life without Marks & Spencer, thatched cottages or muddy country walks.

Nothing more was said about moving until a letter arrived three months later. It contained a hand-drawn card showing a lovely house on a hill, surrounded by olive trees and vineyards.

I read the contents of the card and looked at the photo the couple had taken of my husband lying in a hammock on a cruise ship. Obviously another tough assignment for him.

'It was such fun meeting you on the Star Clipper,' read the card. 'Do come and stay if you're ever in the region, we would love to introduce you to the Languedoc.'

I looked at the drawing of the house again and compared it with the view from our front door. The French house had palm trees, sunshine and a swimming-pool.

Idyllic though the village of Mayfield is, we looked out over a car park and constant drizzle. Next door was the pub, which I had grown to hate. Not so much because it was next door, but because Rupert wasted too much time and money there.

'That idea of yours about moving to France,' I said. 'Let's go and have a look.'

Within a week we were planning a trip to Pézenas, a medieval town twenty minutes away from the Mediterranean. Olivia, our daughter, was then around three months old. We left her with Rupert's parents and drove to Stansted. Just the drive to the airport was enough to make you want to leave the country. Despite allowing for more than two hours to get there we almost didn't make it. We ran on to the plane and arrived at Carcassonne in blazing sunshine an hour and a half later. It was early October.

Peter Glynn-Smith, an attractive man of around 70 with more energy and wit than all the 30 year olds hanging around the Mayfield pub, met us at the airport. It was him Rupert had met in Thailand. Married to Dominique, a French woman, Peter had lived in the Languedoc for 12 years and had grown to adore the region.

'This is a wine growing area, the biggest vineyard in the world,' he said, as we drove from the airport. 'There are a couple of great cities, Montpellier and Nîmes, we are close to Spain—we often pop down there for lunch—there are large sandy beaches, flamingos and oyster beds, and mountains to the north, which funnel the wind in another direction. They say we get more than 300 days of sunshine a year, but when it rains, it really rains. I have lived all over the world, but I like it best here.' The best news for house hunters was that the house prices were a third to a quarter of what you pay in England, helped by the strong pound. We were sold.

The housing market in the Languedoc, when we first started looking, had agents, but they seemed reluctant to give us any information about houses for sale. A former Buddhist monk turned estate agent drove us long distances to look at unsuitable properties. He was deaf in one ear and overtook cars on corners. Another agent, an Englishwoman, was reluctant to sell anything. Rupert explained to her that this was her job.

'Oh no,' she said. 'I don't want the place overrun with foreigners. I liked it best a few years ago, when it was quieter.'

We wanted an old property in the middle of nowhere, ideally with five bedrooms and a swimming-pool. We looked within a 30 kilometre radius of Pézenas for over a year.

Every time we came out we would stay with Peter and Dominique. The problem was that, because Peter is an interior designer, their house is one of the most elegant in the region. We would trawl around wrecks all day and come back to the tranquillity of St Siméon, and wonder if we had started on a mad mission.

To make matters worse, Peter introduced us to all his friends, most of whom he had designed houses for. For example, Norman and Stephanie, who live in one of the most beautifully converted mills in the world. We would go for long lunches on their terrace, which is in between their pool and the vineyards next door. It was the ultimate in luxury picnicking. You felt you were in the middle of the countryside, while sitting at a marble table drinking local wines.

In all we must have made seven or eight trips, some with Olivia, some without. I'll never forget her taking her first bath in the Languedoc, in Peter's beautiful round marble sink. The trips were great fun. Peter and Dominique looked after us splendidly, organising dinners and showing us the region. As soon as we found a house with any potential at all, we would call Peter in to take a look. 'This could be the most exquisite house in the south of France,' he would invariably announce, tape measure in hand. I would stare at three rotting walls and a hole in the roof and try to share his vision and enthusiasm.

By now, of course, I was totally set on moving. I had come to love the way of life I had seen so far. I imagined my children (I was pregnant again) running around Peter's pool with his daughter Laura. I envisaged daily trips to the Pézenas delicatessen to stock up on marvellous cheeses and local goodies. I thought more and more about a life in the sun.

But by now we had also given up all hope of ever finding the perfect place. The isolated house with swimming-pool and five bedrooms didn't seem to exist. We would have to try to rent somewhere and try to find a house once we were installed.

On the final afternoon on what we had decided would be our last house-hunting trip we ended up near Clermont l'Hérault, a small town to the west of Montpellier. Another English agent showed us a couple of properties. He had been a plasterer and came to the south of France ten years ago on holiday. After a week in the sun, he decided not to go back to Bolton. The most impressive thing about him was the amount he drank.

'I start off with beer,' he explained. 'And move on to a bottle of wine and half a bottle of Ricard every night.'

His shape and colour confirmed this.

We told him that we were visiting one more place before returning to England. We were about to give up on the whole thing or try to find somewhere to rent.

'Well, you'll buy it,' he said.

'How do you know that?' we asked.

'I just do,' he grinned, tapping his red nose.

We drove away resolving never to drink as much as he did. But the strange thing was, the minute we turned off the main road to follow the small track to the final property, we knew it was right. The tiny country road ran through vineyards and *garrigue*, the scrubland made up of stunted oak trees, broom, rosemary and thyme.

I was expecting something disappointing around every corner, but instead, three kilometres after we had turned off the main road, we saw the house on top of the hill. Old stones, blue shutters, swimming-pool, roses and olive trees in the garden, and not another house in sight. As we turned up the drive, my nipples stood on end. Historically this has always been a good sign.

I found it hard not to smile as we were taken round. The lady who owned the house insisted on showing me every cupboard in it. I felt like jumping up and down shrieking: 'I don't care if there isn't a single bloody cupboard within a ten-mile radius.'

'Will you stop grinning,' hissed Rupert as we looked round the garden. It was stunning, filled with yellow, pink and red roses. There were palm trees by the pool and olive trees dotted around.

'I can't,' I replied, almost in tears.

The couple suggested we walk up to the vineyard behind the house to get a feeling for the countryside it stood in.

'Just make an offer now,' I said to Rupert. Both he and Peter glared at me.

'I love it,' I said.

'Well of course you do,' said Peter, trying to look patient.

We walked back to the house and I tried to look nonchalant. Downstairs the whole vast room was lined with books. One of our main concerns about moving had been where to put our books. It was a sign. I had to concentrate on not throwing my arms around the owners. Could it possibly get any better?

'The house is called Sainte Cécile,' said Madame Millière. 'She is the patron saint of music.'

I envisaged opera blaring from the house as we swam naked in the pool on balmy summer evenings. Did I imagine it, or did Bea, then in my tummy, do a somersault?

After about an hour we said goodbye to Monsieur and Madame Millière and went back to plan our strategy. There was no question we wanted the house. We could just about afford it, although it would mean re-mortgaging in Sussex. How easy would it be to close the deal?

We spent a night dreaming of life at Sainte Cécile, how the children would learn to swim there, the walks we would take, the dinner parties we would give, repaying the hospitality we'd been shown on our visits to the region.

At the estate agent's the next morning we resolved to play it cool. But we were due to fly out that day and there was no way I wanted to leave without signing something. We were instantly shown in to the boss's office. When I started telling him that there were cracks in the walls, he said that we could arrange a survey if we wished, but the property was sound. Besides, a Swiss couple had already made an offer. Just then, his phone rang. I caught my husband's eye. I thought it was important that he realised how crucial his next move would be.

'If we don't get this house I will never recover,' I whispered.

When the agent came off the phone, Rupert asked him how much the Swiss had offered. What about if we offer a sum £10,000 higher? I will ask them, he replied. We had to sign a formal offer, then the agent drove off to see the vendors in person. We were told to go for a walk and a cup of coffee.

We walked around in the sunshine for an hour, worried to go into any shops in case we lost the signal on our mobile phones. I kept telling my husband to call back and offer the asking price immediately. After an age, the phone rang.

'Please come back to my office,' said a voice.

They had accepted!

We all drove to the house, went on another tour and were shown all the cupboards again. Then we were offered a glass of champagne and some canapés. It all seemed terribly civilised.

'It's a bit less than we had hoped for,' said Madame Millière, patting my pregnant tummy. 'But I wanted the house to go to a young family.'

We sat down and went through all the things they would leave in the house and decided on a date for us to move in. They wanted one final summer there with their grandchildren so September the first was agreed on. This was six months away.

'And you must come and have lunch next time you're down,' said Madame Millière. 'I want to introduce you to my gardener.'

We went back to England with a photograph of the house, which I put on the fridge as I counted the days until the move. It showed the French windows downstairs, framed with roses. You could see the strong sun lighting up the glass.

From then on my life was taken over with 'the move'. I began to arrange the mortgage, the French bank account, how to give birth in France, childcare, having telephone lines installed and so on, all issues I will be covering in this book. I didn't speak any French. I spent most of my later school years in Sweden, where the first foreign language in schools is English. I took this as an opportunity to bunk off instead of doing something useful like learning French verbs. We employed a local French friend, Isabelle, to give us lessons twice a week. But I found it incredibly hard to get my head round the language. With Isabelle's help I fired off faxes to the Post Office, the local mayor's office, the local GP and banks. By the time we moved in September I would be seven months pregnant and wanted to get as much organised as I could beforehand.

The last week in August Rupert left for the Languedoc with Hugo and Julia, his two older children, then aged six and eight. The idea was that he would be there to sign the final papers and sort things out for when we arrived. Olivia and I would travel down a week or so later.

Once Rupert had gone we started putting the whole contents of the house in cardboard boxes. The removal van arrived two days before we were due to leave and took everything out of the house. I was going to spend my last two days in England staying with a friend.

I locked up for the last time and handed the keys over to Pat, our neighbour. Her dogs, Hector and Camber, came out and started running around, barking madly. My appearance was usually a sign that they were going for a walk. I wondered how much I would miss the walk out of the back of the house over the fields, and the views of Sussex I loved. Pat looked as if she was going to start crying and I thought briefly about cancelling the whole thing. What the hell was I doing going to give birth somewhere I didn't even speak the language? What was the French for epidural?

Instead I gave Pat a hug and told her to come and see us. Hector and Camber looked glum as I opened the gate and walked out without them.

Two days later at the Ryanair check-in at Stansted I was thinking even more seriously about going back to the unfurnished house in Mayfield. My main worry was where Olivia and I would sleep. The floor might have been an option for her, but in my advanced stage of pregnancy no way was it for me.

'I'm sorry,' said a particularly po-faced member of the airline's staff. 'You're too pregnant to fly.' Rarely have I come across such unpleasant people, and I am including experience working for a headhunter in the city of London, as I have whilst flying the dreaded Ryanair.

This sadistic member of staff was telling me I wasn't, in fact, going to get on the plane to pursue my dream, that, no, I wouldn't be pruning my roses by the pool that afternoon. Instead I would be driving back to Sussex with Donia and Olivia to Mayfield.

I thought briefly about leaning across the check-in counter, grabbing her polyester necktie and slowly strangling her.

'You're not serious?' I asked, hoping it was all a nightmare.

'I am,' she replied. I could see the beginnings of a smile form under her fourteen layers of cheap foundation.

'But I have flown all over the world while pregnant. I even called BA to check how many weeks pregnant you can be and still fly.'

'Ah, well, they have different rules than us. With us, anyone over seven months pregnant has to have a certificate from their doctor.'

'And if I have that I can fly?'

'Yes.'

'How do you suggest I get you one now? I mean can I call my doctor and get her to fax it?'

'Oh no, I shouldn't think so.'

Olivia started to cry.

I picked her up and looked around me pleadingly. Was there a doctor in the check-in queue?

A colleague of Miss Sadistic came to my rescue.

'If your doctor could fax us something now, on this number, we could let you on,' she said, handing me a piece of paper.

I didn't dare explain to them that my doctor had recently committed suicide and that the lady who had taken over hardly knew me, so it was unlikely she would be able to say whether I could fly or not. I gloomily took the piece of paper and headed for the back of the queue.

Donia, who had been looking for some last-minute supplies of Calpol, joined us.

'You haven't got very far, have you?'

'We're not going,' I said.

She laughed and picked up Olivia who was falling asleep on the luggage trolley.

'No, I'm serious.' I explained what had happened.

I've always found a pregnant woman weeping hysterically is pretty effective in any situation. So when I got through to the secretary at the surgery (thank God it was the grumpy one's day off) I wept and told her what had happened.

She reacted like Moneypenny when James Bond is in a crisis.

'Don't you worry my lovey, we'll send it through straight away. Leave it all to me.'

Less than an hour later we were airborne, heading to our new home. I have never been so relieved to be on a Ryanair plane.

We landed in Carcassonne an hour and half later. It was wonderful stepping out of the plane into what felt like a sauna. I stood at the top of the steps and breathed in the air of my new home: wonderful, if slightly tarnished with aviation fuel. Rupert was there to meet us. He told us that the furniture had finally arrived that morning and the men were busy unloading the truck. Max the cat had made it too but was refusing to come out of the cage he had travelled in from England.

The three kilometre drive from the village to the house was even more beautiful than I remembered. The vines, the olive trees, the huge pines close to our house were all swaying in the gentle breeze. I was desperate to get to my new home and float in the pool. In fact, that day was spent mainly arranging for the beds to be put up so that we all had somewhere to sleep that night—Rupert had so far been camping in the garden.

By early evening the beds were in place and I went for my first dip. It was one of those situations where the reality is better than the fantasy. I felt relaxed and happy, despite the fact that the house was a shambles and there were around 150 boxes still to unpack. Olivia ran around the pool with her plastic caterpillar. Donia was busy covering herself in baby oil to ensure optimum tanning.

After the swim we opened a bottle of wine on the terrace. I remembered a moment of doubt I had had a few months previously about moving. 'I bet you,' a friend of ours in Mayfield had said, 'that after six months you'll be wondering what on earth you've been worrying about.' He was right, but it happened on the first day.

2
One Egg Is un Oeuf

One of my favourite beginnings to any book is 'There was no possibility of taking a walk that day' from *Jane Eyre*. If *Jane Eyre* had been written by a Frenchman, the first line would have been: 'There was no possibility of a baguette that day.' France is a nation obsessed with bread. No meal is complete without it. It melts the heart even of the toughest functionary. I once came back to my car to find a traffic warden about to write me a ticket. 'I was just getting some bread,' I gasped as I ran towards him and my illegally parked car, waving my baguette. 'Oh I see,' he responded, eyeing my loaf. 'That looks good, which baker did you get it from?'

All sorts of bread, not just the baguette, are central to the French way of life. The absence of it is fundamental to the country's history. Would there ever have been a revolution if Marie Antoinette hadn't suggested the peasants eat cake? There are still those in France who make the sign of the cross on their loaf before breaking into it. There are fierce arguments about the decline of bread, the addition of chemicals, the decline of the artisan bakery and its replacement by the bread factories attached to the supermarkets. The relationship between a French person and bread is more than one of food, it is emotional. There is a

French expression: *Triste comme un jour sans pain*. As sad as a day without bread.

You will never go for a meal in France and not be given bread. Whatever the time of day or night, however lowly an establishment, there will be a basket of bread. If you are used to butter with your bread you will have to ask for it, as my father-in-law does. He often ends up with beer instead of *beurre*, but I don't think he minds too much.

This obsession with bread has now reached our household. And not just any bread. Bread with texture and with taste. There are certain bakeries that are to be visited just because of their *pain complet*. Or raisin and nut loaf.

We used to be perfectly capable of eating lunch without a baguette. Not so now. Every time I leave the house the phrase 'will you get some bread on your way back?' rings in my ears. Rupert seems lost without it. If I fail to get bread, he will grumpily search the freezer for some and then complain. 'Would have been nice with a bit of bread,' he'll say, prodding his pasta. How this happened to us, I don't know.

Bread dictates the rhythm of our life. The consequence of this mania for fresh bread daily does actually mean you go shopping every day and therefore end up eating a lot more fresh food. Forced to go into town to buy some bread, you may as well pop into the fishmongers (where you will often be given a recipe to go with your fillet of fish), the butcher or the *crèmerie*, for the perfect cheeses to go with the bread.

This shopping, imposed by the necessity to always have fresh bread, presages what soon becomes a complete dietary transformation when you live in France. The seasons become much more important. We live quite near Bouzigues, which is famous for its oysters and other strange looking crustaceans. They produce 15 tons of oysters a year and 100 tons of mussels. In our local market town, these *coquillages* are sold from wooden cabins in the central square, conveniently between the best bakery, the best *crèmerie* and an interesting wine shop. It is no coincidence that the town statue of Marianne, the bare-breasted revolutionary, is set into the small place separating these businesses. She holds aloft a sign with the rights of man, but she has obviously chosen to take up her position where there will be plenty of good bread, and accompaniments.

One declares loyalty to one shack or the other, and for some reason we have become the customers of Ludovic, who soon gets to know you and remembers what you order and how you wish it prepared.

For example, Rupert will always have the medium-sized oysters, opened. Ludovic sells a dozen for around £3. Although they're said to be the sexiest food going, oysters don't really turn me on. In fact, I find them slimy and faintly gross, which is a shame as they are otherwise a perfect food, no calories and loads of protein. I notice the French like to eat them with bread—but only brown bread.

What does excite me though is the asparagus season. In England asparagus was something we could rarely afford. And even when we could, it wasn't very good. In France, the asparagus is wonderful. You get the thinner or the thicker variety, both delicious. Green or white. Both varieties are better steamed, never boiled. A sage French woman told me an asparagus tip should never touch water. Because I am partly Italian I love them with a sprinkling of parmesan on top. They are also great roasted or grilled. When the season starts you see them everywhere, sold in a *botte*, which is a bunch about as big as both your hands can comfortably go around.

My favourite place for buying asparagus is in our neighbouring village. There is a young couple there who open their garage and set up a table outside it every day during the season between five and seven in the afternoon, lending another meaning to the famous French phrase *cinq à sept*. They are there for a total of about five weeks and during this time I have to eat asparagus every day.

I normally pull up by their stall and they hand me the asparagus without me having to get out of the car, a sort of asparagus drive-through service. One evening I was on my way home from collecting the children and had to stop for my asparagus fix. Rupert was away on some trip to Africa. I had had a very busy day and was keen to get back home to do some more work, so when I saw an old couple standing chatting by the stall I decided to turn the car around first to save time. We have a Toyota Landcruiser, a bigger more cumbersome vehicle you could not hope for—although something resembling a tank is necessary if one is going to survive the drivers in France. I found a side road and drove in, then started reversing.

I did, in fact, see the great tree behind me, and was just wondering why the reversing alarm hadn't gone off when *crash*, the whole back window collapsed.

'Oh,' said Olivia. 'I wonder when Daddy's coming home. He's a very good driver.'

Bea was by now mimicking me, but thankfully getting it wrong and saying 'oh duck'. The asparagus man and his old gossiping couple were looking on amazed.

Still determined to get my asparagus, I drove up to the stall. The oldies moved away pretty sharpish. 'Two *bottes*, please,' I said, trying to control my rage. 'No, make it three.'

Once you have become a serious foodie, it is no longer enough to visit the *crèmerie* for the cheese for your bread, but you will want to make friends with someone who actually makes the stuff, so you can buy it at the farm gate. General de Gaulle famously complained: 'How can you be expected to govern a country that has 246 kinds of cheese?' What is curious about this statement is that the French have not stopped inventing new ones, and this may explain why the country continues to present governance problems. It now has 365 kinds.

One day we spotted goats close to us. In France, this can only mean one thing—cheese. The farm, Mas Roland, has a green and yellow *Bienvenue à la Ferme* sign on the gate—an indication that they welcome visitors and are proud to show them how they produce the products of their particular *terroir* (an almost untranslatable French word which reflects the almost mystical qualities of particular plots of land to produce particular distinctive flavours).

The family here has been producing goat's cheese for 23 years. After meeting the goats and watching some of them milked, you can buy from that day's batch, which is a lovely, white crumbly cheese, or semi-fresh (about two days old) or mature (about four days old). The longer it stands, the creamier and 'goatier' it becomes. Mas Roland is a hamlet perched on top of an imposing hill which is surmounted on a road of many zigs and zags. It's actually easier on a bicycle than in a car.

Bienvenue à la Ferme is proving a wonderful way of bringing the children closer to their food. The farm is open every day between 4.30 and 7.30pm, so we can go there, on the way to the bakery. Until they could say the word goat, my daughters called it the 'baaaa farm'. There is something intimate and satisfying about seeing exactly where your food is coming from.

We also get our eggs from a local farm. Olivia is obsessed with eggs and would eat them at every meal if she could. She can't, partly because too many eggs aren't good for you, but also because every time anyone in the house has an egg, Rupert comes up with his favourite joke:

Why do Frenchmen only have one egg for breakfast?

Because one egg is *un oeuf*.

The girls still don't get the joke but groan in sympathy with me.

In the early 1990s, a French scientist noted that despite the fact that the French eat masses of runny cheeses, kilos of *pâté* and *foie gras*, drink gallons of wine and smoke millions of cigarettes, they are 30 per cent less likely to die from heart disease than their counterparts in the US or northern Europe. He also noted that the southern French were 30 per cent less likely to suffer from heart conditions than the northern French. In addition, just 7 per cent of French people are obese, despite buttery croissants and pastries, compared with 22 per cent of Americans. This phenomenon has become known as the French Paradox.

The French diet is beneficial not just for the heart but also leads to less bowel cancer, fewer circulatory problems, less osteoporosis and other problems. In fact, a recent study showed that men who had already suffered a heart attack and switched to a more Mediterranean-style diet cut their chances of a second heart attack by 70 per cent. A Mediterranean diet is easy to follow wherever you are in France. Choose fish above red meat, olive oil at every given opportunity, and at least two glasses of red wine a day. If you're worried about wine being fattening, don't. A whole bottle of Bordeaux is 680 calories, the equivalent of a cheeseburger and chips, and probably better for you.

When we first decided to move I imagined myself pottering around markets, picking out the choicest peaches and apricots. This does happen, but there are also supermarkets, which are sometimes more convenient. Every Wednesday in our village there is a market which consists of a huge vegetable stall run by a round, jolly couple. There is also a little old lady selling whatever is in season, be it strawberries or asparagus, from the back of her Renault 5, and a van that sells horsemeat. I don't think I've eaten any yet, but Donia (who speaks no French) did once come back from a butcher I know sells horsemeat with something that looked very odd. When I tasted it, it was vaguely sweet. I gave it to the dog, just in case.

The French love nothing more than comparing recipes, they talk for hours about the benefits of vanilla essence versus vanilla pods and other essential topics. The round, jolly vegetable stall lady is a very keen cook and once gave me a fantastic recipe for chocolate mousse. It was incredibly complicated and involved about 12 eggs. At a dinner, once your cooking methods have been dissected, they will ask you where you got your ingredients from. If it was the supermarket, lie.

By far the biggest market in my region is in Pézenas every Saturday. Here you can buy anything from children's shoes to fresh ginger. In the winter it is blissfully local, in the summer every other voice is foreign and there is nowhere to park. On the upside, the stalls are more varied and you can find some real treats. You can find every kind of flavoured olive, ready-made paella, several cheese and meat stalls selling all sorts of things the English will probably never eat.

Proof that Olivia has become totally French came one day when she proudly showed Monika, our Slovakian babysitter, a big fat snail she had crawling on her arm. 'Ugh,' said Monika, reeling backwards. 'It's disgusting.' 'No, it's not,' replied Olivia. 'It's delicious.' I myself have never tried them, but then eating something that looks as if it may have come from somebody's nose has never really appealed to me.

Snails are big business in France. They eat two billion of them a year, one third imported from Turkey and Eastern Europe. In fact, I once saw someone advertising a ready-made delectable dish he described as *escargots aux grenouilles*. Snails with frog's legs. As with everything essential to the French lifestyle, the government is in control of the situation. In 1982 it passed a law that snails could only enter France at designated spots where the customs officials have snail testing machines. These ensure that the snails destined for the French consumer are alive and healthy. The classic French snail is the Burgundy snail, which is light brown, and feeds on the vineyards. They are usually cooked in their shells with a dab of garlic butter in each one, although in Burgundy they are sometimes combined with chanterelle mushrooms.

As a consequence of all this shopping, the most dangerous time

Recently, we were phoned by our primary school because of a storm warning.

'Could you come and collect the girls please?' the head-mistress asked. 'The school will be closed with immediate effect.'

When I arrived, the girls were in the refectory, waiting for their lunch-a four-course, sometimes five-course meal.

'They can't possibly go home now, storm or no storm,' said the dinner lady as the lightning flashed. 'Can you come back after lunch?'

Lunch is the great excuse. When John Paul II visited Lourdes, security was tight; nobody was allowed to cross the road. Nobody, that is, except a furious pensioner who told the policeman that she had to get home in time for lunch.

It is this respect for things like lunch that makes France a pleasant place to live. The French have their priorities right: their main aim in life is to enjoy it, not to earn as much money as they can. 'I would rather have lunch in the garden on a sunny day surrounded by my family than have a new car,' says Georges, a French friend. In France, it's not about how long you live, it's how long you lunch.

The English who move to France adopt the French way of life pretty quickly. I always stop for lunch now. In fact, if I'm not at the table shortly after midday, I start to get nervous. The day is divided up into two parts: before lunch and after lunch. Nothing happens during lunch except, well, lunch.

Another comforting aspect of life in France is that not much changes when you get old: you still play the national sport (boules) and go cycling. A lot of the French seem to spend their life preparing for old age. My daughter's best friend, for example, was very worried the first time she came to visit us, as we had to drive over a bridge that has no barri-ers. She is six. was astounded to see my daughter take off her seatbelt before the car had come to a complete standstill. Last spring, I took the children into town. They were wearing

to be on the roads in France is just before noon. Frenchmen and women with low blood sugar levels, having just had a croissant for breakfast, are rushing home or out to lunch. As the midday meal in France is still a big deal, the whole country shuts down between 12 and 2pm. If you want to get somewhere quickly, that's the time to go out. It's as if a curfew has been imposed. It always reminds me of walking back from work as England was about to play in the semi-final of the 1990 World Cup. Although I lived in central London there was not a soul about. *Everyone* here has a proper lunch. There is no question of grabbing a sandwich on the run. I even read a story recently about two burglars who broke into a flat in Agde. As it was midday, they stopped stealing things and ate a baguette. The police found crumbs all over the floor.

When you go out for lunch in France you will notice that most places have a *menu du jour*. This is usually extremely reasonably priced at between €10 and €15. For this you get four courses, as well as coffee. It is again part of their socialist values. The man in the street should be able to eat well at midday, it's his right, no matter who he is or where he is. In fact, you will find that the price of a coffee, a beer and a baguette is more or less the same throughout France as well. According to Fiona Cantwell, a former chef who now runs the Château Marcenac, you should try the menu of the day when you go out. 'Even if there is some offal on it you would never normally eat. You might like it, and, anyway, with four courses there's plenty of other stuff you can eat if you don't.'

Eating out in France, however, is not always good. I have had some terrible meals. In fact, last time I was in London I was amazed at how well I ate and what good value it was. I suppose I did go for sushi and Italian, both things you are only likely to find in the big cities here. Maybe the quality in general is better in big cites, but I have found where I live you have to be really careful not to go out, eat badly and pay a lot for it. But the French still view

trousers and long-sleeved T-shirts. It was about 16C with not a cloud in the sky.

'Aren't they cold?' asked a young woman who stopped us in the street. 'It's not summer yet, you know.'

'It is to us,' I felt like responding, though I told her I had left their jackets in the car, with their hats and gloves.

I predict the Brits who have moved here for a better life will enjoy ageing disgracefully in France so much they'll hang on to the bitter end. Our children will moan that we're not dropping off and leaving them our money. But the good news for the French state is that when we do die, the cash will come just in time for their long and pleasant retirement.

England as a place with appalling weather and even worse sustenance.

When asked what they feared most about facing the English at Twickenham this year, the captain of the French rugby team replied 'the food'. France's leading lingerie designer, Chantal Thomass, says she dreads going to her factory in Norfolk due to English cooking. 'I have to go on a diet when I get back to Paris,' she says. 'I blame the sandwiches. But what else is there to eat?' During the Jamie Oliver campaign for better school dinners, one French friend of mine suggested we needed a similar drive for the adult population.

France, on the other hand, has always had a reputation for wonderful cuisine. The world's greatest chefs are traditionally French. The French attitude towards eating has always been revered, along with the markets and choice of fresh produce.

As I have said, it is very easy to wander down to your local town and buy any number of delicacies depending on the season. I find there is no need to plan dinner more than half an hour in advance. You just go and see what's around. 'I love the fact that what I eat is

determined by the seasons here and what is good at the greengro-
cer's next door to my house,' says Ken Hom, the celebrity chef,
who has a home near Cahors.

The French custom of shopping for fresh food every day may
be time-consuming, but there is something very satisfying about
coming home with a basket filled with fresh goods that you eat
straight away.

But try to go out for dinner in rural France and you will often
be disappointed. Many restaurants are over-priced, second-rate,
badly decorated and lit by searchlights. Added to which the choice
is often limited. It seems the foodie revolution that has hit England
in the last ten years has yet to reach rural France. Basically the
choice is French food or more French food. Much of it is frozen.
And even though France has this wonderful reputation for food, I
have heard several people complain that they have had the worst
meals of their lives here.

The chef and author John Burton-Race spent six months in
south-western France researching his book and TV series, French
Leave. 'During that time I drove 36,000 miles and ate in literally
hundreds of restaurants,' he says. 'I would say maybe half a dozen
were good. The rest were rubbish. If we served food like that in
England we'd be shut down. They show no imagination and the
choice is so limited. Basically it's duck, duck, duck or duck.'

Burton-Race finds eating out in England a better option. 'I love
France and if I can afford to I will probably end up there,' he says.
'But in terms of eating out we have far more variety, the quality is
better and the prices are good. And it's not even as if we have the
luxury of fresh melons, asparagus and all the other wonderful fresh
produce the French markets offer. I don't think the French restaurateurs have any excuse. They don't seem to have advanced at all
since haute cuisine days.'

Burton-Race concedes that the low quality could in part be due
to the 35 hour week which has led to increased costs. 'Restaurants

are hiring 30 per cent more staff because nobody is doing any work,' he says. A French friend of mine says the locals in rural France aren't that discerning, so restaurants can get away with it. 'They've been eating under-cooked duck here for hundreds of years and can't seem to get enough of it,' he says.

Laurent Pourcel, chef and co-founder of the two-Michelin-starred Jardin des Sens in Montpellier, defends French regional cuisine. 'We have always had great gastronomic areas in France but here in the Languedoc, for example, we were seen as a poor rela-tion,' he says. 'But I think quality is finally improving throughout regional France.'

Pourcel, who recently opened a restaurant in Piccadilly called W' Sens, is not worried by France's low standing in the top ten restaurants list. 'You have to be very wary of fads,' he says. 'Remember that French cuisine has been around for decades and has a lot of history behind it. It is here to stay. We will continue along our path and always be extremely important.'
Yet even he admits that eating out in London is more interesting than eating out in Paris.

Zoe Harris, a new friend of mine, told me a story recently of an experience they had in a restaurant called in Marseillan, a small port on the Etang de Thau, close to Bouzigues. Some very good friends of theirs had come to stay. They had been with them a week and this was their goodbye meal on the way to the airport.

They arrived at the restaurant at 1pm. By 2.15 they still hadn't had any service at all. 'It was mother's day,' says Zoe. 'And I think they were short-staffed, as well as very busy, but they could at least have given us a drink and a basket of bread.' When their food arrived another hour later, the monkfish two of them had ordered was so tough she couldn't cut it. 'I don't know what they could have done to get it to that state,' she says. 'I've never seen anything like it.' Her son had oysters which looked as if they had been left out for hours, and they probably had been. They made him so ill he threw up all the way back to England. 'The other food was barely edible,' says Zoe. 'But, being English, we didn't want to complain too much. It was a terrible end to the holiday for our friends. What really annoyed me most was that they refused to accept they were wrong or apologise. They were so arrogant.'

Restaurants here seem to be divided into categories. There are those where you eat well for a fair price, there are good restaurants, semi-gastronomic restaurants and, at the top, gastronomic restaurants. I have not been to many gastronomic restaurants here but the ones I have been to have been good, if pricey. There are some wonderful semi-gastronomic places on the beaches near Montpellier. There is something glorious about eating luxurious food on a beach, surrounded by teak furniture and fans. You almost feel as if you're in Morocco.

In France, the English have a terrible reputation as big drinkers. In fact, we are now known as the drunks of Europe. Even in my relatively unknown region there is a bar in the next village known as the 'English Bar.' Whatever time of day or night you go past, you can see the Brits with their glasses of beer and copies of some English paper they have just bought. Alex, my French friend and wife of the winemaker Jean-Claude, says the French would never drink like the English. 'They have one glass of wine with lunch and two with dinner. They may not even go that far', she says, 'the culture is changing and a lot of French now only drink when they go out or are entertaining.' There are a lot of Brits who really don't do much else. You see them at the bars, red-faced from the sun and the *pastis*. 'They don't help the reputation of the English in France,' says Alex.

When I asked my friend Caroline what she found most repulsive about the way the English eat, she told me it was the habit of mixing cucumbers and cheese. 'In France a cucumber is an *hors d'oeuvre*. And cheese is, well, cheese.' She remembers an exchange she went on, aged 16, to Coventry. She was with three other French

---

Food and language

Tomber dans les pommes—literally, to fall into the apples—meaning to faint

Couper la poire en deux—to cut the pear in two—to meet halfway

Faire le poireau—to act like a leek—to be kept waiting

Tirer les marrons du feu—to pull chestnuts out of the fire—to be used as a dupe or a tool

Se fendre la pêche—to split one's peach—to laugh uproariously, to split one's sides, to laugh one's head off

Tondre des oeufs—to shave eggs—to be a skinflint

Pédaler dans la semoule—to pedal in the semolina—to take leave of one's senses

Cracher dans la soupe—to spit in the soup—to spoil something so that it can only be enjoyed by you

Casser du sucre sur le dos de quelqu'un—to break sugar on someone's back—to talk about someone behind their back

---

teenagers and every day they were sent off for the day with a picnic lunch. 'Every day we would open our sandwiches and find cheddar and cucumber,' she says. '*C'est pas possible!* Disgusting. We all refused to eat it. The only thing we ate from the picnic were the crisps.'

There are ways the French do things that we find hard to cope with as well. For example, my friend Carla McKay has a house in a village nearby. She woke up one morning to chattering voices outside. Her neighbours were having a gossip. 'How nice,' I thought. 'I'll take my coffee to the terrace and see what's going on.' When she looked over towards the noise, she saw that one of them was holding up a dead hare, while another ripped its skin off. The blood was gushing down the street. 'Now, you don't get that in Lower Heyford,' says Carla.

When I first moved here, I was practically vegetarian. It is really since having the babies that I have started craving meat. But still some of the things they come up with are too much. Tripe, for example. That's what we feed our dog. And why do they insist on eating every part of an animal from its trotter to its brain? They really are not in the least squeamish. Fiona Cantwell told me that when they signed for their *château*, the local mayor came round to take a look. He found some *foie gras* and *pâté* in the cellar that had been there at least 10 years, which he proceeded to eat, declaring it delicious.

For the true difference in culture between the French and the English when it comes to food, you need only look at the word *gourmand*. Its literal translation is greedy, which in English is an insult. In French it means the same thing, but it is not an insult. People are always telling me Leonardo (our son, now one year old) is *gourmand* but it is said with a hint of admiration, as if to say he eats well, as opposed to too much. The word *gourmet* in French means you appreciate good food and good things. This is an enormous compliment.

In a country more recently renowned for critical theory than breakthrough-cuisine, there are agonies in the French culinary establishment over a perceived lack of cutting edge. Jamie Oliver has become an unlikely TV hit here—the irony that an Englishman is now teaching the French to cook is not lost on the French chattering classes.

It is, in fact, the case that if you want a choice of daring restaurants propelled by determination to advance to the very frontiers of culinary experience, you are better off in London than rural France. 'The discovery of a new dish does more for human happiness than the discovery of a new star,' declared the most eminent French philosopher of food, Anthelme Brillat-Savarin. Brillat-Savarin considered the French revolution also as a revolution in the kitchen, inaugurating an era of bourgeois culinary supremacy and the rise of the restaurant. But the new dishes are now mostly being discovered and invented elsewhere. France suffers in the kitchen as in so many other things because it is so bureaucratised. As it is so hard to start a business, there simply isn't the same capital going into catering as in Britain. Many of the professional French restaurateurs seem to have left for greener pastures abroad, running huge and profitable restaurants in places like New York and London.

Nevertheless, the cuisine of the country, the basics of bread, cheese, olives, salads, grills of meat and delicious fish, make the experience of daily eating superior here. Perhaps this is the trick. Expect to eat well, but not always when you eat out. Usually we eat at home. Nothing could be easier than a couple of rump steaks you have marinated in olive oil for 24 hours and some French beans. Finally some fresh goat's cheese. And don't forget the bread. And of course the wine. The food here is more wonderful.

The closeness to food means, too, that entertaining here is easier, and something that most people find themselves doing more of. Entertaining is easier partly because there is absolutely no shame in buying at least your pudding ready made, if not everything you put on the table. Why would you spend hours making a *tarte aux pommes* when your local bakery does it a million times better and for less than €10? The tradition of storing things like the *foie gras* and *pâté* mentioned above is so that the French housewife is able to produce a good meal at any given moment. I have often been invited to an impromptu lunch with Peter and Dominique and out of nowhere she has produced a spread that looks as if she had been planning it all week. If you analyse the ingredients, they are simple. Tomatoes, basil, melon, ham, lettuce, bread, cheese, *pâté*. But on a hot day with a glass of chilled rosé, looking out over their garden, it seems a feast fit for kings.

3
Integration

My father always tells me that the only way to learn a language properly is to have an affair with a native. He speaks nine languages. All, he maintains, the result of his hectic love life.

Interestingly, his English is appalling. I remember him telling me when I was a teenager that the only English woman he had ever had a vague desire to sleep with was the queen. I found this more shocking than his prolific taste in women. My mother, he told me, learnt Italian in about three weeks. She confirms this and says it was because she fell in love, which seems to confirm my father's theory.

If the love-affair option isn't available to you, this is rather a pity. It is essential that you learn to speak French if you intend to build a new life in France, and the alternative methods are by far inferior. I know a woman who claims to get around France letting her finger speak by pointing at what she wants. It would be ridiculous to live in England like this, speaking or making no effort to speak English. Yet there seem to be plenty of Brits who are convinced beforehand they'll get by without speaking a word of French.

I was determined never to be like this. Perhaps I had an advantage. I already spoke English, and studied Italian as a student. It is said that when you already know more than one language, the next one is easier.

But French didn't strike me as easier. And, if spoken as they do in the *Midi*, the south of France, incomprehensible even to most Parisians.

The price of failure is social isolation. I could already see the consequences: to live in an English-only ghetto of teas, bridge and golf that might as well be Surrey.

Learning French is vital but it is very very hard. Most of us learned it at school and arrive here perhaps even with a GCSE or A-level, yet completely unprepared to understand a single word. Although all French children are supposed to do English, it seems they have as much trouble with our language as we do with theirs. Indeed, there are surveys that the French themselves are finding it hard to master their own language.

I started lessons before we moved. I spoke almost no French, added to which, I don't have my mother's natural talent for languages. Learning French has proved to be one of the major challenges in making a success of my new life in France since moving here. Once we got here, I carried on having lessons for about a month, until my French teacher and her husband got divorced and she moved out of the region. It was only four years later that I found another teacher.

Marylène loves teaching me how to speak 'proper' French and delights in telling me how many mistakes the French make and how they can't use the subjunctive properly. She says her neighbour's French is worse than mine. Or rather, his vocabulary is more limited. However untrue, flattering me is guaranteed to keep her in a job for a long time.

Not everyone makes the effort to have lessons and to try to string sentences together in conversation. For me, life has become a lot easier and much more fun since I stopped having to plan everything I am going to say in advance.

There are a couple of things that have genuinely helped me to learn the language, and still do. The first is the radio. As we live in the middle of nowhere, I spend a lot of time driving around. I started listening to non-stop talk shows like *France Inter* and *France Culture* as soon as we got here.

To start with, it was appallingly depressing. I had no idea what they were talking about. Eventually, though, I worked out that the news comes on the hour and I made a point of listening for stories I knew were likely to run.

The second thing was finding a French friend and I was lucky to find one who comes from the north and so speaks the language comprehensibly.

I met Alex because I had become addicted to her husband's wine. He makes a fantastic Chardonnay-Viognier, Vignes de Nicole, which I first drank when we were house-hunting. Some women crave banana sandwiches when they're pregnant—I crave Chardonnay.

Once we had found a house, visitors started to arrive from England. Among these was a friend who had just landed a part-time job as wine buyer for the London Match bars. When he told us he was coming on a wine-buying mission, I was determined to find the maker of the Chardonnay-Viognier. Millions of pregnant women all over London would be eternally grateful, I argued. Jean-Claude Mas, as we found out the maker was called, is a young man with an MBA from Birmingham University and a vision for the wines of the region. We all became great friends, and Alex, his wife, became my most constant source of French.

I also met a lovely Frenchwoman called Caroline, whose daughter goes to school with my daughter Olivia. She and I meet once a week and speak in French and English. Although she is not a teacher, I find my time with her more useful than a lesson because I am just talking and, by doing that, constantly coming across things that I have always wanted to know, like the difference

When to *tu* and when to *vous*?

It's a nightmare, a very complicated issue to which there seems to be very few easily defined rules. I usually *vous* everyone and Rupert goes for the *tu*. As a foreigner it is easier to get away with using the wrong word, the French will just assume you're ignorant and not rude. Personally I find the conjugation of *vous* much easier, so am happy to carry on being ultra-polite. It seems it's OK to *tu* children, but once they get beyond 18 they have to be *vous*-ed. In fact, Jérôme, Peter and Dominique's son, tells me his teachers started *vous*-ing him from around 15. In terms of adults, the more familiar you are (and this is defined by social class, circumstances in which you meet and so forth) the more likely it is you will be on *tu* terms. I would never dream of *tu*-ing Geneviève, my cleaning lady. This keeps a distance between us which we're both happy with. Once, early on, I did *tu* her by mistake. She said she preferred *vous* as it was '*plus jolie.*'

There is a famous story of one of General de Gaulle's generals with whom he had worked for decades. The general suggested they had worked together for such a long time that to *tu* each other would be more natural. De Gaulle replied: '*Comme vous voulez.*' A total snub.

My child minder Chantal and I still *vous* each other after four years. Although we are friends and we have a lot in common due to the children (who call her and her husband *maman* Chantal and *papa* Gilbert) I think we have gone beyond the stage where we can now comfortably change to *tu*. It would just seem wrong somehow.

If you are invited to someone's house and the hostess *tu*'s you, you should *tu* her back (assuming she is not 50 years older than you). It is apparently up to whoever's house it is. My friend Alex *vous* her parents-in-law and they *vous* her, even though they are now related and live in the same house. In fact, she calls them M and Mme Mas. I asked her once why she doesn't call them by their first names. 'They never said to do

between *neuf* and *nouveau* (*nouveau* means new to the owner, *neuf* is brand new).

She also talks me through other cultural differences, such as saying thank you.

The French seem appallingly bad at it. You invite people for dinner and the next day you expect to be fielding calls from admiring friends and neighbours.

'The French say thank you on the evening,' says Caroline. 'And they tell you they have eaten well [only if the have eaten well—if not, they won't say anything about the food] and that's enough. You invited them and so you obviously wanted them to be there, so they have no reason to be overly grateful.' After dinner at my gynaecologist's house, I wrote a card to say thank you. His wife called this a 'charming habit' and told me it was only the English who ever wrote. The same seems to apply to presents. You never get a thank you note for a birthday present to a child.

I made friends with an old lady in the village who does what a lot of them seem to do, sit and watch the traffic go by. She is as broad as she is tall and I suppose about 70. Normally she wears slippers and a pinafore, the uniform of the elderly ladies here. Every time I drove past her, she would glare at me as if I'd pushed in front of her in the bread queue. I couldn't understand what her problem was. It wasn't even as if I had foreign licence plates on the car, so it couldn't be that she hated the English. I decided to smile broadly every time she glared and see what happened. One day, after about a month of waving and smiling at her, she finally gave in. She smiled back. Now she even stands up and waves, especially if the children are with me.

In fact I have found the least welcoming people in France have been my fellow Brits. George Bernard Shaw once said that 'It is impossible for an Englishman to open his mouth without making some other Englishman hate or despise him'. In France he doesn't even need to open his mouth. Forget the French demonstrating in

so,' she replied. 'I think it has to do with their age.'

Her husband, Jean-Claude, says *vous* to her parents, but they *tu* him. When I asked Alex why there was this difference, she couldn't explain. If the French don't know, what hope is there for the rest of us? Arielle Dombasle, the filmstar wife of the French writer Bernard-Henri Lévy insists he call her *vous*.

I remember a male French friend of mine, who shall remain nameless, once telling us that *vous*-ing your lovers was 'sexier' than *tu*-ing them. If you ever saw the film *Dangerous Liaisons* with John Malkovich and Michelle Pfeiffer you'll know how right he is. What struck me as strange about his comment was not that he *vous*-ed his lover, but that he thought it such a normal thing to have a lover and to discuss it openly. Especially as he is married to a friend of mine and she was there at the time.

Guillaume de Perthuis, my aristocratic friend from Normandy, once came home from school aged eight and *tu*-ed his mother. His father slapped him across the face and told him to stop being so insolent. His parents still *vous* each other (and of course he *vous* them). But I am happy to say people like the de Perthuis are in a small minority.

So, in summary, *tu* people you like and want to be friends with and who are of a similar age and social background, as long as you meet them in a friendly setting. If you meet them in a formal environment, you may have to wait to *tu* them. *Vous* those you want to keep a distance from or you are required (possibly due to their age) to show respect to. I tend to take my lead from the French, and so far have not messed up too badly. But if I ever take a French lover, I will insist on being *vous*-ed.

Brittany. The coldest welcome when you move to France will be from the Englishman next door, who will hate you on sight.

'Some Englishwoman has just moved into our street,' an English friend of mine told me recently. 'What is she doing here?

We don't want any more Brits in the village.' Another family I know complained that their new neighbours are from Sunderland. 'Why on earth would we want to live next door to people from Sunderland?' they asked me. 'Because you can understand what they're saying,' I was tempted to reply.

I find this the strangest thing about our life in France. The Brits that are here don't want any more Brits to join them. This despite the fact that most of them, according to the French I talk to, make no efforts to socialise with the locals. 'I would say that 90 per cent of them don't speak French and don't integrate,' says a policeman I met in the Dordogne.

This antipathy towards other Brits has haunted me since we moved here. If I had a pound for every time someone has said to me: 'Oooh, I hope you're not going to do a Peter Mayle on us and bring lots of Brits to the region,' I'd be as rich as he is. After I wrote a column which described the region I live in I had hate mail from a woman living here saying she had been here for 10 years but had the good sense to keep the place secret. Hello? The South of France a secret? I don't think so.

Anything that is seen to encourage the Brits to move to France is frowned upon by other Brits. In fact anything remotely British is despised. There is to be an English grocery store in our local town. 'We think it's terrible,' says one Brit living here. 'A totally retrograde step. We didn't come here to eat baked beans.'

Maybe not, but this denial of one's culture seems a bit forced to me. Rather like a Londoner moving to Cornwall, picking up the local accent and refusing to speak to his townie friends. I have an inexplicable addiction to most things English, so am delighted at the news of the grocery store. No longer will I have to harass visitors to bring stocks of oatcakes and Horlicks with them. In fact, I can now stop inviting people to stay.

Another thing that you will find if you move here is that if you go to a restaurant and there are other English people there, they

My friend Prune. I started going to Prune's gym class, the most brilliant gym class I have ever been to. It started at 8 am when she would rock up in her black Jeep looking insanely cool and glamorous. She always wore great clothes and was beautifully turned out even at that time in the morning. She was a fitness fanatic, but her classes weren't about jumping around. Her whole philosophy was centred on stretching. I still don't know, how, but I have never been so sweaty and out of breath as during those classes. And for two days afterwards I could barely move.

'You must stretch every day,' she told me. 'As soon as you get up, just do it, any time during the day you have a minute, stretch, hold your ankles and count to five.'

I will never forget the phone call from Beatrice who used to come to Prune's classes with me.

'I have some terrible news,' she said. 'Prune, our wonderful gym instructor, is dead.'

She had been out cycling with Jean-Luc on his day off and some lunatic, who was on medication for depression and shouldn't even have been driving, drove into her and killed her instantly. He also hit a 10-year old boy who lost a leg as a result.

The funeral was the following day. The speed at which it happened shocked me. I remember when our neighbour died in Sussex, it seemed an age before we gathered in a cold crematorium in Tunbridge Wells.

The whole town showed up to show its support and sorrow at the Pézenas church. Beatrice and I stood at the back. Her husband and son followed her coffin into the church, weeping openly and leaning on each other for support. School children she had taught could barely speak as they related how she had inspired them. A lady who I think was her mother also spoke. Everyone in the church was crying, including us. I felt devastated. After the service, the cortège walked slowly through town to the cemetery where she was interred in the family

will continue their lunch in hushed whispers once they've realised you also come from Blighty. I asked a friend of mine why this is. 'I didn't move to France to be surrounded by English people,' she said. 'Another table of English ruins my lunch.' If avoiding Brits was your reason for moving to France then you picked the wrong country. Go to eastern Germany. There are no Brits there. In fact I'm not sure there are even many Germans there.

I think the fundamental cause for this antipathy is that when people move to France they can reinvent themselves. Here they can be whoever they want to be, because the French have no idea how to pinpoint their background and education from the way they speak. They don't want to be pigeonholed. Back to George Bernard Shaw.

But this Utopian dream of a little French paradise where you are removed from the outside world is no longer achievable, unless you go way into *la France Profonde*. And why is it so desirable? Would you really want to spend the rest of your days eating nothing but French food and trying to crack jokes with French neighbours who find your accent and sense of humour incomprehensible?

The good news is that despite press reports of anti-Brit feeling, the French still seem to like us. 'I love the English coming here,' says Guy de Saint Victor, a wine marketing executive based in the Languedoc. 'They revitalise our villages, do up all our old houses and buy lots of Languedoc wine.' Another local resident agrees. 'We French are far too insular,' he says. 'I think it's good all these foreigners are coming, they make us more open minded and receptive to change. And now that there is an English grocery store opening, it will be possible to have a decent cup of tea this side of the Channel.'

The key to a successful life in France is, as I have often said, learning the language. An unforeseen bonus to speaking French is that when your new English neighbours turn up on your doorstep,

tomb. A funeral worker dressed in a sort of space suit was charged with pushing her new coffin in among the old, decaying ones. The whole thing was horribly macabre. I couldn't quite believe she was in there. The final part of the ceremony involved everyone lining up to pay their respects to Jean-Luc and Hugo, their son. It was the kind of line you have at a wedding in Britain. I watched people go before me and tried to work out words of comfort before I got to them. This would have been hard enough in English, but in French all I could come up with was 'I'm so sorry'.

The man who killed her got two years in prison and is probably out now, back behind the wheel of a car. As my cleaning lady Geneviève said: 'It just proves that in France you can commit murder, as long as it's with a car.' I still do Prune's stretches every day.

you can pretend to be from Brittany.

Rupert is very friendly with the local French, mainly because he has taken up the national sport of cycling. At first, I thought it was rather sweet. He went off three times a week with a bunch of old codgers dressed in skin-tight lycra, cycled up and down a few hills, and that was it. Recently the whole thing has taken on a rather more serious turn. I found a copy of *Vélo Magazine* under the bed. Instead of poetry, now he talks about gears, heart-rate monitors and some guy called Lance.

But Rupert's cycling obsession has been a very useful introduction to the village and has had something of the effect of a love affair, as his French has improved remarkably—especially when he's talking about gears and inner tubes. Since we invited the cycling team for an English breakfast, they view us with renewed respect. 'Anyone who can eat that stuff is a stronger man than me,' said his French cycling mate Charlie, pointing at a pot of Marmite. The bacon sandwiches, specially imported for the occasion and served with HP sauce, were an instant hit.

We were subsequently invited to the retirement party of one of Rupert's cycling gang. Everyone he cycles with is retired. Except Lilian who is female and one of the fittest (and thinnest) women I know. In between running the local toy shop in Pézenas, she also runs the London and Paris marathons and triathlons throughout France. Cycling with retired old men may seem like a cop-out, but these sexagenarians can whiz up a vertical incline in no time.

The cyclist retirement party started at lunchtime and was held in our neighbour's garden, which is about 500 metres from our house. There were about 70 people there, including the cycling team and their wives. Between midday and 2pm a lot of pastis was drunk. Then it was time for lunch. Oysters and mussels were followed by plates of ham, *saucisson* and *pâtés*, then spit-roast wild boar (ideal for me, a semi-vegetarian who doesn't like seafood). The children all ran around playing, the guests sat at long trestle tables eating and drinking. There were speeches and a small cabaret—mainly Charlie dressing up like a woman. At around 5pm we thought we could politely leave. We said our good-byes and went home for a cup of tea. At around midnight we went for a walk. There seemed to be a lot of noise coming from our neighbour's garden. At first we thought we were imagining it, but as we got closer we noticed that many of the cars that had been there at lunchtime were still there. We bumped into one reveller who told us this was perfectly normal. 'We party all day and all night and then the women drive us home,' he told us. In the background we could hear Charlie singing.

One of our first social events in the region was an invitation for dinner at the home of Jean-Luc and Prune Clerc. They were childhood sweethearts and one of the happiest couples I have ever met. He runs the most wonderful delicatessen in Pézenas, which used to be owned by Prune's father. Everyone loves the deli, mainly because of him. He is the human equivalent of a teddy bear. It was

Our location, two miles away from the nearest village, normally insulates us from local gossip. But news reaches me of a tale so gripping I feel I cannot ignore it.

The story centres on the most important building in the community—no, not the bank, nor the bar; not even the post office. It's the bakery.

It is not my favourite bread shop in the area-the range is a bit limited but, occasionally, I have glimpsed the baker in the back room. Rather a handsome, muscular chap, covered in flour. His wife, a bohemian figure with long, highlighted hair and a penchant for grungy outfits, sold the baguettes and croissants. We were quite friendly, partly because she shares a name with one of my daughters.

However, last weekend, when I went to buy a loaf, I was served by a rather pretty youngster with long, blonde hair. Where, I asked a friend, was the baker's wife?

'You mean you don't know? The whole village has been talking about it!' She steered me towards the local bar and over a cup of coffee outlined the sorry tale.

It turns out that a couple of years ago, a Parisian moved into the village with her husband. She became best friends with the baker's wife. They spent many happy hours together, talking about fashion, food and other French obsessions. But as Coco Chanel was fond of observing: 'My friends, there are no friends.'

When the baker's wife went to visit her ailing mother, the baker took the opportunity of getting close to the Parisian woman. He may not be the first baker to be caught with his hands in the wrong bag of flour, but when his wife discovered what had been happening in her absence, she took it badly. She repacked her bags and left. Nobody knows where she went.

The Parisian thought this might leave her free to move in with the handsome baker, but he apparently rejected her kind offer.

The Parisian's husband was not impressed. He went along to

a great honour to be invited to their home. Our friend Peter told us he had lived here for several years before getting an invitation. It is the most stunning house, a Victorian building hidden away in the centre of town with a huge orangery and garden. The pool looks as if it was built 150 years ago and is surrounded by mysterious hanging plants. The whole house and garden looked to me like a tropical forest, plants and vivid colours everywhere. Inside the walls are covered with paintings painted by Prune, a talented artist as well as a dancer and gym instructor.

We were asked for 8 o'clock and arrived at 8.15. No one else was there yet. I had not yet got used to the *Midi* and the fact that everyone is appallingly late for everything. So we were shown around the garden and the house and then asked to sit down in the orangery. There was a bottle of Laurent Perrier Rosé in an ice bucket and eight champagne flutes on the table.

'Oh brilliant,' I said. 'My favourite.'

Jean-Luc and Prune smiled and carried on chatting. At a quarter to 9 we were still the only people there and the bottle remained firmly closed. The French attitude to drinking is very different from ours. They really do drink in moderation. And as we found out that night, you only open the bottle once everyone is there. During dinner I found the amounts of wine they poured into the glasses ridiculous. Why were they being so stingy? We do live in the biggest wine-producing region in the world. There is hardly a shortage of the stuff. Added to which, two of the guests were winemakers. I've got used to it now. And even if I still drink more than the average Frenchwoman, who will drive you mad by hanging on to the same glass all evening, I prefer my measures small. A glass filled to the brim now seems very gauche.

The dinner was fun. I had some idea of what was going on until about 10 o'clock when everyone got fed up with making an effort and launched into fast, furious French. But even then it felt good to be somewhere foreign, somewhere new—there was so much to

the bakery with his shotgun and loosed off a couple of rounds into the windows. Whether he was aiming at the baker, we don't know. What we do know is that the baker has got rid of two women who were beginning to show their age and, apart from the damage to his windows, has come out of the whole saga unscathed. Moreover, he now has a younger woman handling his baguettes.

What interests me, though, is the reaction of the rest of the village. They are delighted to have something to talk about. 'You'll notice the police haven't been involved,' one village senior told me. 'That's the French noblesse oblige. If a man has been cuckolded, then he is perfectly entitled to take a few pot shots at your window.'

Not that there is much sympathy for the wronged wife. 'She was always very grumpy,' said another villager. 'She would look at me and say, 'What do you want?' when I came into the bakery. 'Some bread,' I felt like responding. 'Isn't that bleeding obvious?''

Nobody has condemned the baker as a cheat and a cad. Everybody thinks he is a jolly good bloke. When I asked another villager if he wasn't shocked by the goings-on at the bakery, he looked amazed.

'Shocked?' he said.

learn and do. Prune and I became good friends that evening and started playing tennis together every week. We would give each other French and English lessons on court.

I soon discovered that there are also a good many traits which the French share with the British. My friend Beatrice left England around 25 years ago to marry into the French aristocracy. She is incredibly elegant, and it was at her house (I use the term lightly, it's about the size of Victoria train station), that I first learnt about French snobbery.

We had dinner in the cave. Luc, Beatrice's husband, makes very good wine which he sells mainly to English supermarkets. There was a roaring fire and about 35 people sitting down to dinner. I was seated next to Luc's cousin and asked him, out of curiosity, if there were words or phrases in French that one should avoid.

'Of course!' He replied. 'Lots of them.'

I asked for an example. He told me about the time his son came home with a girl he wanted to marry.

'When we opened the door, she said '*Bonjour messieurs, dames.*' It was appalling.'

'What was appalling?' Had I misheard this phrase I had thought of as inoffensive up until now?

'You can't say that, it is for shopkeepers, it is terrible, unforgivable.' He looked as if he was going to choke on his *foie gras*.

'What did you do?' I asked, feigning horror.

'We totally ignored her.'

'For the whole weekend?'

'Of course,' he delicately wiped some bread from the corner of his mouth, 'he's married to a perfectly nice girl now.'

The Mills & Boon tragedy of not being allowed to marry someone due to a careless phrase killed my appetite for the dinner but roused my curiosity. Had I really landed somewhere more class-ridden than the home-counties?

There are just as many things to avoid in the French language as in English—maybe more. Phrases and words that you thought were innocuous like *enchanté*, *manger* (only animals eat, humans breakfast, lunch or dine) sound terrible to the wrong ears. Of course, a local neighbour wouldn't be offended if I told him I was *enchantée* to meet him. But a lot of the more educated French would.

In fact, I don't know why I was surprised to find this. I remember my aunt Piera telling me off when I was about 12 years old for starting to clear the table before Bertrand, my uncle, had finished eating.

'It is terribly bad manners,' she told me. 'And it upsets your uncle.' I was amazed. At home, clearing the table was always seen as a good thing. Piera then went on to tell me that Bertrand had been brought up in an extremely bourgeois French family. Before anything was cleared from the table, everyone had to have finished. Otherwise the flow of the meal would be interrupted. His mother once fired a maid for saying '*Madame vous êtes servie*' instead of '*Madame est servie.*' The difference is minimal, but to a sensitive bourgeois lady the thought of being feasted on by her guests was obviously too much.

✳ ✳ ✳

One of the walks is up to the end of the road out house sits on to a vineyard with a cross in the corner. On this walk I pass a small hut with an almond orchard. It looks abandoned and it never occurred to me that anyone would want to do anything with it until I heard it was for sale.

From then on, every time I walked past, I imagined all sorts of awful things that could happen there. A kennel for example; maybe some mad Englishman will show up with his fox-hounds. Or a nursery school. Finally I gave in and drop a note through the owner's letterbox saying I have heard it is for sale and am interested in buying it.

I hear nothing for over a month but one day a M. Bourret calls to say he had seen my letter and that his mother is indeed interested in selling the land. His father had looked after it but he has been dead for five years and so no one had bothered much with it. His mother, who was selling it, wants €9,000.

I am slightly taken aback by the price. It seems like a lot of money to spend on something we really don't need. But I arrange to meet M. Bourret at the plot so he can show me what is included in the sale. We met the following day and I manage to knock him down to €8,000. I ask him for permission to have someone come and prune the 60 almond trees before we sign the final papers. He said this won't be a problem.

Rupert and I decide the purchase might have been a bit mad but is a good investment for the future. The children can have parties there and we can always sell some of the almonds should things get really bad. The main thing is though that we are able to walk past there every day without regretting that we didn't buy it. And it is one of the prettiest spots in the world.

A few weeks later I see M. Bourret driving past our hut. He stops for a chat and tells me how amazed he is to see all the almond trees flowering. 'I thought they were all dead,' he says. 'If I'd known they were alive I would have charged you more.'

I didn't resent him for his comment. I suppose I must be getting used to them. The French and the English are a little like siblings. Very close, almost too close sometimes. One of the most interesting things about living here has been learning about them and what makes them tick. A subject they find equally fascinating when the tables are turned.

A French writer and broadcaster called Agnès Catherine Poirier published a guide to the English. In it she tells the French how to relate to their Anglo-Saxon neighbours. The book investigates our attitude towards things like drinking, sex and Boris Johnson (all in their own way good fun, but best not to combine them would be my advice).

To do my bit for a better understanding of the French, I have compiled a cut-out-and-keep-guide to our Gallic friends. Just follow the simple rules below and not only will your own family cease to recognise you, but the locals will start treating you as one of their own.

The day starts early in France. To help you and your neighbours wake up you should probably keep a cockerel. Once it starts crowing it will wake your dog up who will start barking, along with all the other dogs in the village. It is now 6am. Before you open your eyes have a cigarette. If you're really taking this seriously, have two. Get up and drink a litre of coffee. It is essential that you do not eat anything healthy at this stage of the day. If you feel tempted by anything at all, light up another fag.

False friends

Actuellement means 'at the present time,' and should be translated as currently or right now. *Je travaille actuellement*— I am currently working. A related word is *actuel*, which means present or current: *le problème actuel*—the current/present problem. 'Actually' means 'in fact' and should be translated as *en fait, en réalité* or *à vrai dire*. Actually, I don't know him— *En fait, je ne le connais pas.* 'Actual' means real or true, and depending on the context can be translated as *réel, véritable, positif,* or *concret*: The actual value—*la valeur réelle*.

Affaire can mean business, matter, deal, transaction, or scandal. 'Affair' is the equivalent of *affaire* only in the sense of an event or concern. A love affair is *une liaison, une affaire d'amour,* or *une aventure amoureuse*.

Une affluence is a crowd of people: *Il y avait une affluence attendant à la porte*—There were crowds waiting at the door. 'Affluence' indicates a lot or a profusion of something (usually wealth): the affluent society—*l'ère de l'opulence*. There is plenty of information—*Il y a une abondance d'information ici*.

Agonie refers to death pangs or mortal agony, while 'agony' means severe physical or mental pain, but not necessarily just this side of death: *angoisse, supplice*.

Arroser means to water or spray. 'Arose' is the past participle of arise: *survenir, se présenter, s'élever*.

Assister à nearly always means to attend something: *J'ai assisté à la conférence*—I attended (went to) the conference. 'Assist' means to help or aid someone or something: I assisted the woman into the building—*J'ai aidé la dame à entrer dans l'immeuble*.

The reason you need to starve yourself is so that you have the desire and adrenalin to drive like Luke Skywalker trying to escape from Darth Vader when it comes to midday. While driving to the restaurant of your choice (where you will of course eat a four-course lunch and drink one glass of local plonk) try to stay as close as is humanly possible to the bumper of the car in front of you. If you can, overtake it on a blind corner.

On no account should your knees be anywhere except under a table by 12.30 at the latest. If you miss this witching hour, you're doomed and you will be ostracised by the rest of society. If you ask a waitress for a menu she will shake her head and look at her watch. Although she will pretend to be sympathetic, she will secretly despise you.

Once lunch is over, you should make your way back to the office. But do not hurry. You must on no account work more than 35 hours a week, so if it takes you three hours to get back to your desk don't worry. Have a siesta somewhere en route and don't forget to have a pee in public, obligatory if you're a man.

Once back in the office beware: Someone may ask you to do something slightly out of the ordinary that wasn't decided at least six months ago. Your response to this should be '*c'était pas prévu*' or it wasn't planned. You must refuse to cooperate. Similarly if anyone should have the nerve to ask you to do something at ten to six, calmly tell them you are packing up your pencils and then you have to go.

If anyone tried to engage you in conversation during the day there are two topics of discussion: Politics and food. You must brush up on the names of relevant politicians and be able to hate them convincingly. Should they ever appear on television it is customary to jump up and down in front of the television hurling abuse at them. This swearing must be in French but it is fairly easy to pick up. If you get stuck, just repeat *connard* (jerk) several times.

Avertissement is a warning or caution, from the verb *avertir*—to warn. 'Advertisement' is *une publicité, une réclame,* or *un spot publicitaire.*

Blesser means to wound, injure, or offend. 'Bless' means *bénir.*

Bras is an arm. 'Bras' as the plural of 'bra'—*soutien-gorge.*

Une bride refers to a bridle. 'Bride' is *une mariée.*

Candide means naïve or ingenuous. 'Candid' means open or frank: *franc, sincère.*

Car is most often used as a conjunction: because or for. As a noun, it refers to a coach or bus. 'Car' is *une voiture.*

Caractère refers only to the character or temperament of a person or thing: *Cette maison a du caractère*—This house has character. 'Character' can mean both nature/temperament as well as a person in a play: education develops character—*l'éducation développe le caractère.* Romeo is a famous character—*Romeo est un personnage célèbre.*

Caution is a financial term; it can mean guarantee, security, bail, or backing. 'Caution' indicates *prudence, circonspection,* or *avertissement.*

Célibataire as a noun means a bachelor, as an adjective can mean celibate or simply single/unmarried. *Célibate* is the adjective of *célibataire.*

Chaîne can refer to a chain, a production line, a mountain range, a TV channel, or a stereo. Chain can be a noun—*une chaîne*—or a verb—*enchaîner.*

Chance means luck. Chance refers to *un hasard, une possibilité,* or *une occasion.*

Façon means way, as in *voilà la façon dont il procède*—this is the way he does it. It can be translated by fashion when it is synonymous with way or manner, as in *à ma façon*—in my fashion or my way. 'Fashion' is a style or custom, usually in clothing: *mode* or *vogue.*

Facteur. In addition to factor, it can mean postman, mailman, or maker—*un facteur de pianos*—piano maker. A

The food discussion will be about where you buy your meat, bread, cheese and so on. You should carefully note which bakery has the best baguette and so on. While at the local butcher's (on no account must you buy meat from a supermarket) it is a good idea to antagonise your fellow shoppers by taking as long as you can. Another good trick is to pretend you've finished and wait until the butcher has added everything up before saying; 'Gosh, that ham looks nice,' and making him start all over again. You can easily waste an hour of yours and everyone else's time in this manner, for which they will be eternally grateful as they are all trying to avoid working more than 35 hours.

If you are stuck for a way to spend your spare time should take advantage of the French custom of the *cinq à sept*. Your wife/husband won't mind, as a '*petite aventure*' is all part of your integration process and essential if you are going to learn to be French.

You should talk about all prices in francs, old francs if possible. On no account mention the Euro unless it is to complain about some politician and inflation.

Finally, before going to sleep at night, you should read *Le Monde*. Even if you understand nothing, keep muttering '*c'est pas normal*' under your breath. This is a very useful phrase which you should use if anyone does or says anything at all to irritate you. If you can't be bothered to speak, just give them a Gallic shrug.

* * *

You will find when you move to France that a lot of family and friends will decide to visit you, so you may not need to make many French friends. With so many of ours arriving, our good taste in finding our new home has been rather too exuberantly affirmed— the flow of guests doesn't stop. My parents-in-law came to stay the first Christmas we were here, and never went back. Luckily they bought their own house, and, as one of the things I was worried

'factor' is *un facteur, un élément, un indice.*

Figure is the French word for face, but can also refer to an illustrated or mathematical figure. 'Figure' refers to numbers *chiffres* as well as to the form of a person's body: *forme, silhouette.*

Napkin is correctly translated as *serviette*: I need a napkin—*J'ai besoin d'une serviette de table. Une serviette* on its own is a towel.

Parcelle means a bit or a fragment, or can refer to a parcel of land. 'Parcel' refers to *un colis* or *un paquet.*

Particulier as an adjective has a range of meanings: particular, specific, characteristic, distinctive, special, peculiar, or private. As a noun, it refers to a person or individual.

Pays refers to a certain territory, usually a country, but can on occasion refer to a *village.* 'Pays' is the third person singular of the verb to pay: he pays me cash—*il me paie en liquide.*

Personne as a noun means person, but as a pronoun, it can mean anyone or no one: *Elle le connait mieux que personne*—She knows him better than anyone. *Personne n'est ici*—No one is here.

Phrase means a sentence. A phrase is *une expression* or *locution.*

Pièce means piece only in the sense of broken pieces. Otherwise, it indicates a room, a sheet of paper, coin, or play. Piece as a part of something is *un morceau* or *une tranche.*

Préjudice means loss, harm, or damage. 'Prejudice' refers to *préjugé(s)* or *prévention(s).*

Saler means to salt. 'Sale' is the noun for *vente* or *solde.*

Secret can, in addition to the English sense of secret, mean reserved or reticent: *Il est secret*—He is reserved. 'Secret' refers to something that is not public knowledge.

Sensible means sensitive or even nervous, as in *pas recommandé aux sensibles*—not recommended for people of a nervous disposition. 'Sensible' means to show good sense, e.g., in

about was depriving my children of their family, it has been good having them here.

Jonathan, another very good friend, came to stay about 17 times before we finally told him he had to buy his own place. He dutifully went off and spent a fortune on a house four times the size of ours and had it beautifully renovated by our designer friend Peter. He holds exquisite dinners in his garden but is otherwise rarely here. When he is, he still seems to prefer to hang out with us, so is often found on our terrace, plotting his latest crusade against the BBC or the Channel ferry operators. He is godfather to Olivia and I fear is instilling her with subversive ideals. She has already caused havoc at school. Miller pronounces himself 'delighted' with her.

Of course, you will also find that you are invited by the local British simply because you are an expat.

There are several classes. There are those who have holiday homes and those who live here. Those who live permanently in France tend to look down upon the former. Then, within the living-here category there are those who have recently arrived and the long-timers. Long-timers have been here for 20 years or more and have gone native. In the south of France, some of them even speak with a local accent. You would never think they were English if you bumped into them in the street. They in turn look down upon the 'newcomers', i.e. anyone who has been here less than ten years.

One of my neighbours, Ray, is in this category. The first time I met him, he showed up at my house covered in blood. I was swimming in the pool when Donia, our babysitter from the UK, popped her head over the terrace.

'There's a man covered in blood at the door,' she said, in the same voice you would use to announce the postman. Donia is used to drama. In one year she was taken hostage in the petrol station she was working in and hit over the head with a gun, she crashed her car into eleven others (during the same incident), and she was

making decisions: *sensé, raisonnable, sage.*

Souvenir is the French verb for 'to remember' as well as a noun for memory, recollection, and remembrance. *Un souvenir* is a keepsake or memento.

Spectacle refers to any sort of exhibition: *un spectacle de danse*—a dance performance or something that others can watch: *le spectacle de la rue*—the bustle on the street. *Spectacle* can mean an exhibition, but is usually used with a negative connotation: you made a spectacle of yourself—*tu t'es donné en spectacle.*

Supporter means to support or hold up, as well as to endure or put up with something. 'Support' means all of these things, but in the sense of enduring something, *soutenir* is the more common translation.

attacked by a psychotic heroin addict on the streets of Brighton.

Throwing on a sarong, I rushed upstairs. Ray had fallen off his horse while riding in the *garrigue* close to our house. A rabbit had popped out of a hole. His horse went one way and he went the other. Ray left England 25 years ago to escape borstal and Mrs. Thatcher. He married the daughter of the region's most celebrated folk singer and has made a life down here as a jazz musician. He is known as Ray Trop and has a reputation for being a bit of a madman, albeit an incredibly talented one. He is a brilliant guitarist and singer, and a total flirt.

The girls looked at him in horror as I bandaged him up.

'You've got a big hurty,' my daughter Olivia said.

'No,' laughed Ray, looking dreadful. 'It's only pretend. Just a bit of paint.'

Despite the shared nationality, there is almost more antagonism between the Brits in France than there is between the French and the Brits. As journalists writing about France, my husband and I are always being blamed for 'bringing more Brits' over here. My mother-in-law was recently stopped in the street by a British estate agent who you would think would be delighted to have the place crawling with potential house buyers. 'It's your son's fault there are all these people coming over here,' she said, referring to a book he has written on the region. 'I preferred it when it was more quiet.'

The British, in fact, seem to antagonise each other easily. Another English friend recently bought a house in a village close by and told me that one of her British neighbours showed up on her doorstep soon after she moved in.

'I thought I would come and introduce myself,' she said. 'Us both being English and all that.'

'Of course I immediately loathed her,' my friend told me.

Another friend who wishes to remain nameless tells me she despises the habit the English have of using the odd French word in a sentence. 'They'll say, oh which *boulangerie* do you go to? The other thing I hate is people kissing me three times. Most of them I wouldn't even want to kiss once, but to adopt the local habit of three is unforgivable.'

I have asked people what it is about other expats that bothers them. 'I didn't come hear to hang out with other Brits,' is one common retort. 'They're all so boring. All they want to do is sit around drinking all day and getting red-faced,' is another. 'A lot of people probably move to France to reinvent themselves,' says a friend of mine who has lived here for 14 years. 'It is very easy to be exactly what you want to among the French, they don't know enough about England to place you.'

Despite our efforts, we have not done as well at integrating as I would have liked. I can count my French friends on one hand. I am under no illusion that we will ever be considered French. That much is obvious, however many French lessons (or lovers) we have. There seem to be two worlds which exist next to one another. A lot of dinners we are now invited to are either predominantly English or French, in other words people that speak French along with the

French or just English.

4
Earth, Wind and Fire

The ancients believed there were four elements. In the thorny *garrigue* where we live, between the Mediterranean Sea and the Black Mountains, it is easy to see why. We have regular storms of a ferocity that occurs perhaps once a generation in Britain. The ditches become raging torrents, rivers flood, and every year a number of unwary people are carried away and drowned.

In the summer there is baking heat, the screeching of cicadas and no rain. These *canicules*—literally dog days—can only be endured by sleeping through most of the day and working at night. These heatwaves end in September, with an enormous clap of thunder and brilliant electrical storms, leaving most of the electrical appliances in the house wrecked.

There is the earth, which the French call *terroir*. And then there is the most quixotic element of all: water. Water for drinking. Water for bathing. Water that does not necessarily gush from the tap. It is easy to understand why the old French peasants always have their eye on the sky. I certainly feel we live much closer to the elements here than we did in England. Here, the relationship with water is more intimate, interactive and at times, threatening.

For example, we are dependent on a spring for all our water. So if there is the slightest problem in any part of the complicated system that brings water from the source via a series of underground pipes and storage tanks to the house, nothing comes out of the tap. This has now happened countless times.

The first time, Rupert had just started a new contract helping to arrange a series of educational programmes for journalists on the importance of water. The irony was not lost on me. As he was away somewhere gallivanting about trying to make water flow to the world, here in our French paradise there was no water at all.

The film *Jean de Florette* by Claude Berri, set in Provence in the 1920s, portrays a crippled ingénue played by Gerard Depardieu, dying in agony trying to provide water to his family as malevolent local peasants, played by Yves Montand and Daniel Auteuil, plot to steal his land. It is odd that this film with its dark portrayal of the French rural character became one of the most successful French films of its time. There were not only evil peasants to consider when our water stopped for the first (but not the last) time.

Normally I am stuck in the house alone when this sort of thing happens. Rupert always contrives to be away when there are domestic disasters and phones me from some luxury hotel, pretending to be sympathetic while working his way through the minibar.

The best person to call in a crisis is always my cleaning lady, Geneviève, who has many years of experience in the various disasters that the elements can throw at you here. She thrives on crises, and is brilliant at volunteering her husband Jean-Pierre to sort them out. He has come to my rescue many times as when Sam, our dog, was on heat and seemed to be stuck to some random stray (I had no idea that was how they mated and thought they had crashed into a tube of super-glue or something).

There was the time when the washing machine started smoking and looked as if it was about to blow up. I was convinced we would have to buy another one, but Jean-Pierre fished out a five centimes piece that was causing all the trouble (callously left in a pocket by Rupert). Jean-Pierre also comes to my rescue even when I'm not there. On a trip to England I had a call from Monika, our Slovakian babysitter, who was alone in the house. She has spent a couple of years in Italy where she perfected the art of hysterical behaviour. The lights had gone out. There was an axe murderer outside just waiting to come in and chop her into tiny pieces, after he had tortured her almost to death and stolen all her possessions. I called Geneviève, who told me Jean-Pierre would be there immediately. He got the lights back on and Monika agreed not to leave.

In case of a lack of water Jean-Pierre is phenomenal. He can normally fix the pump, or fiddle with the wiring so the whole thing jerks into action once more. He only failed me once.

'Don't you worry *Madame*,' Geneviève assured me on one particularly difficult occasion, as Jean-Pierre stood looking bemusedly at the empty tank in the garden. 'This is up to the fire brigade now. They can't just leave a pregnant woman alone with children and no water.' She ordered them to deliver a tanker filled with water. Unfortunately the trailer overturned on its way up the small country road. Luckily it was warm enough to have a bath in the swimming-pool.

Even Jean-Pierre was at a loss. The system seemed to be working well, but nothing was happening. The tank was just not filling up. Geneviève said we had probably used up all the water in the source. I was horrified.

How would we survive?

'You need a *sourcier*,' said Jean-Pierre.

'A *quoi*?'

'An expert on natural water sources, he'll tell you if you have any water left.' Jean-Pierre gave me a telephone number.

'Apparently he can tell if you have got any water just by talking to you on the phone,' I told Rupert that evening when I called him in his faraway hotel. 'I would have thought that he could tell that we

It's time to get undressed again,' my husband says to me about once every three months.

This is part of the regular ritual we have to go through to get water into the house, not some south of France swinging club. Our winter in France, as in England, was very dry. I'm sure our system is going to continually seize up, and I will have to spend most of the summer in my underwear scaring the salamanders in the water tank.

You need to beware of idyllic properties in the middle of nowhere: more often than not, there is no mains water. This means that if your well or source dries up, it's your bad luck. Your dream home can suddenly turn into a Jean de Florette-type nightmare.

This has happened to Madeleine Hazard and Charlie Makin. In December 2003, the couple from west London bought a four-bedroom house near a small village called Cucuron in the Luberon region of Provence for €575,000 (about £400,000).

They had been looking for a place for more than a year and were delighted to find it. 'It just seemed like paradise to us,' Madeleine says. 'Just what we were looking for, set in a stunning garden full of olive trees, high above the village.'

They knew the house didn't have mains water, but had the well tested as part of the survey and were told it was fine.

'When we had the survey done in winter, the output/supply of water was fine,' explains Madeleine. 'You are advised to ensure that you have a minimum of three cubic metres per hour, which we did.'

They went out the following spring and built a swimming pool. It was then they noticed something was wrong. 'The water pressure just didn't feel right,' Madeleine continues. 'There was a great big drop. Then the people that had built the pool told us there wasn't enough water to fill it.' They had to pay for a company to bring tankers of water to fill it from Aix-en-Provence.

When they came back to the house for the summer, there was no water at all. Their friendly Spanish neighbour still had

didn't have water by the fact you were phoning him up,' was his response.

Tony, as the *sourcier* was called, arrived the next day. He was Spanish. I was slightly concerned to discover that he spoke a French as unintelligible as my own. But he also spoke good English. He walked over to the source and produced a two-foot long strip of plastic. Wearing a rather thoughtful look, he moved it around. Suddenly it started twitching in his hands.

'You 'ave water,' he said. 'We know that,' I replied. 'The trouble is that we don't have it in the house.' I explained to him the Byzantine workings of our water supply. It flows from the source into a small tank; this is transferred into a neighbouring tank, which is then pumped 40 metres across the garden into a four cubic metre holding tank, from where it is pumped into the house. Tony wandered around, then came up with the solution. 'This tank 'ere is leaking. Buy some special cement, slap it everywhere, and all will be right as rain,' he said.

He explained to me about springs. I had thought that behind the rock was a large underground reservoir, that once tapped, would spring into life like an oil well. Apparently not. Springs are more like underground gutters, which channel water down through the rocks. Springs can dry up. The water can just go somewhere else. 'Don't be alarmed,' he said. 'I think you will be fine.'

I asked him whether he thought we were using too much water. 'You cannot use too much water,' he said. 'If it is coming out and you don't use it, it will just go to waste.'

It was nice to have one of Geneviève's doomsday theories trashed. Tony relieved me of €30 and disappeared in his white van. Then Jean-Pierre showed up. I told him what we had to do. He did not think there was a leak from the tank. He went down to the large holding tank and got inside. 'There is no water coming in,' he said.

So now we had water coming in from the source and disappearing magically somewhere in the garden. I went down to look at him

water and allowed them to link a hose to his supply and fill up their bathtub as an emergency measure.

Madeleine asked the mayor what it would cost to bring a water supply from the village and was told the bill would be about £60,000. She approached her neighbours to see if they wanted to share the expense. 'Their attitude was that it was their right to have water and they shouldn't have to pay for it.' This is not the case. If you have bought a house with a well or a source, the responsibility of how to get water to your house rests with you.

Madeleine and Charlie have solved their problem by buying a 10,000-litre tank and burying it in the garden, at a cost of £8,000. It will need to be refilled every 10 days at a cost of £120 throughout the summer. They are looking forward to the day when mains water is finally connected...

squeezed in the tank.

'What is that floating on the bottom?' I asked.

The floating ball had fallen from the ceiling of the tank. It was not what was preventing the water from flowing in, but we could see there was another opening that had jammed shut. He opened it and we heard water flow, a dim sound, but as pleasurable as that of a waiter bringing you an iced vodka and tonic.

'We must wait and see,' he said.

All that day I checked the tank to see if it was filling up. There seemed to be the sound of running water, but I wondered if I was imagining it. That evening I went and sat by the spring, watching the small holding tank fill up with water, three litres a minute. After half an hour the moon came out. Then there was the unmistakable sound of a pump. I ran from the tank to the reservoir by the house. There was the sound of running water. From somewhere indoors came the sound of a washing machine starting up and a dishwasher coming to life.

On other occasions, we have problems with too much water. Before we invested in a huge four-wheel drive, we really were often completely cut off during the winter. There are rivers to either side of the house and during the storms we often had to leave the children with the babysitter until the water subsided. Rupert and I would drive as close as we could to the water and assess the situation. Was it really worth risking the car, and the children, just to get them home for the night? They would only have to make the same perilous journey the next day to get back to the babysitter. And what if it rained even more and we were stranded at home with the children? Possibly even more terrifying than being stranded without them.

It is the elemental quality of France that for me, having spent years living in the cramped, temperate UK, is so surprising. This is a place where the forces of nature are genuinely overwhelming. Your everyday life is affected by the elements in a way it is so rarely in England. When did you last not go shopping because it was too hot?

Or when did you last not get on a plane because the airport was closed due to flooding or snow? The French have learned to cope with these natural disasters. They have efficient forces of firemen and rescue workers. The regular floods that burst from the Rhône cause devastation but this is quickly cleaned up by the emergency services. Angela Thomas was very impressed after her house was flooded. 'There was no shortage of organisations coming round to see what I needed,' she says. 'They provided me with a new fridge and all sorts of things I had lost.'

When the *garrigue* catches fire in the summer, spectacular water bombers arrive. I remember seeing a fire over the hills one night, I wasn't sure what to do but thought I ought to call someone. In France the emergency numbers are split up. You call 15 for an ambulance, 17 for the police and 18 for the fire brigade. I dialled 18 and was politely told that they were already aware of the blaze.

Ten minutes later the planes arrived and the fire was under control. Around us they cut fire breaks. When I first saw the great machines in action I thought they were razing the ground to build a housing estate. Not so, I was told by the friendly forest ranger, who then offered to cut a circular walk for us on the hill opposite and called it '*La Promenade des Anglais*'.

When the storms come we have to unplug all the computers and the phones. In fact, it was Geneviève who first told me we needed to do this. I of course ignored her, for she is extremely dramatic at times and I thought she was exaggerating. When I went to switch on my computer the hard drive had failed. The phone line was working but crackling terribly. The insurance covered the cost of replacing the computer and France Telecom sorted out the phone. In terms of insurance though, you need to be careful. A lot of policies do not cover natural disasters.

All this is slightly humiliating. Whereas in Britain the transport system can collapse because of rain or the wrong kind of snow or leaves on the track, disasters seem to be on a kinder, more gentle scale than those here. The winds here are usually that much stronger, sometimes just walking into the wind can feel like a workout. The bolts of lighting—the *sturm und drang* from the heavens—is just on a different scale. In places like India, Africa, and the western parts of the United States, there is a similar respect for the rage that nature has in reserve.

It is hard to describe just how hot it gets here in summer. I remember one of the first mornings after we moved in. It was the beginning of September and we set off at 7am to buy our morning bread from the village bakery. Buying my morning bread is one of the things I had been fantasising about us doing since we signed the contract to buy the house. I was heavily pregnant (for a change) and wore a sarong and a T-shirt. All went well until we started for home. By now it was almost 8am. Suddenly the sun tripled in strength and at one stage I thought I was going to have to lie down in the road. I took my T-shirt off in an effort to cool down. Luckily there was no one about.

Seeking the shade is a concept so alien to anyone who lives in England. But during July and August when I go shopping I will cross the road if there is shade the other side. Carrying out any chores is a nightmare, you come back home feeling like you've been bashed over the head with a cricket bat. The heat is so intense around the house you can actually hear it—a sort of buzzing noise combining cicadas with relentless hot air. By the end of August the garden looks as if it's been burnt, everything is dry and yellow.

We have had plenty of problems with electricity since coming to France. When we first moved here it kept cutting out for no apparent reason. We would know it had cut out, not only because there were no lights, but the house alarm would start a high-pitched squeal, usually when we just got the children to sleep. There seemed to be no reason for the constant cuts.

In the summer, I wondered whether it could be the heat. I thought it might have melted the cables. I also used to blame the power cuts on the wind. We don't have the infamous mistral here, but we have what seems to be its younger brother. Once I went for a siesta and woke up to find the three metre square pool umbrella snapped to bits in the water. The wind had lifted it from its stand.

Our most memorable power cut was during our first year in the house on Christmas Eve. We had invited 12 people for a Swedish dinner. Just as we raised our first glass of schnapps, the lights went out. Luckily we had bought a lot of candles from the Toulouse IKEA, along with the schnapps. We lit about 20 of them and waited for the electrician to show up. It was rather romantic, the whole atmosphere suddenly changed and became more intimate. There was a feeling of siege around the table as we fumbled around for the herring. The electrician showed up about 20 minutes later. He is a local man, but married to an Englishwoman. He speaks good English but with an extremely pronounced French accent making it rather like having Inspector Clouseau checking your wiring.

'Theez is most strrrange,' he told the candle-lit company, as he wandered from fuse box to trip switch prodding things. He couldn't understand why some circuits worked and not others, there seemed to be no rational explanation for it. Eventually all the lights came back on, but we decided we liked it better before, so once he had gone, we turned them all back off again.

The electricity still goes off periodically, but we have dismantled the alarm, so I don't really mind too much.

5
Sleeping with the Enemy

When we first moved to France I had no fixed idea how I would make a living. So I invited the letting company Bowhills to come and see me in my new home to tell us if we could rent it out for the summer. My plan was that we would decamp to England or Sweden for two months.

'You'll have to change a lot of the fittings,' said a rather sniffy woman as she walked around the house grimacing. 'It's all a bit, well, shabby.'

She went on to tell me all the things I would have to provide prospective tenants with, from new linen to swimming-pool towels. 'The good thing about it though,' she looked at me and started to fill in some dreadful looking form, 'is that it's big enough for two families with several children between them to share.' The thought of someone else's children running around my house was enough to put me off the idea of renting forever. I told Mrs Sniffy that I would have to think about it.

A lot of people who move to France decide to make money by renting out their homes. The formula is simple. You sell up in England, buy somewhere here for a quarter of the price, and convert part of it into a *gîte*. If you have no mortgage, you don't need much of an income and so you can live off the rent from your *gîte*.

Or you keep a smaller place in the UK and rent out your house in France during the peak summer months when you can get literally thousands of pounds a week. This pattern has become so widespread here that it is now known as *la maladie anglaise*.

The formula may be simple, but it is an area full of unexpected pitfalls. Penny and Alan, friends from Sussex, for example, have a house nearby and rent out a cottage attached to it. Their first tenants came from Birmingham and were due to stay for two weeks. 'We rushed around like mad getting the whole place ready for them,' says Penny. 'We had done a lot of work to the cottage and were really pleased with the results. We had always planned to buy somewhere where there was the possibility of an income,' continues Penny. 'Our idea was that once Alan retired completely we could downsize at home and live here almost all the time.'

The guests arrived a sunny Wednesday morning and Penny showed them around the newly converted cottage. 'I felt proud and happy showing them around,' she said. 'It was like the beginning of a new era for us.' Everything seemed to be fine until they found their tenants outside the following morning with their bags packed. 'They had been kept awake all night by scratching and scrabbling in the attic, and they were convinced the place was infested with rats,' says Penny. 'I was horrified and tried to calm them down, but they were having none of it. They upped and left, leaving us an address to send the refund to.'

In fact, their cottage isn't rat-infested, it is home to a small mouse-like creature indigenous to the south of France called a *loir*. It is translated as a dormouse in the dictionary but it has small circles round its eyes, rather like a raccoon. The next day, the Hastings-Jones called in the pest control people. 'This man arrived with a box of carrots and a bag of poison,' says Penny. 'I couldn't believe it. And all he did was roll the carrots in the poison and shove them under the tiles in the roof where the *loir* go in and out. He charged us £100 and cluttered off, warning us not to tell the authorities we had done this as the *loir* is a protected species. I have to say, I rather liked the look of them and felt really miserable about the idea of killing them.'

The following day, Penny went outside expecting to see the garden littered with dead creatures. Instead she found a row of carrots that had been neatly pushed out. 'It was as if they'd been offended by this foreign object,' she says. 'They had just pushed them out, without so much as nibbling on them.'

Alan and Penny have decided to let them stay and now warn tenants about them with a description and picture in the information manual. 'We've tried to make it a positive thing,' Alan explains. 'To make it part of the whole experience of being here, as opposed to just a pest.' So far, they have had no more complaints.

Not many people let strangers rampage through their home for their own enjoyment. It is only driven by necessity. Another of my friends who rents out her house over the hill from us calls her tenants 'the enemy'. She arrives at the beginning of every letting season with bags of supplies. 'I've just got to get the place ready for them,' she says. 'God knows what state it will be in once they've all gone.'

When Selina Howard decided to build a £1 million house on the French Riviera, the future rental income she could get was very much part of the equation. 'I figured that if I could get £3,500 per week for the whole of the summer, the house would at least run itself in terms of costs and any profit could be put towards the mortgage.' Her house was barely finished when her agent told her she had some tenants. They were a New York family with one small child. He was an investment banker, she a housewife. The fact that they had decided to rent the house for the full six weeks was a huge bonus. 'I was delighted,' she says. 'It seemed too good to be true, I hadn't even had to go looking for anyone.'

Claire Gooch of Riviera Search International, the agent dealing

The French created the perfect village. There are examples are all over France; Beynac in the Dordogne, Tourtour in the Var, Olargues in the Hérault, all exquisite in their own way. The church is normally at the centre, cobbled streets winding down from it, the *hôtel de ville* stands proudly in the main street, along with the butcher, the baker and post office. In the village square bereted men play *pétanque* in the evening sun. When I first moved here I was convinced they were sponsored by the French Tourist Association This idyll may soon be challenged.

Where I am, in the south, we are seeing a process of destruction as criminal as it is rapid. On my school run in England I used to drive through the suburbs of Crowborough, a more depressing start and end to the day is hard to imagine. Now I drive through three medieval villages. One of them even has a real-life fairy tale castle, just like the one you see at the beginning of Disney animated films. When I first moved here four years ago I used to look forward to the school run. It was a good chance to see if the local prince was home. Now it is almost getting depressing.

The sudden migration into the region by northerners from all over Europe has put immense pressure on the housing market. The French have responded by allowing a housing estate or lotissement epidemic. The south of France is the new Florida. And just like Florida land it is being sold off in parcels to the highest bidder.

The definition of a *lotissement* is one plot of land divided into two or more individual plots for housing. Once in possession of one of these plots the locals, either individuals, companies or the council, will build concrete house covered in *crépi* or rendering of questionable taste. One really choice example I saw the other day was actually painted mauve. The effect will be completed by a breezeblock wall to keep out intruders. As if anyone in their right mind would actually want to go inside one. But the point is this: Tragically the French seem to have lost touch with their traditional building methods, materials and

with the property, said they should have seen the warning signs. 'I only had contact with the wife before they landed, and she seemed OK, if a little demanding. They wanted all sorts of child-safety equipment, and were very insistent on having a king-size bed.' The owner assured Gooch that the bed was king-size and left for England. When the couple arrived, they took one look at the bed (queen-size in the US) and threatened to sue. Gooch spent the rest of the day locating a king-size bed. 'The man was incredibly aggressive,' she says. 'He was furious at the inventory the owner had left, which was 10 pages long and listed everything in the house. The client threw all the papers up in the air and shouted: 'does she really think I've flown all the way from New York to steal a corkscrew?'

Gooch and the house manager managed to calm them down, but not a day passed during the six weeks when they didn't phone up to complain about something and threaten a lawsuit. In addition, they had demanded air-conditioning units in every room, at a cost of £250 a month each, as well as barriers around the swimming-pool, which cost another £1,000.

Howard was lucky she had appointed an agent to deal with it all and gone back home. 'I would strongly advise anyone thinking of renting to get professional help,' says Gooch. 'If at all possible, go for a local British agent and stay away from the whole rental process, let the professionals handle it.' This could either be an agent, or someone living locally who does this kind of thing for a living. An agent is likely to be more expensive, charging up to 25 per cent of the rent. The going rate for an individual is around 15 per cent of rental income.

When we'd been in our house for about six months, I met a charming man who lived in the nearest village to us. He wasn't here during the summer months and suggested that I take on the renting of his house. He would pay for all the advertisements, I would take the bookings and see people in and out, making sure the place

above everything the way they laid out their towns to be genuinely functional. Instead of cohesion we now have sprawl.

Some would argue that the reason for all the cheap housing is that we Brits have moved in en masse and bought up any old wreck for an inflated price, thus making the only choice for the locals a cheap concrete monstrosity on a housing estate. Granted, house prices have gone up, but give a young French family the choice of an isolated old farmhouse with cracks in the wall and no central heating (like ours) and a nice spanking new house close to the school with all the mod-cons and about 99 per cent will go for the latter. This passion for old stone is a particularly British affair. In one of the medieval villages I drive past every day there was a building that resembled a shed but was in fact a medieval nail factory. It was one of those buildings that used to make me happy just looking at it. Lots of old stone, all expertly laid on top of one another to form a structure that had lasted for hundreds of years. One day it was gone; smashed to the ground by the local farmer that owns it. A few weeks later he had built a replacement shed, out of breezeblock, where he now stores his tractor. Every time I drive past I feel like getting out and letting his tyres down.

Some friends of mine bought a lovely house in a nearby village a year or so ago. They are now thinking of moving as plans have been agreed to build 98 houses in the field next door to them. The field was a vineyard, looked over by most of the village which is built, as so many French villages are, on a hill. This latest housing estate will ruin the character of the village, and for what? To line the pockets of the family who own it.

If you are buying a property in France the first thing you should do before you start imagining drinks on the terrace overlooking a vineyard is to find out what the *plan locale d'urbanisme* is for the land around your property. You can get this information from the mayor's office. If the area is lodged as high/medium residential then you need to ask if anyone has lodged an application to build a *lotissement*. But bear in mind

was clean and so on. It seemed like an easy job. He was charging £1,300 a week and the house was quickly booked up for July and August. Six weeks before the tenants descended, the whole of their rent had arrived in my bank account. I would have to think about giving it back to the owner when the time came.

We had agreed that he would give me 30 per cent of the rental income, which was a very good deal. The first visitors came from Israel. There were two families with teenage children. The men were all huge and the women tiny and beautiful. I showed them around while silently cursing the lunatic nextdoor neighbour who had chosen that moment to move his collection of tractors around his rather unsightly plot.

'It's wonderful,' they all said. 'And so peaceful compared with Tel Aviv.' Their stay was marvellous, except for one of the huge men going through a sun-lounger. I was particularly struck by how much one of the mothers appreciated getting up in the morning and just going for a walk in the countryside. Something I do every day and had started to take for granted.

The problems started with the arrival of the next guests, some rather grumpy types from the north of England. Suicide bombers did not frequent their daily lives so they found the neighbour irritating and noisy. In addition, the sanitation system collapsed on their second day and the downstairs bath filled with sewage. I was telephoned at 11pm and told to do something about it. I explained that French plumbers only work 35 hours a week (at best) and that they were unlikely to come and see to a sewer at that time of night. I promised I would have one there the next morning. That night I lay awake trying to work out how to keep my promise. One of the worst things about living here is getting anything done. Plumbers, electricians and so on, are horribly unreliable.

The first two plumbers I called at 8am couldn't do anything for a week. The third one said he would be there at midday. I called the house and told them I would send the cleaning lady in to clean the

that the *plan locale d'urbanisme* can be revised by the commune or the state at any time.'

A French friend of mine once said: 'The French don't appreciate France, only the English do.' I found it an outrageous comment at the time, but I'm beginning to agree with him. It is an ironic footnote that the people complaining loudest about the destruction of the countryside in France are the British.

sewage-filled bath and see them there at 12pm. They seemed to have calmed down and I thought the worst was over.

At noon, I was there, as were seven rather hot and irritable people waiting to have a bath. The plumber, of course, failed to show up. And by then it was too late to do anything until at least 2pm as France shuts for lunch. I offered bribes of wine and baths at my house but my suggestions were met with stony silence. I couldn't really blame them. As Marcelle Speller, of Holiday-Rentals.com says: 'People who come on holiday just want it all to be perfect, they don't want to deal with things they have to deal with at home, they just want to relax.'

The sewage saga continued throughout the summer. It would be fixed by some mad plumber only to break down again. Finally it was concluded that the fault lay with the person who originally converted the place for putting in a pump that was too weak to do its job properly. But I had eight weeks of disgruntled guests, which was hellish. And not an experience I am keen to repeat.

Luckily my friend has decided to stop letting out the house. He says the damage caused by the tenants, such as a tear in the swimming-pool lining and breaking the automatically closing gates, negates the profit.

'People on holiday will behave in a manner they wouldn't even think of at home,' says Alexandra Wills. She bought her house on the outskirts of a small village close to Toulouse for £150,000. She put down £50,000 and has a mortgage for £700 a month. She lets the house for £1,300 a week during July and August. 'I realised that I could work from anywhere and thought it would be great to be able to come on extended holidays with my daughter but not feel like I was wasting time. Also, prices in this region were still relatively affordable when I bought this. I think it was a very good investment.'

Alexandra tells stories of cream sofas covered in chocolate stains and horrendous telephone bills. 'It got to a stage where I almost said no children. Get a hefty deposit, that's my advice, and throw the phone out. Everyone has mobiles these days.' She says she will carry on letting her house. 'It gets easier as the years go on, and you learn what not to put in it, like cream carpets that need to be steam cleaned. The sad thing is, you end up furnishing it for eventual disasters and not for yourself. And the thought of other people trashing your house is awful. It is very hard to tell what they're like over the internet.'

According to Gooch, who deals mainly with up-market properties, no amount of deposit, however, will safeguard you from some tenants. 'In some of the real luxury homes, even a £10,000 deposit won't cover the damage. It is mainly caused by Russians, who have that kind of money, along with a complete lack of respect for other people's property. In fact, a lot of clients, not only Russians, have an 'I've paid a lot of money, so I'll do what I want attitude.' Gooch tells of a collection of several precious antique vases being smashed as they were thrown at the husband of a family who rented a house in St Tropez. 'He was a British peer, with his own manservant and two wives. I don't know which of the wives did the damage, maybe both of them. I think they got fed up with him going out partying all night with his mates from Monaco, really not the kind of behaviour one would expect!'

Jeffrey Quirk of JQ International, a tax and law firm based in southwest France, maintains that most unpleasant rental experiences are the fault of the owners and their desire to save money. 'Nine times out of ten it's the owners who create the problems,'he explains. 'Most expats leave their brains behind on the airplane. They come out here and expect to do it all on their own. They forget how they would do it at home and try to do it all under the table as cheaply as possible.'

Quirk's advice is not to cut corners. 'Declare everything and get a proper contract drawn up, otherwise you have no recourse. And get a reputable agent involved, decide on the commission and all the terms before you start.' He also advises vetting your potential tenants. 'Some are a higher risk than others. The jet-setter hooray-Henry types tend to want to get wrecked and then wreck your house.'

Anyone looking to rent should take into account all costs and taxes before they think about making a profit. 'There is not only income tax but wealth tax, property tax and residential tax,' Gooch says.

The *taxe foncière* (property tax) is calculated according to how much land you own, how many buildings you have and so forth. It is payable even if your property is empty, providing it is habitable. Gooch quotes a client with a house of 400 m² with 2000 m² of land. They pay around £2900 a year in property tax.

The residential tax (*taxe d'habitation*) is payable by anyone living in the property and is levied by the town where the property is situated. The amount is calculated by the land registry and based on the average rental value of the property in the previous year. They will take into account the living area of the property, including outbuildings located less than one kilometre from the main house. If the property is the main family home there are reductions for dependants, which are calculated as a percentage of the rental value. This tax is not paid by those exempt from income and wealth tax. According to Gooch, it is normally around the same figure as the *taxe foncière*. It is worth noting that even if you don't live there full-time, if you occupy the building on January 1st, you are liable to pay the residential tax for the full year.

In terms of declaring your rental income, if you are not a French resident you must still declare it in France. You can declare the income and French tax paid on your tax return to the UK authorities. But there may be some additional tax to pay if you have not paid as much in France as you would at home.

If you are a French resident, *any* income has to be declared in France. You have to declare the amount you made on your annual French tax return. The authorities will deduct 72 per cent of that income and tax you on the remainder on a sliding scale according to how much you earn.

There may not be much left to declare once you've paid all the costs of running a house. 'Cleaning staff will charge you around £6-10 an hour—that's if you can find any,' says Gooch. Even if you can find staff, they are not always reliable. One agent tells the story of a cleaning lady near Avignon who cleaned three houses one season and they were all burgled during the winter. She was never seen again. 'And if you pay a cleaner or a gardener legally, you have to pay 40 per cent social security costs on top of their salary.'

Homeowners who go by the books are not likely even to cover their costs. Gooch continues, 'There are also all the other costs such as insurance, water, electricity and gas, which are all very expensive. In addition there is the general maintenance of the house. We specialise in the Côte d'Azur and there might be floods one day and scorching sun the next, and when there's not enough water, concrete structures can crack. Talking of swimming-pools, there's the cost of that.'

The issue of swimming-pools has been worrying renters in France ever since the Prime Minister's nephew drowned in one. The so-called Raffarin Law declares that any pool, rented or not, must have a barrier of some sort to prevent people falling into it. In typical French fashion, the law was announced and a deadline

A few months ago some people from the Aveyron bought a piece of land next door to us. We had been offered the land by its owner, who used it as a garden. It is a plot of about an acre and he wanted £60,000 for it. We took the view that for that amount of money we could buy a garden in Chelsea, so we declined his generous offer.

On the piece of land is a hut, rather less attractive than the one Sting is complaining about, but I had never given it much thought. The site is classified as terrain non constructible-land where no building is allowed-so nobody could move in and spoil our peace. Or so I thought.

The first thing that alerted us to our new neighbours' presence was the fact that they filled up our bin with rubbish. One of the things they had thrown away was a box for a kettle.

'Why would they want a kettle when they don't have any electricity?' my husband asked. There's no fooling him.

The next thing we heard was a generator. Then we saw satellite dishes and solar panels going up. One day a man from a fosse septique company stopped to ask us if we know where the plot is.

Suddenly there were two more huts; Sting would have been apoplectic by then. These people were clearly planning to move in. And what's even worse, they were planning to move in with two barking dogs.

My husband was furious and wanted to report them, saying that the French have a noble tradition of denouncing their neighbours. I suggested the best way to deal with the situation was to make friends with them. So we went over with a bowl of cherries from the garden and introduced ourselves.

We couldn't hear ourselves think over the din of the dogs. 'I like the tranquillity here,' said our new neighbour.

We asked him what he does for a living. Surely if he has a job he won't be able to spend too much time here?

set before they had even decided on the details of it. For those with rental properties, the deadline for putting in place a security measure was January 1st 2004. But, even as the deadline passed, the government had not announced what was acceptable under the new law. Finally, they have since issued further rules, and it seems that those rushing to put up expensive fences (which can cost thousands of pounds) may have been wasting their money. A simple alarm, available for around £500, is enough to meet the legal requirements. However, it is worth checking with your insurance company what sort of security device they will accept, as some of them will only take on liability if there is a fence. This could leave landlords in a very awkward situation should an accident occur. Also you should remember to turn your alarm off at night if it's very windy. I have been woken up at night several times by it going off due to a violent gust. This is obviously only safe providing your children don't sleepwalk in the garden and you remember to turn it back on in the morning.

Quirk, who runs *chambres d'hôtes* (bed and breakfast) himself, says he has between 30 and 40 people a year coming to stay who are looking to-buy-to-rent. According to a survey carried out by www.holiday-rentals.com, 80 per cent of owners are not renting out their properties to make money. 'They do it to keep their dreams,' says Speller. 'They rent out the properties so they can use them and enjoy them, it is not a money-making scheme. This fact is further reinforced by the statistic we came up with when we asked what their future plans for the property were. One hundred per cent said they planned to keep it or leave it to their children.' Paul Beaufils, who runs a website called www.buyahousein-france.com, agrees. 'Everyone I have come across looking to rent out their place is doing it to cover the mortgage,' he says.

Despite all the downsides, Ruth de Latude, who lets out four converted barns on her estate, loves it. 'We get to meet people from all over the world,' she says. 'Last Christmas we had eight

'I've taken early retirement,' he said. 'I got throat cancer from smoking. My wife and I will come down most weeks.'

He was true to his word, spending most of the summer in his shed, rather like Stig of the Dump. Every time we stuck our heads out of our front door the dogs barked.

My husband decided we needed to take action. To be honest, we really wouldn't have minded the huts, the satellite dishes or even someone leading a gypsy-style existence next door, but the dogs had pushed us over the edge. One of the reasons we bought our house is that it is in the middle of nowhere. If we had wanted to live close to barking dogs we would have considered other options, such as a village house, which are a lot easier, and cheaper, to come by.

'Take him a packet of cigarettes,' was one helpful friend's advice. 'Shoot the dogs,' suggested another. We found both of these solutions slightly harsh. Instead we sent a message to our neighbour through the man that sold him the land saying it was difficult for us to work or sleep with the noise of the dogs and could he keep them under control. This had no effect whatsoever.

Finally, we visited the mayor. He admitted that the original hut is illegal, but as it has been there for a while there was nothing he could do. And as for the dogs, well they are just doing their job. What is it about French people that they seem to be immune to the sound of incessantly barking dogs?

'So they can just do what they like?' asked my husband.

'Ils sont chez eux,' said the mayor. Case closed as far as he is concerned.

We went to an English lawyer for help. 'Land classed as non-constructible in France can be misleading, as certain building will still permitted,' said Dawn Alderson, a solicitor. 'But what actually passes will depend very much on the individual mayor.'

As the law was clearly not going to help us, we decided there was only one thing for it: make friends with the dogs.

Californians staying when the gas in their barn ran out. They had no hot water or heating for seven days, and it was freezing. They ended up practically living with us, became our best friends and even came to our wedding.'

One of the ways we encourage people not to come and stay with us again is to convince them to buy their own house. Rod and Fee Thompson, for example, have been bothering us for years. They arrive every summer with undrinkable bottles of Cahors which they force my husband to stay up until three in the morning consuming. One year they even broke a bed. I mean, please, these people are over 40.

This year, after their obligatory annual visit to us, they rented a lovely farmhouse in the Midi-Pyrénées. Passing an estate agent in the local town, Rod spotted a picture of a château for sale. 'It was wonderful,' he says. 'In the middle of what seems to me to be God's own country, with 17 bedrooms.'

It seems like a good idea at the time. The sun is shining, the wine is good (providing Rod didn't buy it) and the countryside is spectacular. The trade in seems like a no-brainer. A terraced house in Clapham for all this? Why not buy a place and live in this paradise forever?

But before you commit to spending the last day of your holiday in the *notaire's* office signing for the dream house, there are some things you should consider. First, is buying a place really the best option? The rental market has very flat for a while, so you may find some bargains, especially off season. If it is a holiday home that interests you, consider that you could stay for at least eight weeks a year in the luxury hotel of your choice for the cost up the upkeep on a second home in France. And you would never have to worry about burst pipes or burglars.

According to Bill Blevins of Blevins Franks International, who has been watching Brits move to France for nearly two decades, the most common mistake they make is the lack of research. 'Carry out

We explained to our neighbour that the dogs irritated us. He
was surprisingly nice about it and suggested we take Snoopy
and Unis for a walk so they could get to know us. Now, every
time they see us they don't bark, but wag their tails in antici-
pation.

a full analysis of what you are seeking to achieve from moving
abroad and then spend as long as possible reviewing all the possibilities re the areas and then precise locations in those areas,' he
says. 'Check out the selected location at all times of the year. Some
places are very hot in the summer but suffer from unexpected cold
and wet in winter. Some places are a dream in the winter and a mass
of tourists and the related activity in the summer. For example, fun
fairs, noise, night-clubs that are open all night in summer but are
virtually invisible in the winter.'

If you do find a wreck in the middle of nowhere that looks too
good to miss, try to get a precise costing for renovation before you
buy it. Many people assume that because property prices are
cheaper in France, building work is as well. This is not the case. In
fact paint is hugely more expensive in France than in the UK.
Gavin Quinney, a wine maker who did up a château outside
Bordeaux actually found it worthwhile driving back to England to
buy paint, and luckily he was able to coincide his paint runs with
Chelsea games.

Tony Tidswell, a friend who lives in a nearby village, rents out
gîtes. He recently had someone to stay who fell in love with his
whole set up and made him an offer for his crumbling and beautiful stone house he simply couldn't refuse. 'He said 'I want to buy
your life',' says Tony. 'And he has the money to finish renovating
the house in a way we just can't.' Tony and his wife Carole plan to
use the money to build a new house. A British family in a French
new build. That really is integrating.

Sadly Rod and Fee didn't experience quite the same rush of blood as Tony's guest. I even offered to lend them the money for the château. 'Oh no thanks,' was the response. 'We'd much rather stay with you.' Oh well, better buy a new (sturdier) bed.

✳ ✳ ✳

All we wanted to do was sell our almond crop at the local market. It is 7.30 in the morning and I am in the courtyard of the mayor's office in Pézenas. No, I'm not in trouble with the authorities—I'm here to sell fresh almonds.

There is a bustling market in Pézenas on a Saturday, and my husband's latest money-making scam is that we sell the almonds from our almond grove.

In order to get a stall at the market, one has to queue up with about 30 other hopefuls at the crack of dawn. Needless to say, my husband is still in bed and I am queuing. My stepson, Hugo, has agreed to come with me, with the proviso that he is home before the start of the test match.

I was amazed when I phoned the mayor's office earlier in the week to ask what one needs to do to secure a stall.

'Just show up,' said a seriously surly woman, who was clearly already bored even though it was only 9am.

'That's all? No papers to fill in? No birth certificate translated by an official translator? No need to know what I'm selling?'

'No,' she said.

I could have been coming along with pornographic literature for all she knew. Or, even worse, Wellington memorabilia.

But as we check out our fellow stallholders, I realise things aren't that simple.

In front of me in the queue are two men. They not only have papers with them but are also clutching great folders of official-looking documents.

I explain our plan, and they both shake their heads.

'They won't let you do anything without papers. We've been coming here for years, but we bring them every time,' says one, waving an impressive folder in my direction. He tells me he is here to sell goat's cheese. The other plans to sell fruit and veg.

'One man last week drove three hours to get here and was turned away because he had no insurance certificate,' adds the fruit and veg man. Our little venture seems doomed to failure.

'I know!' says Hugo. 'If we don't get a stall, the fruit and veg man could take our almonds and 50 per cent of the profit he makes on them.' This boy will go far (he is 14).

I suggest Hugo's plan to the fruit and veg man, who agrees it's a good one. Hugo then suggests we could take 50 per cent of the profits he makes on his sales as well, but he doesn't seem so taken with that idea.

I ask our new friends how the system works, and they tell me you have to register the goods you are selling, then you are given a ticket with a number on it. At eight o'clock there is a raffle, and if your number is picked, you are taken to a corresponding spot in the market.

Finally, the door opens and we start to file into an office. Behind the desk sit a police officer and a woman from the mayor's office.

'Oh, dear, this looks scary,' says Hugo. 'You're going to need all your French for this.'

As he speaks, he leans against the wall, inadvertently turning out the lights in the room.

'Uh-uh, that's not a good start,' he says, switching them back on as the policeman behind the counter sighs.

'You can always tell the newcomers,' smiles the goat's cheese-seller. 'They invariably lean on the light switch. We all know it's there.'

Finally, we get to the front of the queue.

'We're selling almonds,' I tell the policeman.

'What?' is his response.

'Almonds,' I repeat. I have changed nothing in the way I pronounce the word almonds, but this time he seems to understand.

'Where are your papers?' he demands.

'We don't have any, this is just a one-off. We're selling the contents of our almond grove.'

He and the woman look at each other in despair.

'You can't just sell to the public without any papers,' thunders the policeman.

'You need papers. Everyone before you had papers. You need to be a member of the Chamber of Commerce; you need insurance.' His list goes on and on. I am beginning to understand how an illegal immigrant trying to bluff her way into France must feel. In fact, I'm amazed they have a problem with immigrants here at all, such is the efficacy of their bureaucrats.

Hugo and I have no option but to walk out of the office without our ticket to the day's lottery, heads bowed as the rest of the queue stares at us.

Once outside, we try to find our fruit and veg man. He is nowhere to be seen. But we find the cheese-seller, who asks another stallholder he knows if she would like to sell our almonds.

'No, we don't even bother picking ours,' she says. 'Nobody wants them. The only place you can sell them is the beach.'

We walk past our friend Jean-Luc's grocery store.

'Couldn't sleep?' he asks, looking at his watch.

We tell him what has happened.

'Bring your almonds here,' he says. 'I'll sell them.'

We collect the almonds. Jean-Luc weighs them: there are 9kg.

'How much were you going to sell them for?' he asks.

'I thought €5 a kilo.

'That's what you get for dried almonds,' he tells me. 'It's too much.'

I do some shopping while I'm there. My bill comes to €44.

Jean-Luc charges me €28 and says the balance is for the almonds. We have made a total of €16 on the sale of almonds. As the saying goes, God hates a primary producer. Even in France.

6
Lucky Bastard

There will be a moment in every business phone call you'll make from France when you know that you are going to have to admit where you live. You are probably sitting on the steps, overlooking the pool and the pine trees, with the blue sky in the distance. You have seen on the television that it is raining in London, but here in the south of France it is another perfect day. Then the question comes.

'But you are not in England, are you?'

'No, I live in France.'

'Paris?'

'No. The south.'

'Ah.'

In their mind this is no longer a work call. They visualise the blue sky, the bottle of rosé wine for lunch, the afternoon siesta in the hammock.

'Lucky bastard.'

Daily abuse from harassed and envious colleagues and business contacts in London is just one of the normal trials of escaping England for a life abroad. The idea of escaping when you are retired, and fifty something, is to do so after having paid off life's mortgages, cashed in on long-appreciating UK property, and resettled for a life of essentially retirement, albeit with a bit of light activity interspersed.

But when you are twenty years younger than that, have a huge mortgage, children to bring up, and must depend for future income on a business plan that is entirely untested, it is somewhat different.

It is a good thing we did not know how hard the move would be, or we might not have had the courage to move in the first place. Our self-confidence sprang mainly from ignorance.

While it seems, in theory, that in an era of ISDN and now broadband (though not yet in our village), it is possible to substitute telecommunications for travel, and carry on with the same jobs as before, reaping northern European income streams to sustain a life of bread, wine, cheese and olives, in practice it is not so easy.

We reckoned that as journalists, and with my own sideline in lucrative corporate headhunting, we would have no problem. And this was the extent of our business plan.

In fact, we very nearly came unstuck while one child followed another. We have a big house, which means enormous out-goings and when things get bad we are often forced to take out money from maxed-out credit cards to put in the bank to cover the mortgage.

So here is the brutal reality of moving to France and taking your jobs with you. It is not impossible. But you will have to have nerves of steel to see it through. We started in a kind of haze of enthusiasm and then travelled to the depths of despair before regaining some financial equilibrium.

Rupert is a great person to live with when things get bad because he always believes something will come up. Incredibly, it does. He also says one should spend one's way out of a crisis which is why, despite looming poverty, even at the worst of times we seemed not to lack for wood in the hearth and food on the table. (Still, there are times when it is scary.)

'But what will come up? From where?' I often ask while staring at horrible letters from the bank.

'Don't panic, it's all under control,' he replies.

* * *

For journalists, writers, designers, artists, financial professionals and others, the appeal of sunshine, cheaper housing and plentiful inexpensive red wine needs no further explanation. Cheap flights, mobile phones, the internet and satellite television makes it technically more feasible than ever to work from almost anywhere.

The trick is to organise your professional career. In practice, this means building some entirely new networks, and recognising that some of the older ones may wither away.

I was quickly made redundant by my firm of headhunters. The economy was down, business dragging, I was a long way away when it came to plotting the corporate cull around the West End water cooler. Besides, if anyone has to get the chop, it is bound to be the smug git in the south of France, while the rest are slogging their way to work on the Northern Line.

Despite the difficulties that can accompany getting professionally established in France, and I have not yet come to the bureaucratic madness, the tax system, many more people are trying it. We are not the only northern Europeans here. There are winemakers, shopkeepers, designers, artists, journalists, novelists, estate agents, restaurateurs, and many others, all making a go of it. I reckon that for us, servicing clients in northern Europe and America works best—it keeps you farther away from French officialdom. But it is also possible to make it on a local level. However, one difference in France is that, unlike in Britain, your growth is limited because you are unlikely ever to want to employ anyone due to the high social charges.

There at least 500,000 British people living in France. Although

I am finally able to compare the criminal justice systems of England and France, having been in police custody in both. The first time was in England almost 20 years ago. The latest, in France, rather more recently.

I recently had an accident, or rather a frenzied French-woman had an accident with me. I was on my way to the cinema with three friends when we were diverted onto a small country road due to a serious pile-up on the main one. I was driving slowly, discussing the perils of French driving, when a black car came speeding towards us. Just as I thought it was going to race past, it crashed into us.

This is the third time I have been crashed into since I moved to France. You might, as my husband suggests, think this has something to do with my ability to drive. But the first time I was stationary and the second time I was on my side of the road. Sadly, so was the car that ploughed into me.

This time I was as close to the kerb as I could be but still the oncoming driver couldn't avoid hitting me. I stopped and got out, as did the other driver.

'You squashed me,' she told me angrily as I approached.

'That's funny,' I replied. 'I had the same sensation.'

A 15-minute argument ensued. The other driver refused to swap details; she said she wanted to wait for her husband. I was in no mood to wait-he might try to drive into me, too. In addition, traffic on the tiny road was heavy due to the diversion and I was worried we might cause another accident. The woman became increasingly unreasonable.

'I've spent 15 years working in accident and emergency,' said Beth Anne, a doctor friend who was with me. 'This woman has what we would define a hysterical personality. We need to get out of here.'

I took the arrival of a tour bus beeping behind my car to do just that. On we went to the cinema, reasoning that it was her fault anyway and that would be the end of it.

Imagine my surprise when the police showed up a few days

many of them are retired or rich, there is a growing number making a living here. Paul Vernon, for example, fled from England over twelve years ago. His first step was to open a restaurant on the Riviera, even though 'I did not speak French and knew nothing about restaurants'. The California Republic was a raging success, so much so that he sold it to a Frenchman after a year. Then he lived for nearly ten years on a hillside, enacting his own French version of the 'Good Life'. With no running water or electricity, and relying on firewood for heating, it was hard work. Now he works for I2I Europe, an internet company that puts on special events for companies such as Microsoft, Gateway and AMD. Vernon organised the first live interactive pub quiz from a bar in Monaco, with Prince Albert as a competitor. His company also staged the first live web transmission from the Cannes film festival. Would he go back to England? 'Never,' he says. 'The quality of life is so much better here. I love everything about it.'

For those who choose to move to France and decide to work there as well, the most obvious form of income is *gîtes*. However, there are now so many Brits offering compatriots places to stay that they say there are five *gîtes* for every guest.

A more imaginative approach is *chambres et tables d'hôtes*, an upmarket bed and breakfast. This is what Fiona Cantwell and Tony Archibold have created at the Château de Marcenac, close to Rodez in the Aveyron.

Tony has been mesmerised by castles since the age of five. His parents were posted to Geneva and there he saw his first castle, the Château Chillon. 'From then on, they became an obsession,' he says. 'I would ask to visit the castle every weekend, to me it was such a magical place.' Tony studied architecture at Oxford and never stopped visiting castles. He met Fiona and they moved to a terraced house in Reading. He worked as an architect whilst teaching at Oxford. Fiona was flying around the world cooking for the Ferrari Formula 1 racing team. 'We really only saw each other

later asking for my husband.

'What has he done?' was my first thought. As he spends most of his time cycling, I wondered whether he'd been caught speeding on his bicycle.

'There was an accident a few days ago,' said the policeman, as his Inspector Clouseau-like younger assistant waved a familiar-looking, broken wing mirror in front of us. 'Would you like to tell me about it?'

'No,' said my husband. 'But she would.'

I was asked to go to the police station. Naturally, I took Beth Anne with me as an expert witness. The woman who drove into me had come up with a very different version of events to what actually happened, even telling the police she was injured.

'I'll see you separately,' the grey-haired policeman from the previous day told us when we arrived. I followed him into an office with two tables in it. There was a chair against one wall that he told me to sit on. He sat behind his desk and began typing my details into a large, old-fashioned computer. The room was shuttered to keep out the sun; Roujan police station does not have the luxury of air conditioning.

After 10 minutes laboriously spelling the names of every living (and dead) relation I have ever had, he asked me to tell him what had happened.

Halfway through my statement, the young officer from the previous day's home visit joined us. They were both charming to the point of being flirtatious. Just what you need when you're in a spot of bother.

Whenever the phone rang the younger one would leap up to answer it. Most of the calls were from a mad woman who spends her whole day calling. You'd think she'd have better things to do, like driving into innocent foreigners.

'Do you know how we found you?' asked the senior policeman after I had signed my statement. The car I had been driving is a friend's Jaguar with a personalised number plate that I

about once a week,' says Tony. 'She was always travelling. It began to feel as if we were living to work and not the other way round.' Fiona agrees. 'Our hours were completely different to everyone else's, so we were not part of the community and not really involved in anything.'

They decided to sell up in Reading and fulfil Tony's lifelong ambition to live in a *château*. 'We would spend the evenings searching on the internet for castles while everyone else was watching television,' says Fiona. 'Our plan was to buy something and run it as a bed-and-breakfast to be able to maintain it. We picked the Midi-Pyrenées because it still has a slight frontier feel to it.'

'And because of The Hundred Years' War, it is full of castles,' adds Tony.

They sold their house in Reading and moved to a half-built *gîte* in the region. This was to become their search headquarters. 'We knew we had to save every penny we could, so we went for extremely basic accommodation,' says Fiona. 'And we just prayed things would go smoothly.'

After weeks of visiting castles and discussions, they made an offer of just over £500,000 on a fantastic property on the edge of a village. They had prepared a business plan in French, Abbey National France had agreed to lend the money, it was now just a question of signing. The day before the signing was due to happen, Abbey National France pulled the plug. 'It was terrible,' says Tony. 'You put everything on the line to buy something and then you find there's no back up. In my opinion, they say yes to too many buyers and then cherry pick, thereby letting a lot of people down. We heard from the agent we were by no means the only people this had happened to.' Barclays eventually agreed to step in and lend the money but by then it was too late. They had lost the property.

'We were devastated,' says Fiona. 'It was such a dream place, and to make matters worse, the buyers have done nothing with it, I've been to look.'

always imagined would be impossible to track.

'No,' I replied. 'How?'

'Your licence plate is untraceable. We had been looking for you for a few days when we saw your car by chance at a garage,' he told me. 'Are you having the oil changed?'

'No, I took it in to fix the wing mirror.'

'I asked the mechanic why it was there and he told me he was just changing the oil,' said the policeman. 'I asked him about the broken wing mirror and he told me he knew nothing about it.'

It's not called the Garage Siciliano for nothing.

'By the way,' he added. 'Your car is still on the national search system, so if you get stopped just tell the police it has been dealt with.' Great, so now I'm going to be stopped by eager gendarmes every time I go shopping.

I am waiting to hear what happens next regarding the accident, but I understand we both have to sign some form saying it was nobody's fault and that will be an end to it.

Even if I end up paying for the damage to my friend's car, the whole experience was much more civilised than my encounter at Stoke Newington police station in north London all those years ago. The police there cared nothing for justice but were interested only in convicting someone, anyone, for some class C drugs they found in the glove compartment of a car I was in. They weren't my drugs, but as I was the only one in the car without a criminal record the police convinced me it would save my friend (a rock star with a long list of convictions) from going to jail if I took the blame. Luckily, when it came to court, the judge realised what had happened.

Along with integrity, the other thing that Roujan police station has, and that was sadly lacking at Stoke Newington, is a Babyfoot table in the garden.

As in so many things that really matter, such as the health service, education, public transport and pastry shops, the French come out on top.

On to the next castle. Another stunning property, just outside a village. They prepared all the paperwork and the business plan in French, a process that took almost two months. At the last minute, the regional council decided it wanted to buy the castle. In France, the council has first refusal over any property within its jurisdiction.

'We were still living out of a suitcase and watching our capital slowly dwindle,' says Fiona.

They had been in France for almost three months by the time they found Château de Marcenac, which was on the market for less than £500,000. Again they found it on the internet. The castle is further into the countryside than the other two they looked at— next door to a farm where they now buy a lot of their food. It had been owned by a family who had used it as a holiday home for two or three weeks a year for 30 years. It hadn't been lived in full-time for over 100 years. The sale went smoothly. 'We finally have our dream,' says Tony. 'But as we're doing everything ourselves, there's not much time to sit about and enjoy it.' They have repainted a lot of the main rooms, using the original method of mixing linseed oil, water and lime—partly to create an authentic effect, but also to save money as paint is very expensive in France. They are renovating the bedrooms they will rent out one by one. So far two are complete. The plan is to provide luxury bed and breakfast and fantastic food. Fiona is a professional chef.

'Our aim is to be able to make enough money to maintain our lifestyle and the castle,' says Tony. He has already registered with the local professional architects' association and will continue to work as an architect for private clients.

'We may never be rich,' says Fiona. 'But we're living in this fantastic place, eating beautiful food and meeting interesting people who pass through. And seeing each other more than once a week, which was really the whole idea behind the move.'

Making money from wine is another option which a lot of

people moving to France consider. But unless you have the capital to buy a huge vineyard, your choices are limited. One option is to focus on selling it, which is what the creators of www.picwines.co.uk are doing. Helen Genevier and Julie Statham met on their first day at university over 20 years ago. In 1997, Helen, who married a Frenchman, moved to the Pic St-Loup region in the Languedoc. Julie was working as a stockbroker for Deutsche Bank in Frankfurt when she decided she needed a change of career. 'I was fed up with stockbroking and fed up with working for a political organisation,' she says. 'I looked for a house for a week and when I saw the one I bought I decided I didn't want to go back to Frankfurt.'

It was during a dinner with friends who were visiting from England in the summer of 2002 that they came up with the idea of Pic Wines. 'We were talking about it half-jokingly, about how everyone that comes here goes home with boxes of local wine. Our friends said we should go for it, that they would definitely buy the wine from the web rather than cart it home.'

They spent two years preparing to launch the business. This included going on wine-tasting courses, writing hundreds of letters to local domaines to see if they would be interested in them selling their product, and a horrendous amount of paperwork.

'The last six months before the launch we were working on it full-time,' says Helen. 'Mainly sorting out the administrative stuff—the SARL, French and UK customs and VAT, and delivery. French administration is quite baffling, complex and littered with unhelpful staff.'

'Actually all the bureaucracy was really long-winded and depressing. We just wanted to get on with the business but there was always some piece of paper missing,' adds Julie. 'We couldn't sell a bottle until we had the right piece of paper, which we had to wait six months for.'

They chose 25 domaines out of the hundreds they had written

to. 'We have to be reasonable and keep the number limited so we can generate a certain amount of volume,' says Julie. 'But there are still lots of vineyards out there we would like to work with. Our aim is to get a good spread of styles to reflect what the Languedoc has to offer.'

Their first sale was in October 2003. 'A magical moment,' says Helen. 'It was wonderful going round the various domaines collecting the wine to ship, that's definitely the best part of the job.'

When Teddy Hutton and Nicola Russell decided to move from Oxford to France at the beginning of the 1990s, they were fleeing from Margaret Thatcher and the British weather. Teddy was a teacher of problem children and blamed Thatcher for the cuts in funding. Nicola worked as a publicist for various theatres such as the Royal Shakespeare Company and the Watermill Theatre in Newbury.

'My French grandmother died and left me £50,000,' says Nicola. 'This acted as a catalyst. We thought we would create a place where actors could come and rehearse. However, no sooner had we done it than the tax rules were changed and companies found it cheaper to rehearse in London.'

To begin with, life was a struggle. When the actors failed to show up, Nicola was forced to attract other types of activity. She contacted hundreds of people to offer them a venue to run courses. Nobody was interested. Nicola discovered that the only thing that worked was actually getting them to the place and showing them how it worked and the facilities. Now she runs courses in yoga, jazz music, creative writing, script writing, choral singing and there are plans to run a series of gardening courses.

Their first course began on July 27, 1997, teaching people how to be pop singers. 'I remember it well because at the end all the women were clustered around the television, weeping at the death of Princess Diana. It was all rather surreal.'

One of their most popular courses has been a fertility course, where people gather to discuss methods in how to conceive. 'It was also to help childless couples come to terms their infertility,' says Teddy who, when he isn't busy helping to run the place, works as a wood sculptor.

In order to pay for their French adventure, they sold half their Georgian house in Oxford's St John Street to Teddy's sister for £100,000. 'It's probably now worth £800,000,' says Teddy wistfully. A few years later they sold the other half to Teddy's mother.

Like many people before them, they went first to Provence, which they found overcrowded and too expensive. Gradually moving west, they discovered the Languedoc. Here they found a *chambre d'hôte*, where they based themselves over the next three years while they looked for a suitable property. 'We wanted it to be large enough, but in a village, not isolated. Teddy was very clear about the fact that he wanted neighbours. And there needed to be facilities for running courses, and not for running a hotel.

'We did not want to be hoteliers. What we have is a venue that people can rent for £2,500 per week in high season. Then we try to leave everything else up to them, although it never works out like that. We have to be here all the time and be involved, otherwise things don't run smoothly.'

When they came to the Maison Verte, they found a well-proportioned bourgeois house built in the 1830s, together with a two acre garden, outbuildings and winemaking facilities. 'It was big enough to do something barking mad,' says Nicola. Having bought it for £140,000, they spent £40,000 on it immediately, which included putting in new bathrooms, converting some of the outbuildings into *gîtes* and building a pool. 'I told Teddy that a pool would help attract the clients, but really it was quite self-indulgent,' says Nicola. 'I wanted a house with a pool.'

Six years later, the courses are full. The business is registered in France as a *Micro Entreprise*, which, although it does not give them any grants, means there are low rates of tax, provided they don't earn over £50,000 per year. They say that they don't earn more than this, but they have a good life.

'It is hard work,' says Nicola. 'We tell the guests that we employ a team of electricians, plumbers, gardeners, and cleaners. When they ask what they are called, we say they are all called Teddy and Nicola. Employing people in this part of France is expensive and difficult.'

However, the satisfaction comes from people returning year after year. 'It is interesting to watch the guests arrive stressed and finding everything foreign,' says Teddy, 'and to see the transformation after a few days of playing boules and sitting by the pool. Also you can watch them develop. I always say that here we grow people as well as plants.'

Lorna Macleod fell into giving courses almost by accident. In 2000 she bought a large house in Uzès in the Gard in the south of France. She carried on working at her job as head of communications at the London Business School, until one day she decided that there was more to life than sitting at a desk. Happily ensconced in her house with a swimming-pool for which she paid £300,000, but which is now worth considerably more, she was attending a photography course in the Lubéron hills in Provence when she was struck by an idea.

'As I was driving home, I suddenly realised that I could do exactly the same thing,' she says. She began gradually by converting a large room into an atelier, and doing up the small house in the garden so that it could accommodate guests. She experimented with a small course in May, during which four people stayed. In the day, a local artist taught them painting. In the evening, they either ate with Lorna or ate out at restaurants. 'The whole thing was such a success that I am playing a fuller programme in September, including creative writing courses, photography and possibly even silversmithing.'

She is running the business as *chambres d'hôtes*, which means that there is a minimum of paperwork and bureaucracy, as the rules are not too cumbersome. However, she is aware that she may have to look into planning restrictions if the courses increase dramatically in number.

'So far it has all been very good fun,' she says. 'Marketing is via word of mouth or a website. The bonus is that I meet lots of interesting people, who so far have not complained and appear perfectly satisfied. They all seem very pleasant.'

The guests either stay in the *gîte* in the garden or at a local *chambre d'hôte*. Lorna provides a light lunch of salads, *pâté*, cheese and bread, while in the evenings people are encouraged to sample the local restaurants. On the final night there is a dinner for the whole group in the house. Prices for tuition and food start from €250 per week. Accommodation is additional, around €300 for the week. She decided to leave people to make their own arrangements to either fly Ryanair to Nîmes or take the TGV to Avignon or Nîmes.

Some people with an extraordinary talent might find that they are able to take advantage of the teaching opportunities, without all the hassle. Simon Fletcher left England 21 years ago because he wanted to work in Europe. An established artist, painting in watercolour and pastel, he also runs seminars for people who already know how to paint, but who want to improve their technique. A five-day course costs around £600 including half board and tuition, but he leaves it to other people to organise the courses.

'I work on a number of different courses, the most popular of which are the three-day courses,' says Fletcher. 'I will meet the people, normally around ten of them, and then we will go on a little walk to find a suitable subject to paint. I start painting. The people on the course can either watch me do it, or paint themselves. Then we have lunch together, more painting in the afternoon, then *apéritifs*, during which they can ask questions. The people who come are baby boomers: architects, designers, professional people who don't want to lie on a beach. Recently, younger people are getting interested. I reckon I can show them more in a week than they would learn in six months at art school.'

Simon and his wife Julie sold a Victorian house in Oxford for £50,000 back in 1982. Simon spent two weeks looking in the south of France, before buying a *maison de maître* for £12,000 in the foothills of the Cévennes. It is a large house, with beautifully proportioned rooms, and two terraces with splendid views over the hills.

'We have been doing it up ever since we bought it,' says Simon. 'We spent the first six months working flat out, so the place was a building site. Once it became habitable, we carried on improving the house whenever we had some spare money. But it remains a work in progress. There is always something to do.'

When they moved to the village they were the only foreigners in the place. 'People used to ask us, why have you come to live in our village? But they couldn't have been more hospitable. The children fought to play with our two boys, and when my wife became ill with hepatitis, the villagers rallied round and looked after all of us. On a professional note, living in France has enabled me to have a more varied and interesting career than I could have enjoyed in England.'

It can be much harder. Michael Simon, a 37-year-old IT Consultant, moved to Montpellier in the south of France to make a new start after his business went bankrupt in the UK. Even though he knew France relatively well and spoke the language fluently, he found the first six months an administrative nightmare. 'They are quite rigid,' he said. 'If you don't have the right bit of paper it just doesn't work.'

Eventually he and his wife settled in, they had two children and he found work for a French IT company. After four years he lost his job. 'I started going to interviews and was told that I was competing with between 900 and 1,400 applicants for each job. All my

One of the first things I did when I came to France was attend a demonstration. I am not normally one to pick up a placard and take to the streets, but I felt strongly that I wanted to protest against Le Pen. Along with a couple of hundred locals, I marched around Pezenas in protest. But, like Marie Antoinette, Le Pen comes up with catchphrases that you can't help but notice. He says of France: 'Aimez-la ou quittez-la.' In other words, love France or bugger off.

You have to admire the French for their Frenchness. Unlike the diffident English, who are suddenly tearing out their hair trying to work out how to adapt to a multicultural society where the sons of immigrants try to blow up people, the French have made it clear all along that to live here you must behave like a Frenchman.

In many London schools, the children hardly speak any English. This situation would never arise in France: in the primary school where our daughters go, there are other English children. But if at any stage their chatting in their native tongue interferes with their progress in French, the teacher calls for a time out, and a strict diet of French-only is imposed. When an American company in Paris tried to make it compulsory for its staff to speak English in the office, the French staff rebelled and told them where to go.

If you don't make an effort to speak French here, the locals will look at you with ill-concealed disgust. The worst insult a French person can levy at a foreigner is that they don't speak a word of the language.

What I love about the French is that they don't give a monkey's about being rude or politically incorrect: if a woman has nice breasts, they tell her.

A London trader friend of mine came to work in Paris recently and was told he had to be friendlier to the ladies. 'Open doors for them,' his boss told him. 'Tell them they have nice legs and that their clothes look good; you're so indifferent, they all think you're gay.'

qualifications are English and they just didn't want to know. They simply don't accept them over there. Either you have a qualification from their *Ecole de Commerce* or *Ecole d'Ingénieurs* or you're a nobody.'

Michael and his family lived off his unemployment cover for several months but when that ran out he decided to go back to England to find work. 'I got a job straight away at home,' he explains. 'But my wife and family stayed down there. So I started commuting. Obviously this put a strain on the marriage and we eventually got divorced.'

Susan Wyles, a qualified nursery nurse had a similar experience. She moved from Canterbury to the Dordogne to set up a bilingual nursery school. The authorities would not let her start her business and demanded a translation of her whole three-year course into French. This still wasn't enough, so Susan, a single parent with a teenage daughter, did a degree at the University of Toulouse. This also proved to be insufficient for the authorities and after three years of struggling she gave up and went back to England.

Starting a business in France is really tough. There is not only the bureaucracy to deal with, but the whole mindset of the French. One business woman said to me: 'France has been practically communist in its outlook for so long that I think small businesses are really frowned on and not supported at all.'

Tony Tidswell, who runs several websites offering advice and help to potential settlers, says there is no point in coming unless you have thought it all through very carefully. 'The realities of coming to France and working in France are not encouraging,'he says. 'Unemployment is officially 10 per cent (in the south it is up to 30 per cent), so for a non-French person the chances of getting a salaried job are very low, even for a short contract. Without fluent French, which will take you over five years of immersion, and an educational diploma or degree from France, you are likely to be unemployed. Part-time work also requires fluent French and is

Coming from London, he was terrified to even look at the women, lest he should be up on charges of sexual harassment. In France, if you're not sexually harassed at least once a day, you're either having a bad hair day or you ate too much garlic for lunch.

This attitude extends to their immigrant population. No, you will not wear veils in school. Schools in France are of the state, not the church, and as such, religious signs are not acceptable. You don't like it? Tant pis. That's the way it is.

very hard to get. Just 'getting by' is difficult unless you have some invested capital generating some income. You cannot start any business here without being registered and/or licensed and many trades are restricted 'professions' such as real-estate, travel, legal, insurance, financial, medical etc. Anything else and you have to pay in advance for the right to work and the taxation/social costs start at 50 per cent of your turnover (yes turnover, not profits). Working illegally as a non-registered alien will get you into serious legal and financial trouble. A local 'sport' is denouncing people working illegally as the 'denouncer' gets a cut of the penalties.'

For my own career, however, moving to France proved the best thing I ever did. Thanks to a very good friend, I started writing for the *Sunday Times*, mainly about Brits living in France which in turn led to a column. A publisher then contacted me after the first one was published and I wrote this book. Rupert's improbable optimism has paid off.

7
Père du Village

Short of bad news about the children, it was one of the most worrying answer-machine messages one could receive. 'This is Gregory Guida,' said a French voice in good English. 'I need to talk to you about a large construction project that will seriously impact the value of your property.'

He left a phone number, but it was already after office hours. We spent much of the evening discussing the problem. What could it be? A new road? A housing estate? A nuclear power plant?

Whatever it was, the mysterious Frenchman certainly had a sharp idea of what it takes to penetrate to the core of Anglo-Saxon anxiety. The British, living on their overcrowded island, are obsessive about property; the French tend to have a more relaxed, continental attitude. If an official in Paris draws a line across a map and decrees it to be the route of a high-speed rail line, it will not be too long before the bulldozers appear and not long after that when the first TGV whistles past at 300 kmh. France is such a big country—three times larger in area than the UK—that policies on the use of land tend to be pretty relaxed. The result is that large parts of France are becoming quite similar to suburban Kansas City.

Virtually every French town and city is now surrounded by hideous strip shopping malls and new housing estates. This carefree attitude to land use—in essence, use it up because there is always more—is one of the reasons why the British have

An Englishman in possession of a house in France must be in need of a builder. Brits are famous for buying wrecks that the French wouldn't touch with an extra-long baguette. They then spend years doing them up. Years, because it takes so long to find somebody to do the work. *A Year in Provence* might as well have been called A Year Waiting for a Plumber.

When Nick Sole and his wife, Sally, wanted to install a complicated geothermal heating system in their home in Nizas in the Herault, they opted for contractors from Newcastle. 'It was a huge mistake,' says Sole, 'but I was nervous about the language issue and also thought I could trust the company in question. In reality, we ended up spending a lot more money than we would have done locally. The job also took several months longer than it should have and we also missed out on subsidies that the French provide for green heating.'

As a result of their bad experiences with the heating contractors, the couple hired local builders to do the rest of the work on their gîte. 'My advice to anybody is to look at the local options before importing workmen,' says Sole. 'Unless, of course, you're after a plumber, and then it's quicker to have one walk from Poland than it is to wait for a French one.'

But even if you can find a French plumber, will you be able to understand him? 'People are scared of misunderstandings and problems due to the language barrier,' says Paul Beaufils, an estate agent in Beziers.

You no longer have to bring over builders from the UK, though. There is no shortage of expat workmen-at least in our region. 'They're like the 'FILTH', the traders who fled London in the 1980s for Hong Kong,' my husband says. 'Only now it is 'Failed In London, Try the Hérault'.'

found it so easy to settle in France. As the French have abandoned their old houses in the villages and towns, and moved to the new estates, the British have simply moved in behind them, taking over the old properties and often caring for them with a punctiliousness that is pretty alien to the natives.

'You can tell in any village where the foreigners live. They are the only ones who have painted their houses,' says one of my friends, only half joking. Gregory Guida says the mentality here is very different. 'In Britain you are much more densely populated,' he says. 'So the quality is much more important. In France it doesn't have to be pretty. In Britain if you go to any random village everything will be perfect. In France, three houses will be perfect and they will be owned by Brits. The French have only just discovered the countryside, a little too late I think because the English have made it unaffordable.'

Shortly after we moved in we bumped into a local man pacing up and down the field opposite us. He wanted to build a weekend home there, he told us. I went white and almost fainted. But the mayor wouldn't let him, he went on, the land does not have building permission. We tried to look sympathetic and skipped off home, vowing to vote for said mayor in the next election. Since that day though, we have been on tenterhooks, waiting for something to ruin our view, our peace, in short our pretty perfect location. We were even conned into buying a worthless plot of land adjoining the property for a couple of thousand pounds. The owner of it only had to mention the word steel dump and our cheque book was open.

The evening of the phone message from Gregory we went for a walk and tried to imagine the various hillsides covered with houses, or a road going through the valley. It was a horrible thought. Our rural idyll was over. We would have to go and live in Wales.

When we finally spoke to him the next day, we learned that

Some Brits opt for multinational workforces. Michael Derrington used a team of builders from France, England and Scotland to do up his house in the Languedoc.

'They all worked really well together,' he says. 'They had the same common aim: to do a good job. And, of course, to have a good lunch. In my view, this is key my skills as a cook came in very handy.'

it was not our view that would be spoilt, but the view around Pézenas. The mayors of two small neighbouring villages had approved a plan to erect 11 giant windfarms, nearly 400-feet in height on one of the most visible plateaus in the Hérault. We were happy that this wasn't happening on our hill, but appalled that this could even be contemplated without lengthy consultation with the locals.

'I only found out by chance a week ago,' said Gregory. 'We have about a month to try to stop it.' His English neighbours, Jonathan James and his wife Anne were equally surprised. They bought Domaine St Hilaire 18 months ago, to escape from the bustle of suburban Dulwich. The vineyard contains fruit trees, olives and wild flowers. Now there is the prospect that they will have giant towers overshadowing the wildlife. Each rotor will be the length of a Boeing 747. The towers will be four times the height of a water tower or electricity pylon—they will become the tallest buildings in the Hérault.

'It is unbelievable,' says Jonathan James. 'We would have thought twice before buying the domaine if we had thought such a thing could happen. We found out by chance a few days ago. Now we have less than a month to act.'

Many of the local French seemed either unconcerned or resigned to the fact that the windfarms would happen. But the British community of Pézenas, some 200 strong, leapt into action. Peter Glynn-Smith, says the very idea is an outrage. He renovated his house, rebuilding Roman walls, and creating an enormous garden with a dining area where guests can look out south to the sea. Now that view is about to be ruined forever.

'It seems astonishing that such a unique area of outstanding natural beauty as the Hérault should even consider introducing windfarm pollution to its landscape,' he says. 'We have always believed that this part of France had learnt from the mistakes of other Mediterranean tourist communities. Greed or ignorance today by a few will have a long-term financial impact on thousands.'

This would sound reasonable except for the attitude of many French. Not only do many locals think the wind farms are actually attractive, but they are queuing up to sell their land to the wind farm developers. It was becoming a curious situation where the conservationists seeking to preserve the beauty of the landscape were mostly foreigners, and those seeking to despoil it were the natives. As Guy de Saint Victor, a French friend of mine who has lived in England says: 'I really have nothing against the Brits arriving in such huge quantities. At least they are environmentally friendly.'

Gregory found it extremely difficult to motivate the local landowners into any kind of action. 'They just don't believe me when I say that the value of their property will be halved if there is a windfarm next door to it,' he says. 'They think the increase in value they have seen over the last five years is set in stone.'

The International Press Club of Pézenas (members: my husband, Jonathan Miller, Frank Johnson, another neighbour and journalist, and of course Peter Glynn-Smith, our official photographer, and me) organised a wind and wine evening. It was held at Jean-Claude and Alex's castle, Château de Conas. The mayor of Pézenas was invited, along with several local British winemakers and members of the expat community. The mayor had expressed an interest in meeting them and the expats wanted to tell him what they thought about the windfarm. The evening went well, the wines were good but not much was achieved. The mayor was predictably non-committal and said of course no decision would be taken that was detrimental to the region. In other words, he would watch the way the wind was blowing and vote accordingly.

The British activists, more potbelly than Swampy, decided their best bet was to target some of the 22 estate agents in Pézenas. Foreigners won't buy and you'll lose your fat commissions, they warned. The estate agents looked horrified and started frantically taking notes.

One British homeowner who has already had his property ruined by a windfarm is Nick Rogers who lives in Surrey. He decided to buy a holiday home in Brittany, along with a friend. 'We always went on holiday together, so it made sense to buy a place together and split the costs and the work,' says Nick. The two men went house hunting and found the ideal property close to Guerlesquin, a house split into two cottages. 'It was great, a lovely place tucked away in the middle of nowhere, the nearest building was a farmhouse about 50 yards away,' says Nick. Because it was so perfect for them, they decided to buy it without their wives seeing it. 'We took lots of video footage home to show them and they were delighted.'

The sale went through smoothly and a couple of months later the families went out to spend Easter in their new holiday home. As they were coming off the motorway exit they saw nine windfarms shimmering in the distance.

'Oh, I wonder where they are?' Nick said to his friend. As they got closer to the property, they realised the turbines were not far away. When they turned onto the lane towards their house that they realised they were right next behind their place.

Nick is fairly sanguine about it. 'At first we contacted the agent, Vivre en France, and went crazy with them. They said they had no idea. I don't believe that. The guy who sold us the property was a Brit and I think they must all have known about it. The fact is they are at the back of the house so they don't spoil our view. Of course they have affected the resale value of the property but the children like them.'

If Nick had gone to his local mayor's office (*mairie*) before signing, he would have seen the plans for the windfarm. When we bought our house, we had no idea how important the mayor is, but if you do one thing before you sign, go and check out your property and the land surrounding it. The mayor's office will tell you whether there is any public access to the property, whether the land around it is building land or not, whether there are any major projects in the pipeline and so on. You just have to show up with the details of the property or the parcel number of the land it is on. The mayor has the *Plan d'Urbanisme* (habitation plan) for the village and its surrounding areas. This will show you exactly where you can and cannot build. Do not be tricked into buying land and told it has planning permission without checking. However, you should bear in mind that the mayor is under no obligation to tell you of any developments. In the case of windfarms, for example, the village or region will gain from them financially. In addition he is unlikely to give you an honest answer if it means the loss of a sale to a local resident.

The role of the mayor in France cannot be exaggerated. Every village has one, even if it doesn't have a baker, and he or she is involved in everything. A friend of mine who wishes to remain anonymous says: 'I have always believed and advised anyone that if you fall out with your local *maire*, it's time to move home.'

Jacques Kuhnlé, a retired English teacher living near Nancy, confirms the importance of keeping in with the mayor. 'When I built my house in the Alps, I was careful to invite the mayor to see the house and drink a glass of pastis,' he says. 'At first he didn't like the place but after the wood panelling was stuck over the concrete he said it was all right. Thank Goodness! My neighbours have a piece of sloping land which keeps collapsing on to the road. They managed to have the commune buy the part of the property that crumbles to avoid costly maintenance.

One of the most active protest groups in my area was set up to save a bar. It wasn't just any bar: it was the only one within a 10-mile radius. The Parisian who owned the house next door was fed up with the noise from rowdy pastis-drinkers (mainly from Birmingham, as far as I can make out).

'It would have been terrible,' one activist told me. 'Where would we have gone to watch England beat France in the Six Nations?' Unluckily for the Parisian, the village mayor took the side of the drinkers, and the bar is still open.

A few miles away from me in the High Languedoc, two mayors have agreed to a proposal for a landfill site. The plan is to destroy more than 60 acres of natural park by digging a hole in which to dump household rubbish. In addition to the hole, there will be 30 trucks a day negotiating windy roads through medieval villages to get to the site.

Understandably, most local residents are up in arms, including some English people. Simon Fletcher, a landscape artist and architect, and his wife, Julie, have lived in the village of St-Gervais-sur-Mare for 25 years.

'I will lie down in front of the lorries if necessary,' says Simon. 'This is a mad scheme with very serious implications. Three water sources below the proposed dump supply more than half of the drinking water to the Hérault.'

Simon and Julie are among a growing number of Britons campaigning alongside their French neighbours. When Robin Boxall, president of Brits Nîmes (an association based in

They couldn't have done that if the mayor hadn't been a friend.'

I remember when I first visited our mayor to talk about some land that was for sale near to the house. I wanted to see whether or not it was designated building land. He showed me a map of the village and surrounding areas. It was rather like those old-fashioned maps of the world you used to get in schools, where all the pink bits were British. Here all the pink bits were protected. The plots that were allocated building land were blue. Luckily the land close to us was pink. I noticed that just outside the village was a whole swathe of pink bits with one little blue bit stuck in the middle of it. I asked him what the blue bit was.

'Oh that's the house the previous mayor is building for himself,' he told me.

Jean Martinez, the mayor of my neighbouring village, Caux, describes the role of mayor as being 'like the father of the village. You are involved in everything, from the psychology of the people, to their quarrels, to the water supply, the school, rubbish collection. In short, anything related to the life of the people.' Jean is a Professor of medicinal and organic chemistry at the University of Montpellier. He has worked and lectured all over the world and speaks flawless English. He is the head of one of the major experimental laboratories at the University, but on Tuesdays, Thursdays, Saturdays and 'Sundays if necessary' he is mayor of Caux, a village with a population of just over 2,000.

'I have always looked after people,' he says. 'And I love this village. This is something foreigners will never understand, this love we have for our homes. It's a kind of atavism. If it hadn't been for the village, I would have stayed abroad, the career opportunities are much better. But the village is the only thing that you never leave, you even end up buried in it.'

If you are planning to do anything at all with your home in France, or even if you're not, it is well worth cultivating your

Nîmes that has 230 British members) heard that the local airport was going to be closed, he and his fellow expats sent out letters to 35 mayors across the region telling them how bad the closure would be for the local community.

Ryanair brings 200,000 people a year to the area, who spend an average of €66 (£44) a day. 'But it is also great for local people who want to go over to England for football matches,' says Boxall. 'If you have property here and pay taxes here, there is no question you have just as much right as anybody to fight for something you believe in.

'While the chamber of commerce was fighting on behalf of local business to save the tourism trade, we were fighting on behalf of individuals that live or own property here. Some use the airport 25 times a year to come to their holiday homes.'

The message is clear. It is the mayor you need to chat up if you want to get anywhere. My advice to anybody moving into a French village is to invite the mayor for a drink, even if you're not expecting a landfill site, wind farm, motorway or anything else you might not like. Don't just sit back and let it happen: foreigners who live in France have as much say in what happens to their surroundings as their French neighbours.

One second-home owner I spoke to said she didn't feel it was her right to get involved in local opposition projects. 'I only show up for a couple of months a year,' she says.

I don't see why how long you spend in a place should have anything to do with it.

However small your stake, would you put money into a company and see it ruined without complaining?

For the Fletchers and their neighbours, the battle goes on. Meanwhile, one Englishman trying to sell his house has been told by local estate agents they are not taking on any properties in the villages affected by the landfill site as nobody will buy them until a decision has been made about the proposed location. Property prices have already fallen by more than 10 per cent.

local mayor. He or she will be able to make most decisions that affect you and your home. In terms of planning permission, the decision rests with the mayor unless the land is protected, in which case the mayor would have to refer it to the DDE (*Direction Départementale de l'Equipement*). But don't forget, whatever the mayor recommends will be taken into account. If you live within 500 meters of a listed building, any change you want to make will have to be passed by the equivalent of the English Heritage, *Bâtiments de France*.

Mayors are elected for a period of six years. In the country they are elected on the basis of personality rather than politics. 'Here people have known me since I was knee-high,' says Martinez. 'It is only really in the bigger cities you have to belong to a political party.'

When we first moved here our mayor was a retired colonel who drives a vast motorbike. He seemed like a perfectly nice chap to me, but Geneviève told me that he sided with the far right in the last election. There was a plan to remove him and he has been replaced by a communist. The last time I saw him before his removal, he looked stressed. His plans to create a village square had been rejected, he told me. He wanted to knock down the post office, which also houses the doctor and the hairdressers and make that area a place to sit. The post office, doctor and hairdresser would be moved to a new building down the road.

'It's impossible,' he sighed. 'People here want to die as they were born.'

I think they have a point. I rather like the crumbling old post office. And it's not as if the villagers miss having a square. They find plenty of places to sit and watch the traffic go by, even if they have to bring their own chairs.

So the power of the mayor is not limitless, but it is a force to be reckoned with, as Sophie Randall found when she moved to the Mayenne in northwest France with her husband David and their three children.

They ended up buying into a nightmare situation. First, the farm was owned by two families, with five people still involved in the property, including a M. Poulletier, who had a vegetable patch there and grew cider apples. Although the agent who sold it to them had told them it was not occupied, another member of the family still rented out one of the small buildings on the farm. They moved to France with their dogs and had specifically asked the agent if the property was suitable for dogs. He had said yes, although he must have been aware of the law that if you have more than three dogs you have to be further than 30 metres away from your nearest neighbour.

After about a year in the house, they had both failed to get jobs in France. Sophie is a teacher and David is an accountant but their qualifications were not accepted here. They decided to set up a dog breeding business. 'We had bought a legal book on rules and regulations governing breeding livestock which was recommended by *Nos Chiens* (a French glossy dog magazine) but it was desperately out of date,' says Sophie. 'This is yet another lesson that we have learnt, that systems are so complicated in France that no one anywhere seems to know the definitive answer.'

The Randalls sent off their application, put several bitches into pup and sat back and waited. 'It was very nerve-racking,' says Sophie. 'But I felt we might just muddle through until we could start selling puppies.'

The minute Poulletier and the other family member, M. Edard, realised what they were doing, they started a campaign to evict them. 'They knew that if we got authorisation they would be never make any money from the property because no-one can build or live on land within a 100 metres of a breeding kennel, which meant that they couldn't develop the site,' says

Sophie. 'We didn't of course know but Poulletier is an ex-coun-
cillor, a friend of the mayor.'

Poulletier went around to all the neighbours and told them
to complain about the Randalls' dogs. 'Everyone is the village is
frightened of him,' says Sophie. 'The next thing we knew the
DSV (*Département de Services Vétérinaires*) came round to
close us down. The guy in charge was only slightly apologetic
and said we should just go back to England. We couldn't really
believe it was happening to us as, as far as we knew, we had done
everything right. But we are English so as usual fair game.'

The Randalls refused to move. Then things turned nasty.
'Poulletier started coming around drunk and frightening the
kids and leaving poison about for the dogs,' says Sophie. 'The
mayor stepped in and told us we had to move the dogs or he
would get the SPA (The French equivalent of the RSPCA) out
to put them down. He also told us that we should go back to
England. I told them all at this point that I was going to take
them all to the European Courts as technically they didn't have
a leg to stand on.'

The Mayor then brought in the region's head vet to
strengthen his case. 'Fortunately for us, she is a woman. Not
only that, a very tough one who has presumably had to fight
men all the way to get to the top and she certainly didn't appreciate the mayor telling her what to do! I don't think she could
give a damn about fairness or justice but she certainly wanted to
teach him a lesson and so told him that it was nothing to do with
him at all, but that it was her decision. After all the anxiety it
was at least quite good to see him storming off in the rain with
his deputy holding the umbrella for him so his cashmere coat
wouldn't get wet!'

Finally her decision was that they would have to move the
dogs, but she put no time limit on it. The Randalls found somewhere else to house the dogs. 'Poulletier had the last laugh

---

French workmen

When dealing with French workmen, there are some useful phrases whose real meaning you should be aware of:

Je ferai le maximum (I will do my best) = I'm late for lunch

Ce n'est pas normal (This is most unusual) = Too complicated for me

Je vais vous envoyer un devis (I will send you a quote) = You'll never see me again

Je vais passer en début d'apres-midi (I'll be there early afternoon) = I'll be there this week

Je vais passer dans la semaine (I'll be there this week) = I'll be there this month

Je vais réfléchir (I'll think about it) = I'll think about it for the next 10 years, by which time I shall be retired.

---

though,' says Sophie. 'We couldn't go home as we could no longer afford to buy a house anywhere in the UK so we decided to sell the building and put the money into building up the dogs so we could make a proper living out of them. We put it on the market, but every time the agent took someone to look at it, Poulletier was there and he would charge up to them and tell them that if they bought it, he would make sure they were sorry. Eventually we had to drop the price and sell it for probably half of what it was worth to one of his mates.'

Sophie and David have now bought the house near the piggery that houses their dogs. They now have 40 dogs and are selling them all over France and winning prizes for them. 'Fingers crossed, we are a little bit wiser and are not going to get cheated a second time,' says Sophie. 'I would certainly advise people to avoid friends of the village mayor.'

While you are making friends with *M. le Maire*, you should also try to make friends with local artisans. Down in the south, reliable builders, plumbers, electricians and so on are notoriously difficult to find. I must have made almost 100 appointments to see various people, and only half have even shown up. The other trick is to come and give you a quote and then disappear. Or, as in our case, come and take away your TV satellite box to fix it and then vanish. Four years on we have heard nothing from the rather handsome man who showed up in a white van and said he'd be back in a week.

There wasn't much building work to be done, but when we bought our house it had a huge atrium; a sort of death trap for children and also a waste of space. Although it had been very useful for shouting at Rupert to come upstairs when he was watching the cricket, after a year we decided that Olivia and Bea's survival thus far had only been a matter of luck and that it was time to fill in the hole. According to our interior designer friend Peter Glynn-Smith you should always live in a place for at least a year before undertaking major construction work, you need to see what it's like through all the seasons and get a proper feel for the property. We asked a local English builder to come along and take a look. It was such a relief to speak to someone who answered back in English and seemed to understand everything I said that I didn't worry when he said he would have to fit in the job with tending his vineyard. In fact, tending his vineyard was the least of our problems. The family only had one car, so when his wife needed it, he couldn't come. He was a keen tennis player and obviously couldn't miss any games on account of our atrium. After six months we were still living in semi-chaos. But eventually the job was finished and we had another room upstairs. When we decided to put a fireplace in, we went for a local builder. He showed up at 8am every morning and worked solidly until 6pm. The whole thing was finished in ten days.

Even if you find it tough dealing with local builders, using foreign help is not to be recommended. A couple who wish to remain nameless managed to alienate the locals by importing workmen from England. They bought a barn in the Aude valley for conversion last spring. Nine months after they moved in, they still had no electricity or running water. Finally they hired a local architect to take over the project, but by then they had so alienated the local community that even he got nowhere. 'Every time I submitted absolutely water-tight planning permission on their behalf, it would be turned down for some reason. It clearly just wasn't going to happen for them here,' says the local architect, who wishes to remain nameless. 'They came into the community, didn't introduce themselves to the neighbours or the local mayor and then proceeded to use a builder from England to do all the work.' He goes on. 'But these were not nasty people, they were just naïve. And they didn't speak French.' Eventually they sold at a loss and went home.

It is inevitable, especially in regions like the Languedoc where house prices have risen by 30 per cent in the last four years, that there will be some resentment towards the foreign invasion. I went to buy some meat in a local butcher's a year or so ago and was told by the man hacking up my beef with a 10-inch cleaver that it was my fault his children couldn't afford to buy a house. Others are more pragmatic and say that the Brits and most other foreigners too only go for the old houses the French don't want. But still it is true that even a house on a *lotissement* (housing estate) now will cost around €100,000. When we first started looking here you could get a huge old village house for that price.

However, as always the French state is on hand to help. In the village where my girls are at school they are about to build 60 low cost houses for low income families. The villagers are up in arms, saying they will have to build a new school as well to accommodate all the children. No doubt the Brits who live there will get involved. I heard a story recently of a fight in a village nearby to keep a restaurant open. The snooty Parisian lady who had a holiday home next door to it wanted it closed because of the fumes it produced. Colin, a friend of mine who lives there, said the local Brits were at the forefront of the fight to keep it open. They have won the battle and also made a lot of friends in the village. Parisians down here are less popular than the foreigners, so it was an extremely unwise move on her part.

Last time I saw Gregory, he told me the latest news on the windfarms. He and his father Umberto, a charismatic, handsome gentleman, have managed to use their connections to get a commission to look into the project. This commission then advised the Montpellier authorities that the project shouldn't go ahead. 'After that, we were told the building permit would be refused,' says Gregory. 'But the head of the council has not made a decision either way. I think there is tremendous pressure from politicians in Paris, as well as pressure from big business.'

Another worrying development is that there is a plan to change the law so that mayors can accept a windfarm project without having to go to the regional council. 'This is truly scandalous,' says Umberto. 'In effect the mayor of a village of a few hundred people could give the go-ahead for something that could affect thousands.'

The Guidas question the feasibility of the windfarms. 'Our analysis of the whole problem is that it could become one of the great scandals of the 21st century,' says Gregory. 'Thousands of windfarms will spring up across the country only to placate the eco-Nazis, who don't even live in the countryside. But when the power companies tire of overpaying for this extremely undependable source of power, the windfarms will be left to rot, their thousand ton concrete bases as shameful a remembrance as WWII bunkers. The greens argue that we should put them where man has already ruined the landscape. The landscape around Pézenas has not been ruined, but it soon could be.'

As Umberto sums up: 'The sword is still hanging over our heads.'

8
Still a Supermodel

I was doing some late-night admin in my office when I heard my daughter Olivia run downstairs. The two girls, Olivia who was then aged four and Bea three, insist on sleeping in bunk beds in the same room. I use the term sleeping lightly, they rarely stop chatting and playing before 10pm. So to hear her come down at 9.30 was not unusual.

'Daddy,' I heard her say to Rupert, who was watching the news. 'There's a big, big problem.'

So far I was still only half listening. It was the next sentence that had me jumping from my chair, screaming as I ran upstairs.

'The torch fell out of bed and Bea has got blood on her head.'

I found Bea in the bathroom with Monika, the babysitter, who was trying to stem the relentless flow of blood. The wound was on her forehead and looked deep.

My husband and Monika were a lot calmer than me. In fact, Bea was a lot calmer than me. I started phoning every doctor in the region to find out what we should do. I spoke to one who said she might need stitches. So off we went to the local hospital, with Bea wrapped in a blanket. Visions of similar situations at hospitals in London came to me.

'We'll be there for at least four hours,' I said to Rupert. 'Why

Postnatal care

You will have a check-up two months after giving birth and
your doctor can then prescribe a course of pelvic re-educa-
tion. This is normally carried out by a *Kinésithérapeute,* who
is a cross between an osteopath and a masseur. Currently this
is still reimbursed by the state, but according to my *Kiné*, it
soon won't be. It is a most singular experience and you
should go wearing your best underwear, which you will have
to take off. He measures how fit your pelvic floor is by asking
to squeeze his fingers (this is not something for the chronical-
ly shy). 'That's not bad after three children,' I was told.
'With some patients, I ask them to squeeze and I feel nothing.'

The aim is to get your nether regions back into shape
after childbirth, whether this is to keep you or your husband
happy, I'm not too sure. Or maybe it's for the amusement of
France's *Kinés*.

didn't I bring a book?'

We parked right outside the door of the *Polyclinique Pasteur*
and rang the emergency bell. A nurse opened the door and asked
what had happened. She asked how old Bea was and then led us to
an operating theatre. There seemed to be no one else in the hospital. About five minutes later a young doctor straight from ER
arrived looking very cool in his surgeon's kit and black scarf. He
greeted us all and looked at the wound.

'She'll have a small scar,' he said. 'But with stitches it will be
minimal.'

Bea looked horrified.

'Don't worry,' said her father as they placed a gas mask on her
face. 'You'll still be a supermodel.'

The nurse asked Bea to blow into the balloon. After a few sec-
onds Bea started giggling, then she fell asleep. About half an hour
later we were home. The whole episode, including getting there

and back, took less than an hour. Admittedly we live near a small town, so maybe we were shielded from the crowds of drunks and drug addicts one would find in any major metropolis, but, in England, there wouldn't have been a hospital there.

The French pride themselves on their health system. And it is true that after giving birth here (twice) and living with three small children who spend a lot of the time being ill, I have been very impressed with it. It seems to mix the private and public in a way that the English haven't been able to.

But getting onto the system is a nightmare. Because it is so comprehensive (for example, I paid nothing for Bea's treatment) they are not keen on letting foreigners onto it. They kept turning me away and telling me I was covered in England, until I finally got a letter from the social security there saying they had nothing more to do with us and that we were resident in France.

The brilliant healthcare system does not come cheap. For every employed person around 45 per cent is contributed to the state for social security benefits and healthcare compared with 22 per cent in the UK. 'This percentage is split between the employer and the employee approximately 30 per cent to 15 per cent,' says Sarah Vedrenne, an accountant with CAC Languedoc. 'In France when we talk about what we get paid, we talk in net terms. If I look at my salary slip it's heartbreaking, but that's the price we pay for the benefits system.'

As most people with a business to run in France will tell you, the system is not sustainable. It is just too expensive to employ people. Ruth and Charles Simpson who run a vineyard told me that the people that owned the business before them used to employ eight people. 'We now employ one,' says Charles. 'And for this one person we pay another 100 per cent on top of his salary in tax and contributions. It's a huge problem in France. The system is so punitive it forces people to go underground. If we didn't have to pay such huge charges we would almost certainly employ more

> The French equivalent of Calpol
> A word of advice from my friend Ruth who gave birth to
> their first child in Narbonne. 'I had been in my hospital for
> about an hour when the contractions started to get just a little
> bit too painful. The nurse offered to get me a painkiller. I said
> yes please. She came back minutes later with a bullet-type
> pill. I suddenly realised what I was supposed to do with it.
> Charles and I looked at this thing and then at each other. 'I
> love you very much Ruth,' he said. 'But there's no way I am
> putting that up your bottom.'
>
> The French are mad about suppositories. You will find as
> soon as you have children here you get very used to
> administering them as they see them as a cure-all, the French
> equivalent of Calpol.

people. As it is, we just can't afford to.'

***

Finding a doctor is easy in France. The French are as interested in their health as they are in their stomachs. There seem to be doctors for everything, and when you see them they prescribe huge amounts of pills and potions. When all three children are ill at the same time our kitchen looks like a pharmacy. If you don't like one doctor you see, you can go to another, you just pay €20 each visit. There are several doctors in the neighbourhood. Our favourite is German. This is partly because he speaks English, but also because he doesn't just hand out antibiotics every time you visit him. He tells me that all is not well in the French system. I asked him if it is, as the French declare, the best system in the world. 'There are worse,' was his reply. However, he points out that in Germany there is a choice of 16,000 different types of medicines. In France there are fewer than 5,000, with brands being discontinued every day as the government tries to save money. I can confirm this. Two medicines I tried to get to treat my six-month old son's bronchitis were no longer available.

Dr Hirner, our German doctor told us the first time he saw Leonardo that the little boy needed a circumcision. We spent months traipsing backwards and forwards to a clinic in Béziers where a rather sadistic skinny doctor tugged his foreskin back repeatedly and told us all was fine. I was told I had to keep doing the same thing and putting cream on it. 'It will loosen,' said the sadist. Leonardo didn't seem to agree. He wept hysterically every time I started to touch him. This news came as a surprise to one of his uncles who said he had always welcomed such female attention. But the sight of my son screaming and weeping sent me back to Dr Hirner who repeated his earlier prescription and sent us off to Montpellier.

Sadly now both Dr Hirner and Leonardo's foreskin have gone. Leonardo had an operation the day before his second birthday at Lapeyronie Hospital in Montpellier. Once again the French health service was incredible. We were in a private room, offered tea and coffee and the whole thing was over by 9am. The villagers of Roujan, sadly, didn't take to Dr Hirner and eventually he gave up and left. He swapped jobs with a doctor in Guadeloupe and as far as I know is happily integrating with the islanders.

But despite drawbacks, the system is magnificent. Where else can you give birth for free and be looked after in a private room with air conditioning and television? Where else can you walk into a hospital at 10 o'clock at night and be given the service we were with Bea?

Posy and Mike Fallowfield had a terrible health scare almost as soon as they moved to France. Mike was suddenly taken seriously ill with a critical heart condition. 'We knew he had a problem before we left England,' says Posy. 'But we didn't realise how serious it was.' The local doctor told them to go and see a specialist in

Auch. He ran some tests. He said the results were serious and suggested they go to the Clinique Pasteur in Toulouse for an angiogram. 'We showed up at the hospital on the Thursday before Good Friday like innocents abroad,' says Posy. 'We didn't realise

Useful medical terms	
allergies	*les réactions allergiques/ allergies*
anaesthesiologist	*un/e anesthésiste*
anaesthetic	*une anesthésie locale/générale*
ache	*le mal*
blood	*le sang*
blood vessels/arteries/veins	*les artères, les veines*
blood test	*le prise du sang*
cancer	*le cancer*
chills	*sensation de froid*
a cold	*refroidissement*
to cure	*guérir*
diabetes	*le diabète*
fever	*la fièvre*
'flu' ('feeling unwell')	*le rhume*
inflammation	*l'inflammation*
influenza	*la grippe*
itching	*démangeaison*
medication	*les médicaments*
migraine	*la migraine*
muscular tear	*un claquage musculaire/une élongation*
on an empty stomach	*à jeun*
pain	*la douleur*
pins & needles	*des fourmillements/des fourmis/des picotements*
Repetitive Strain Injury (RSI)	*les microtraumatismes permanents*
shooting pain	*une douleur lancinante*

this meant he would have to stay there. He didn't even have his toothbrush.' The test was carried out and they were told that Mike had four blocked arteries. He would either have to have open heart surgery or have four stents (a small cylindrical piece of mesh which opens the artery) inserted, one for each blockage. 'Luckily they opted for the stents option,' says Posy. 'Otherwise it would have meant six months of convalescing in the caravan which probably would have killed us both off.' Mike stayed in hospital for four days. 'Even then, he was desperate to get out,' says Posy. 'He told me he felt like jumping around.'

The whole process, from the first visit to the GP to the convalescence took exactly three weeks. 'I'm not saying that we wouldn't have got good treatment back home,' says Posy. 'But I am sure it wouldn't have happened so quickly.' Mike is certain it made a huge difference. 'I think being here saved my bacon,' he says.

Because his condition is chronic, the medicine Mike has to take every month is 100 per cent reimbursed. His treatment cost £8,000 in total, 90 per cent of which he got back from the state. At the time, he and Posy were covered with an E106. They are now fully paid-up members of the French system. If they had had a *mutuelle* at the time of Mike's operation, they would have got everything back.

Sadly this all-encompassing health service is under threat. The government has been trying to introduce healthcare reforms and according to a recent survey, failure to do so could see healthcare expenditure of £85 billion a year by 2020. Health spending accounts for nearly 9 per cent of GDP compared with 7.1 per cent in the UK. There is an unpopular plan called 'Hospital 2007' which proposes management reforms and a new emphasis on cost management. The core suggestion is that citizens must pay more and doctors must change their behaviour. The French consume almost three times as many antibiotics as the Germans, for example. I have tried to go down the homeopathic route, until my GP retired. His

insomnia	*l'insomnie*
a splint	*une attelle*
surgeon	*un chirurgien*
surgery	*la chirurgie*
swelling	*c'est gonflé/enflé*
to treat	*soigner*
vertigo	*le vertige*
whiplash	*le coup du lapin*
X-ray	*une radio(graphie)*

replacement was not *conventionné* (ratified by social security) so the visits became too expensive at £30 per child. One of the ways the state is looking to save money is to reduce the number of alternative, and so-deemed non-essential, treatments available.

We kept Bea at home the day following the torch incident, just to make sure she was all right. At one stage I went to check on her. She was playing with Monika and her Barbie dolls. She was holding a particularly stunning example of a Barbie doll with fluorescent pink hair and a princess dress. Monika was holding Ken.

'If you don't love me any more,' Bea's Barbie was telling Ken, 'then I'm going to tell my mummy.'

I think she is going to be all right.

9
Enfants de la Patrie

About three years after we moved to France, I was hauled up in front of the headmistress at my daughter's school. I had done nothing wrong, although it's amazing how a headmistress's office can make you feel guilty whatever your age. The problem was my five-year old daughter, Olivia. She had apparently bitten a classmate's bottom. 'Was he cute?' was my first question.

'No,' said the inappropriately named Madame Jolly. 'It was a girl and she has teeth marks on her bottom. This behaviour is inexcusable. What are you going to do about it?'

To make matters worse, the girl's mother then phoned me. She was furious. I thought briefly about cheering her up with my husband's helpful comment that he had often wanted to bite her bottom (she is a very attractive single mother) but decided instead to opt for surrender and promise to take Olivia to see a child psychiatrist.

I asked Olivia why she had bitten the girl's bottom. 'She kept following me around,' was her rather surly response. I told her bottom biting was wrong, but my husband and mother both took a more lenient view and said that kids behave like that.

They might in England, but not over here. At least not without the whole village establishment taking notice.

Education is a pressing concern for many people buying homes in France. Some see it as a way of getting out of school fees in England. For us, the thought of the expense of sending all our five children to boarding school was enough to make us leave the country.

In France there is little social cachet about sending your children to a boarding school. In fact, it is traditionally those who are bad who get sent away. We have become good friends with my gynaecologist and his wife, Kati. He is a rather good-looking man, known in the family as the Dashing Dr Denjean. She is incredibly glamorous, your average French nightmare, a size 8 (if that), impeccably turned out, with beautifully manicured nails. Their daughter is ten and whenever she misbehaves, Kati threatens to send her to boarding school. Our friends Peter and Dominique Glynn-Smith epitomise the culture divide. He was very keen to send their son to Bedales where his children from his previous marriage were educated. She wouldn't hear of it.

'Private' schools, however, are still popular. In total around 15 per cent of the French send their children to private schools compared with 5 per cent in Britain. The private schools were all traditionally religious schools, but there are now some international and bilingual schools. The main difference, it would seem, is that the private school teachers don't strike as much as the state ones. In fact, every time Olivia and Bea have a day off due to a strike, I call my friend Alex to see if her daughter Elisa is around to play. She never is. Alex pays €84 (around £50) per term to send Elisa to a private school and this sum will remain constant as she grows up. French private schools are fully regulated and partially subsidised by the state. The international schools are much more expensive, some are on a par with English public schools.

Several parents of English children I have spoken to have found there is more support for their children within the French private system than the state one. Private schools are more likely to allow more time for French as a foreign language tutoring and there seems to be a consensus that they look after the individual needs of the child. The most important thing is to check with the individual schools and teachers in the region you live in or are moving to as there are of course variations.

My two girls go to school in the village where my babysitter lives. When I tried to enrol Olivia in the local village school here, it was full. To enrol a child you will need immunisation certificates and a piece of paper from your insurance company which provides cover for them at school. Sometimes the insurance company covers the child inside the school but not during outside activities, like trips, so it's worth checking. You will also need to provide proof of residence.

Chantal, my babysitter, was already looking after Bea when Olivia first started school, so it was also more practical to have them both in the same place. In addition, she was only going in the morning as she was just over two. So far, I have been extremely happy with the way things have gone. The school itself is a lovely village school, the teachers seem great and she is doing very well. Last term she came home with top marks in every subject, except pronunciation, which she got the second top mark in. I was over-joyed, but the somewhat overprotective headmistress has insisted I take her to see a speech therapist. This seemed to me a little ridiculous, but I am going along with it—he may be able to do something about my pronunciation at the same time.

Olivia speaks just about perfect French, so imagine what the teachers would say about an English child moving over aged, say ten. An estimated 50,000 Brits a year are moving to France, and there must be a lot of school age children among them. It is difficult to say what the ideal age is to move to a different culture, although the earlier the better if you want to speak French like a local. When we moved, Olivia was just over one, so barely speaking. My other two children were born here. Bea, now three, speaks

There are times when I realise we bought more than just a house in the south of France. Such as when French presidential candidate Nicolas Sarkozy commissioned the French playwright Yasmina Reza to write a portrait of his existential inner being.

Most people will, like me, probably struggle to remember what existentialism is, if they ever knew. But the strange thing about living in France is that my children won't. They will soon start learning about existentialism and all aspects of philosophy at school. (If you would like to know what existentialism is, it's all about understanding the human condition. If anyone asks, just tell them it's the opposite of positivism. That should shut them up.)

My children's cultural identity is already taking shape aged six and seven. Every two weeks they come home with a poem that they have to learn by heart. This is in their cahier de poésie, their poetry exercise book, a concept I find irresistibly charming, even if learning the poems does cause a lot of stress.

These poems are not about the things you might expect six-year-olds to be learning about, such as fluffy sheep and cute kittens. No, they are about things like snow falling and surrounding your heart like a soft mousse or the rising sun casting shadows over ploughed fields.

And the children are judged on how well they recite them. Competition may not be allowed to flourish in the French high street-Swedish chain store Hennes was recently banned from opening a branch in the Champs Elysées because the government wants to give smaller players a chance to operate-but it is alive and well in the French classroom.

Ever since my seven-year-old daughter, Olivia, received only an orange dot-as opposed to the top mark, a green one-she has been more determined than ever to learn her poem perfectly. The last one about the snow we heard so many times that her younger sister and brother were also reciting it by the end of the week. Even the cat purred along.

English with a charming French accent and is always being corrected by her older sister who seems to have English somewhere deep down in her memory. In his book *Buying a House in France*, André de Vries, suggests that children under seven settle in most easily. 'Any older and the language deficit, combined with the rigorous nature of the French education, could make their lives unbearable'.

Liberté, égalité, fraternité,

I wasn't worried about sending my children to school in France when we first moved here. They were so little I knew they would adapt easily. But the more I learn about the system, the more concerned I become. The first thing you need to remember is that it was set up by Napoleon who decided that all French children should study the same subject at the same level in every region so that the local differences (and objections to his dictatorship) would disappear over time. This gives the whole school system a uniformity, which I suppose is useful if you move within France.

Some 200 years later, however, this fundamental concept remains largely unchanged. According to a French friend, 'We were being attacked from all sides, mainly by the British as usual and so we set up a lot of military schools. Sadly nothing has changed since then.' To illustrate the difference between the two systems, he tells the story of one of his sons who is at Cambridge and decided to go travelling in Peru. He went off happily with a rucksack and came back after two months having had a wonderful time. 'My other son who is studying in France went to Marseille for two weeks and was terrified the whole time. Children in France are just not taught to cope in the world and to think for themselves. The system allows no self-reliance. You learn and shut up, that is it.' Another French friend argues that Marseille is terrifying and far more dangerous than Peru, but that's a different argument.

My cultural initiation also includes reading the French edition of Glamour magazine. Coming back from Paris once (surrounded by French people reading very highbrow books) I was flicking through an article entitled 'My Best Ever Night of Sex'. After looking around to make sure nobody was watching me, I read about a girl who was on holiday with her best friend somewhere hot and steamy. They came across a stranger on the beach and had sex with him. Like you do. I was rather surprised, though, to find that at the bottom of this saga was an analysis from a leading psychiatrist, who concluded that 'the girl is clearly in love with her best friend, as she never once mentions the stranger's penis'.

After six years of living here, I think we have moved further away from the English attitude. My husband, for example, has become addicted to Proust. He has even signed up to a website called Salon Proust. Yes, in France, men don't spend their time drooling over sites like 'Am I hot dot com' but rather they swap anecdotes about Marcel and his madeleine moments.

I have grown rather fond of it. Intellectualising can be good fun and is cheaper than shopping. Sadly, I think one of the reasons the Brits are less intellectual than the French is the fact that we are so busy earning money. As Samuel Johnson said: 'All intellectual improvement arises from leisure.' There's another good reason to hang on to the 35-hour week.

The other thing you have to remember is that teachers are civil servants, employed by the state to make children perfect little French citizens. 'They are like soldiers in an army,' says a friend. 'Individuality is frowned upon because it can cause dissension in the troops.'

Though the job of the teachers is to produce little republicans, the '*égalité*' breaks down quickly. They are all supposedly teaching the same subjects at the same times, but not all schools are created equal. There are some inspiring professors but many others who just go through the motions. The Bac (equivalent to A-levels) has supposedly been reformed and it now comes in several flavours and just like in Britain, the pass rate constantly goes up. 'But if your plan is that your gifted child should rise to be admitted to one of the *grandes écoles* like the famous ENA, more selective even than Oxbridge, you had better move to Paris and send your child to one of a very strictly limited number of the grandes *lycées*,' says Guy Veillot, a French friend. 'Admissions to these tends to come via connections and is not coincidental with residence in the better post codes. And so the elite renews itself.'

This is not a view shared by all. Rory Clarke, chief editor of the OECD *Observer* magazine, says France is ahead of England in terms of equality in education. 'I wouldn't like to be guilty of dewy-eyed romanticism,' he says. 'But I think the system favours ordinary people with brains in France, whereas well-off people with money and not much in grey matter are guaranteed very little indeed. If you like, it is one of the better vestiges of the revolution. If you compare the two countries' exam results, in Britain, broadly speaking, those who do well come from good backgrounds and those who do badly from poor ones. In France the background is more mixed.'

But still there are elements of French education that are paradoxical. By attempting to reconcile the often contradictory tenets of French Republicanism, it has produced a system where quirky children can be overlooked or ignored. At the same time, the French system somehow produces writers, thinkers, musicians and artists of towering genius. It is like so much about France—hard to figure out.

The marvellous film *Etre et Avoir* offers a glimpse into the survival of traditional schooling, especially at the primary level, which looks rather inspiring. Olivia, aged five, is already doing the beautiful joined-up writing they learn and I am very proud of her, but

My husband has a foolproof method for ascertaining just how French our children are becoming. Every Sunday morning, as we tuck into our boiled eggs, he asks them two questions: what is the best football team in the world, and was Napoleon a good bloke? The children dutifully reply: 'Chelsea, and no.' But I wonder if one day my husband will find himself choking on his toast soldiers as they nominate Marseille and start reeling off Napoleonic victories.

'Aren't you worried your children will grow up French?' I am often asked. Worried? Yes. About almost everything there is to worry about, and plenty more. About them growing up French? No. It seems to me a pretty nice thing to grow up into. And when they're ready for their first job, they can go on the French version of The Apprentice. Instead of being told, 'You're fired,' you're told, 'You're completely useless, so you've got a job for life.'

The question of national identity is one that every parent should think about when they uproot their children and take them to a foreign country. Strangely enough, the children feel strongly about the issue as well.

My daughter, Olivia, was only one when we moved to France, but she maintains she wants to live in London and has a strong preference for all things English.

This includes her choice of friends at school. Although they are now only six years old, four of them hang out in an English clique. I can't decide whether I'm appalled by this or secretly quite pleased that she is exposed to English culture outside the home. At least they can discuss Peter Rabbit and Winnie the Pooh without having to explain who they are.

But how much of a difference does living in another country make to their character? Does it mean they become less English? Will they feel more French when they're 18 and renounce their British passport in favour of a French one? Will they refuse to eat Marmite? Will they start demanding snails for lunch? Who will they support in the World Cup?

she will end up with the same handwriting as millions of other children in France, except those who are left-handed and can't cope with writing right-handed. It is peculiar that they all learn to write in exactly the same way. Children will learn how to spell and surf the internet. But it is an open secret (and a comfort to British immigrants) that many French people never really master their own language and are condemned to menial jobs on the minimum wage, or worse, because if you don't pass the French language section of the Bac you get nowhere.

Reform of the education system has been continuous and the results decidedly mixed, or at any rate minimal. Often obstructing change, the teachers tend to be left-wing and also deeply conservative. As soon as the government wants to change something, they strike.

Despite the changes some basic inequalities between schools remain. If you are the sort of parent who cares about this (and not everyone does to the same degree), it is, in fact, exactly like education in Britain and everywhere else—it is absolutely crucial where your child goes to school.

According to Nick Rowsell, who was an English teacher in France, a lot of expat children have problems with the French system simply because they are different. 'One of my American work colleagues was told time and again that her kids were failures,' he says. 'On the advice of teachers, they spent their formative years being shunted around educational psychologists. In later years, in *lycée* and *collège*, their major crime was that they 'didn't fit in.' My colleague's kids have now finished with the system. However, for us the nightmare is just beginning—my daughter has been assigned a special needs teacher because she is 'different'. The French way of education can cause a lot of emotional trauma to non-French parents and their offspring. Even if their children have never set foot in a British school, the simple fact of one parent exerting a British or English linguistic and cultural influence on the

Our babysitter, Miranda, 17, who has English parents but has lived in France for 15 years, says: 'England when I'm in France and France when I'm in England.'

I am always amazed by how English her accent is: you'd think she had been brought up in Surrey.

'But I am English,' she says when I tell her this, although she admits that when she visits her cousins in England, she is appalled by several things. 'They all drink, smoke and have sex, all the time. If a girl behaved like that over here, she'd be known as a slut,' she says, before adding in an even more horrified tone, 'and they never eat bread with their meals'.

I have noticed my children becoming French in some ways. I took Olivia to a museum a few days ago. There was a part of the room that was cordoned off. 'We don't have the right to go there,' she told me very seriously. 'We can go here and there,' she said, pointing to the non-cordoned-off parts. 'But not there.'

Although part of me wanted to skip over the cordon singing Rule Britannia, I actually quite like the French sense of what is right and what is wrong. One of the worst things that you can say to someone here is 'it's not right', and can be used to describe anything from genocide to a badly cooked piece of duck.

I didn't move to France to become French. I moved to France for a better life-although I have noticed I have a growing obsession with introducing the children to Beatrix Potter, Mary Poppins and Orlando the Marmalade Cat, among other thoroughly British institutions. If they choose to ignore them and opt for The Little Prince instead, that's up to them. I suspect the English culture that I am so keen to expose them to comes from an England that no longer exists. Which is another reason why we moved.

child, will set him or her apart from the system.'

Nicole Kuhnlé, a primary school teacher I interviewed, tells me that foreign children are often different from other kids, but usually for positive reasons. 'They are usually better pupils than the rest of the class,' she says. 'I have had countless children from Arab countries, some not speaking French at all, an American, a South Korean, Yugoslavs, Turks, Albanians. And they usually coped quite well or even were top of the class after a few months.'

Stephanie Godwin lives in the Mayenne and her three children are going to school in the region. She has encountered terrible problems, and puts it down to them being English. 'They seem to equate someone who is English with someone with learning difficulties,' she says. 'Joseph's (her five-year old son) teacher told me he would have to stay back a year after teaching him for four mornings. She says she hasn't got the time to teach an English child to read. There are only 12 kids in his class!' Stephanie advises anyone looking to move here to check out the attitude of the local mayor towards the British before they buy. 'I have just discovered that it is the mayor who controls all the primary schools and that is why we have had such a bad time here, as he doesn't want any English kids in the school.'

She also says that bullying is a huge problem in France and that it starts with the teachers. 'They just don't want any extra work so they try to get rid of English children as soon as possible by sending them to another institution like SEGPA (special educational institutions for children with learning difficulties or behavioural problems). This they achieve by being foul, running the kids down as much as possible and refusing to help them in any way.'

As in all schools there are stories of bullying by other children from France. I have had lots of letters from readers on the subject. One from a couple who recently moved to Perpignan with their boys aged seven and nine. They were picked on for being the only English children in the school, the younger boy was hit on the head so hard (by a girl) that he had to be taken to hospital in an ambulance. They also found that the teachers were far more violent than in England. 'To start with our eldest son was in a class where his teacher would suddenly shriek at one child or another and then strike them,' says his mother, who wishes to remain anonymous. 'Our child was never hit, but he was always on edge, not knowing what the others had been hit for.'

My primary school teacher friend Nicole Kuhnlé says that she has given a few smacks in her career, when it was still not illegal to do so and when the child was really uncontrollable. 'Today whenever a child gets hit, a rare occurrence, it usually ends up in court,' she says.

According to Nick Rowsell 'anyone moving to France for the sole purpose of the better quality education their offspring might receive should themselves go back to the classroom. It is a loopy idea'. Nick trained as a teacher here and says that what he saw of the education system was enough to make him leave it. 'French schools might look good on paper,' he says. 'But they don't half screw up your kids. French education is all about following instructions to the letter, and that starts in the first year of infant school.'

Jacques Kuhnlé, Nicole's husband and a retired English teacher himself, says that may be true, but he defends the French educational establishment. 'Seeing bad manners and the way children are (not) educated at home by their parents, I don't find it shameful that someone should set limits to what children can do or not do in the company of others, even in the first year of school,' he says.

To illustrate his point on limits set, Nick tells the story of his daughter, Lena, when she was five, being asked to draw a picture of a Father Christmas (she goes to a nursery school in Bourges in the Cher). 'Just before Christmas, my daughter's class was told to draw a Father Christmas on a sheet of A3 paper. My daughter duly drew a nice Santa, but she added a Christmas tree and presents. With the approach of Christmas, Santas appeared all around the classroom on the wall from all the children, apart from our daughter. When my daughter's work did appear, it was a minuscule Santa since the teacher had cut the offending items out the picture, so it would match the others. I told the teacher that it showed imagination and initiative and was met with a stony silence, followed by: '*votre fille n'a pas suivi la consigne*—she didn't complete the assignment.'

One of the most common criticisms of the French system and the thing that most worried me is the lack of opportunity for self-expression. Pupils are force-fed information like a goose being fattened to make *foie gras* and just expected to regurgitate it when asked. 'This is reflected in the fact Cambridge alone has won 80 Nobel prizes against 50 for the whole of France,' says Alaric Wyatt, a private tutor now based between Oxford and France. 'True and deplorable,' says my friend Jacques. 'But the reason is not so much the lack of freedom given to an individual as the amount of money scientists have in their labs.'

Children are also likely to find there is much more homework than in the UK. Ruth de Latude who brought her three children up in France remembers them having an hour's homework every night from as early as seven years old. She found the system a harsh one. Ruth's eldest son Thomas suffers from epilepsy and has had to take drugs all his life to fight the condition. 'These make your thought process much slower so Thomas found it very hard to keep up at times,' she says 'Here they seem to have either schools for severely handicapped children or nothing at all. And in the normal school you either keep up or you're out. Thomas was terribly unhappy and in the end I took him out aged 16.'

Indeed, the French system is not famous for dealing with any special needs well. Leslie Sorbie from Newcastle-upon-Tyne is considering a move to France with their daughter and two grandchildren. Her grandson Sean is 11 and has Down's Syndrome. In France, says a source at the British Down's Syndrome Association, they are way behind England in terms of education. 'They do not, as we do, offer children with Down's Syndrome access to mainstream schools as a matter of course, although I think things are better in the rural areas.' Jean-Charles Wiart from FAIT 21, the French Down's Syndrome Association, agrees that in France there are vast regional differences. 'In theory parents have the choice of whether or not to integrate their children, but in practice it depends on the region and what is available there.' In France a child with Down's Syndrome will be 'shadowed' by a carer in normal school, and some regions do not have this facility. In Nancy, for example, there is the choice of integration in an ordinary school or a special class in a local school.

Some friends who live near Montpellier have a daughter who is dyslexic—which is not a condition the French look upon as seriously as the English do. 'It has been really tough for Georgie,' says her mother. 'And as far as I can make out, they don't really get much of an education anyway. The teachers are always off sick and the girls are sent home early. When they do get taught it's very old fashioned and they seem obsessed with results.' They moved to France when their triplets were 11 years old. Mike, her husband, is in the army and was posted here. 'There was no question of leaving them behind,' he says. 'That's not what we had them for.' The girls were taken out of the English public school system and put into a school in a village close to Montpellier. It wasn't just Georgie who had problems. 'They absolutely hated it at first,' says Mike. 'I remember one time Jessica calling me to tell me that she was outside the school and all three girls had locked themselves in the car. There was a time when I think they would rather have done anything than go to school.'

Other people, like Melissa Miller, have moved their children back to England to get away from the system. They moved to France when their children were six and nine. 'There was a lot of shouting, humiliation and smacking. And the children, who had nothing to play with but a ball made from old newspaper, did a lot of physical fighting and bullying.' Her daughter did very well.

After 10 months she had mastered the language and was among the top of her class, but her son was placed in a remedial class because he refused to speak French to the adults. 'I also found the method of teaching very parrot fashion and narrow-minded,' says Melissa. 'They leave no room at all for imagination or creativity. In the classes for the younger children homework consisted of learning long poems by heart. Older children were taught by copying long passages from the blackboard and learning them for tests. In the end we decided to come back to England for the sake of the children's education. We did not want them stifled. We were grateful for this short educational experience. It did them no harm and there were some great benefits.'

Paul Beaufils, a former naval officer who moved to Béziers just over two years ago to set up a property business, is very happy with the French system. When they first moved here, he told me the school took the arrival of their two daughters very seriously. They were nine and thirteen and neither of them spoke French. 'They got all the governors and the teachers together,' Paul told me. 'They had a meeting that went on all afternoon. I was panicking thinking they weren't going to let them in or something. Finally the headmaster appeared and said they had made a decision. 'I know what we're going to do,' he told me. 'We're going to speak French to them.' I could have told them that!'

His daughter Laura learnt the language easily and is now top of her year. 'She loves school,' he says. 'And is particularly good at history.' One day he asked her why she liked the subject so much. 'It's pretty easy Dad,' she replied. 'All you have to remember is that the French lost everything except for Africa.'

One of Tony Tidswell's best memories is his daughter's first day at the village school of Nizas in the Languedoc. Miranda was three at the time and he remembers another three year old girl coming out from the classroom, taking her hand and leading her in. 'It was such a poignant moment,' he says. 'And they are still the best of friends.'

What will be the right school will depend on your region. There are notoriously bad schools in the suburbs where it is unfortunately true that very few learn anything much. Most people seem to encounter problems in regions where there aren't so many expats and where the children are the only foreigners at the school. Jacques Kuhnlé says 'generally speaking, *maternelles* (nursery schools) are excellent. Primaries are quite good. *Lycées* are fine. Naturally this is a general assessment. You will find poor or lazy teachers even in the best places. The real problem is in *collèges*. Their location is critical. Try to avoid *collèges* or *lycées classés en ZEP* (*zone d'éducation prioritaire*). This means difficult suburbs, problems of discipline and pupils' motivation. As for private schools, beware. They are not all good. Far from it. Some are excellent but the others (I would say over half depending on the region) can be just awful.'

The most important thing you can do as a parent is to stay positive. If you accept the different life, methods of doing things, so will your children. If you are planning your move several months in advance, get your children a French teacher. If you are already here, get a tutor; someone who can come in every afternoon and help with the homework, the syllabus, and of course the language. The tutor can also help your children get used to the endless tests he or she will encounter.

Your child may have been top of his or her class at home and will probably come bottom for a while. This will be very hard to adjust to and demoralising. On the positive side, a huge number of Brits I have met who have children in the system here find they eventually overtake their French counterparts. Some parents have chosen to take advantage of the system here and then send their children to private school in England to complete their education. 'Our daughter was going to be held back for a year here aged 13,' says an Englishman who has lived in Paris for 30 years. 'She avoided that by going to England and also has come out with a more rounded education.'

Educational experts say it takes five terms for a child to fully settle in and learn the language. This period may be shorter if they are very small, and of course it gets more difficult the older they are.

Don't forget that their English will deteriorate and it will be up to you to reinforce it, as the level at school is not going to be high enough. At home, we speak English and Swedish, and videos and TV are only allowed in those two languages. If a book is English (like Harry Potter), it is read in English and never in the French translation. I encourage the girls to speak English together and so far they do. Chantal, their babysitter, says she loves listening to them chat away, although she has no idea what they're talking about.

Another common complaint among expats is of bias in the teaching in French schools, so you may need to correct that. A wine-making friend of mine in Bordeaux says he will send his son to school in England: 'I'm terrified he will grow up thinking Napoleon is a good bloke,' he says. ('What does he expect?' asks Jacques. 'Nelson presented as a hero or Waterloo as a great victory?')

The mother of the bullied boys above tells me they were extremely surprised by the history material the boys came home with one day. 'We noted with interest that the French teach them that Franco-American forces landed on D-Day and went on to win the war,' she says 'On the plus side, our son has overcome his aversion to Maths, as it is a subject he now really fully understands.'

You will also have to have a decent level of French to be able to help them with their homework as they get older. All conversations with teachers will be in French and you will also need to communicate with your children's friends. Assuming you're not moving to the Dordogne, they are likely to be French.

My stepson Hugo will be 13 next year and has been offered a place at a good school in Britain. There is a good reason he won't be going. It costs a fortune.

I have started to look into the alternatives for Hugo in France. In total there are around 25 international schools here. Some of them, like the British School of Paris, offer a British education up to A-Levels. You can even play cricket there. According to Richard Woodhall, Head of the Senior School, their aim is to provide a totally British education away from home. 'Although we have pupils from 55 countries here, this is an English education in France,' he says. 'Parents looking for that should beware of some of the international schools that purport to offer that but are in fact French with just a bit of English on the side.' The fees at the British School of Paris for a 13-year old are €15,500 a year. Your child could also live with a host family close to the school at an additional cost of about €600 a month. The total cost then is about €22,700 or about £15,000. A lot less than the equivalent in Britain but still not a steal.

If you feel like educating your child among the jet-set of the Riviera there is the Mougins School near Cannes. The fees are less than in Paris, €11,250 a year, but again you would have to factor in the cost of a host family. 'We have students from 22 countries who end up in universities all over the world,' says Sue Dunnachie, Marketing Consultant at the school. 'I think in terms of the British universities coming from an international education is an advantage. One of our students has just got into Oxford.'

With international schools there is a concern that the students are only passing through and so never really settle in. According to Dunnachie, this is changing. 'We are finding that the pattern of students is changing, rather than the children of people who have been posted here, we are seeing a lot of children whose parents can work from anywhere in the world and have picked the sunny south of France.' Also on the Riviera is

Graham Richardson, who moved to Montpellier with his wife Karen and their children ten years ago, has three daughters who have been through the French system. He advises throwing children in at the deep end. 'When we first got here, Charlotte was eight,' he says. 'There was a French-Canadian girl in her class who spoke good English so we thought it would help her to sit with her and learn from her. Not a bit of it. Whereas Sarah (ten at the time) and Josephine (four at the time) both picked up French in two months, after six months Charlotte still wasn't making progress.' In the end, Graham told her that if he ever heard her speaking English to her friend she would never see her again. 'That was a turning point, after that she was fine.'

Graham's girls are among those that love the system here and have had no problems at all. 'They have responded well to what is really a very structured and organised system,' says Graham. 'They seem to enjoy the constant scoring that goes on.' A small blip came early on when Josephine found she was losing a mark on every test at school, even if she got all the answers to the questions right. She asked her teacher what the problem was and was told that she was spelling her name incorrectly, she needed to put an accent on the first e. 'But I'm English,' Josephine told the teacher. 'That's not how my name is spelt.' 'It *is* in France,' was the response.

Higher education

The higher end of the French system is even more impenetrable than the English. There are the *grandes écoles*, the top schools, and then everything else. Only a small percentage of *grandes écoles* students come from a working-class background, although there are efforts to change this. The *Sciences Politiques* school in Paris, for example, recently opened admission to suburban schools where the students are traditionally French lower-class of Arab origin.

Graham Richardson's daughters Sarah and Charlotte have both

the Sophia-Antipolis School, which runs parallel courses following either the French state system or the International Baccalaureate (IB). According to Peter Arnold, a teacher there, it is a good alternative to the 'fiasco' of the UK system. 'Universities love students that come out with the IB because they know it's such a rigorous academic course,' he says. 'It is the equivalent of getting three of four A-grades at A-Level.' The fees are €8,500 a year for the IB and only €2,000 for the French system. However, Arnold advises anyone that has not had any previous French against going for the latter option. Added to this there are boarding fees of €10,000 a year.

Up country in Bordeaux is an international school with a small-school feel. Although in the centre of town, Bordeaux International School has only 100 students. It takes students aged three to 19 and teaches an English curriculum. It seems more French than the other international schools, it has a French headmistress for example, and the students integrate a lot with students from other local schools. Fees start at €9,900 a term for secondary students and host families charge around €6,000 a year.

Of course one of the brilliant things about living in France is that the state education system is so much better than the one in the UK. Maybe Hugo will just have to learn French and come out of school thinking Napoleon was a good bloke. A teacher I spoke to here says it takes about three terms for a foreign student to learn French and settle in. It will be a tough three terms for him, but what admissions officer from a UK university will be able to resist a bilingual boy with an IB and a suntan?

got extremely good Bac grades and are carrying on into higher education. Sarah is doing *prépa* (intensive teaching in smaller classes which the top 10 per cent of the Bac students have the option of doing) at the *lycée*, and may go on to one of the sought after *grandes écoles*. Charlotte has decided to go straight to university to study law. 'We moved here to give the children a better education without having to pay for it,' says Graham who is preparing to move back to England to become a teacher. 'I think we've achieved that.'

The problem is the low standard in the universities has made it even more essential to get into a one of the *grandes écoles*. 'Now that the government has decided everyone needs to pass their Baccalaureate, the standards at universities have gone down so the only people who will get decent jobs are those who make it to the *grandes écoles*. And to make it to them you have to have the right family, not just for support, these students work from 8am to 11pm, but also the contacts,' says Guy Veillot.

Many people don't agree and maintain that as it is all based on your exam results there is no room for elitism. 'The written part of the exam is nameless, precisely to ensure that only the best succeed (the old republican principle of equality),' says Jacques Kuhnlé. 'Only at the orals (when they exist) can the examiners see who the students are. And even then, letting in a bad student because you know him or his parents is dangerous, not only legally: if he fails miserably the other teachers will demand to know who let in that awful student,' he says.

'Most people think that the Bac is equivalent to English A-levels but it's not,' says Graham. 'The real selection for top grade higher education takes place the following year at the universities themselves where a huge percentage of the intake fail to carry on. I think this is an interesting twist because it means that everyone who gets even a mediocre Bac [80 per cent pass rate] can go to university [*égalité!*]. And then they find themselves sifted ruthlessly before being kicked out if they are no good. Which means that just like anywhere else, the French have an elitist system but are clever at pretending otherwise.'

In order to get into a *grande école* you have to be at the right preparatory school. Peter and Dominique Glynn-Smith have been forced to run two households so that their son can go to school in Montpellier. This is the closest city that has a school that is a feeder for the exclusive preparatory schools everyone is aiming for. Once you have got into the *prépa*, you have two years of unimaginably hard slog ahead before the ultimate prize of the *grande école.*

Jérôme did get into the *prépa* in Versailles, in fact, he came top in the whole of France in Geography and History in the Bac for his year and was even telephoned by a government minister who congratulated him. Astoundingly, the very first question he was asked in his interview at the *prépa* was: 'Here in Paris, we have the impression that in the south of France you find it difficult to work hard. What do you think of this?' My friend Jacques would say that the fact the interview took place is proof that there is no prejudice or elitism in the system. Jérôme comes from a family who live down south with no smart Paris address.

As far as the expense of the best education in France is concerned, now that Jérôme has got into his *prépa*, his parents will have to find around €2,000 a year tuition fees and at least €600 a month living costs. 'There are very few boarding facilities,' says his mother Dominique. 'And in France not everyone gets a grant.'

The Arts

One of my main concerns about the educational system is that there is really not much beyond academic subjects taught at French schools. In primary schools there is no art, music or sports to speak of. In secondary schools, according to Jacques, they have one or two hours of music a week, the same with arts and sports. Drama is not usually on the syllabus. Originally Wednesdays were free because of an arrangement with the Catholic Church so the children could go to catechism in the morning. Nowadays the idea is that pupils have Wednesdays off to pursue their interests. This of course is difficult for those who have parents who work and can't drive them to which ever club they want to go to.

Sarah and Matthew Cookson have decided, after 12 years in France, to move back to England with their children Rosie and William for secondary school. 'I'm fed up with driving around the county all the time,' says Sarah. 'If we want them to get a balanced education we have to take them to the various clubs or classes ourselves.'

Sarah recommends finding out about something called the *Forum des Associations.* This is an open day, usually a Saturday, where all the associations and clubs display their courses and you can register your children for them.

This lack of sporting and artistic culture means that if your child is incredibly sporty but not keen on course work, he or she may never be seen as anything but a low achiever. 'If your child is not academic, he or she may not be very happy in the French system,' says Laurence Micklethwait, who is French and married to an Englishman. 'They will feel like a failure all the way through.' Laurence has decided to send her two boys to French school for the moment, partly because the English schools around Paris are so expensive and because she feels the academic level in French schools is higher. 'This may change,' she says. 'My husband was at boarding school in England and he may want to send the boys there one day. I'm not against the idea.'

There are special schools geared towards dance or sport, so if you have a child prodigy who is not academic, he or she could go to one of those. But remember they are not in every region. I am worried Bea will not be academic. She seems to have more of a crazy Viking Swede gene in her than her sister, and she is definitely the actress of the family. When Olivia was her age she would come back at the end of term with a folder full of work with little smiley faces the teacher had drawn on. This is their system of marking little ones. Smiley faces means good, non-smiley means mediocre and turned down mouth is bad. Bea has more of the latter two, but

I guess there's still time.

I am keeping an open mind. So far the girls are happy where they are and they will stay. Our older children, Hugo and Julia, will stay in England. Hugo has an unconditional place at Eton and if we can afford it (no chance) we'll send him there. Julia wants to go to her local comprehensive because she likes the red uniform (there are worse reasons for choosing schools). When the little girls are older I may decide to send them to the international school in Montpellier, or even England for a year or so. I would like to think they will grow up truly bilingual (with enough Swedish to talk to attractive Scandinavian men when they come across them) and I don't think they will do that if they are educated here 100 per cent. Leonardo will never learn to play cricket if he is educated here, unless his father teaches him. But I guess he will play rugby and I never really understood the rules of cricket anyway.

Whatever else, it's a lot better than Heathfield Comprehensive or 15 years of trying to find £4,000 a term each for some middle class training ground in the home counties.

10
Hell on Earth

The intransigence of the French might be scary, but the tax and social security regime is positively terrifying. France is well known for being impossibly bureaucratic and punishing. For French friends who run successful businesses here it has got to the point where they are considering moving them to the UK. Bill Blevins, of the financial advisers Blevins Franks, tells me one of his most successful French clients in Paris is moving his whole operation to London. 'Despite the prices there, he will save around 40 per cent in costs due to the punishing social security regime in France,' he says.

A lot of English people who move to France or have a second home here think that they can simply stay out of the system. As a warning to them I quote a terrifying statistic from a book written by a former tax inspector. He states that if you are a French farmer, you are likely to be inspected by the tax authorities once every 135 years. If you are a foreign entrepreneur you are likely to be investigated once every six years. Is this institutionalised racism?

'I don't think that tax offices target foreigners specifically, but in areas where there are a lot of foreigners there are often various forms of abuse going on, some of which they catch up with eventually,' says Dawn Alderson, lawyer at Russell Cooke. 'Some people think they can go and live in France and pay tax neither in England nor France. It's just not realistic.'

Despite doing everything legally, Tony and Carole Tidswell have been through the hellish experience of a tax investigation. Bill Blevins describes the process similar to 'having a concrete mill wheel around your neck'. Those who have been through it agree.

Tony and Carole were wrongly advised when they first moved to the south of France over ten years ago. 'As a self-employed person, I was told I had to register my profession with the relevant association or *Chambre*,' says Tony. In France there are several *Chambres des Métiers*, one for commercial professions, another for artisans and another for writers and artists. As they were in the process of setting up an internet business, Tony registered as a photographer—which had been his previous profession. Belonging to a *Chambre* means that you pay a monthly contribution to your social security and pension payments. Tony ended up paying €500 per month over six years, even though they had no income at all. They were living on capital whilst doing up their home and starting the internet business. 'What we did was totally wasteful and unnecessary,' he says. 'Although I had several meetings with tax people and accountants here not one of them gave me the right advice. If you ask five people the same question, expect five different responses and often conflicting replies.'

Finally they went to a UK accountant for advice. He told them they only needed to register with the *Chambre des Métiers* if they wanted to operate any business or trade in France where they were going to invoice people locally. They then resigned from the *Chambre des Métiers*. 'Immediately we were jumped on for tax on all income that had gone through our bank,' says Carole. 'This included the sale of our personal effects, private loans and expenses we were paid whilst trying to set up our business.'

The tax authorities are not allowing any expenses they have incurred during the years they are investigating to be offset, so

Tony and Carole now face a tax bill of around €17,000 on 'non-existent income.'

'For people coming into the French system', says Tony, 'just appointing an accountant or talking to the tax people is not enough. It is really necessary to dig deeply into the implications of trying to work in a system where you will be assumed to be guilty of trickery and are guilty until proven innocent.'

Brent and Susan Calvert moved to the Dordogne in 1995. Brent had owned a number of estate agent offices in Blackheath, but when he was offered a substantial profit by one of the large mortgage players, he decided to take his money and flee abroad. He moved first to Andorra, but after seven years of skiing and hill-walking he bought a large farmhouse with land in the Dordogne area of France. Immediately they ran into trouble with the French taxman. 'Looking back on it, maybe we were a bit naïve,' says Brent. 'We declared everything we had and once we had done that, we didn't stop paying. Even though we love France, it couldn't continue. I was paying more tax than I was earning. I said this to the taxman and he just laughed and said 'sometimes it is like that'.

The easiest way to avoid trouble with the French taxman is to work for a French company. This way your employer gets to pay for your social security contributions (around 40 per cent on top of your salary) and deal with the authorities. However, the average wage is only €800 per month net, hardly enough to pay most mortgages. Nick Rowswell, head of studies at the French Air force language school in Avord, south of Paris, has been in France for 13 years. 'Since the introduction of the Euro,' he says, 'living and working as the French is getting harder. I have an annual salary increase of 0.5 per cent, inflation stands at 2 per cent and prices have risen by 17 per cent.'

You should also take into account that you may have to pay wealth tax (*Impôt de Solidarité sur la Fortune* or ISF) if you have net assets which are valued at over £500,000. This applies to anyone who is resident in France or has assets in France on January 1st of more than £500,000. When calculating the value of your assets you have to take into account things like your car, furniture, yachts etc. You may also be asked to produce receipts to justify your valuations. You will pay a percentage of the value of your assets calculated on a sliding scale at 0.55 per cent on assets of between £500,000 to £770,000 up to 1.80 per cent on assets of £10 million and above.

The capital gains tax law changed recently. This tax is paid when you make a profit on a property that is not your principal home. A French resident selling a property that is the principal residence will not be taxed on any capital gains. Residents and non-residents from the European union selling a property, where it is a second home, within five years of purchase will be taxed in full at 16 per cent on any profit. Residents from outside the European Union will be taxed at 36 per cent. Between six and fifteen years after purchase any gain on the sale benefits from a discount of 10 per cent for each year of possession, thus after 15 years of owner-

---

Don't mention the War

In small communities across France there is still much bitterness going back to the Second World War. When Francis Cammaerts, a celebrated British secret agent who helped the French resistance during the War from within France, moved into his new house, he made friends with his next door neighbour. About a year later, his neighbour's wife showed up at his house in tears. 'I can't tell you the difference it has made,' she said. During the war, the Germans had said they would release one imprisoned French soldier for three workers. Her husband had, mistakenly, thought that by volunteering they would let his favourite uncle come home. The villagers had shunned him ever since, until the British secret service hero became his neighbour and friend, nearly 60 years after the end of the War.

ship no tax is payable. The cost of property extensions, major improvements and renovations, supported by receipted accounts, may be deducted from the gain. Bear in mind that social taxes, in some cases as high as 10 per cent, are also payable on any gain from property sales, although not by non-residents.

There are several property taxes you need to be aware of. First and foremost there are two types of local tax: *taxe d'habitation* (residential tax) and *taxe foncière* (property tax, similar to council tax in the UK). Residential tax is payable by anyone living in a property in France, property tax is paid only by the owner of the property. Both taxes are payable on main or second homes and whether you are a French resident or not. If your property is habitable (ie furnished) on January 1st of any given year, you are liable for tax for that year. The amount of tax you pay will usually be based on the rental value of the property for the previous year, as well as the living area and factors like whether or not you have central heating, a swimming-pool, location and so on.

You must also pay tax on any rental income received in France. It does not matter where you live, where you collect the rental money for your home in France or where your personal tax is paid. If the house you are renting is in France, all income from it is considered as being earned in France and tax must be declared on that income in France. Tax must be paid in France, even if you declare and pay tax in another country.

If you are already making a tax declaration in France you can add the property income to your declaration, deduct all relevant expenses and you are liable to tax at 25 per cent on the balance. If relevant expenses are greater than your income no tax is due. If you do not already send in a tax declaration, the simplest system for your property is a *régime micro*. Under this scheme, you are only liable for tax on 30 per cent of the income; they allow you the balance as expenses. You pay tax at 25 per cent on the 30 per cent of the gross rental income.

In addition there may be local tourism and occupancy taxes. Your local *mairie* or *préfecture* can help with this information. These taxes are usually payable per bed, and are usually around one Euro a night.

You are not likely to face double taxation if you have paid your taxes in France and then take the balance back to the UK. You can ask in person what forms are needed at your local tax office. They are usually helpful. More information can be found at the government site (www.service-public.fr).

The one piece of advice everyone gave us when we moved here was that we should keep all our accounts in England.

As it turned out, it just wasn't a realistic option. You have to pay tax in the country in which you live and with children at school here, there is no way we could avoid that. In fact, ultimately the children were the answer. The French are extremely keen on population growth and there are all sorts of benefits for '*familles nombreuses*'. This is classified as a family with more than three children. You get to go on the train for half price, for example. In terms of tax, the level you pay is reduced drastically with every child after the third one. With five children between us, the tax man is very nice to us.

11
Mad Dogs and
Englishmen

In Conan Doyle's story *Silver Blaze*, Sherlock Holmes is able to deduce who nobbled the horse from the fact that the dog did not bark. If Holmes had been in France, he would never have solved the mystery, because there has never been a French dog that did not bark.

One of the few drawbacks of living in this fine country is that, wherever you are, somewhere in the distance you will always hear a dog barking. In villages some owners seem to encourage their dogs to bark to dissuade intruders.

The first house we wanted to buy in France was a relatively isolated property, about half a kilometre between two villages. We liked everything about it until my husband went for a walk in the fields and came across the footings of a building. When he asked what they were for, he was told 'kennels'. Although the owner assured us that if we were bothered by the noise the mayor would have the dogs removed, we preferred not to take the chance. Passing the property by chance recently, we stopped to have a look. As our car pulled to a halt in front of the kennels, 50 dogs jumped up and started howling.

These dogs were kept purely for hunting, a practice that is common all over France. Even though we live in the middle of nowhere, we can often hear two dogs kept in a cage barking from across the valley. 'These animals are not normally regarded as pets and once they stop being useful are usually shot,' says Stephanie Godwin, the English breeder based in the Mayenne. I often feel like wandering over the hills to let them out, but as the hunters traipse around my house with rifles for much of the year it's probably not a good idea.

My friend Carla, who is mad about dogs, says she could never live here because of the way the French treat their animals. She once went to stay with a friend in Provence. Close to the house were two dogs, locked up in a shed, which the owners used for hunting now and again. 'It was appalling,' she said. 'They would throw them bits of stale bread once a day, the poor creatures were starving and frantic.' One evening she could stand it no longer and let them out, having fed them a dinner bought especially from the local butcher. The next day the owner of the shed arrived at her friend's house, furious. 'He knew that only the English would let his dogs out. We had to own up and my friend apologised for my behaviour. I just wanted to kick him.'

Julie Fletcher says that when they first moved here they used to see a hunting dog tied up all day long across the river from their house. 'He was never let off except to hunt,' she says. 'They would throw him some scraps and give him water every day. We got so distressed that we approached the people one day and talked to them about it. 'Oh don't worry about him,' they said. 'He's used to it.' 'Eventually he died, and still attached to his chain they carried him off to bury him.'

How does one explain this fundamental difference in attitude? The dogs I describe above are purely for hunting purposes. But it is not only hunting dogs that are cooped up all day long. Guard dogs in France have a pretty bad time as well. These animals are seen as purely functional and are not part of the family or kept for pleasure. At Château de Conas, they have an Alsatian called Bush (named after the elder American president) who is a guard dog. He is tied up most of the day and barks whenever anyone arrives. Alex, my friend who lives there, would as soon take him for a walk as invite him to dinner, although her father-in-law does take him round the vines occasionally.

One of Simon and Julie's neighbours, François, has a dog called Bruno. Bruno spends 22 hours out of 24 locked in a pitchdark basement. At 8am every day, François brings him out and ties him to the railings in the road. Bruno then stands there barking for an hour while François gets ready to take him for a walk. 'If we've had a late night we always sleep in the spare room at the back,' says Julie. 'Otherwise we get woken up by poor Bruno who comes out literally blinking at the light.'

But does every French person behave the same? Curiously it was a Frenchman, Blaise Pascal, a 17th-century philosopher, who said 'The more I see of men, the more I admire dogs'. But maybe this says more about French men than French dogs. Pierre Desproges, the French stand-up comedian (an extraordinary thought in itself) came up with the following:

Plus je connais les hommes, plus j'aime mon chien.
Plus je connais les femmes, moins j'aime ma chienne.
(The more I know of men, the more I love my dog.
The more I know of women, the less I love my bitch.)

Pascal seems to be in a minority. I have never seen so many stray dogs and dogs left tied up as I have in France. Why would a dog never be tied up and left to bark in an English village? Because someone would report it to the RSPCA. Here it is such common practice that the French equivalent, the SPA (*Société Protectrice des Animaux*) would be snowed under.

Although I have never seen dogs cooped up in England and let out only to defend a property or hunt, Laurent Garosi, a French qualified vet who has been practising in Suffolk for seven years, says the Brits are as bad as their French counterparts. 'The main difference, at least in the south of France, is that dogs are sometimes kept outside,' he says. 'Obviously then they are less a part of family life but I wouldn't say there is any difference in their treatment.'

Not all vets agree with him. I spoke to one based in the Loire. He preferred to remain anonymous. 'I hate the way the French treat animals as something to make money out of,' he says. 'They have no feelings. They only see animals as objects. I can't wait to get the USA, Canada or Britain where I will no longer feel like I'm battling against the rest of the population.' He thinks vets in France are undervalued and underpaid.

There is a huge difference in mentality and it goes all the way up to government level. In the UK so-called puppy farms have been wiped out because of new Kennel Club rules that took effect in the

---

Caroline and Charles Hiscott bought an isolated farmhouse four years ago. Some people have recently bought a plot of land close to them-they camp there four nights a week and have two dogs that bark every time the Hiscotts open a door. 'Are they allowed to camp like this?' asks Caroline. Unfortunately, the answer is yes.

There is no limit to the amount of time you can camp on a piece of land if you own it. If they had a caravan, however, they would not be allowed to stay for more than three months without permission. According to Dawn Alderson of Russell Cooke Solicitors, the Hiscotts could take action because of the dogs. 'The highest court in France has confirmed that animal noise that is excessive and repeated can constitute 'un trouble anormal du voisinage' (abnormal disturbance caused by a neighbouring property),' she says. 'In these circumstances, you might be able to bring an action claiming damages or an order preventing the noise. This would be a last resort, but the law is on your side.'

year 2000. These rules state that any breeder of pedigree dogs is only allowed to register one litter of puppies a year. In France, no such rules exist and consequently unscrupulous farmers are breeding two litters a year from young bitches until they are aged three and four. Then they sell them on to even worse puppy farms where they breed them to death and take their offspring to the markets where unsuspecting people buy them. Clearly these will not be very social or healthy dogs.

I heard about Thérèse Pelon, a Frenchwoman who has dedicated her life to dogs. She was a vet but decided against having a surgery and began studying dog behaviour. She also started to breed Leonbergers, a fine old breed measuring over one metre at the withers. The French canine society found that selling the dogs was easier if they were smaller and more aggressive, so they encouraged breeding with the runts of the litter. Thérèse gave her breeding card back and decided to go it alone. She has thus saved this race from extinction. However, the canine society has refused to allow her to call them Leonbergers, so she has given them the name *Lion d'Occitanie*, from the region in which she lives.

When we first moved here people would ask me if there was anything I didn't like. There are two things, the drivers and the dog poo. My local town is a beautiful medieval town with a wonderfully illustrious history and stunning buildings. When my mother first came to visit she said she felt like writing a letter to the mayor that read: 'Dear Sir, I have enjoyed my trip to your glorious town enormously. I would have liked to look up at the historical buildings, but was too busy scanning the streets for dog poo.'

Montpellier, another elegant place, has become a meeting place for Europe's down and outs. If you were homeless, where would you rather sleep rough: in the sunny south of France or in Glasgow? Many vagrants have dogs because the French system is such that arresting someone with a dog involves so much paperwork the police can't be bothered. These dogs live, eat and defecate all over the city. There are specially equipped little vans that go around cleaning up, but wherever you step in the exquisite pedestrian centre you have to watch out. I once asked an official at the mayor's office what they were doing about the problem. He conceded that it was a difficult issue but said that it was really up to the police.

If you complain to your local mayor about a dog wandering around loose or barking, he or she will write a letter to the owner or visit them. 'Dogs are a big problem in villages,' concedes Jean Martinez, the mayor of Caux. According to Martinez, it is the foreigners (and by that he means not only the Dutch, English, Swedish, German and so on, but also the people from northern France) who have a problem with dogs. 'If you are born in the village, dogs wandering around is part of daily life. You don't see it as a problem. It is only those who don't come from here who complain about them.'

I have always thought of myself as a cat person, probably because I was bought up with a mother who surrounded herself with cats and found dogs 'smelly'. But since I came here, my life has become linked with dogs in several ways. The first thing that happened was that the house came with a dog. I remember the first time we came to see it. As we drove up the drive, a wolf-like creature came bounding towards the car, frothing at the mouth. We sat in the car while it circled, looking menacing. Eventually the owners came out and released us. Jazzy, as he was called, turned out to be friendlier than we first thought. In fact, when we sat down in the drawing room on our second visit, once the sale had been agreed, he sat next to Rupert and put his nose in his hand.

'I see you like dogs,' said Mme Millière, the previous owner of the house.

'Oh yes,' nodded Rupert and smiled, anxious not to offend her or jeopardise the sale.

'Good,' she smiled back. 'Because it's his house. He belongs here. We can't possibly take him with us to a flat in Nîmes. Anyway, you'll need a guard dog here.'

It seemed like a fine idea. In fact, we were both so overjoyed at the thought of moving there she could have said she was leaving her ten grandchildren and we probably wouldn't have objected.

We took a picture home with him to show Hugo and Julia. They were delighted. In fact, they seemed more interested in him than the house itself.

When Rupert arrived to take possession of the place, a few days before me, Jazzy was there to greet him. At that stage our furniture hadn't arrived and Rupert slept in the garden while Jazzy guarded the entrance of the house.

He was an extremely effective guard dog. He would bark if there was a car within a few hundred metres of the house. He was a brilliant alarm when you were swimming naked in the pool. Jazzy was also very good at keeping guests under control. That first summer a rather hungry friend of ours was staying. When she got up for a midnight snack she found Jazzy blocking her path to the kitchen, snarling menacingly.

The problem with Jazzy was that he was slightly unstable. He would chase cars and bark at them as if they were trying to murder us. He once chased a lone jogger into a water-filled ditch, and only a few very fast cyclists made it past the house without being overturned. The previous owners had got him from a rescue home and, although no one knew anything about his background, he gave the impression that he'd been badly treated. The other disadvantage was that he had cataracts in one eye so would often knock over the babies because he couldn't see them.

But the climax of Jazzy's menace came one night during a dinner. We had started with homemade saffron risotto, and were finishing off a leg of lamb when disaster struck. Our friend Norman is extremely fond of dogs and had spent the evening telling us how lucky we were to have Jazzy. 'He's a great *dawg*,' he said, in his New York accent. A former chief executive of a car manufac-

turer and big player on the stock market, he was talking about the
world of high finance when Jazzy slunk in from the terrace and sat
next to him. I briefly heard Norman talk about some director or
other whom he had known, before I went into the kitchen to check

Dog laws in France

* The land belongs to private owners. You are only allowed to
walk on designated tracks and footpaths across it. (Look for
yellow and blue signs.) Your dog could be shot if found running free in a hunting reserve or on farmland.

* Most walks around parks or leisure environments demand
that you keep your dog on the lead. You are also supposed to
have a rabies certificate with you at all times to show the
authorities if required.

* You can face a prison sentence of up to six months if you
abandon your dog. Your dog must be identifiable at all times;
breeders like Stephanie sell puppies with a microchip and a
medallion to wear so that people can take your dog, if found,
to the vet to be identified. Make sure they wear this on their
collar at all times!

* Have good strong fencing to prevent your dog escaping and
think of getting third party liability insurance for him/her.
Remember that healthcare is private in France, and if your dog
causes a car accident, someone—in all likelihood the owner—
has to pay for the ambulance, hospital, and the fire brigade.

* Put a notice on your gate warning people that they enter at
their own risk. (Do not, however put one of those '*chien
méchant*' signs up as you may be admitting liability.) If your
dog bites anyone who enters uninvited, you are covered. If
your dog attacks under other circumstances, you could face
hefty fines and even prison.

* Watch out for ticks, they are much more dangerous than in
the UK. You need to get a potion which you put on your dog
when the tick season starts in the Spring. We have a plastic
contraption with which you get them out, and it doesn't risk

on pudding.

A minute later I heard an awful howling noise. At first I wondered whether it was Norman getting dramatic while telling a story, or whether he had been given some bad stock market news. I was on my way to see what had happened when Georgia, Peter Glynn-Smith's daughter, came into the kitchen looking pale.

'Can I have some ice and some tea-towels,' she said. 'Jazzy has bitten Norman and it looks bad.'

I gave her the ice and towels and ran after her to see what was going on. Norman was leaning back in his chair, with blood pouring from his nose.

'Stand aside,' said one of the guests in a rare display of energy. 'My father was a doctor.' (A psychoanalyst, it later turned out.)

He put the ice and tea towels on Norman's nose and declared he would have to go to hospital. Peter's wife, Dominique, being French, was volunteered to go with him.

'It's only a scratch,' said Norman, as we all tried to stop him looking in the mirror as he left the house. 'Don't remonstrate with Jazzy,' were his last words as he was led off to hospital. Jazzy was outside on the terrace looking sheepish.

I went to sit down when I spotted something on the floor. It could have been a piece of lamb but looked a little undercooked. I went white and pointed.

'It's not Norman's nose,' said Rupert, grabbing a piece of kitchen paper. 'But I'm going to make an executive decision and remove it anyway. We don't need it here.'

The next day we visited Norman in hospital. He had had a serious operation, whereby they grafted some skin from his thigh onto his nose. He was absolutely wonderful about it all.

'Don't do anything to that *dawg*,' he told us. 'It was my fault.'

Rupert told me that Norman had hugged Jazzy after feeding him a piece of lamb. Jazzy had got frightened and lashed out. There was much discussion as to whether the dog was to blame or not, but I

leaving anything embedded. Dogs die of so-called tick disease in France and you need to take precautions.

* Issues about noise with neighbours are always difficult. In France, the basic rules are that you can have up to nine dogs in kennels without having permission, and any number of them in the house! You are definitely allowed one guard dog, which can bark when visitors arrive. Beyond that, if someone wants to complain to the mayor they can, and it will be investigated. The best thing is to be at least 100 metres away from your neighbours. At a distance of one kilometre, you are generally safe. As a rule of thumb, allowable noise is determined by the type of neighbourhood. If you live by a busy main road you can make quite a lot of noise; if you live in a secluded hamlet virtually any noise will be frowned upon.

* No one can stop you from having dogs in rented accommodation. If your dog damages anything, you obviously have to pay for it, and it will be grounds for terminating your lease.

* You can take your dog on holiday with you to campsites and hotels, as long as it is well behaved and covered for rabies. Dogs are also allowed in most shops and restaurants.

think we all knew there was only one thing we could do.

The dog had to go. But where? France is not like England. There are not mad people on every street corner willing to take on a nose-eating, cyclist-chasing Alsatian. There are over 10 million dogs in France according to the *Société Centrale Canine*, (compared with 6.8 million in Britain) and not much of a support system.

This became evident not only when we were looking to re-house Jazzy, but when Cordelia and Tim, friends of mine who eventually bought a house down here, rescued a dog.

They were driving to meet us for dinner in a café on a particularly nasty road called the D13 when they saw a small dog thrown through the air. The car that hit him simply carried on and as they drove past they saw the dog lying in the middle of the road bleeding. Tim turned the car around and pulled over. Cordelia and the children, Katie aged 17 and Orlando aged 12, stayed in the car as Tim braved the relentless traffic of the D13 to reach the dog.

'It was awful,' says Tim. 'He was lying there with blood coming out of his mouth. The only part of his little body he could move was his tail, and he wagged that when I spoke to him. My French really isn't good enough to soothe someone, so I spoke half in French, half in English.' By now other cars were stopping to see what the problem was and one lady telephoned the fire brigade.

Up at the café, some other friends arrived who had driven past the scene on the road. They hadn't recognised Tim but when they told me that there was some dog dead on the road 'and some lunatic with it,' it didn't take me long to work out that it had to be him.

The firemen arrived and Tim was convinced they would just scoop the little dog up and that would be the end of it. 'They were amazing,' he says. 'So careful and gentle.'

The following day they went to the fire station to see if the little dog had survived the night. They were told he was at vet's in Clermont l'Hérault and so they went up to see Roujan as he had now been named, because they had been on their way to the village of Roujan when they'd rescued him. They were told he was a wonderful patient and had charmed all the staff at the clinic. He had some terrible injuries including a ruptured stomach and a broken back leg.

'I think by this stage our fates were intertwined,' says Tim. 'We asked what would happen to him if no one claimed him. The vet just shrugged her shoulders. I asked if we could take him and she was visibly delighted.' They were told that if they wanted to take him on they would be liable for some of the costs of his medication, as well as ongoing treatment and vaccinations. But they said they would stand the cost of the operation to insert a clamp in his leg.

'In total we would have to give them about €400 and so we

decided to adopt him on the spot. He really was such a lovely dog and I'm convinced he recognised my voice from the day before. The only question then was what to do with him for the six months' quarantine before we could take him back home to Scotland,' says Tim.

But the problem of where to house him for six months was getting urgent. They were leaving in two days' time and Roujan needed a home. It was after the second visit to the vet and about two weeks into Roujan's quarantine that Jean-Pierre and Geneviève showed up at my house looking slightly embarrassed.

'Madame,' said Geneviève, wringing her hands. 'It's about the little dog.'

'Oh God, what's happened?' I asked her. My first instinct was to panic. Cordelia and Tim would be heartbroken if anything happened to him.

Geneviève beamed. 'Nothing has happened to him. But he's adorable.'

'Yes?'

'Madame, Jean-Pierre and I were wondering if we could look after him until he goes back to Scotland.'

Sadly for Jazzy, we couldn't find anyone willing to take him on. We thought about keeping him as an outside dog, but it would have meant we could never ever relax with the children around. They didn't understand that he could be dangerous. Julia had had a scary moment with him some months earlier when she got her head too close to his and he snapped at her.

There was only one thing to do. I called the vet to make an appointment.

Sometimes life in France can seem really complicated. This was one of those times.

'You can't just bring him in for an injection,' said the vet. 'He has to come in and be psychologically assessed. This takes at least three visits. If, at the end of the third visit, it is deemed the logical solution, then we will put him down.'

This seemed like a ridiculous way to deal with the situation. In the end, Rupert and his brother took Jazzy for a final walk with a gun borrowed from Ray, our neighbour. It seemed a more dignified way of dying than an injection from a vet following psychoanalysis. One minute he was wandering around the mountains, the next he was gone. It was one of the most difficult decisions we ever had to make.

We decided to get a new dog almost immediately. Partly because the house felt empty without Jazzy, but also because Geneviève said we couldn't live here without a dog. It wasn't safe, she told us.

After much discussion we agreed on a Labrador puppy, though quite what we thought it would do if we were ever threatened by burglars I don't know. Anyway, I remembered my grandmother's Labrador with much fondness.

I started scouring the small ads for a suitable candidate. For some reason we decided it had to be female and a purebred, in some moment of madness we must have thought about breeding from her. We found a dog for €280 in an ad. She whimpered on the way home as she snuggled into my shoulder. This little bundle obviously wanted her mummy. Sam, as she was now, grew. And grew and grew. A fatter dog I have never known. We decided what she needed was a friend to run around with. When a neighbour of friends was about to drown 11 puppies we said we would take one, Coco. We had had Coco for about a year when our third dog arrived. A stray Alsatian, he was attracted by her being on heat. Sam had also had her admirers, one a rather mangy-looking longhaired stray, who was nicknamed Shoe. This is because every time I saw them I would say 'shoo', so Olivia thought that was his name. When his even less attractive mongrel friend arrived for a piece of the action he became known as Box. These two quickly went away again once Sam was off heat. But Wolfie, as we'd nicknamed him, showed no signs of leaving. This was probably because I kept feeding him. He was painfully thin, and, although Rupert kept telling me not to feed him, because 'the last thing we need is another dog,' I just couldn't help myself. I later found out that Monika was doing the same thing.

Wolfie was very shy and would keep away from everyone. Sometimes on a walk he would lift his head as he passed me and lick my hand, which I think had something to do with the fact that I fed him. I adored him; he seemed to have such a noble spirit, unlike the two Labradors who were sweet but terminally stupid.

But Rupert was just not happy with him around. 'Remember what happened with Jazzy,' he warned me. And then one night Wolfie started barking at 3am and wouldn't stop. When the French want to get rid of dogs, they just abandon them. I have always found this an abhorrent practice, but now found myself agreeing to do the same.

'Wolfie will be fine,' said Rupert. 'He's a survivor. He'll find another home. We just do NOT need a dog barking all night.' As we drove away, I watched him look at the disappearing car and felt horrible. He was intelligent enough to understand what was happening. I would almost rather have left one of the others behind.

It was around lunchtime the next day when Rupert walked into the kitchen looking amazed.

'You will not believe who is wandering up the road towards the house,' he said.

I rushed out and there was Wolfie, looking a bit thinner and certainly stragglier than the day before, but fine. And he was home.

'Oh well,' said Rupert. 'I guess it was meant to be.'

Wolfie settled in well. He began to nuzzle Rupert's hand as well (once he'd forgiven him for trying to abandon him), and it seemed to me a little as if we had resurrected Jazzy.

12
Living on Water

Watermills are a popular choice with Brits settling in France, the threat of floods notwithstanding. There are an estimated 5,000 watermills in southern France, many of them derelict, waiting for an owner with money and taste to restore them. The Romans introduced them into France as a key source of power. Many were used to grind flour and olives, as well as irrigating the land. Later they were used to make paper and in the 18th century to power looms for weaving cloth. With the introduction of steam-powered engines they were largely abandoned.

There are two key issues for anyone contemplating buying a watermill. First, check that you get the sun. Second, find out if there is running water in the summer. In the Languedoc, for example, a lot of the rivers dry up in the hottest months. The only way you can verify whether or not the river will run dry is to check with local records at the *mairie*—the mayor's office—or, if you are lucky, you will find a local historian who may be able to provide some data.

The best place to look for watermills is near the rivers that come down from the Massif Central. The *départements* of the Lot and the Tarn are two areas where there are a good number of mills, and to date these areas have not become as popular or developed as

Tips for buying a watermill
— Beware of flooding
— Check for rot
— Find out if the river runs all year
— See if there is sunshine—in fact, this applies to any house, if you're mad about the evening sun, make sure the house you're thinking of buying actually gets it.
— Be prepared for high maintenance costs

some of the regions bordering the Mediterranean. Prices vary sharply depending on location and condition.

There is a watermill in the Minervois region of the south of France whose location is a closely guarded secret of the London family who have spent the last 20 years restoring it. To reach it you have to drive four kilometres down a stone path, which is often cut off in the winter. There is only solar heating, no telephones or television. 'It is our bandit's lair', says the owner.

When the family bought the mill, it was derelict. Working mainly with the family and co-opted boyfriends of the daughters, along with a retired hippy who got lost on the Croisette in Cannes many years ago, it is now an exquisite home that can sleep 16 family members in comfort. On a summer's evening in June it is an idyllic place to linger over a bottle of local wine, listening to the birds and the water.

But this serenity can be seriously disturbed. Rain in the mountains can send a wall of water hurtling towards you at high speed, sweeping all in its path, and often with very little or no warning. 'Three years ago in November there was a sudden huge flood,' says the owner. 'The river rose more than 18 feet. The house was six feet full of water. Trees were uprooted and turned into giant battering rams. The damage was colossal.'

One of the most stunning houses I know is the mill house

owned by the writer Stephanie Keating and her husband Norman
Berke, a retired American businessman. The first time Peter
Glynn-Smith took us there for lunch we were still house hunting.
It was one of those lunches you never forget, lots of wine, won-
derful food, interesting conversations and sunshine all day long.
Stephanie is an amazing character and legendary hostess. Norman
is fascinating, one of those people who has done everything.

Their guests are always interesting. On any given day you might
find an Oscar-winning screenwriter swapping recipes with Boris
Berezovsky's chef; Norway's most famous artist dancing with a
local matador; or the organiser of the Rhino Charge, East Africa's
most gruelling charity event, holding court in the corner with a
glass of whisky, surrounded by attractive women.

Their mill, set in rolling countryside with the hills of the High
Languedoc to the north, is on the edge of Saint Chinian, one of the
best wine-producing appellations of the Languedoc. They bought
the house in 1995 from a French philosophy professor and sculptor, who had been a friend of Samuel Beckett. The house dates
from the 17th century. The mill is a later addition, probably from
the 18th century. The power from the river was used to power
looms to make uniforms for Napoleon's army. The house is set off
back from the road, down a drive of enormous plane trees that
must each be at least 250 years old.

The house is not only surrounded by water, there are channels
that run underneath the house. During one flood the water rose
almost up to the dining room windows. But Stephanie has taken
heart from a comment from the French philosophy teacher who
sold them the house. 'She told me that if we loved the house it
would look after us,' she says. 'The first year we were here, the rain
came pouring in. I found myself at 1.30 in the morning sandbag-
ging the place and mopping up with towels. In frustration I went
outside and looked at the water rising in the river. But remembering what she had told us, I went to bed. In the morning, the water

had receded. And ever since I have slept soundly here, confident that we will be all right.'

If you are looking for a mill you should contact one of the agents dedicated to locating them. I have never really thought about it, but agree that the sound of water would be lovely (not much chance round our way). Others love the proximity to the river, watching the birds and fishing from their bedroom windows. In the south of France there is the bonus that you have access to water all the year round to irrigate your garden for free. Whatever the merits of owning a watermill, it is the housing equivalent of owning a classic car or a Fife schooner. You are likely to end up spending as much time working on the place as you will enjoying its benefits.

Doug and Bethanne Hazelton live on the water at Sète, on the Mediterranean coast close to Montpellier. They have converted a 90-foot former cargo vessel called Sinbad into their home. Doug has been mad about boats since he was 12 and lived on them since 1967. He met Bethanne in the Caribbean, where she was working at the time.

Although he was in the process of building a house for a girl-friend at the time, he and Bethanne ended up at the top of a mast of a boat. 'I guess that's where we fell in love,' says Doug. 'That was the end of my girlfriend's house and we moved on to a trawler.'

Shortly afterwards, they were married on the island of Saba, a volcanic island in the middle of nowhere in the Caribbean 'I wanted some place our relatives would have a hard time getting to,' says Doug. After their children, Antaris and Azura, were born, they spent several years travelling around the world to Thailand, Venezuela, Indonesia, Fiji to name a few places. They settled for a while in New Caledonia where the children went to school, but apart from that Bethanne taught them on the boat through a French correspondence course. 'We got into a routine,' she says. 'We would get up early and do a couple of hours before breakfast, then some more afterwards. We were normally finished by lunchtime,' she says. 'The children got on very well and loved having all that free time. It meant I had to get my French up to speed which was great.'

The most surprising thing they have found about living here is how cold it is, even though they are in the south of France. 'We had no idea the winter would be so tough,' says Doug. 'We were wearing every piece of clothing we had. I don't think we owned a jumper between us.'

Once the summer is over they will go back to the Caribbean, although Doug is full of praise for France. 'If I were a land person I would live in France,' he says. 'It's a great place, in the summer. The people have been really helpful and I like the French system. In some places in Europe we've been treated like waterrats but not here.'

Bethanne agrees. 'It's been great to have a year in France,' she says. 'I have thoroughly enjoyed being here, but then I thoroughly enjoy being anywhere. The only downside about Europe is that you can't anchor at sea, so here we are next to the road the whole time. We're used to getting up in the morning and going for a swim.'

They make a living on the boat from the odd charter and salvage work. 'It's what I call my golden egg theory,' says Doug. 'If you're in a plodding job you won't see the golden egg. Times can get a little tough, but that golden egg always comes by in the end.'

13
La Vie en Rouge

There aren't many jobs more demanding than running a vineyard. First, you are a fruit farmer, tending the vines, pruning and picking the grapes. You are open to the vagaries of the weather, such as hailstorms during harvesting and attacks from beetles and bugs. Then you become a chemist, blending the produce until it becomes drinkable. Then you become a marketeer and salesman, trying to persuade sceptical consumers that what you have bottled is nectar, not nettle juice.

If it is so demanding, why do so many people try it? To do so as a foreigner in France, still the world's most famous wine-producing country, is difficult and takes enormous guts. To succeed you need to be clever, as well as lucky.

One of the biggest costs in the wine business is the price of the land in the first place. The best way is to inherit a vineyard, but that mainly happens to lucky Frenchmen. Englishmen need to buy their way in.

Jonathan Maltus, an Englishman who grew up in Nigeria, together with his wife Lyn, had the good fortune to possess both the inclination and the money to buy a vineyard at a time when many growers in Bordeaux were desperate to sell. In 1991 heavy frosts in April devastated much of the crop in the region. By the following year, prices in St Emilion had almost halved. Maltus had sold an engineering company and at the age of 36 was looking for a new challenge.

'My wife Lyn and I had just married,' he says. 'We decided to take a bit of time off, so moved to Cahors in France. One of my neighbours was having trouble selling his wine. So I helped him out by selling a large consignment to Oddbins. I thought, 'this wine business looks easy'. Gradually I became more interested in it. And I soon discovered that it was not as easy as I had thought.'

He bought Château Teyssier, an estate in St Emilion, for £1.2 million, and began restoring its fortunes. Both the *château* and the vineyard had been neglected. Serious work was needed on the five hectares (about 13 acres) of vines. What he hadn't bargained on was how long it would take.

'You forget that there is a long period of time before you can sell your wine,' he says. 'In the beginning you have a large outlay and the income of a small sweetshop. You need much more money than you think to tide you over these lean periods.'

Fortunately for Maltus, St Emilion suddenly became sexy in 1996. It was the beginning of the so-called *garagistes*, 'garage wines', in Bordeaux. Growers were cultivating small parcels of land, tending the grapes carefully, handpicking them, and making them into wine. The small quantities produced meant that there was more demand than supply. Prices of the best garage wines start at around £150 per bottle and keep going up. Hew Blair, the buyer for Justerini & Brooks, helped launch their wine. He tasted the vats, walked round the vineyard and agreed to take all the production on the spot. Maltus was made. His winery is now a mass of stainless steel tanks for the Château Teyssier wine, while the much sought after Le Dôme has its own micro-brewery, containing four oak vats. Elsewhere there is a barrel cellar that can hold up to six hundred barrels. The place is as neat and tidy as a Swiss post office. Even so, Maltus pushes a

No wonder they have made a film about him. Hugh Ryman's life contains all the essential elements for high drama: a multi-millionaire father, fine wines, family feuds and, most essential to the plot, a 16th-century chateau in France. Ryman's experience making wine in Provence was the inspiration for Sir Ridley Scott's film A Good Year.

'I hadn't heard about it until three weeks ago,' laughs Ryman, 45, standing on the pebbled, yew-lined drive in front of the Chateau de la Jaubertie, seven miles from Bergerac, where he spends his weekends with his biologist wife, Anne, 42, and their four children.

It was Ryman's father, Nick, the stationery tycoon, who came to France in 1973 after selling his business for £8m to the Burton Group. 'My father had always said to my mother they would end up in France one day,' says Ryman. 'He loves wine and said that he had drunk a lot of bad wine in his lifetime and wanted to do a better job.'

'He fell in love with the place,' says his son. It is easy to see why. The chateau, believed to have been built by King Henry IV for his mistress, Gabrielle d'Estree, is not immense but is beautifully proportioned and very elegant.

The main three-storey building has seven bedrooms; on either side there are small pavilions. At one stage it was owned by Marie Antoinette's favourite doctor, and she provided him with the parquet for the main salon.

The purchase was not easy: the chateau was owned by a divorcing couple, and the wife did not want to sell. They lost 80 per cent of the harvest in a hailstorm. 'That was our welcoming present,' says Ryman, who was 13 at the time and had chosen to move with his parents and two sisters rather than stay at boarding school in England. 'To break up the clouds, the locals were firing rockets, which narrowly missed us. It was not an ideal beginning.'

Things did not get easier and, with cash-flow problems looming, Ryman Sr found the only way to finance the chateau's

hose aside in disgust. 'I am sorry it is so untidy,' he says.

The price of land in St Emilion is ridiculously high. A hectare of good vineyard will set you back around £150,000-£300,000, depending on the location and the age of the vines. Over in the area known as Entre-Deux-Mers—the land between the Dordogne and Garonne rivers—land is much cheaper, more like £20,000 per hectare. What's the difference? Wine growers will tell you it is all in the *terroir*—a word that in the case of wine includes the soil, the subsoil, the climate and even the history of the place and its winemakers.

In 1990, Esme Johnstone and his wife Sara bought Château de Sours, one of the prettiest estates in Bordeaux, for around £1 million. Their timing could hardly have been worse. Prices were high, but then the devastating frost of 1991 hit. Their yield for that year was tiny. The wine they produced was not much good. 'It was a disaster,' says Esme.

However, he and Sara persevered. Michel Rolland, Bordeaux's most celebrated winemaker, visited and advised them to make more rosé wine. Tell most producers this in the Entre-Deux-Mers and they will walk away or hit you. It is considered something of a failure to make rosé. But Johnstone's rosé caught the attention of a number of critics, including Auberon Waugh. 'Like the dozy apprentice who fell asleep and invented Guinness, Esme Johnstone has chanced upon possibly the best rosé in the world,' said Waugh.

As the man who helped create Majestic Warehouse in England, Johnstone understands the importance of marketing. 'It's quite good fun,' he says. 'But the job of winemaker is 365 days a year. It is hard work. It is all about attention to detail.' He does not recommend it as a life for somebody who is retiring from the city. 'It is a young man's game,' he says. 'You need money and you need energy.'

The Johnstones have also converted one of the houses on the estate into a guesthouse. At Domaine de Sours you can swim in the

renovation was to raise £1m by selling bonds in the winemaking business. The investors, initially friends and relatives, each put in between £1,500 and £4,000, and in return received five to 10 cases of wine a year.

His son, meanwhile, was hooked on winemaking, studying in Bordeaux and in the great French chateaux of Yquem and Latour before attending Australia's leading wine school near Adelaide. In 1985, he returned to work at Jaubertie, building on his father's use of New World winemaking techniques.

Father and son did not get on, however, and three years later Ryman left to work as a 'flying winemaker', creating a range of wines at vineyards around the globe aimed at average consumers.

In 1992, Ryman, by then living in Bordeaux, heard that his father, who was due to undergo a heart bypass operation, was on the verge of selling Jaubertie. 'I desperately wanted to keep it in the family,' he says. 'So my business partner and I put together a package to buy it.'

In 1996, Ryman's property, wine and consulting business-which he ran with Esme Johnstone-the man behind Majestic Wines-was running into trouble, too, and the pair realised the only solution was to sell some of their properties-among them, Jaubertie. 'The thought of it was heart-breaking, but there was no other choice,' he says.

It was easier said than done, not least because his father was still living in the chateau and trying to buy it back himself. Ryman Sr finally moved out, but, according to his son, took almost everything with him. 'Most of the furniture was owned by my father and some things did belong to the property,' Ryman says. 'But when you start taking the doors, that really is going too far.

Ryman still lives in Bordeaux during the week, but spends as much time as possible at the chateau. 'We all love it here,' he says. 'I was very lucky my wife is as keen to keep it in the family as I am.' His father, who has also remained in France, is

pool, sleep in one of the three bedrooms, and dream that you are making wine, without any of the effort.

The Bordeaux boys say that good wine can only be made in their region. But in the last ten years, the price of land and *châteaux* has risen by at least three to five times. This makes it prohibitively expensive for newcomers. It is also tempting some people to prove them wrong by creating great wines in other parts of France.

One person doing just that is Patricia Atkinson. Her remarkable story began in 1990 when she moved to France with her husband who had always wanted to live here. They bought a *château* close to the Dordogne with a small vineyard (four hectares), but had no plans to become winemakers. Instead they worked as financial consultants while restoring the property. Shortly after they moved, Patricia's husband was taken ill and went back to England. She was left alone, spoke hardly a word of French and had to work out a way to make a living. The small vineyard became her only hope of an income. She learnt how to become a viticulturist, winemaker and estate boss. A decade on, the small vineyard Patricia started with has grown to an estate of 21 hectares. She has won countless awards for her wine and is the author of a best-selling book which tells her story.

Another city person turned winemaker is Graham Nutter. After a successful career in banking he has bought a vineyard in the Minervois, together with his French wife Béatrice. The Minervois is a relatively new appellation in the Languedoc, making wines that would sell for about a fiver in a British supermarket. This is the place for people to go who are looking for a lifestyle as well as a place to make wine. The land and buildings are cheaper. The weather is better. The *terroir* is as yet unproven, although many good wines are beginning to be made there.

'I want to create something splendid here,' he says. He started looking for a place in 1999. 'I visited nearly 40 properties,' he says.

writing a book about his experiences and is reluctant to comment on his dealings with his son.

'If I had my time again I would do everything I did, but I'd pay more attention to overheads and working capital,' he says. 'I don't think I've had a very tough ride, but I think I have perhaps gained a little too much experience.'

'They were either too big, too small or too near the road. My wish list was quite simple. The property needed to be isolated, and the vineyard needed to have the potential to make a good wine.'

He says that when he drove up the avenue of St Jacques d'Albas, they knew this was the right place. 'I strongly believe in the soul of a place,' says Béatrice. 'We fell in love with its soul.'

There was much work to be done. The 28-hectare estate has the capacity to produce up to 150,000 bottles of wine a year. Much of the production was sent to the local cooperative. The previous

Buying a Vineyard

Do
— Have a bigger budget than you think you'll need.
— Know something about farming and the wine business.
— Have a clear idea of your market—who is going to buy your wine?
— Talk to people who have done it.
— Try some of Jean-Claude's wine.

Don't
— Spend all your money on the property. You will need to invest and upgrade the winery.
— Try and drink all your production.
— Expect to make a profit in the first few years.
— Imagine it will be easy.

owner had not had the money to invest in either the land or in the cellar.

'I wanted to get some of the wine away from the Minervois co-op,' says Nutter. 'The president told me that it was all or nothing. I had a word with my local *notaire*, who knew the president from their school days. After another conversation, we managed to reach an agreement.'

As well as upgrading the house, building a new cellar, tasting room and storage facility, Nutter is also planning a five-year programme to improve the quality of the vineyard. 'You have to invest in the soil,' he says. 'We are trying to re-establish the mineral content of the property.'

There is still much work to be done. Nor does he think that because he is in his 50s, he is too old.

'I have a lot of energy,' says Nutter. 'After living in New York, London and Paris, I still wanted to achieve something else. I think where a lot of people go wrong is they spend all their budget on the property. You need to put a third into the property, a third into improving things, and keep a third for marketing and contingencies. If it all goes wrong, at least we can say that we tried.'

Jean-Luc Colombo, a Rhône-based winemaker and consultant, applauds Nutter's choice of region. 'Without question, Languedoc Roussillon is the area to buy a vineyard in France,' he says. 'Buying anywhere else is prohibitively expensive, assuming you can get hold of a vineyard in the first place.' The regulated French wine business—particularly in Burgundy or Bordeaux—discourages foreign ownership. The price of land, due to the wine boom of the last five years, means that a decent hectare of vines could cost anywhere from £20,000 to £100,000. But a domain in the Languedoc, together with vineyards, can be bought from around £750,000.

However, the process is by no means straightforward. Many sales are handled privately, so it is very hard to know what is on the market until it is too late. The first step for many would-be buyers is to contact the *Société d'Aménagement Foncier et d'Etablissement Rural*, known as Safer. This bureaucratic body was set up 40 years ago to help young winegrowers find vineyards and finance. It has now moved more into the property business. There are also a number of estate agents who specialise in selling vineyards, such as *France Vignobles et Propriété* and *Jean-Pierre Rambier* in Montpellier.

But even if you manage to buy a vineyard for £750,000, it is important to bear in mind that this is just the entry cost. 'Once you have bought an estate, unless you are very lucky, you will need to spend £100,000 on the cellar, £50,000 on equipment, and there are annual running costs of around £3,000 per hectare,' says Jean-Claude Mas, one of the area's most celebrated winemakers and husband of my friend Alex.

While it is tempting to think that you can cover these costs from selling the wine or even just sell the grapes to a *négociant*, over-

---

Classification

The organisation of the French wine industry is based on a system of classifications, which guarantee the origin of a wine from a certain area. Its specific purpose is to guarantee authenticity however it is now thought to protect the producer more than the consumer. The system was developed by the Ministry of Agriculture in the 1930s after pressure from producers of high quality wine who were concerned with the over-production of low quality wine during this period. This pressure resulted in the establishment of the *Institut National des Appellations d'Origine des Vins et Eaux de Vie* (INAO). The INAO consists of twelve regional committees: Alsace and Eastern France, Champagne, Southwest France, Loire Valley, Burgundy, Languedoc-Roussillon, Rhône Valley, Provence-Corsica, Vins Doux Naturels, Cognac, Armagnac and Eaux-de-Vie de Cidre.

supply in the wine world has led to a glut of grapes on the market. The bottom has fallen out of the *vin de table* market; even *vin de pays*—wine that is not *appellation contrôlée*, has declined in price by 25 per cent in the last few years.

Ruth de Latude came to the Languedoc 25 years ago from Yorkshire. Together with her husband Gilles, she runs the Domaine de Bourgade. With over twenty hectares under vine, including Cabernet Sauvignon, Syrah, Grenache and Mourvèdre, they have found themselves caught in the falling price trap. With *négociants* offering them 10 per cent less for their grapes each year—around 25 pence per kilo—it is hard to make any money from the vineyard. 'We are making much more money from the cottages that I have converted on the estate,' says Ruth. Despite this, Ruth and Gilles have recently invested in a winery and are now producing their own wine, called *Les Trois Poules*, thereby bringing the winemaking tradition back to Bourgade. According to Ruth, they found remains of Roman pottery at the domain which showed wine was probably made there over 2,000 years ago. 'It was always a working farm,' explains Ruth. 'But we used to sell the grapes to local winemakers. The price they paid gradually went down until it wasn't really worth our while. We decided that it was time to take the whole operation under control. We started this year and did everything by hand that we could, partly for reasons of quality and partly to save on costs.' Their first vintage will be ready in time for next season's guests. 'There will also be plenty of picking to do,' says Ruth. 'So we will be putting the guests to work.'

The Languedoc has come a long way in the last ten years in the wine world. If it continues to develop—and winemakers like the talented Jean-Claude Mas continue to work from here—the price of a hectare of vineyard will soar. Ten years ago, Jean-Luc Colombo was buying land in Cornas on the Rhône for £2,000 a hectare. Now it is worth anywhere from £20,000 to £100,000.

Charles and Ruth Simpson, both in their 30s, were attracted to the Languedoc region due to its potential. They were living in Azerbaijan when they decided they wanted to get into the wine business. 'Basically we had a lot of time to talk,' explains Charles. 'We didn't really know anyone and there wasn't much to do. So during those long dark winter evenings we chatted about what it was we both wanted out of life.' At the time, Charles was general manager of Glaxo-Wellcome in Azerbaijan and Ruth was working as a consultant for various charities. 'The way things were going with my job, we realised we would be forever moving and not really

---

Appelations

AOC (*Appellation d'origine contrôlée*). Still seen as the highest level of French wine, used to be strictly controlled and regulated. There are over 40 *appellations* in France. In general, the laws of any AOC control the following: the area entitled to the name; permitted grape varieties; density of vine plants; minimum alcohol levels; and yields. Within many regions there can be a hierarchy of *appellations*. The AOC classification is however no longer a guarantee of quality. The AOC laws have come under increased criticism as being outdated and anti-competitive, providing only a collective marketing facade behind which some mediocre wine producers can shelter. The limitations imposed by the system have meant that some producers choose specifically not to classify their product as AOC in order to retain maximum flexibility in their viticultural and winemaking techniques and in order to compete with wines from the New World.

VDP (*Vin de Pays*): Good quality drinking wine that has to come from a certain region. For example, Vin de Pays d'Oc must come from the Languedoc.

Vin de table: The lowest classification of wine. Can be bought directly from co-operatives for around £1 a litre. Drinkable, but only just.

---

together much at all. Which is not the reason we got married.'
Charles and Ruth considered several options, including estate management in Scotland and commercial forestry. They wanted something in which they were both interested and to which they could
both add value. 'The idea of being involved in wine seemed very
romantic,' says Charles. 'Although I'm not sure I would describe it
as that now that we've actually done it. In addition, we both have
experience in business management, strategy and marketing, so we
felt we could work on that side of things, although we knew nothing about actually making wine. We were both fascinated by the
fact that a bottle of wine can cost between £2 and £2,000. And the
difference in the price is purely to do with marketing and reputation.'

Charles and Ruth bought Domaine Sainte Rose, a stunning
estate outside Béziers, in June 2002. The domain itself is 16th century but the *château* was rebuilt after a fire around 100 years ago.
They paid around £1.2 million for the property, which includes 46
hectares of vineyards and another five or so hectares of parkland,
a winery and of course the *château*. 'Anyone wanting to set up here
wouldn't need to spend as much as we did,' says Charles. 'You can
buy planted land for between £10,000 and £15,000 per hectare.' If
you do need to raise substantial funds, one option is to copy Charles
and Ruth's model. They raised a third of the money themselves, 80
per cent from personal funds and the balance from investors, each
paying about £5,000 to become members of a group of 12 people
who are entitled to free wine as well as an annual dinner at the
château. A third came from a bank loan and the final tranche in the
form of so-called vendor finance. 'We told the previous owner we
couldn't afford the whole lot at once, and because he wanted out he
agreed to let us pay him a third over time,' explains Charles.

The philosophy of the business has been to define the target
audience and then make wine to cater for that audience. 'Our typical customer is a person who is interested in wine, is looking for

---

Terms

Bouchonné. Corked. An 'off' characteristic in wines due to imperfect corks. Often caused by the chemical compound trichloroanisole or TCA. Cork taint is believed to come from fungi that are not detectable on dry corks, or by cork processed with chlorine. TCA diminishes the fruit character of the wine, producing a stale, woody, mouldy smell and taste, possibly accompanied by oxidation of the wine.

Négociant. The English translation is 'merchant'. Alternative definition: A wine merchant who buys grapes, must, or wine, blends different lots of wine within an *appellation*, and bottles the result under their own label.

---

something different and wants to be close to the product,' says Ruth. 'It's the kind of person you would get buying their meat from a butchers' shop instead of the supermarket.'

'It was always our dream to own the relationship with the customer,' adds Charles. 'As a UK customer you can click onto our website, order some wine and it'll be there within 48 hours. The downside with our method is that it all depends on personal contact. It's hand-selling, so the business takes time to build up.'

Perhaps any non-professional winemaking person should follow the lead of our friend Peter Glynn-Smith. Having sold his Islington-based design business, he bought one of the finest houses in the Languedoc, together with a small two-hectare vineyard. His Cabernet Sauvignon grapes are tended by a local man and sold to the local cooperative. The grape harvest is just enough to pay for his hobby, while he has the satisfaction of owning a vineyard. 'There is nothing better than sitting on my terrace in the evening, watching the swallows drink from my pool, and see the grapes ripening on the vine in the distance,' he says.

14
Dreaming Spires

When we were looking for our house, we were briefly tempted by a crumbling *château* for sale about five kilometres away, for the same price. Even we could see this was reckless. It is a most striking building, with a stunning façade that looks down the valley towards the village of Gabian. There is an 11th-century Romanesque church attached, very useful for weddings and christenings, and when we looked at it, there was even a camel in the courtyard, extremely good for keeping the lawn looking neat. But the upkeep would have been impossible. My stepson, Hugo, is still mad about the place. 'I can't believe we could have been living there,' he says whenever we drive past (which is most days). 'It's so cool.'

Cool? Try bloody freezing. A *château* in the winter has to be one of the most inhospitable places in the world. We once stayed with Lucy Archer and Colin Winter at their *château*, which they were restoring slowly, bit by bit. A warmer welcome you couldn't have hoped for, but the temperature in their bedrooms was probably hovering around zero. I have never before or since seen Rupert sleep with his socks on. The huge pile of our great friends Beatrice and Luc does have central heating, but it's too expensive to use. In the winter, you go to dinner there dressed in your duvet.

It was not only the cold that put me off buying Château de

Cassan. The scale is just too vast. It's rather like having a Ferrari, every time something goes wrong it costs you more than it would to buy a normal car. Also there are about 200 windows. By the time you'd have cleaned the last one, it would be time to start again.

Still, the phrase 'a *château* in France' has a particularly nice ring to it. You immediately imagine dreaming spires, large grounds, marble staircases, fine wines.

However, the French seem to classify much that does not live up to that description as *châteaux*. Cynics say that a more literal translation of *château* is 'cow-shed'.

Sarah and John Colvin, a couple I met from London, said when they were house hunting in Bordeaux they had told the agent they wanted a *château*. 'By that we meant somewhere with spires,' says John. 'They showed us everything from farmhouses to glorious wine estates. I'm sure in England if you ask to see a castle you don't get shown a two-up, two-down terraced house.'

This could be because there are so many castles in France. According to Stéphane Gondoin, editor-in-chief of the website www.casteland.com, there are over 30,000 *châteaux* and medieval fortifications here. 'Many of these sites offer no or little interest for the general public,' says Stéphane. 'Or they are difficult to get access to (private property, wooded or rough terrain, under water even) and only a few thousand are open to visitors. I personally visited about 1,000 of the more inaccessible sites, most of the time with rubber boots, heavy-duty clothes and not forgetting a compass to find my way around.'

At least in part, the French have the English to thank for their abundance of *châteaux*. During The Hundred Years' War (1337–1453) the French were forced to build thousands to defend the northern coastline. Further south in the Dordogne, the English and the French both built castles to defend their land. At one stage, Edward III had possession of one third of France. All along the Dordogne River are the monuments to the struggle for territory between the two countries. Some joke that the Brits have finally won the war, as they own so much of the land.

The *châteaux* in the Loire date from the 15th and 16th centuries and were built by the French royalty. The Loire was their playground and the hundreds of *châteaux* there were built as statements of power and wealth. The ultimate statement is of course further north, at Versailles. 'Louis XIV took the royal power to its ultimate conclusion,' says Colin Winter, who has been fascinated by castles since he was a little boy. 'Versailles is the epitome of the power of the French monarchy.'

Further south, mainly in the Languedoc-Roussillon region, are the Albigensian *châteaux*, built by the Cathars in the 13th century to defend themselves against the Catholic crusaders out to destroy them. Among these are some of the most impressive castles in France, built on top of huge rocks in stark landscapes. Along the Pyrenées are the relatively small 'commanderies', big box castles, built by the Templar monks to defend themselves against invasion from the Moors in the 11th and 12th centuries.

According to Colin you have to be 'mad and impassioned' to go through with buying a French *château*. 'It is not necessarily a rational decision,' he says. 'Unless you have masses of money, they have to be in some way commercial. We run *chambres d'hôtes* which is never going to make us rich, but the hope is that it will generate enough of an income to look after the building for you.'

In fact, the castellated *châteaux* that are the glory of so much of France still contain, remarkably, a wondrous and almost surreal cast of penniless aristocrats living in poverty on a huge scale. It can be argued that this verifies the theory that you would have to be mad to live in one. These are the houses where the *Marseillaise* is actually banned, as at Château Bourgade, between Pézenas and Béziers, where the count (and his English wife Ruth de Latude) are holding out for a restoration of the Bourbons.

Some English people end up in a *château* without even looking

Tips when buying a château
1. Do triple your budget
2. Do employ local architects and workmen, but keep an eye on them. Don't leave even the smallest decisions to someone else.
3. Spend the money where it is needed and not, like Gavin did, on laying down the cables for outdoor lighting in the future. He says it's unlikely he'll ever be able to afford the lights.
4. Remember that a big property has high running costs, long after the renovation costs.
5. Do check references of local builders and architects or look at work they've already done.
6. Before signing anything, check out any future building developments of the local town, and roads etc.
7. It used to take between 20 and 30 years to build a château. Don't underestimate the time it will take to restore one today.
8. Fiona recommends always being ready to open a bottle of wine at any time of day and have a drink with neighbours and workers.
9. Do introduce yourself to the mayor. He or she can be very useful.
10. You may be eligible for grants, check with the local mayor's office or talk to *Bâtiments de France*.

My top tip is to ignore all the above advice and don't be so silly. Rather than buy a château, it's much cheaper to stay with those who have.

for one. When Fiona De Wulf started looking for a place to live, she was thinking about a cosy cottage somewhere in the Dordogne, Normandy or even the Loire Valley. She was 30, newly married to a Frenchman, and keen to settle in the country. One rainy day, driving through Burgundy, she stopped to look in the window of an estate agent's office. What she saw would lead to nine years of heartache, interspersed with fleeting moments of elation. A picture of a crumbling *château* covered in ivy caught her eye. She did not know then that there were great holes in the roof, and that the place had been largely uninhabited for over 70 years.

'The agent suggested we go and look at the place,' says Fiona. 'It was raining, and there wasn't much else to do. We looked through the gates and drove away laughing. I asked my husband who would be mad enough to buy a place like that?'

However, over lunch they found they kept talking about the *château*. Bruno, her husband, was bored of farming and wanted to do something different. She was looking for a challenge, and liked the Burgundy countryside.

'It reminds me of Surrey and Sussex where I grew up,' she says. They finished their wine, paid the bill and went back to look around the derelict property. They were horrified by what they saw. The ceilings had fallen in. There were pigeons and squirrels living in the roof. However, the original floors and doors were still there, even though the latter were hanging off their hinges.

The *château* had been built in 1650 by Antoine Comeau, Lord of Créancey. It had been passed down through his family for generations. During the Second World War the Germans used it as a local command post. After that it was abandoned, until some locals bought it in 1959 for use as a wine store. They lived in two rooms, without hot water or central heating.

Fiona and Bruno knew that years of neglect meant that it would be a monumental undertaking to restore it. But at least it had not been spoilt by tasteless renovations. So they made an offer for the *château* and five acres of garden. For £250,000 it was theirs.

On May 31 1994 contracts were exchanged and they were given the keys, even though you could walk into the *château* through holes where the windows had been. 'It was so daunting that we did not know where to start,' says Fiona. 'We started by pulling the ivy off the walls. This should be practised on a regular basis by anyone trying to keep their sanity when a wild and devastating project is trying to get the better of you. However, once that was finished, we had to decide what to do next.'

Finally they settled on doing up the cottage in the garden, which would give them a place to live while they finished the rest of the work. 'I thought if we could make the place respectable it might keep my mother happy,' says Fiona. However, even in the cottage there were problems. The ceiling had caved in on the old furniture, the main beams were on the floor and water was pouring in all over the place.

Fiona employed a Paris-based architect, but found that nothing got done. 'The workers kept promising to finish things, but nothing ever happened,' she says, 'three months passed and all we got was stories of in-grown toe-nails and stone masons' wives expecting babies. Eventually we were asked if we had been in touch with *Monsieur* B, a local architect and great expert in renovations. We finally got the message, explained the situation to our Paris-based friend and hired *Monsieur.* B. That was Thursday morning. On Monday morning, a whole team of builders showed up and work got under way.'

Monsieur B soon moved on to other jobs, but by then Fiona had established a good relationship with the builders. From then on she ran the site herself. They spent two years working out how the *château* could function. Heating specialists came to make estimates of how to make the place warm. Then they had to sell Bruno's farm in France to pay for the work.

'Work on the *château* started in 1997,' says Fiona. 'We took all the doors off their hinges, numbered them and stored them in an outbuilding. Then we began at the worst end of the building,' she says. 'There were lorry loads of rubbish, with occasional jewels such as a missing piece of the staircase. Then we had to do structural work, to hide pipes and wires. We took the roof off to get pipes and drains in.'

After about a year, the sheer scale of the project suddenly hit Fiona. 'I remember collapsing one evening in despair. I really thought we would never complete it.' Then fate intervened. A local worker was called in to take down some trees in the garden. Fiona asked him if he knew anybody who could come and help run the site. After a month he returned, saying that he was the man for the job.

'We would never have managed it without Henri,' says Fiona. 'He worked from seven in the morning until seven at night. We would have to tell him to stop.'

Along with Henri, Fiona cooked lunch and dinner for six or seven workers every day. 'It was great fun,' she says. 'The people in Burgundy love to work hard, but also to play hard. Builders round here love working for the English because we make them cups of tea. In addition, Bruno's wine cellar got quite badly decimated.'

French bureaucracy turned out to be relatively easy to negotiate, at least in the beginning. The *château* is a listed building, so there were a couple of grants from *Bâtiments de France*. However, Fiona cautions that the language difficulties can be hard for people to overcome at the beginning.

Several years of hard work and £600,000 later, the *château* has been fully restored into an elegant home. During renovation Fiona and Bruno hardly had time for a holiday. 'It was very hard to get away,' says Fiona. 'We could escape for a day or two, but either nothing happened while we were gone, or something dreadful happened. The builders seemed keen to use their initiative, often with disastrous results. And besides, we got so interested in the work that we did not want to leave.'

There are still things to be done. Fiona wants to redo the garden, clean up the woods and renovate the greenhouse. There is a pigeon loft that needs sorting out. There is also a rumour that there is a buried treasure under a blackberry bush. 'The trouble is, the place was full of blackberry bushes,' says Fiona. 'We haven't found the treasure yet, but we plan to keep looking.'

To help offset the running costs, some of the bedrooms and the cottage where it all started can be rented out. Fiona says the whole project has been immensely rewarding but extremely tiring. Would she do it again?

'Only if Henri were 10 years younger,' she says. 'And fortunately he has just retired, so I'll just have to stay here.'

Bordeaux is another place famous for *châteaux*, built on the profits of the wine trade. It can be a dangerous place to visit, for it is easy to fall under the spell of these romantic buildings. Gavin Quinney had led a fairly unremarkable life until the age of 40. He was living in Wandsworth, married with two small children, working for a computer company. But in June 1999 he found himself at Vinexpo, the Bordeaux trade fair. Instead of coming away with a couple of cases of wine, he bought Château Bauduc, a beautiful property on the edge of a busy market town called Créon, 20 miles southeast of Bordeaux. So what brought on this moment of madness? Was it the wine?

'Don't ask,' he says. 'I guess I was looking for a new challenge. I'm sure if I had the decision again I might do things differently.' In one respect he was lucky. The computer company for whom he ran the sales side had gone public in 1998, leaving him with a windfall of shares. He cashed in his options, and headed to Bordeaux with his family for a new life as a winemaker. Bauduc was built in the 19th century in the style of the belle époque and is surrounded by woods and a park. It has a 75-acre vineyard and 125 acres of woods and fields, as well as an apartment for the vineyard manager and an old farmhouse. The whole property cost around £1.7 million, about twice the price of a decent place in the 'Toastrack' of Wandsworth.

Buying a *château* in Bordeaux often means buying a working vineyard, which is what the Quinneys ended up with. 'Wine actually was the driving force behind us coming out here,' explains Gavin. 'It wasn't an interest or a hobby, it was a passion.' Angela was aware of this passion but didn't give it much credence. 'He'd talked a lot about buying a vineyard,' she says. 'But I didn't for a minute think he'd actually do it. I thought he'd forget about it, but it didn't go away and here we are. It was quite stressful doing up the *château* at the same time as trying to organise the vineyard, winery and the harvest.'

'The *château* is not enormous, despite its grand symmetry,' says Gavin. 'But it needed totally restoring in places.' The Quinneys moved into the farmhouse on the estate with their two children, Georgia and Sophie, then aged four and two. They had both done up houses in London and knew the key was to get a good team together. 'But it is very different here,' says Gavin. 'In London you just get a builder to organise the whole thing and bring everyone in. Here each part of the project requires its own artisan.'

Through a series of enquiries they put together a team of plumbers, electricians, stonemasons, carpenters, roofers, painters and decorators. 'It is essential to find the right artisan for the job,' says Gavin. 'We were lucky, we had to do a lot of fundamental work like rewiring the place, if we'd had some cowboy involved he could have caused serious problems. I would advise anyone doing the same to live in the region for a while before starting the project and to find out who is good and who is not.' Gavin and Angela started with a team of an electrician and a carpenter whom they trusted. They then brought in other artisans, at any one time there were around 15 working on the project.

Even without involving cowboys, the project had its problems. While doing some earth moving in the garden they suddenly discovered a huge hole. As the days passed, the smell from the hole got worse and worse. Eventually they brought in professionals who told them that it was the old septic tank and it needed replacing. They ordered one to replace it and meanwhile applied for all the relevant permits with the local *mairie*. 'A septic tank specialist came from the town hall and told us we not only had to replace that one, but that there was another one on the other side that needed replacing too. By that stage we had already ordered the new tank with a capacity of 8,000 litres. We then doubled that, as well as the cost. £6,000 later we have enough capacity to last several lifetimes, even with all the friends we have staying in the summer.' Another big issue was the overall plumbing. The previous owner had used the cheapest possible materials, 20 years ago, so all the pipes needed replacing. In addition, the whole *château* needed rewiring. In the grounds, one of the biggest expenses was knocking down the 20 or so telegraph poles that lined the drive to the house and putting all the wiring underground. 'Luckily EDF (Electricité de France) were doing some work at the time,' says Gavin. 'So we just combined it with them, which cut a lot of the cost.'

In terms of the decorating, the whole place needed an overhaul too. 'When we first walked in as the owners, we got a bit of a shock,' says Gavin. 'It's one thing seeing a place with all the furniture in place and pictures on the walls, but when it's all been shipped out, you notice that bits of skirting are missing and a lot of work needs to be done.' They decided to start more or less from scratch. 'We gutted the whole place,' says Gavin. 'We kept the original floors and ceilings but everything in between had to either go or be rebuilt.' They were very keen to keep the original look of the *château* so they decided not to change any of the dimensions of the rooms and to replicate as many of the original features as possible. 'In the drawing room, for example, there was an old marble fireplace that was falling to bits. After much advice on the subject, we decided it was better to get rid of it and buy another one from the era to replace it. It took months, but I eventually found one that was exactly the same size and shape in an antique shop in Bordeaux.' They kept the original parquet floors and the bevelled glass doors. There are seven sets of doors, each of which had to be removed and treated for weather damage. '*Châteaux* can sometimes be quite gloomy places,' says Gavin. 'But these doors create the most amazing amount of light. They are incredibly heavy though and, as well as being weather damaged, some of them were actually sagging in the middle and needed their balance redressing.'

In the kitchen they found that the fixtures and fittings they had thought were part of the sale such as the fitted cupboards had been removed. 'This is not unusual for France,' says Angela, Gavin's wife. 'I've heard of plenty of cases where they even took the light bulbs.' They invested in a butcher's block from a Bordeaux antique market and then built an oak and marble island as the centrepiece of the kitchen area. They had ordered a cooker from Lacanche but when it arrived it looked swamped in the huge kitchen space. 'We sent it back and got the professional size, which fits beautifully,' says Gavin. The fireplace, although oak, was stained a dark, sombre mahogany colour. They removed it to have it stripped and repainted before putting it back. 'It meant living with a hole in the wall for the five months it took to do it, but to do the job properly took a lot of time,' says Angela. The dining room is an extension of the kitchen and looks out over the colonnaded terrace to the south. This was landscaped by a local *paysagiste* with whom Gavin worked very closely. The view is breathtaking, downhill towards a single walnut tree in the middle of a green sloping field. On either side there are oak trees and beyond them vineyards.

They also remodelled the entrance to the *château*. 'When we arrived, everyone would literally park with their bumpers up against the main steps of the house. I wanted to change this and create a proper entrance by removing the cars from the front door of the *château*,' says Gavin.

The *château* has nine bedrooms, three of them with en-suite bathrooms. 'The French don't seem to like showers,' says Gavin. The master bedroom has a bathroom in one of the turrets and another small bedroom off it, which Gavin and Angela now use as a dressing room. 'The sad thing is, we can't afford to put any cupboards in now we've done all the other work,' says Gavin. 'All our clothes are still on IKEA hanging rails.'

Gavin and Angela chose all the colours for the walls themselves.

Gavin would pick up the paint stocks from England on his frequent trips over to see his football team Chelsea play. He is still a season-ticket holder at Stamford Bridge and goes over around 20 times a year. 'Paint is so much cheaper in England,' he explains. 'And the quality is so much better. Even so, I think we spent around £25,000 on the painting of the interior. But we're really pleased with the results.'

The restoration of the *château* took around nine months and cost the Quinneys an estimated £150,000. Gavin also says that anyone thinking of taking on a *château* should do the sums again and again and again. 'With a house in London you might at most double your budget. But here with a *château* there are several issues you might come across, like we did—the septic tanks, the damp, the ceiling caving in at the farmhouse—that will all cost you £10,000 each to fix. And then you've got four bathrooms at £10,000 each before you've even started on anything else, although we were lucky in that a couple of the original baths were in good enough condition to keep.'

Despite having spent his windfall and more, Gavin and Angela have no regrets. Their wine business is going well. Gordon Ramsay chose one of their whites as his house wine and Rick Stein recently added them to his wine list. They rent out the farmhouse they stayed in while doing up the *château* and it is fully booked for the summer months in advance. The pace of life in Bordeaux suits them. In London, Angela worked at Condé Nast and rarely had time for herself or the children. 'I would leave the house before they got up and get back home when they'd gone to bed, this is so much more fun. I also find it a much simpler place to live; it's less stress-ful, less materialistic. The French aren't fussed what kind of car you have, the focus here is very much on food and wine, which is a relief after London.' Gavin agrees. 'It's amazing, we have only just got a front-door key,' he says. 'For two and half years we couldn't lock the *château*. Imagine that in Wandsworth.'

15
La Chasse

In France there is really no noticeable anti-hunt movement. When we first moved here I was amazed to find what looked like a sniper pacing up and down the path to my house. I asked him what he was hunting.

'Anything,' was his response. I hoped this didn't include mothers and small children. But I knew better than to complain. Hunting is part of the culture here and I suppose because it has none of the snobby connotations it does in Britain, it is generally accepted as something people are free to do, even close to your house.

The hunting fraternity in our village is very powerful. That's one reason I don't complain about them, however disconcerting it is to be out walking with the children among armed men. Once I was jogging at about 8 o'clock in the morning. A shot was fired. I could smell the smoke from the bullet. But rather than lodge a complaint I have given up jogging (I hated it anyway). We live in the middle of the countryside and I am sure it is partly the power of the hunters that keeps the housing estates away from our valley.

I have yet though to see people on horseback charging past the house. Fox hunting has not caught on here yet. The French tend to hunt what they can eat. When the police appear at a hunt in

France, they are there to help the huntsmen and the hounds, not to arrest them. Henri d'Origny, a designer for Hermès and a regular at the Rallye Trois Forets hunt north of Paris, says the gendarmes queue up to attend. 'Their job is to escort the hounds across the

Some Brits move to France to play golf. Not that golf has been banned in the UK (yet) but the weather sometimes makes playing more difficult than any balaclava-clad protestors could.

There are only 450 golf courses in France as opposed to over 2,000 in the UK. The French are getting to grips with the game, but slowly. Try to name a famous French golfer and you'll be hard pushed to. The only one I can come up with is Jean Van der Velde who so excruciatingly lost the 1999 Open at Carnoustie by fluffing the final hole and then losing the play-off. If he had won, thousands of little French boys would probably have taken the game up. Instead golf in France remains a sport played by only a few. Some Brits see this as a good thing.

Horror stories from all over the country reach me. French players are pushing in, wearing strange clothes and even driving their golf carts into the bunkers to take shots. There are at least two places you will find snails on a French golf course. One is in the restaurant, where they will be marinated in garlic and served hot. The other is on giant posters on the course, encouraging people to play faster. While players tuck into the snails on their plate, they ignore the signs on the fairway.

'They have a typically French attitude towards rules which is to ignore them,' says one exasperated expat from Provence. 'For example if they miss the ball, they don't count the shot.' Another expat based in the Languedoc complains that they play winter rules all year round. This sounds heinous-but what does it mean? Apparently it's all to do with the rule that you can pick the ball up in winter to wipe mud off it without counting it as a shot. The French, however, do this in the summer as well, when there is no mud on the ball. Worse, they

roads. They hunt three times a week and get paid for it. It is one of the best jobs going.'

This approach is encouraging some British huntsmen to move to France in the face of the ban that-bar delays resulting from legal challenges-is due to come into force in England and Wales next month. 'Hunting is part of my life and I am not prepared to give it up,' says Simon Wright, who hunts twice a week with the Southdown and Eridge hunt. 'I am a Sussex man, born and bred, but this is enough to make me leave the country. My 14-year-old son, Marcus, loves it and I don't see why he should have to give it up.'

The French, who have grown accustomed to the arrival of the British diaspora over the past five years, are bracing themselves for a new influx, together with horses and hounds. The arrivals will have a largely sympathetic welcome. 'Hunting is a symbol of England,' says d'Origny. 'This is fascism and totally ridiculous.'

Venetia Winborne, who hunts several times a week and has lived in Normandy for more than 20 years, says a ban would never happen in France: 'If they tried it here they would have people with pitchforks marching on Paris.'

Wright is looking for a house close to Pau, where foxhunting was introduced by the Duke of Wellington more than a century ago. The Victorians went out in hordes because of the benign climate and, at one stage during the 19th century, 20 per cent of the population was British. There is a Rue de Buckingham, an 18-hole golf course and tearooms all over the city. Pau is still known as La Ville Anglaise. 'There are already lots of Brits here but we have been in contact with several hunts in England that are making plans for the future,' says Paul Mirat, head of international relations at the Pau tourist office and a keen huntsman.

Jeffrey Quirk, who runs riding and hunting holidays at Chateau de Sombrun near Pau, is planning to take a pack of hounds over from Hertfordshire: 'We are going to create a truly English fox

are also accused of picking up balls in the rough.

I visit Souillac Country Club in the Dordogne to investigate these slanderous accusations. This is a club run and owned by Brits, but with 250 local members. According to club President Sylvie Delcamp, they are trying to follow the rules. 'But it is really something you invented and we try to follow,' says the glamorous Madame Delcamp (nicknamed Golfing Barbie by the male members).

Sylvie admits that the French aren't so hot on dress code and that their manner can be a bit more laid-back than your average British player. They often wear shorts and T-shirts, although Sylvie tells me bare chests are frowned upon (unless it's hers I presume).

During competitions the locals repeatedly have to be told to take things seriously and not to cheat. The French golfing association even runs courses to teach players etiquette and instil in them the importance of replacing divots. 'But the upside is that we don't have your snobbish attitude and ridiculous rules against women,' says Sylvie. 'In Britain it is a more macho game.' In France 40per cent of registered golfers are female, compared with only 20per cent in the UK.

I talk to Pierre, a local farmer, who has been a member of the club for two years. He plays once a week and is astounded by the Brits on the course who show a dedication to the game he has not seen among his compatriots.

'They are on the course at 8.30 and they leave at 17.00,' he says. 'They don't even stop for a proper lunch and what's more they do this every day. They don't even have weekends off. It's incredible.' If you want to ensure an empty course in France then you should play at lunchtime. The French see golf as something for before and after food, not during it.

hunt here.' Quirk predicts more packs will move to France. 'I think it's going to go absolutely crazy,' he says. 'You are looking at 250 hunts that will be unable to function after February. It's either move or shoot the hounds and sack the staff. I am investing in another 15 Irish hunters to cope with demand.' Quirk is in talks with Diana Pyper, joint master of the Puckeridge hunt in Hertfordshire. 'The hounds have been in my family for more than 100 years and their pedigrees go back to the 17th century,' says Pyper. 'I couldn't bear to put them down, so moving to France is one possibility.'

Stephen Sherwood, an equestrian property consultant and former joint master of the New Forest Hounds, moved to France three years ago to escape the ban on hunting.

He says those considering moving their packs out should look into it carefully first: 'There is so much work involved in getting the licences to hunt here. You have to sit a really tough exam, organise insurance, get local permits to hunt and so forth. They would be better off developing a relationship with a French pack.'

All around the country the hunting community is gearing up for an influx of Brits.

'I think we will see a lot of them coming over,' says Jane Hanslip, who runs riding holidays from her home outside Bergerac in the Dordogne. 'I am planning to run two hunting weekends a year from my property.'

Hunting with hounds in France is mainly for stag and wild boar. As Lady Winborne puts it: 'The French rarely chase anything inedible.' The culture here is also very different. In England, the emphasis is on the horse. In France, it is the hounds that really count. The French have managed to turn hunting into something altogether more cerebral than the British. They call it the art de venerie the art of hunting. Apparently it is all about how the dogs work together to outwit the animal they are chasing. And the animal they are chasing has to be considered worthy, which is why the French don't often chase foxes. 'It would be a bit like chasing a rat,' says Sherwood.

For those from an Anglo-Saxon culture, this can all be a bit too much. D'Origny's American wife, Sybil, doesn't hunt in France. 'She finds it too intellectual,' he says.

16
Disasters

Someone told me recently that 60 per cent of Brits who move to France give up and go back home within the first two years. At first I thought this couldn't be possible, but the more I meet people who have moved here, the luckier I realise we have been.

We came here with no real idea of what we were doing. I spoke almost no French at all and was heavily pregnant. We arrived in a house we knew nothing about except that we loved it, in a region we had only seen as house hunters. I had no idea who would look after our children when I was working, or even if I would be able to continue to work.

After we had moved, people kept telling me how brave we were. It didn't seem brave to me. All we had done was swap a stressful life for one where the fundamentals, such as our home and the climate, were so much better. Already that made a huge difference to our lives. Then there are all the other factors like good state education, a safe environment, fantastic healthcare, great food and so on. It seemed to me it would have been braver to stay in south-east England. But when I see the sorts of awful things that have happened to people on moving here, I can begin to understand why people thought us brave, or even mad.

Countless things could have gone wrong which would have

It isn't until the priest opens his mouth that I remember I am in France.

The ladies look like they are dressed for Ascot. The first reading is the one that begins: 'Though I speak with the tongues of men and angels, and have not love' which we have all heard a million times, the hymn 'I vow to thee my country'. It is all so comfortingly familiar. And then the priest speaks: 'I am so 'appy to welcome you.'

I am at my first English wedding in France. My friends Peter and Natalie are about to be married by Inspector Clouseau.

Oddly enough, they are already married. Priests do not have the right to marry you in France. The only person that can marry you here is a mayor. This is all part of the French laïcité, the separation of church and state, which dates back to the revolution and is why girls were banned from wearing veils to school.

Still, it is a beautiful service, which my husband sadly misses on account of the fact that it is the FA cup final. Yet another great British tradition upheld in France, getting married on cup final day.

We are all dressed up, the women in strappy dresses, some of the men in morning coats. I don't know what the villagers make of it all as we leave the church. I am told by one of them that for a little village wedding like this the guests will normally wear jeans.

We go from the service to the reception. Some Spanish musicians are playing Gypsy Kings-style music. At last something foreign, if not French. The guests jig about in an effort to keep warm; one of them even goes back to her hotel to get her coat. So the weather is English too.

During the excellent speeches I get a text message from my husband: 'Slight delay. Extra time.'

I ask one of the waiters if there is a big difference between English and French weddings. This is his first English wed-

made our lives extremely difficult. They could still go wrong, but I hope now that we're settled here we will be in a better position to handle them.

James and Alice—a nightmare sale

James and Alice are good friends of mine from Sussex. They had always wanted to move to France and finally bought a lovely house in a village near to us two years ago. 'Living in France had always been James' dream,' says Alice. 'He had quite a continental upbringing and works in the wine business. He was so enthusiastic about it that it became my dream too.' When James sold his shares in a wine freight business, they had the money to start looking. They decided to look close to the city of Montpellier and the beaches, with the benefits of the Mediterranean climate.

'We'd been down several times and really hadn't seen anything we liked. Then we saw this place and just fell in love with it. It had everything we needed. We wanted to be in a village, to be able to walk to the bakery and the bar, and to be involved in village life,' says Alice. During the sale there was just one point that worried them. There was a right to buy on the part of the council for a piece of land in their garden. Four metres of their garden could be taken, if necessary, to build an access road from the main road, down the side of the property to a vineyard, which was designated building land. 'We were not unrealistic about living in a village, we know they expand, and four metres we could just about cope with. It still meant we could build a swimming-pool, which was something we had stipulated as a condition to the sale all along' explains Alice. 'We were assured by the vendors that there had been talk about this project for years and that it had never come to anything. They said the project would never happen because the bend in the road was far too dangerous.' They had a London-based *notaire* handle the sale and, satisfied with his findings, the sale went ahead.

ding, he tells me. But he has noticed that all anyone wants to drink is champagne.

'What do they drink at a French wedding?'

'Pastis of course.'

As with anything remotely official in France there is lots of paperwork involved in getting married. The list of what you need is bordering on the ridiculous. It includes a medical certificate to prove you are in good health which is not more than two months old and a birth certificate which is not more than six months old. As a foreigner you need certificates proving you are single (a note from your last girlfriend confirming she happily dumped you won't be enough). Any documents will have to be translated into French by an officially approved translator. The wedding has to be announced publicly for at least ten days outside the mayor's office. You will also need to live in the area for 30 days before you get hitched. This can be waived in an emergency according to my local mayor, for example if the bride-to-be is pregnant. You will also need an EDF bill or similar (the key to a trouble-free life in France) to prove your residential status. Most preposterously you have to vow to be faithful. This from the nation that invented the cinq à sept (5-7pm fling)? Seems a little excessive.

The disco kicks off with Thriller and the dance floor is filled with men doing Michael Jackson impersonations. I see the French look on in bemusement and wonder how many drunken English men they will be fishing out of the pool before the evening is over. At least this time it won't be my husband. As an avid Chelsea fan he is too busy complaining about Arsenal's stolen victory to drink too much.

Once the sale had gone through, James and Alice discovered that the project was far from dead. In addition, the reserve was not for four metres, but for eight. And there was going to be a housing estate in the field next door to them. 'This will ruin the property, the whole ambiance will go,' says Alice. 'In addition, we won't be able to build a pool. Our home is going to be decimated. It is a very stressful experience. I always knew they would build something on the land, which I had accepted, but never imagined half our garden flattened to make the access road.'

James and Alice's first mistake was to trust the vendors. Because they were English, they believed them when they told them the project was dead. 'When we signed, the previous owner was busy cracking open bottles of champagne,' says Alice. 'I realise now that they were more for them than for us.' The building work on the estate starts in a few months. There are going to be 55 houses and the only access road will be the one they build by taking part of James and Alice's garden. Alice is being pragmatic. 'We will just let them get on with it and then eventually build a big wall to regain our privacy,' she says. 'Once it's all done and the garden has grown back up again we'll decide whether or not we want to sell it.'

To add to the stress of the housing estate, James and Alice's 17-year-old son Adam was attacked by a dog as he stopped at a nightclub on his brother's birthday to find out what time it opened. 'He was approaching the barrier to the car park when he saw a man with a dog. He just had time to say '*Excusez-moi monsieur*' before the dog jumped on him, bit through the muscle in his forearm and took two chunks out of his leg,' says Alice. 'The man then called him off, but not before he'd done a lot of damage.'

Adam's brother and sister-in-law took him to hospital where they treated him for the bites. The next morning the police were called and took a statement. An identity parade was organised but Adam couldn't positively identify the owner of the dog, so the case was dropped. 'I can't fault the police,' says Alice. 'They came straight away and were very professional. But you wonder what sort of people would set a dog on a boy who was just asking for some information.'

The dog incident was James and Alice's second encounter with the local police. Just a couple of days before they had been broken into while out at lunch with friends. 'We left around 11 and when we came back the place was ransacked. I have no idea who could have done it, but there were a few people in the street as we waved goodbye to our neighbours.' They were told by police that it was quite a common occurrence and that a house just up the road had been burgled three times recently. 'They knew exactly what they were looking for, just cash, credit cards and jewellery. In fact, the most valuable thing in the house were my pearls, which they left. They probably thought they were fake. I'll never leave money or credit cards in the house again.'

James and Alice's whole French experience seems to be jinxed. About six months ago the sewers in the village broke and the sewage poured into their garden. James decided to do something about the mess and started clearing it up. He was already practically blind in one eye due to glaucoma. Whilst he was cleaning the mess up, a small particle got behind the retina of his good eye, causing a serious infection. They rushed back to England but after much treatment the doctors declared they could do nothing to save his eyesight. He is now almost blind, is unable to drive and can't carry on working, which means they have no income. Despite all this, they still love it here and want to move here full time one day. 'In spite of everything, I just relax as soon as I get here,' says Alice.

Angela Thomas—death and floods

Angela and Ken Thomas retired to a village in Provence called Vallabrègues in 1996. They had come from Wrexham where Angela was a night theatre sister and Ken was a crane driver. They had always loved France and Angela spoke French. 'We thought about going around the world,' says Angela. 'But then we thought, what's the point?   What do we end up with at the end of it.

Better to invest in a house in the sun.'

They had been living in Vallebrègues for seven years when Ken had a stroke. 'I came downstairs one day and found him with his head in his hands saying he didn't feel well,' says Angela. 'He looked terribly pale, so I called the doctor.' The doctor was there within ten minutes and immediately called an ambulance. Ken was taken to hospital where he was given all manner of tests within half an hour and Angela was told he would have to stay in for a few days. She moved into hospital with him and only went home to feed their cats and tend to the garden.

Ken was not in a good way, hardly speaking and losing weight. He hadn't spoken to her for three weeks when one day, as she was straightening his arm, he looked at her and asked: 'What are you doing?'

She was taken aback. 'I'm straightening your arm,' she replied.

'Oh why don't you piss off you soft sod,' was Ken's response.

'I have never been so happy to be told to piss off in my life. I cried and hugged him and it felt like I had my Ken back.'

Ken seemed to make a remarkable recovery. He started moving, eating a bit more, and talking. The doctors couldn't explain what was going on but agreed he could go home. Angela was given a pre-scription for all the things she would need like a wheelchair, an electronic bed, an invalid armchair and went off to kit the house out. She didn't have to pay anything for any of this and in addition a nurse came twice a day, as well as a home help three times a week.

Ken was delighted to be home. He spent a lot of time talking to his cat and watching sport on TV. But after a few days he started to develop a terrible rash. Angela called the doctor again who said an emergency blood test was needed. At 6am the following day, a nurse came round and by midday they had the results. They were not good. Ken's kidneys were malfunctioning. He would have to go back into hospital. This time Angela was not able to stay with him so she commuted from their home to spend the days with him.

Then it started to rain, and rain and rain. 'It seemed like it was never going to stop,' she says. One morning she was about to leave when she heard the flood warnings on the radio. They were telling people to cancel all non-essential journeys because the roads were too dangerous. 'I called the hospital and told them what had happened. They said he was fine and that they would send him my love. I told them to tell him I would be in the following day.'

Angela had a visit from the fire brigade, asking if she wanted to be evacuated. No, she didn't. She was told to move as many belongings as she could to the top floor and to turn off the electricity if the water started to come in through the front door. Some friends offered to move her car to a hill above the village. Her neighbour Marie arrived to stay in her hall, as she didn't have a top floor. Angela had also rescued a cat she found hanging onto a piece of wood floating in her garden. She carried what she could upstairs, including all her bottles of wine, and she and Marie lifted the heavier furniture like the sofa onto tables.

The next day there was no way she could get to the hospital. The water was now all over the first floor of the house and the streets were full of water gushing past. She called again to make sure Ken was OK. He was fine, they told her. That night the stray cat and Ken's cat had a fight and knocked Angela's stack of wine bottles down the stairs. Now the house was not only flooded with water, but wine, and broken glass. Angela was clearing away what she could when Marie came downstairs.

'Aren't you cold?' she asked her.

'It was only then I realised I was picking up the broken glass stark naked,' says Angela.

They were four days into the siege by this stage. On the fifth night she spoke to the nurse on duty at the hospital, a man she and Ken had got to know well.

'He's not good,' he told her. 'He's not talking to me any more. I think you'd better get here.'

Angela managed to get to the hospital by taking a hugely roundabout route. When she finally saw Ken, she was shocked.

'He had lost so much weight, he looked terrible. I went completely mad with the staff and asked if they were trying to starve him to death.' Angela moved back into the hospital to be with him. A day later she went off to get a coffee and on her way back to room was met by a nurse.

'She told me Ken wasn't well. I told her I knew that. 'He's really not well,' she said. I said I knew that too. But when I opened the door I saw what she meant, he was an awful ivory colour. I ran over to him and took him in my arms, I told him we would never be apart and that I loved him very, very much. Then he died.'

'I felt like death was trailing me around like a cloak. I went back to England for Christmas, and on the boat over it got very choppy. We're all going to sink, I thought to myself, and it's my fault.'

Angela's advice to anyone who goes through what she did is to have someone at your side who knows how the system works. For example, as with births, deaths need to be registered within 24 hours. At least in the south, the French are much keener to bury or cremate people quickly, the norm is within 48 hours. The custom here is also to put a table with a book of condolences outside your house. According to a friend who lives near Nancy in the Lorraine region, things are different up north. People either offer their condolences at the cemetery when the bereaved are standing in a line after the burial or people leave their card in a basket at the entrance of the church.

'I was amazed at how many people signed the book,' said Angela. 'Even though Ken didn't speak any French, he was universally liked in the village because he was such a happy person.'

Ken was cremated and Angela has kept his ashes. 'The agreement was that whoever died first would keep the ashes of the other one. When I die our ashes will be mixed together and put in the garden of our house.'

There is no question of going back to Wrexham though. 'My life is here now,' she says. 'I like the people and the way of life.'

Wanadoo—but can't

It's a funny thing about communication companies, but whenever you want to get hold of somebody, there's nobody to talk to. Just recently I've been very keen to get hold of somebody at France Telecom. And shake them. Then strangle them, slowly.

This urge to inflict grievous bodily harm all started when Ghislaine, a sweet-talking lady from the French telecom provider, gave me the glorious news that we could receive a broadband connection. Our neighbouring villages are all connected, but as we live in the middle of a vineyard, we have repeatedly been told it is impossible for us.

Prior to this I tried to install satellite broadband. I bought two different systems. Sadly there was no one in the whole county with the technical ability to install either. The technical help desks at both companies assured me it was perfectly possible to do it oneself. Call me unadventurous, but I don't find clambering on top of roofs putting up satellite dishes straightforward. I then tried an internet version called 'just like broadband'. Just like broadband except it didn't work. My whole computer crashed and refused to do anything but give me error messages.

So when Ghislaine broke the news to me that broadband was ours for the asking, I thought all my Christmases had come at once.

'Are you sure?' I asked.

'*Pas de probleme, madame,*' said Ghislaine. 'You can have broadband, faster than anything you would get in England.'

I couldn't believe it. Proof at last that France was a technologically superior country and that Britain was still in the Dark Ages. This is where it gets technical. Yes, we could install broadband on our ISDN line, they said, but it would have to be changed to an analogue line first. They would send a man along to do that in 10 days' time. After that we would be part of the technological revolution. I was overjoyed. Soon all my problems would be over. I could listen to Radio 3 while sending emails and downloading short adult films. Ghislaine rapidly became my new best friend.

There followed a series of minor disasters which I took with saint-like calm as I anticipated the day my emails would download at 8 Megabytes (four times faster than in the UK). For example, our internet service provider owned and operated by France Telecom, Wandadoo—nicknamed You Wanadoo But Can't— seemed to have even less idea of what was going on than we did. It changed our account to a broadband one in preparation for the great event. This meant we had no internet access at all. I had to keep calling Wanadoo, at a premium cost of 34 euro centimes a minute, only to be kept on hold for 15 minutes each time listening to David Bowie wailing 'We Can Be Heroes'. They might think they are heroes but I don't: Blondie's Hanging on the Telephone would have been more appropriate. The technical support team kept sending me back to the commercial team and vica versa. I asked them if they couldn't sort this out between themselves. 'We can't talk to each other,' I was told by one member of staff. 'That's just how it is.'

Once the man had come and ripped out the ISDN line I was told by various staff at Wanadoo and France Telecom that it was just a question of waiting for the broadband line to arrive. Meanwhile the box was ready and waiting, all configured to my computer by my local technical support team, Lizzie from the neighbouring village.

There was more action around the broadband box than the Christmas tree as we waited for the magic red light to come on. Nothing happened. We waited until Christmas Eve and then started to call people again.

'It's all fine *madame*,' I was told. 'But nothing will happen until after Christmas.'

The day after Boxing Day I rushed into my office to see if the little light had come on. It hadn't. I called the broadband technical team in Montpellier.

'You can't have broadband,' I was told by a rather snotty woman, in the way only the French can be snotty. 'You're too far away from the exchange. In fact the request for broadband on your line was rejected on December 13th.'

I asked said snotty woman what we could do to get broadband? 'Move house,' she said.

Of the 25 or so people I had spoken to at both Wanadoo and France Telecom over a two-week period, none of them had breathed a word about this development. I called Ghislaine. She said she was sorry and would get the ISDN line back. Then we had the charade of trying to get back to where we were before we started the whole process. One mess up followed another. For example, the man that showed up to fix it had no idea of the saga we had been through and just took the first line that came to hand and changed that to ISDN. So we had no phone lines at all for a week. Finally someone with a bit more acumen showed up.

'So let me get this straight,' he said. 'What you really want it to have it just like it was before?'

France Telecom is claiming that 95 per cent of France will have broadband by the end of 2005. And Napoleon was a good bloke.

My advice to anyone planning to install broadband is to double check that you are eligible for it before taking any action at all. Always get the name and the number of the France Telecom or Wanadoo representative you speak to so you can go back to them should it all go wrong. Don't be fobbed off by them, they are very good at telling you to ring another number. Tell them you already have and insist they help you. Finally, be proactive. If I hadn't hassled them we would still be waiting for our broadband connection. And the whole mess would probably have taken until next

Christmas to sort out.

My top tip is this: if a Wanadoo representative comes anywhere near you, run screaming from the room or reach for your shotgun. As I write I am still battling with them. For some inexplicable reason they have just switched my account to a broadband one again. This means I am in limbo—I have no broadband and so can't access the internet. More David Bowie. If I ever hear that song again it will be too soon.

Colin and Tuk Hudson—a swimming pool saga

Building a swimming pool is a top priority for many Brits coming to live in France. Our pool was already here, but I had a swimming pool drama about a year after we moved here. Having handed over £1,800, 30 per cent over the original estimate, to change my pool from a chlorine to a salt system, I watched it turn from crystal blue to murky green.

The crunch came when a guest asked if it was safe to go swimming, or 'are there alligators in the pool'? I called my pool man to ask him to sort the problem out. The system he'd installed obviously wasn't working. His response, 'read the instruction manual. If you want me to come out it's €95 a visit.' I was furious. Rupert threatened to throw the man in the pool if he showed up and tried to charge us €95.

Finally I telephoned the manufacturer of the salt system, they promised to sort out the problem. A technician arrived at 9.30pm the next evening and checked out the whole operation. 'Your pool man didn't put enough salt in,' said Nicolas Tedesco, Export Manager of Pool Technologie. 'Add a bit of hydrogen peroxide to get rid of the green and salt and then it should all be fine.' A week later I had my blue pool back again. I thought maybe I had been foolish to go for a small operator and that maybe a big name with a reputation to protect would be safer.

Not so. Some friends of mine, Colin and Tuk Hudson, ordered a pool from Diffazur in Montpellier for their house in France. Diffazur is one of the biggest names in swimming pool design and manufacture. Just after Colin and Tuk paid their final installment of €4,500 the Diffazur office they were dealing with went bust. They were left with a concrete bunker having paid almost the whole cost of the pool. 'We made several calls to the head office,' says Tuk. 'They have been incredibly bad at responding. The work was supposed to be guaranteed but they refused to confirm that at first.' Meanwhile the Hudsons, who paid for three quarters of the pool up front in order to get it finished before the summer, were left in the sweltering heat looking at a hole in the ground where mosquitoes breed. Finally Diffazur took responsibility for its franchise and finished the pool.

Anonymous—divorce in France

Divorce laws in France are quite different from those in England. When I first moved here a lady got in touch with me who had been the victim of what can only be described as a confidence trickster. They were married in England when the lady, let's call her Susan, was around 30. Her husband, we'll call him Tim, didn't work but was instead going to do up the house, which Susan had bought and they had moved into. Susan worked full time as a psychiatrist. 'He did nothing,' says Susan. 'He told me he was depressed and that he wanted to start a new life. By this stage we had a daughter and she was having a terrible time at school in England, so I agreed to sell up and buy a place in France.'

When they bought the house in France, although it was all with Susan's money, it was easier for inheritance tax purposes to put it in their joint names.

'As soon as the deal was done, he changed. He became violent, cruel, even lazier than he had been at home, simply horrible,' says

Susan. 'I put up with it for three years and then eventually told him to get out. He turned to me and grinned. 'I think you'll find my dear, that the law in France is very different to the law in England. Here this house is half mine and there's nothing you can do about it'. We sold the house and he took half. I was forced to move into a small flat with our daughter. Looking back on it, I think the whole move to France was just a way to get some money for nothing.'

In a recent case, a family had been living here three years outside the French system. The husband worked for cash as a plumber and the wife looked after their five children. He then ran off with someone else, leaving her alone with the kids and no income. As they had not been paying any social security contributions, she is not on the system and therefore not eligible for help. It is worth remembering that you do need to register with the social security otherwise you could find yourself seriously strapped if you become ill or, as in the case above, your source of income runs off with a local doxy.

A friend of mine is just going though a divorce. She and her husband have three children together. When they bought the house, they bought it in his name. 'It never occurred to me that we would ever fight about ownership,' says my friend. Because the house is in his name, she has no right whatsoever to any of the proceeds from it. In fact, her husband doesn't even have to sell it. In addition, as her husband has been working for cash and declaring his income as nil to the tax authorities, any judge will assess him as unable to pay any alimony at all. 'Quite how I'm going to survive with three children, I don't know,' says my friend, who is now struggling to find a job having been a housewife and a mother for the past ten years.

James and Barbara Sands—cash come-back

A lot of people who buy properties or land here pay a portion in cash. This means that both parties avoid tax and is often seen as a goodwill gesture. The problem with doing this is that you have no recourse should things go wrong, as James and Barbara Sands found when they bought a fishing lake in the Mayenne. They took a career break from their jobs in a police force in the north of England to move to France and set up a Carp fishing holiday business.

'We were fed up with the massive stress we were under at work, the rising crime rate and the rat race that is life in England,' says James. 'It sounds cheesy, but we wanted to give it a go and live the dream while we were still young.' James and Barbara, both in their early thirties, sold their respective houses in order to buy a lake with four hectares of land. 'I'm a keen angler and Barbara is a keen gardener,' says James. 'We both love the outdoors so this was an ideal thing for us.'

They paid for the land and the lake above board, but paid £8,000 for the stock of fish in cash. When they got to France, they paid a company £1,000 to net the lake so they could see exactly where they stood in terms of fish stock. There were only four Carp left in the lake. There should have been around 150. When they asked their neighbours what had happened they were told that the previous owner had had a party there a couple of nights before they got there, had the lake netted, killed all the fish and sold them.

'We have absolutely no comeback,' says James. 'But we were in the wrong for agreeing to buy them for cash in the first place, but that's just how it works over here, everyone seems to do it.'

James and Barbara's problems continued. They had been told when they bought the land that they could have a mobile home on it and that getting mains electricity and water to the land wouldn't be a problem either. When they applied for permission to put a mobile home there, they were told that this was not possible. They could have a static caravan but not a mobile home. They bought a second-hand caravan from some people in Nantes. It was only when they got it home and told their neighbours about the transaction that they realised they had been tricked into paying VAT on it. 'You don't pay VAT on second hand goods in the UK, but here I didn't know what the form was so I just paid up,' says Barbara. 'It seems to me the locals here see the Brits as having more money than them and something to fleece at every opportunity. Every single time we have bought materials we have been quoted a price and then told to pay way over that price at the end.

On top of this, James and Barbara had their applications for mains water and electricity turned down. They are going to have to dig a well and pump out water from that. 'Our wonderful neighbours, who are from Paris, have agreed to install a second meter and we will run an underground cable from that for the electricity,' says James. 'But we're going back to the UK in the winter, we have to go back to work. I'm told 50,000 Brits are leaving the UK every year to come to France. They need to know it's not all as rosy as it is on the TV. If you come out here with your life savings, they soon disappear. And people might say we were naïve, but isn't everyone when they move to a foreign country?'

James and Barbara will carry on with their plans to run fishing holidays but only as a sideline. 'All this has put us off moving here full time,' says Barbara.

Driving in France

I have had more car accidents in the short time I have been in France than the rest of my life put together. It's true that one of the incidents did include me backing the car into a tree, but whose idea was it to put giant trees so close to the road? I blame Napoleon. The other two incidents were typical of France. In one I was innocently driving to see a friend when someone came round the corner on the wrong side of the road doing three times the speed limit and drove straight into me. In the other I was barged into by a Lafarge lorry when the driver ran out of room on his side of the road. Better to take out the pregnant woman and baby in a Golf than the lamppost.

The French around us are appalling drivers. Around midday, when they are rushing to get to lunch, they are downright dangerous. Having had nothing to eat since a croissant at 7 am, their blood sugar levels are dangerously low as they negotiate corners at 80 kilometres an hour while thinking of their *steak frites*.

But it is not only the French that present a threat. My charming neighbour Virginia recently arrived at my house in a flap. She had just had lunch in a restaurant where she had drunk two glasses of wine. She was so terrified of making the dreaded mistake of driving on the wrong side of the road when she got into her car that she kept chanting 'I must keep to the left' to herself. She was amazed a few hundred metres down the road to see a Frenchman coming straight towards her. 'I almost killed the poor man,' she told me. 'But he was perfectly wonderful about it.'

When Virginia goes back to England she lends me her car, a Peugeot convertible with English plates. I thought it would be a good experiment to see if the French reacted any differently to me whilst driving an English car. Would they be even more pushy and dangerous? No, is the answer. In fact that's probably not possible. There really isn't much difference in their reaction, except I once drove past a man pruning a vine on a roundabout. I had the roof down as it was a gloriously sunny day. He threw down his secateurs, raised his arms in the air and yelled 'I love you'.

I meet some very interesting people, and the question of how long one can have English plates on a car is one I am often asked. According to Ivan Tredinnick who runs an insurance company here, there is no time limit. 'The French authorities will try to put pressure on you to change your licence plates, but under European law you are under no obligation to do so,' he says. 'The only problem is finding an insurance company that will insure a UK-registered car here, as most of the French ones will not.' But in terms of the law, as long as a car is legal in the UK, it is legal in France.

Another frequently asked question is what does one do if one has an accident? Alison Hall, a media headhunter with a company called The 7 Arts Consultancy, recently drove into a deer on the motorway between just outside Cahors whilst on their way to her house in the Gers. 'My advice to anyone taking a car to France is to make sure you're fully covered in case of an accident,' she says. 'I dread to think what the recovery of the car, let alone the deer, would have cost us. You should also bring plenty of water with you. Our son was in shock after the accident and we had to try to keep him cool in temperatures of over 40 degrees. And don't be tempted to ignore the warning signs for deer, which we used to laugh at.'

Getting insurance that will cover you in France is complicated. Most UK policies stop at the Channel so you need to check with your insurance company what they cover. If you have an accident the first call you should make is to your insurance company, unless of course it is an emergency. Then you need to call 15 for an ambulance, 16 for the police and 18 for the fire brigade. There is also a Europe-wide number, 112, which works all over Europe alongside the national numbers.

For those of you wondering if you can get away with speeding in an English car, the answer is no. Mark and Claire Grogan wrote to me to tell me they were recently caught doing 185 kilometres an hour on their way to a ski resort. They were pulled over at the *péage* and Mark was frogmarched to a police car (in front of his three children) and driven to the nearest town. The three police officers escorted him to a bank and demanded he take out €750 on the spot and hand it over to them. 'It was terrible,' says Mark. 'The bank wouldn't take any of my credit cards so I was then driven to a hole on the wall and made to take the cash out there.' As well as the fine, Mark had his driving licence taken away and was given a three-month ban. They drove off after the incident, with Claire at the wheel. Unfortunately she is as hopeless at keeping a check on her speed as her husband and 15 kilometres down the road they were stopped again. 'I don't know what we would have done if they'd taken my licence away as well,' says Claire. 'The children are all under ten so just that bit too young to drive.'

David and Jan Denholm—insurance, what insurance?

David and Jan Denholm bought a holiday home in the Languedoc and insured it with Groupama, the French insurance company. During severe winds one winter, part of their roof was blown off. As a result, their bedroom was flooded and everything in it ruined. 'The walls and ceilings were stained,' says David. 'The bed and mattress ruined. We came to France immediately and repaired the roof with the help of a local builder.' They went along to the Groupama office to deal with the insurance claim and were told that under the section dealing with floods none of the roof repairs were covered, as they were caused by natural events.

'We were amazed,' says David. 'And we also felt we didn't get satisfactory answers to our questions like, what if we had neglected to mend the roof and the rain had eventually caused it all to collapse?' The Denholms were only given 50 per cent back on the cost of replacing all the bedroom furniture and had to pay for the painting, roof and repairs to the walls and ceiling.

According to my friend Jacques, this happens all the time. 'If the village is not declared the victim of a *catastrophe naturelle* by the *Conseil des Ministres* after studying the dossier presented by the commune, the expenses are yours to cover,' he says. 'After the last earthquake in eastern France I noticed a few cracks in the walls. But apparently there were not enough people who had suffered damage and the town has not been declared *catastrophe naturelle*.'

The moral of the Denholms' story is obviously to check your insurance policy very carefully. If you don't speak good enough French have it translated, or if you live in a region that is likely to flood then ask specifically about the cover for this. Don't assume that things are run in the same way as in the UK. Stephanie Godwin (mentioned below) found her premium was too much one year so decided to cancel the policy and buy another cheaper one. You can't do this in France, you have to give at least two months' notice by registered letter. Her old insurance company is now trying to sue her for the premium.

Stephanie and Jeremy Godwin—not qualified to work

Stephanie and Jeremy Godwin moved to the northern Mayenne in search of a better life for them and their three children. Originally from Beaminster in Dorset, their children were being bullied at school for wanting to study and they were generally fed up with England. Jeremy had worked as an accountant for 15 years and Stephanie had worked as a teacher for 15 years. 'I have a PGCE and an MA in education, as well as my 15 years' experience,' she says. 'But when I tried to get a job here, they told me I had no relevant qualifications and no relevant experience. It was the same story for Jeremy. The only place he could get a job was with an international firm in Paris. The French system is impenetrable.'

A lot of people I have spoken to have found that there is no way you can carry on with the career you had at home without getting the equivalent French qualifications. 'Most of the English out here are broke,' says Stephanie. 'They just can't get work. We've used up all our equity just keeping going. Now we can't even go back.' Stephanie and Jeremy decided to abandon their job search and have instead started breeding dogs, something they started while still in England. 'Thank God we brought some of the dogs with us,' says Stephanie. 'At least we can start trying to make a living from them.'

Jacques says Stephanie was unlucky. 'It sounds as if she didn't knock on the right doors,' he says. 'In my 32 years at the university I have used the services of countless English people as teachers. They set themselves up as *professions libérales*, which is a little tricky at first (tax, URSSAF tax etc) but quite feasible. And there are also private schools which don't have the same requirements as public ones.'

In my experience, those who have best succeeded here are expats who work for companies in the UK. They get paid well and they don't have the hassle of trying to make it within the French system. If you have a job that is transferable, like teaching, you should talk to your local education board or equivalent and find out exactly where you stand before you move.

Gavin and Juliette Morton—denounced to the tax authorities

Denouncement is a phenomenon the English normally find hard to cope with, although it is quite common in France. 'It's just not part of our culture in the UK,' says Juliette. 'However much I hated someone, I would never denounce them to the taxman. It's just not something that would ever cross my mind.' The French are constantly wary of denouncers. They advise you not to get a new car, in case your neighbour denounces you. All the local artisans I know are always extremely wary of working for cash anywhere they might be spotted by the village denouncer. This is obviously a habit that goes back to the war when the French were busy denouncing each other to the Germans.

If you denounce someone, the taxman has to look into it. So the person is faced with the enormous hassle and expense of a fiscal investigation. If the taxman gets any money out of this, the denouncer gets a percentage. It reminds me of the secret police in communist Russia, the whole system is too nasty for words.

The person who denounced them had contacted Gavin with a

view to offering him his services in terms of advice on tax and insurance matters. He visited him and talked to him about their situation. 'After some meetings and general discussions it become clear that the advice was not relevant,' says Gavin. 'And I told him I didn't want his services.' The man then said Gavin owed him £250 for the time he had already spent with him. Gavin told him not to be so ridiculous, paid him £100 and told him to go away. A few days later Gavin and Juliette received a very threatening letter from the man saying that if Gavin didn't pay the balance he felt he owed him, he would report him. 'You might consider it unwise to build up a collection of disgruntled ex-advisors and helpers who know—or can guess at—the foolhardiness and danger of your background,' he wrote.

Gavin ignored him and a few weeks later he found out he had been denounced and the investigation began.

Over the next six months the tax authorities demanded a series of interviews and examinations where every penny which was paid into any bank account anywhere in the world for a two-year period was scrutinised and, unless they were able to prove with certified documentation that the money was not income, tax was demanded.

Under French law a person accused of anything has to prove their innocence. The proof required is dictated by the tax inspectors and this invariably means only officially stamped and certified documents will be accepted. All receipts are treated as income, no expenses of costs are allowed or offset so Gavin and Juliette are now having to pay tax on personal items they have sold as well as loans from friends they have had and repaid. 'Apparently what we should have done was get a contract drawn up and signed in front of a lawyer stating that this money was a loan,' says Gavin. 'But when a friend helps you out, you don't think about doing that.'

Having gone through their bank statements, the tax authorities decided they owed them €17,000. They appealed against the decision and I went with them to the tribunal just outside Montpellier. It was a terribly impersonal building and there was no indication of where we had to be. Even the receptionist, when we showed her the letter stating room C1 in some annexe was confused. Eventually we found our way to the right place, but the tribunal was running late. There were two other cases to be heard before Juliette and Gavin's. We were shown into a waiting room and after a few minutes a rather pinched looking woman showed up and started rustling papers. Juliette and Gavin both nodded towards her. 'That's the woman who's ruining our life,' said Juliette.

Juliette, who speaks flawless French, spoke to the woman and explained that they had new evidence to show the tribunal. They had managed to get their bank to find the originals of cheques the tax authorities had labelled as non-declared income and this was proof that they were, in fact, not revenue. The tax inspector took them and added them to her dossier.

After about an hour's wait, we were shown into the hearing room. Inside there was the judge, two men from the tax authorities and two others whose role it was to ensure that there was a fair hearing. The judge started off proceedings by going into the background of the case. Then it was up to Juliette and Gavin to defend themselves. Juliette explained that during their 14 years in France, they had tried to do everything in the right way and that they had not tried to hide anything. She was incensed that they were being told to pay tax on the sale of highly personal possessions like a painting she had sold that her father left her and Gavin's camera. The judge nodded and said that was all very well but in France you have to declare everything. He then asked the tax inspector if she had any additional information to bring to the hearing. She told him about the photocopies of the cheques Juliette supplied. After that we were allowed to leave.

The judge upheld the decision of the tax authorities and Gavin and Juliette are paying the €17,000 off, in instalments. 'It is so galling,' says Gavin. 'Because we don't owe one penny of it and we're now really up against it.' To add to their problems, Gavin recently had a letter from the fraud squad who have demanded an interview with him. 'At first I thought I had been denounced again,' he says. 'But apparently the fraud-squad investigation is a procedure that follows automatically after a tax inspection.'

Mrs X—compulsory purchase

When Mrs X (who wishes to remain anonymous to avoid further proceedings from her local authority) moved to a lock keepers' cottage on an island in southwest France, she imagined a stress free life listening to the sound of the river flowing by. She had been there for two years when she received a registered letter from the county council.

The letter informed her that the council wanted to purchase half her island, restore the locks and put interlocking steel gates across the island to stop water from seeping into the ground. This would effectively cut her island in two. 'It's amazing how really bad post always arrives at the weekend when there is nothing you can do about it,' she says.

Mrs X, unlike most foreigners that buy in France, had had the foresight to meet the mayor before buying the property. 'We discussed the possibility of making the river navigable again and opening the locks before I bought the cottage,' she says. 'The mayor seemed perfectly reasonable and I even confirmed in writing that, if it would come to it, I would gladly grant the necessary rights of way to enable the river to be navigable again. I therefore thought this registered letter was a mistake.'

As with all compulsory land purchases, there would have to be a public enquiry. During this enquiry, Mrs X reiterated that she would not stand in the way of the project. 'Because I did this, the council could not proceed with a compulsory purchase order,' she says. 'They had to come up with something else. I was completely floored by what it was.'

The council told Mrs X that although she had bought the property, including the lock, from a private individual, she was in fact not the owner. The council had made a mistake, they told her, when they said they wanted to buy the lock, because it wasn't hers to start with. It was already theirs. While the public enquiry had been going on, they had bought a water mill further up the river which they maintained gave them a right to the lock right in front of her lockkeepers' cottage. 'At some stage in the 1960s the properties had all been owned by the same proprietor,' says Mrs X. 'According to them, they had simply become the owner of the lock when they became the owner of that water mill. You have to hand it to them, it's highly creative.'

Mrs X decided to get a lawyer involved. What followed was six years of legal wrangling and stress. At one stage 17 people showed up to start work on the island, including two policemen and two lawyers. Mrs X and her lawyer saw them off.

'The thing you must remember if you're going to take on the authorities is never to be intimidated,' says Mrs X. 'I was determined not to give in. Their attitude made me apoplectic with rage and fired me to continue the fight, despite a lot of people around me saying I should just give in.'

Mrs X thinks that she would still be fighting the case today if there had not been a change in personnel at the county council. 'Some new employees at the council were given the case, possibly because the others were worn out or bored with it,' says Mrs X. 'Anyway, it suddenly became possible to discuss matters. Someone realised I had not been hindering the project and what should have happened six years earlier happened in 2000: we started discussions. We agreed that the council could take 300 square metres of my island, namely the two sides of the lock and the water in between, instead of the proposed 3000 square metres. They paid me a symbolic Franc.'

Compulsory purchase rights (the right of the local authority to buy the property) are often overlooked by Brits buying property in France. 'The laws have come about because in France land is often divided up into small parcels. This makes it very difficult for the community to carry out any major projects so it has to earmark land for development and collate it as and when it comes up for sale,' says Dawn Alderson, solicitor with Russell Cooke Associates

According to Dominique Semenou, the mayor of a village called Souilhe in south west France, cases like Mrs X's are extremely rare. 'We don't compulsorily purchase land on a whim,' he says. 'We would try to come to an amicable agreement. I have only had to expropriate land once, when we needed to build a purifying plant and the owner of the land wanted to sell it at several times the market value.'

Epilogue

Almost everyone from England I meet asks me the same question. Will we ever go back?

There are plenty of reasons for staying here. Climate, healthcare, value for money in housing market, quality of life. The list goes on and on. Where in England there are frustrations getting from A to B, here the roads and trains are superb. The doctors here wait for you, not the other way around. The schools are good. The quality of life is hard to beat. The bread is fresh daily. But there are also some reasons for returning to England. Language, culture, sense of humour, friends, Waitrose.

There was an astonishing opinion poll reported recently in Britain in which three-quarters of people asked said they would leave the UK if they could. Certainly for those coming to France the formula is superficially simple. You leave England with some money in the bank, having sold your house at the top of the market. You buy somewhere in rural France, which is five times the size of your terraced house in England, and you still have some change left over. 'Twice as nice for half the price,' as one estate agent neatly puts it. The rest will see you through until you can get your career started again, from your new headquarters in the middle of nowhere. The children will go to the village school, where they will be fine, even though they don't speak French. You will have lovely family dinners together made up entirely of fresh produce purchased from your local market and a bottle of wine from your new winemaking neighbour and soon to be best friend.

It used to be that the people who moved to France were retired. They didn't need to make a living. They had their pensions and their savings and muddled along quite happily. The kind of people who are moving out here now are different. Of the estimated 50,000 Brits who relocate to France a year at least half, if not more, are young families who need to earn money. In France, earning money is not as easy as it is in England, which could be why there are 250,000 young French people living in the UK, because they cannot get jobs at home. The options open to a Brit moving here are even more limited than those open to the locals. First, the language barrier is a problem. Unless your French is fluent, you're going to have to get a job that only requires English. Even if your French is fluent, a professional qualification from the UK doesn't necessarily translate in the French job market. You can set up your own business, but the administrative nightmare associated with this is horrendous. You could also end up like Gavin Morton, the subject of a tax inspection. The French taxman doesn't on the whole like entrepreneurs.

The people who seem to do well here in my experience are those who can still work for people in the UK. Of course you have to pay tax here, but the whole thing is less complicated. You also don't have to struggle to find work here and the money is often better.

I have never heard of anyone giving up and going back because of the bureaucratic nightmare that life can be here. But there were times when I felt like it. Getting onto the healthcare system was almost impossible. Getting our *Carte de Séjour* (a residents' permit, now no longer a requirement) was tougher than A Levels. When the time came to get my *Carte Grise* for our new car I was terrified that I would have to spend more than half the day fighting with bureaucrats.

As it turned out, the official couldn't have been more helpful and the whole thing was over in ten minutes. I think what had happened is that by then I had learnt not to fight the system. The bureaucracy is unbearable, but it works. And if you have the right piece of paper then it all goes well. The problem with coming here as a foreigner is that you often don't have the right piece of paper. For example, as a foreign family we will never have a *Livret de Famille*, an official record of your family. This means that to get a family railcard (50 per cent off rail travel if you have three or more children and lots of other perks) we have to produce all sorts of other documentation that I still haven't had the time to do. I spoke to the regional council about this problem and asked if there was any way at all I could get one. 'Oh yes,' came the helpful reply. 'Marry a Frenchman.' Seems a little excessive just to get cheap train tickets. If you're not already married and intend to get married, you can beat the system by getting married in France. That way they have to give you a *Livret de Famille*.

Many older people I have met have gone back because they miss family, especially their grandchildren. I came across one couple who had lived in Provence for 12 years and were moving back because the wife wanted to see their grandchildren grow up. Not having family and friends around is undoubtedly one of the big downsides to living in France. We have been quite lucky as most of our friends and family seem to have bought houses here as well. But it's true that some of my good girlfriends are still in England and I do miss seeing them a lot. Some argue that it's nice, because when they come out and stay you get to spend much more time with them, but in my view nothing quite compares to seeing someone every couple of weeks.

When you start a new life in a different country, you have a lot of expectations. You expect things to be better than they were at home. You have an image of your new life and the way you will settle in happily. This image can be very easily damaged if the reality is that your children, for example, are totally miserable.

Renting before you buy is a good idea for some people, though we didn't do it because once we saw our house we knew we didn't want to live anywhere else. It means you can get to know the area you are thinking about moving to and really see if it's for you.

One of the problems a lot of Brits find is that rural France, however idyllic, can be quite limiting. If you come from London and are used to how things work there and having everything around the corner, ending up in a big farmhouse in the Auvergne might sound like a blissful idea. But you should think about the practicalities of living somewhere where the nearest supermarket might be 40 minute drive away. You should also be aware that the people in rural France can be quite conservative and may not be as friendly as you'd hoped. I have found everyone here extremely nice, but I think they're quite used to foreigners by now. In places like the Mayenne and Lorraine there are those who have found they are not. But wherever you are, if you learn the language and join in, you will be accepted. That is easier said than done.

Moving house within the same country is a stressful experience. Add to that a change in culture, language and bureaucracy and you can begin to imagine how tough moving here can be. The language thing is something that gets a lot of Brits down. Moving abroad is not a new concept for the British. They have been moving abroad and taking over vast parts of the world for centuries. But nowhere in those former colonies did they have to learn another language. They simply imposed their own system. In France you can't. You will find that a lot of people only speak French. I was amazed when I first came here at how few of the locals spoke or understood any English. In retrospect this was typically British of me. Why should they speak English in the south of France? How many Devon farmers speak French? The English are notoriously bad at languages. And French is a notoriously difficult language. Something somewhere has to give. And I don't see the *Acadamie Française* budging.

In answer to the question will we ever go back—ever is a long time. But at the moment I really can't see it happening. We have sold our house in England now, so even if we wanted to it would be difficult. I thought I would get very emotional when it came to selling up, that it was the final link and so on. Of course it's not. We will always go back to England to visit people and maybe the children will be educated there in part. England will always be there. And even if we live here for the next 50 years we will always be seen as '*les Anglais à Sainte Cécile*'. We will never be French, however much we integrate and however long we live here. I don't think our children will be either. But does that matter?

It is a difficult place to live in some ways, for many of the reasons I have written about in this book. But the upside is huge. A German proverb speaks of 'living like God in France.' It's the German equivalent of living the life of Riley. Most days, that is exactly how I feel.

Why France?

And what to do once you get there...

People often ask me why we moved to France. I can't pretend to be one of those people who have been coming here for decades. I hardly knew the place before I lived here. But I was attracted by the whole adventure of a new place, a new language and life. I didn't have any idea really what that new life would be like. Warmer certainly, and perhaps more exciting than village life in England, however pleasant that can be.

Most people say they move to France because of the lifestyle. They like the idea of living somewhere cheaper, less crowded, warmer and less stressful than the UK. But there are those who move here for very specific reasons. A local agent I speak to says golf is one of the main reasons people move to France. 'They can buy a house next to the course and play golf all the time,' says Melanie van der Meer from Vallée de la Dordogne. 'There is really no reason for them to leave the club at all.'

Mike Connor, a solicitor from Manchester, bought a three-bedroom cottage at Souillac in September 2002. He paid €200,000 for it. He and his family come out for all the school holidays. 'For us it's not really the golf that attracted us, it was the fact that we could have a house that would be looked after when we're not here and also see the same people and their kids every holiday,' he says. 'It's great for the kids and safe.'

I ask Pierre if he can imagine living at the club. 'Oh no, I would miss my cows,' he says. 'It's a nice course though. Apart from the Brits complaining about us pushing in.' I agree with the saying that golf is a good walk spoiled. My favourite thing is walking. I probably go for an average of three walks a day. A lot less stressful than golf, but possibly more expensive.

We ended up in the Languedoc by chance. But there are probably those of you out there willing to do some research and come to a decision on where you want to end up based on facts, as opposed to some guy on a boat. There are many things to consider.

Of course, the first thing you need to decide before you pick a region is exactly what you are moving to France for. If you're going for sunshine, don't move to Brittany. If you love wine, you should probably look at one of the many wine regions. If you're an aeroplane fanatic, try Toulouse.

Do you need to commute back to England for work? If you do, it would be wise to move somewhere within easy reach of several airports and the TGV. Do you speak any French at all? If not, pick a region that is used to foreigners, where they have language courses and where some of the locals speak English.

I have not covered the whole country here, but start with a summary (and in some cases a score on a scale of 1 to 10, that is in the case of Brit Alert 1 means there are no Brits, 10 means the place is crawling with people accessorised with an English newspaper under their arm.). At the back of the book you will find each region in France listed with all sorts of useful data like the nearest IKEA and what to avoid once you get there.

Alps (Brit Alert: 9 Value Increase: 5)

A place for ski enthusiasts. The three valleys, Courcheval, Meribel and Val Thorens offers some of the best skiing in the world. The longest, widest, smoothest runs anywhere. So much so that the Chelsea owner Roman Abramovich tried to take over an entire village. He was rebuffed by owners. Meribel is the most child friendly of the three. Serious Brit skiers go to Val d'Isere and Tignes where the night life is as lively as the mogul fields. For sophistication head to Megeve; St Tropez in snow boots. Probably best to avoid Chamonix, the place is so overrun with Brits the locals have been protesting. According to Stuart Law, Managing Director of Assetz-France, the Alps is increasing in popularity. 'We have seen an increase in buyers as part of the overall trend for moving abroad," he says. 'But in addition developers are finding land in the south is now so expensive they are moving to the Alps to build." For a chalet in any of the better resorts you will pay at least €500,000. A one-bedroom apartment will set you back around €150,000.

Auvergne/Massif Central (Brit Alert: 3 Value Increase: 7)

Finding a British person living in the Auvergne is not easy. They are rare and want to keep it that way. The region is possibly one of the only ones in France that has yet to be invaded by northerners looking for a new life in *la France profonde*. Part of the reason is its inaccessibility.

The Auvergne is part of the Massif Central, the vast plateau that expands over the middle of France and encompasses the Auvergne, Limousin, the northern part of the Midi-Pyrenées, some north-eastern parts of the Languedoc-Roussillon, the eastern fringe of the Rhône-Alpes and a small part of the Bourgogne Region. The Massif Central is the size of Scotland and covers 1/7th of France. In fact it has more in common with Scotland than just size. It is sparsely populated and freezing cold. Parts of it are almost 2000 metres high and during the winter the landscape is covered in snow. It is a dramatic landscape, combining green (once the snow melts) rolling hills, volcanic peaks, valleys lakes and gorges.

Aurilliac in the Auvergne has the dubious honour of being the prefecture in France furthest away from a motorway. Even now with the completion of the famous Millau Viaduct in December 2004, it seems a long way away. Henry and Eve Platt moved to a small hamlet outside the town of Jussac just north of Aurilliac four years ago. 'We had been living in Amiens,' says Henry who has been in France for over 20 years and worked as a teacher before becoming a translator. 'We knew the region from holidays and just fell in love with it. Like many city rats, we were craving the country life.'

They bought a 19th century five bedroom farmhouse with a hectare and a half of land for £180,000. 'We spent two and half years looking,' says Eve. 'Then one day I just saw it in the window of an estate agent's. 'That's the one I want', I said to Henry. It was over our budget but it was perfect. Although to be honest I'm not such a Francophile as Henry, if I could move it all to the Cotswolds I would.'

Henry and Eve have not done much work to the house but Eve is a keen gardener and works in the garden most days. 'I have introduced the concept of hanging baskets to our neighbours,' she says. 'They're all very friendly and we're delighted to have found the place.' Henry agrees. 'The other good thing it they're all French, I couldn't bear to be in a British enclave.'

To find another British couple you need to travel about 35 kilometres from Jussac to the ski resort of Le Lioran in Saint Jacques des Blats. Since the opening of the Millau Viaduct, the Le Lioran ski resort has become the closest in terms of driving time to the city of Montpellier. This means new business for hotels at the foot of the 44-run resort like the Hotel des Sources recently bought by Janine and Neill Murray. Janine and Neill sold their respective homes in London and Berkhamstead to buy the 14 room hotel in September last year. 'We wanted a change of life and to live somewhere we could have two seasons for the hotel,' says Janine, aged 37 who left her job as a technical manager for Marks & Spencer to move to France. 'Here we can do the skiing season, as well as mountain biking and walking in the summer months.'

They bought the hotel for €190,000 and have so far invested about £20,000 in doing it up. 'We plan to close later on in the year for four months to reduce the number of bedrooms so we can add bathrooms and get a classification,' says Neill, who is 41 and a former postman. 'There are grants available but I would expect we'll spend around £100,000.'

They have both been extremely impressed with the welcome they received from the locals. 'They have been incredibly friendly and kind,' says Neill. 'All the firewood we have we have been given, one chap kept coming up here every week with a basket of vegetables and would take no money for them. Another couple that own one of the hotels in town have been really helpful and full of good advice.'

Janine and Neill would advise others thinking of buying a hotel to work out the finances very carefully before going into it. 'We based all our calculations on 50 per cent occupancy,' says Janine. 'But the most successful hotel in town has an average occupancy of only 38 per cent. You should also be wary of buying places that have been empty for years, there is probably a good reason why they have been, either they need rebuilding or they don't comply with health and safety regulations.' Janine and Neill say the most difficult part of setting up the business has been the red tape and regulations. 'We couldn't have done it if we didn't speak French,' says Janine.

Colin and Linda Newman got the idea of moving to the Auvergne from a local kitchen and bathroom furniture supplier that Colin had been working with for many years. Colin was a long-distance lorry driver and had been delivering the kitchens and bathrooms made in the region for distribution in the UK. It was getting increasingly difficult to meet the delivery deadlines and still keep within the legal limits of speed and time spent driving. 'One day I went to talk to the owner of the business and explained that I wouldn't be able to carry on,' says Colin. 'He asked me if it would make any difference if I lived down here. I said yes it probably would and it all took off from there. We had been coming here for years and knew and loved the region in every season.'

Linda agrees. 'It was one of those opportunities that we didn't want to miss,' she says. 'The children were off our hands and it suddenly seemed possible.' Colin and Linda decided they didn't want to leave Linda's mother Audrey behind and asked her if she'd like to go with them.

'I said yes straight away,' she says. 'They asked me if I didn't want to think about it and I said no, I didn't.'

They moved to the village of Polminhac in the county of Cantal in the Auvergne, along with Linda's mother Audrey Brooks, in September 1993. They had decided to rent somewhere until they could find the right house. 'This proved a little more difficult than we had anticipated,' says Linda. 'We needed somewhere my mother could have an apartment on one level and also to be close enough to the village to walk there so she wasn't dependent on us. After two and a half years in tiny rented accommodation with no heating we were still no closer to finding our own home.'

When a plot of land came up for sale, they decided that the best option would be for them to build a house. The 1500 square metre plot cost just over £13,000. The 150-square metre house cost around £75,500 to build but took a lot longer than anticipated to complete. 'Colin did almost everything himself except for the foundations, walls and electricity,' says Linda. 'He even did the plumbing, all the interior walls and so on. We only finished our bedroom last year so from start to finish it has taken almost eight years.'

The Newmans have no regrets. 'We are really happy and settled,' says Linda. 'I can't see us ever going back to Essex. The only reason we would leave would be if all the children decide to move to New Zealand or something. The best thing about the region is the people; they're hospitable, polite and really helpful.'

Linda says the only downside is missing the family. 'Whichever way you look at it, it's a long trip from Rodez back home,' she says. 'But luckily some of the kids are looking for a plot of land to build on here at the moment too.' The Newmans are now retired but run some B&B rooms.

Property Prices in the region are still relatively low compared with the rest of France. Now that the A75 and the Millau Viaduct has opened there is a cheap (toll free bar the viaduct) and fast route from Clermont-Ferrand through to the south. Clermont-Ferrand is also linked to the A72 eastwards towards Lyon, the A71 northwards towards Paris and there will soon be the

A89 towards westwards to Bordeaux. 'There is no doubt the region has really been opened up with the viaduct and also since Ryanair started flying to Rodez a year ago,' says Myriam de Mahe who moved to the Auvergne seven years ago and acts as a bridge between the local sellers and property hunters. 'I think we will start seeing a filter-trough effect on the house prices.'

At the moment you can find a four bedroom farmhouse with some land for around €200,000. A small town house somewhere like Aurilliac will set you back around €150,000. Unlike the more popular regions of France, there aren't new builds round every corner and housing estates springing up. There are plenty of old stone houses and lots of space; the two things Brits are predominantly looking for when they move to France. It surely won't be long before we see them lining up along the Millau Viaduct in search of their dream homes.

Béarn

Some people say they move to France because it is like England was 50 years ago. If you want somewhere that is like England 100 years ago, then you should move to Pau and join the English Club. Entering the splendid villa set in a park in the centre of the city is like walking into Britain's imperial past. There is a vast marble bust of Queen Victoria and on the walls hang paintings of the Pau Fox Hunt. There is a plaque commemorating gentlemen that died in the Great War. At the bottom of the plaque is a section for their servants.

Pau and the surrounding Béarn Region (part of the Pyrénées-Atlantiques and the Pays-Basque in south-west France) is a place the British have been welcomed since Wellington first came here in 1814. 'It was built by the British, for the British,' says Pierre Truchi Director of the Tourist Office and Palais des Congrès. 'In 1880 out of a population of 25,000, 8,000 were British.'

Now the population of Pau is 83,000 but the percentage of Brits has dropped, although since RyanAir arrived in May 2004 there has been a dramatic increase in property hunters.

Jane Dickinson, originally from Keighley in Yorkshire, has lived in the region for eight years. Jane works in a hotel in the historical centre of Pau and says she can't believe the amount of guests that are house hunting. 'They've all got this dream of a house in France,' she says. 'I used to help them but then I thought hang on a minute I'm going to be surrounded by Brits if they all come here. Now I just tell them it rains a lot.' It does in fact rain just as much in Pau as it does in London, but in half the amount of days.

Joy Askew, a singer-songwriter who has worked with, among others, Peter Gabriel, Laurie Anderson and Joe Jackson, was attracted to the region because of its beauty. 'I was on a tour with Peter Gabriel,' she says. 'We were on one of those tour buses. I was half asleep and then woke up to see the

Pyrénées appearing like a mirage. At first I thought I was imagining it, but they became stronger and stronger. At that moment I knew I wanted to get to know the area better.'

Joy, originally from Newcastle-upon-Tyne, has been living in New York for over 20 years but decided she wanted to establish a foothold in Europe. 'I'm not American,' she says. 'But I didn't want to go back to England because the climate is so bad.' At a dinner party she met a man from Yorkshire who had just bought a place in South-West France for £50,000. 'I started trawling the Internet and made a total of three trips out here,' she says. 'But of course since the Yorkshireman had bought his place, prices had doubled. I was being shown absolute crap for €200,000 and was getting increasingly disillusioned.'

Finally in May last year a German agent came up with a three-bedroom farmhouse outside Montardon in the northern part of the Béarn region for €150,000. The house, which is 150 years old, has been restored by its previous French owner, a local farmer, using traditional building materials. It sits in five acres of land with views in all directions. 'The minute she took me through the gate I knew it was the right place,' says Joy. 'And when I got up to the oak-beamed bedroom I saw the view of the Pyrenées. Now I look out for them every day I'm here, sometimes they appear and disappear like ghosts, they're incredible. I love it here, it's very French, very rural and very local.' Joy has a large barn which she hopes to turn into a music studio and workshop.

According to local agent Jonathan Lewis who works for Property 64, the number of Brits looking in the region is increasing and they are all after the same thing. 'They want the classic old farmhouse to renovate, with some land,' he says. 'The typical budget is around €150,000.' For that you can buy a three-bedroom farmhouse which needs work. If you're after a property that has already been renovated prices jump to €300,000 for a four to five-bedroom farmhouse and €600,000 for a large house with six to eight bedrooms. 'The stone used to build these houses comes from the river basin and is called Galet stone,' says Lewis who moved to Pau from Australia five years ago. 'It comes in various colours but is essentially pale and very pretty. That's what the Brits want.'

Tim Robinson has just that and has now lived here so long he is almost as local as the stone. He first came out to Pau to race some horses and has now been here for 27 years. He married Marie-Françoise, a French woman, and in 1989 they bought the farmhouse outside Marciac. It has five bedrooms, 25 hectares of land, 25 stables and it cost them £50,000. 'It is a wonderful region,' says Tim who breeds horses. 'People are always asking us where we're going on holiday and I tell them we don't need to go on holiday. We have the mountains for skiing one hour away and Biarritz and the sea an hour away.' Their house has now been valued at £150,000 for the property not including all the land and stables. 'It is true that the English invasion has driven up prices,' says Tim. 'I don't have much to do with them, there are 80 people in our village, five of the families are English but I've never met them.'

According to Paul Mirat, Head of International Relations at the Pau Tourist Information Board, the enquiries from Brits are increasing every day. 'It is just snowballing,' he says. 'Every day I have someone calling and asking about property. The other day some friends of mine were sitting in their garden and some English came along and made them an offer for their house they just couldn't refuse. It's incredible.'

According to local agents like Claudine Laborde-Sallenave prices have risen in the last couple of years reflecting the increase in demand. 'But it's not only that,' she says. 'There are now a lot of English agents operating here and they price the properties much higher than we do.' She says prices have risen between 25 and 30 per cent over the last two years.

Edward and Angelika Rich bought the Château de Ledeuix half an hour south of Pau six years ago. They paid £130,000 for what was essentially a ruin with a new roof. 'The council had put on the new roof but then it had been abandoned due to lack of funds,' says Edward. 'The wooden panelled dining room had been transformed into a sheep pen and the courtyard was a local rubbish collection point. Over 850 panes of glass were broken.' Edward, a furniture and interior designer and his German wife Angelika, a furniture restorer, had already renovated one château in France and were keen on another project. 'It has an amazing view of the Pyrénées,' says Edward. 'And the building itself is stunning, we love it here. The boys adore it, there's so much space and they can play bows and arrows out of the slit windows.' The restoration is still going on but the family has suffered one major setback. The council is going to build a housing estate on the land in front of the château. 'This is despite our offer to buy it and build houses in keeping with the château ourselves,' says Edward. 'It is a devastating blow. And ironic considering the same council saved the building from the bulldozers in 1989 because they didn't want to see their historical patrimony becoming a housing estate.'

Housing estates aside, the Béarn has some wonderful countryside, rolling hills and magnificent woods. Added to which, weather permitting, you have the view of the mountains. 'I was astonished visiting the region after living at the other end of the Pyrénées, on the sun-scorched Mediterranean coast, at how still, green and peaceful it was in the Béarn,' says Rosemary Bailey, author of *The Man who Married a Mountain*, a travel memoir about Count Henry Russell the 19th century Pyrenean mountaineer who grew up in Pau. 'I could really understand why so many of the English were drawn there in the 19th century and continue to be drawn there.'

The English club in Pau, founded in 1828 by a local British reading group, is still going. 'We only have three English members now out of a total of 64,' says Erik de Salettes, vice-president. 'But we are trying to attract

more of the English moving in.' To become a member you have to be proposed, seconded and above all, male. Some things never change in colonial
Britain. But it's a great place to live.

Bordeaux (Brit Alert: 10 Value Increase: 7)

Wine is obviously a big attraction for people wanting to move to France and
the most famous of all the wine regions is Bordeaux. For centuries the region
has been sending its bottles to London and the world, growing rich in the
process. But there are many other facets to it. The Atlantic coast is easily
accessible, as are the Pyrenées. It is the fifth biggest city in France with many
cinemas, theatres and cultural events. It is a great transport hub, with a
choice of several airlines and two airports, as well as the TGV. The climate is
good and the food delicious, particularly if you like duck.

David Eley, an artist who moved to Bordeaux in January 2002 with his
wife and two children, advises Brits thinking about moving to the region
against falling for the classic rural idyll. 'Don't automatically go for the
château in the country, you can get far more out of life by being in the city,'
he says. He tells a story of a poodle parlour two minutes down the road
where a parrot serenades poodles with the Marseillaise while they have their
trim. 'You wouldn't get that in the middle of nowhere,' he continues. 'And,
in fact, the countryside is only 15 minutes away.'

The Eleys moved from Hampshire, originally with the thought of
buying a country property. 'I am very lucky in that I can work from anywhere so I thought why not? Also most of my work is related to the wine
industry, so Bordeaux was a natural choice.' He explains that when they saw
their apartment, it just seemed like the perfect place. 'It has three terraces,
one of which looks out over the Roman amphitheatre. This really is a wonderful city.' None of the Eleys spoke French when they arrived and the girls,
were sent straight into the French educational system. 'We're really proud of
them,' says David. 'Within three months they spoke pretty good French and
within six months they were, by my standards anyway, fluent. Nowadays I
really don't know what's going on when they speak French among themselves.'

Townhouses in central Bordeaux start at around £200,000. 'For £300,000
you can get something really special,' says Karin Auriol-Andrews, who has
been working as an estate agent in the region for eight years. 'There is no
doubt that Bordeaux is undervalued compared with other major cities in
France.' There may be a good reason for this. Bordeaux has a reputation for
being a very unfriendly place. David tells me that during a recent heatwave
his wife got stuck in the lift. After half an hour she could hardly breathe.
'The agent's response was to tell me to learn to speak better French'.

David has since had a series of other misfortunes and is close to giving
up on life in France altogether. 'I feel as if I've been abducted and incarcer-

ated in a torture chamber and that there is no way out,' he says. 'It's curtains for us, our whole world has crumbled.'

His disaster story began the day he asked France Telecom to come and mend the back-up mechanism on his computer, a problem they had created whilst installing an ADSL line. The technician who arrived not only wiped out his whole hard drive, but also all his back-ups. In a rare moment of bureaucratic brilliance, David made the technician sign a piece of paper admitting liability. Without that he would have had no recourse at all. What he lost was a new business he had been working on for 18 months, as well as every bit of correspondence he had ever had. 'It was rather like arriving home to find your house had burnt down and all that was left was a sock. But rather than it happening in the security of England, it happened in France where I didn't know any of the rules or what to do.'

David is still fighting to get compensation for his losses. They haven't even agreed on a preliminary amount to pay him while they decide. He and his family are completely destitute. 'I have had countless meetings with lawyers and so-called experts,' he says. 'What is most galling is that they act as if I don't exist, arguing and laughing around me in my own home as they go through the finer details of my personal life. And all in front of the idiot who messed up my life, who for some reason has a right to be there. People keep telling me that it's the Latin culture, but in my view there is still right and wrong.'

For those looking for a place outside the city of Bordeaux, Mary Wakefield, a tourism consultant who has lived in the region for eight years, recommends Entre-deux-Mers, a wine-growing region situated between the Garonne and the Dordogne rivers. 'There are extremely few new developments there,' she says. 'It is all vines or forests and beautiful old houses. It is a lovely hilly region with beautiful views and there is unlikely to be much development as the vineyards simply don't come up for sale.' A large family house in the Margaux or Entre-deux-Mers region will cost around £500,000.

Jill Joiner, an estate agent who has lived in France for 15 years, says she is astounded at the number of British people coming to the region. 'I suspect they are escaping the house prices in Britain and looking for a better way of life,' she says. 'But these Brits are not retirees, they are young professionals, mainly in the IT business, whose main criteria is to be within an hour's drive from an international airport.'

Brittany (Brit Alert: 10 Value Increase: 5)

The Breton village of Bourbriac is where the anti-Brit riots took place last year. You'd think they would be used to us by now. The Brits have been emigrating to Brittany and Normandy since the Roman Empire. Brittany actually means Petite Bretagne or Little Britain. Some of the villages are now practically British and there are locals who resent the hike in house prices.

However, many concede that the Brits tend to buy up old ruins and have revitalised many of the villages that were dying. There is over 1000 miles of coastline and lots of medieval towns and castles for history buffs. Rennes, the capital of Brittany, is only two hours from Paris by train. It has two universities, a lovely historic centre and is famous for its cultural festivals. It is a good city for the young; there are more than 60,000 students there. House prices pretty reasonable apart from the south side where they reach Riviera proportions according to agent Bob Pearson from Breton Homes. 'Some areas, like the Blavet Valley, have quadrupled in price during the last four years," he says." A four-bedroom house will start at around €180,000. This region won't suit those moving to France for a climate change. During the winter you may as well have stayed in Blighty. There are some members of the Breton Liberation Front left but you're more likely to run into your neighbour from Manchester.

Burgundy (Brit Alert: 7 Value Increase: 8)

The countryside in Burgundy is extremely reminiscent of England and this was another region we considered moving to early on in our French house search. I knew it quite well as my aunt and uncle have a house there. It is a place that most British people drive through, or at best, stop for a night on the way to somewhere else. You turn left off the A6 at Châlon Nord to go skiing in the Alps. You turn right at Châlon Sud to go west of Burgundy towards the centre of France. Or you head south on the A6, the Autoroute du Soleil, thundering to the fleshpots of the Mediterranean coast. Any turning to the right between Dijon and Beaune will lead you to a village familiar from a wine list.

Burgundy isn't so much a place as a name on a wine bottle. If you pull off the motorway you will be surprised to discover villages that you already know from the expensive shelf of your local wine merchant's: Fixin, Gevrey-Chambertin, Chambolle-Musigny, Nuits St Georges and Vosne-Romanée. Except for this small area, it is surprising how few vineyards you see, unless you go looking for them. Otherwise the countryside is reminiscent of parts of the Cotswolds, with hills, forests and large fields.

The price of properties varies according to their proximity to the wine regions. For example, around the Côte de Nuit—the hilly strip of land between Dijon and Beaune, where the best wines have been made for centuries, the houses are relatively expensivenothing like prices in the south of England. To the west, around the Parc de Morvan, houses are less expensive. Further south, where even the wines get cheaper and more cheerful, the housing is more keenly priced.

'We bought a house here because it is eight hours drive from Calais,' says Malcolm Hogan, a retired diplomat. 'This way our impoverished offspring can visit us with their children without having to spend a night in an hotel on the way.' The Hogans bought a pretty house near the village of Brionnet four years ago for less than £60,000. 'The countryside round here is rolling hills, full of Charolais cattle,' says Hogan. 'It is pretty unsmart. Not much English is spoken. But it suits us.'

For many years in the Middle Ages Burgundy had been a separate kingdom to France. But the ill-fated siege of Nancy (1477) by Charles the Rash emboldened no doubt by a few bottles of decent wine, was the beginning of the end. The lands became incorporated into France and its leaders enjoyed the spoils. Its rulers were crowned in Reims. They drank burgundy wine, leaving claret from Bordeaux for the English.

Burgundy only became a place on a map again in 1964, when the four departments of Côte d'Or, Saône et Loire, Yonne and Nièvre were grouped together by a bored bureaucrat. Its administrative heart is Dijon, a place better known as a producer of mustard. It is a pretty, bustling city, with multi-coloured roofs and a fascinating old town.

Christine Jacob was a litigation lawyer in Hong Kong until she met a French winemaker on a junk on the South China Sea. She abandoned the law for the vineyards of Echevronne. 'It's a fantastic life,' she says. 'We are doing something others dream of.' Her estate, Domaine Lucien Jacob, covers over 19 hectares of Burgundy's best wine growing areas. They make around 100,000 bottles of wine a year.

The house is in the middle of a small village, with their cave a short walk away. She took me on a tour of her vineyards, some on slopes that seemed almost impossible to walk up. All the picking and pruning is done by hand. The views are breathtaking.

'Burgundy is a fabulous place to live,' she says. 'We eat well, drink well, have lots of fun.' She says that you could buy a very nice village house in Echevronne for £100,000, and the *château*, if it were for sale, for around £400,000.

Richard Parsons has been living in Burgundy for nearly 40 years. He came for the canals, and claims to be the first person to navigate them all as a traveller. He set up Continental Waterways, which sends nearly 7,000 people down the rivers and canals every year. His partner Susie Hopwood runs Burgundy Villas, which has a network of properties for rent all over Burgundy. She arranged the accommodation for Juliette Binoche and her staff during the filming of *Chocolat*, which took place in the pretty village of Flavigny sur Ozerain.

Susie Hopwood says that she came to Burgundy in search of some good luck. Since then she has fallen in love with a man and the region. 'I love the food here so much,' she says. 'We are going to start setting up cookery courses, so that people can come here with something worthwhile to take home.'

But her partner Richard cautions that life in Burgundy is not for the faint-hearted. 'People shouldn't come and live here just because the price of property is cheap,' says Richard. 'People have to realise that moving here will mean a change of culture and you need to adapt. Even so, for £300,000 you can buy an amazing place.'

I looked at a few places in the region, including an old village house with four bedrooms and a large garden. It was priced at £275,000. There were cheaper properties on the market that needed more work doing to them. Those who like town life should consider Beaune, where you can buy a three-storey town house for £200,000. Nonetheless, according to local agents, prices in the region as a whole have gone up by over 30 per cent in the last three years.

Joff and Mary Williams, both still in their 30s, got to Burgundy before prices went up. They moved there over ten years ago to set up a pottery. 'We had been living in Wales,' says Mary. 'I thought anything must be better than that.' Joff agrees. 'We were about to become the fourth pottery in a little village in Wales. I had heard of Burgundy in the film Passport to Pimlico. I suggested it to my wife as a destination, then, a week later, we saw a cottage advertised in an estate agent's in Ipswich. So we called the number, and came out.'

They looked at four houses, one of which they bought. Their son Isaac was ten days old. Joff had studied O-level French. Mary did not speak the language at all.

'I didn't speak for a year,' she says. 'I just listened to the French people who came to our house.'

Four years ago they sold the original house and bought a former *épicerie*—grocer's shop—for £40,000 in the pretty village of Vandenesse-en-Auxois. It had been in the hands of the same family for eight generations, but was in need of considerable work. There was even a tree growing through the kitchen floor.

'It took about five months to make the place habitable,' says Joff. He turned the next door workshop into a pottery, where he works and runs courses in the winter.

'We are never going to be rich,' he says. 'But we have a lovely life. Of course, it is not always the idyll that people imagine. You are always going to be a stranger. And it gets quite cold in winter—colder than England, although it is hotter in the summer. But we love it here.'

Dordogne (Brit Alert: 3 Value Increase: 7)

The Dordogne is back. Thirty years after the English first discovered its rolling hills and beautiful houses, the region is once again in fashion. It is hardly surprising the English love it: it looks just like home, English is spoken almost everywhere, there is more sunshine and properties are a third of the price. The countryside is stunning, the houses magnificent, built in limestone that is reminiscent of the Cotswolds. And since the budget airlines started flying in four years ago, the demand for property has spiralled.

According to Jérôme de Chabaneix, an estate agent with Orpi, France's largest chain of agents, prices rose by 50 per cent last year alone. 'This is more or less due to the English,' he says. 'Seventy per cent of my clients are foreign and of them 90 per cent are Anglo-Saxon.' In his newly refurbished office in the picturesque town of Lalinde, he explains that nowadays most buyers are cash buyers and that they're almost all after the same thing.

'They don't even have to sell their houses in the UK,' he says. 'They just release the equity and then come looking for old stone houses and space. Most of them have a budget of around €300,000 and are moving here permanently.'

De Chabaneix says that only 25 per cent of his English clients are moving to the Dordogne to retire. So what are they doing to make a living? Simon and Karen Colebourn, both in their 40s, moved to the medieval village of Eymet in January 2003 and now run an internet café there. They bought the whole property, including a 375 square metre ground floor space and four bedroom apartment above with two terraces for €100,000. 'I like living here because it's like England 50 years ago,' says Simon. 'Having said that we have kept our home outside Bath just in case.' Simon and Karen had a holiday home in Brittany for 16 years before they moved to Eymet. 'Then suddenly it all just came together,' says Simon. 'The partners in the PR company I was working for decided they would be better off without me, I had a minor heart problem, the children were at the right age to move and the business opportunity came up.' The property they bought was an old grain store and was completely derelict downstairs, although the apartment above it was habitable. They spent six months and around €70,000 renovating it. 'We have a good mixture of clients; French, English, Spanish and Italian,' says Simon. 'A lot of them come down from the Buddhist retreat nearby where there is no internet access.'

If you are moving to the Dordogne in search of a job and you don't speak any French, then Emyet, or Little England as it is also known, is the place to be. It seems one can manage there without so much as a '*parlez vous anglais?*' The local newsagent says he sells more English newspapers than he does French, Nathalie, a French girl working in a computer shop called MCD Informatique (owned by a Brit) says 80 per cent of her clients are English. 'But most of them don't speak French,' she says.

'It is amazing that some people have been here 35 years and still don't speak any French, you certainly couldn't get away with moving to England and not learning English,' says Simon. 'The locals are really receptive considering it's like a re-invasion of south west France. Having said that 15 years ago Eymet was run down and forgotten. Thanks to the influx of foreigners it's booming.'

Kevin Walls has been in Eymet for just 10 weeks. He bought the English grocery store there and so far is doing a booming trade. 'I just got fed up with the government and the rat race over in England,' he says. 'It's a great way of life here.' Walls has both English and French customers and says the most popular thing is Walker's Crisps. 'I have renamed the shop *Le Magasin Anglais*, it used to be The English Shop, which I think was a bit unfriendly towards the locals. All the other shop owners have welcomed me with open arms and people come from two hours away to buy their bacon and shredded wheat.' His house in Norfolk is stuck in a chain but once it is sold his wife will join him. 'We're looking at some places in the countryside,' he says. 'We've found some nice ones for about €180,000 with three to four bedrooms. Basically places that if you picked up and put in Kent would cost you half a million pounds.'

Most Brits that move to the region are not looking to set up a business but rather to do up a stone house, rent out part of it as a *gîte* and live in the other part. It's a formula that has worked for years. 'Don't even think about it,' says Jane Hanslip who runs a rental business, as well as French language and horse riding holidays from her manor house just outside Bergerac. 'There are so many Brits moving to the region and most of them have a plan to rent something out as a form of extra income. They are in fact not only adding to the supply, but also reducing the demand for holiday homes. It's what I call a double whammy.'

Jane bought her nine-bedroom farmhouse in 1989 for £175,000. She has since spent thousands of pounds doing it up. 'Another thing people don't realise is that the cost of renovating here is much more than in other parts of France,' she says. 'And that is because the demand is so huge.' For example, the cost of renovating a classic Dordogne stone roof is around £300 per square metre. Builders working for cash charge between €150 and €200 a day. 'That can quickly add up to €1,000 a week,' says Hamish Eadie. 'Not an easy amount of money to find if you're not working.'

Hamish Eadie was made redundant from the city in 2000 and moved to the medieval village of Beynac on the Dordogne River with his wife Xanthe and two sons Gus and Rory. They bought a restaurant business and have spent the last four years serving the French and English that live in the region with vegetarian alternatives to the local fare of meat and garlicky potatoes. The business was a huge success, but Hamish warns those thinking of moving here to start a business not to underestimate the difficulties setting up in France. 'The French do love a tax,' he says. 'And you end up paying 60 per cent social charges on anyone you employ. Having said all that, we love it here and are looking for our next big project.' Anyone interested in buying Hamish's restaurant should contact Lily Bayliss from Francophiles on the number or email address below.

Stephen and Carelle Sherwood moved out just over four years ago. They sold their house in the New Forest in 2000 and bought a 16th century manor house built by King Henry IV. They decided to leave England mainly due to the ban on hunting that they saw the government pushing through. 'I have been hunting since the age of four,' says Stephen, a former master of the New Forest Foxhounds. 'It was the Bournemouth protest that made me realise it was time to leave. We had a pilot arranged to fly with a protest banner in front of the hotel where the Labour Party Conference was taking place. The police said if he came within a mile of the hotel he would never fly again. It was this heavy handed approach that made us decide to get out.'

Stephen and Carelle got out a map of France and the French hunting yearbook. They pinpointed the greenest areas of the country and those with most hunt kennels. They settled on the region around the Forêt de la Double close to Périgeux and paid £230,000 for their house along with 100 acres of commercial woodland. 'We moved out with our hounds, horses and peacocks,' says Stephen who is now running an equestrian property consultancy while doing up the house. 'I was going to start fox hunting but the hounds have started hunting wild boar and are enjoying it enormously.'

Carelle loves the way of life in France. 'We lived in the New Forest for 27 years,' she says. 'But towards the end all you could hear were the lorries changing gear as they went up the hills. Here I wake up every morning to the sound of bird song. It really is stress free.' Stephen agrees. 'I have no regrets. My French is coming along, although I must admit getting the *permis de chasse* (hunting permit) was a bit of a challenge. I have only been back to England twice in four years, once for the Countryside Alliance March and once for my son's wedding.'

The relentless stream of newcomers does not seem to be slowing down. But one downside with the influx of Brits is that there are now almost no classic old stone houses to be had. 'Stone and space is all the English ask for,' says de Chabaneix. 'They are going to have to start looking at alternatives soon.' One couple that has done so is Nina and John Parr who moved to Villefranche de Lonchat three years ago. Villefranche is a bastide founded by Edward I around 1280 situated between the Isle and Dordogne Rivers, 38 kilometres from Bergerac. John is a builder and Nina runs a property business. 'We have bought a plot and are going to build our own home,' says Nina. 'In fact we're going to build three and sell two. It seemed the best option for us, especially as we can do most of the work ourselves.'

Another option is to try the neighbouring region of the Lot. There are plenty of stone houses, even more rolling countryside and prices are much lower. But there you'll have to learn to speak French.

Ten things you (perhaps) didn't know about the Dordogne

It is the third largest *département* in France
It is the second most visited region in France (after Paris) with more than two million visitors a year
It is the wettest region in France
It is made up of the Perigord Blanc, Noir, Rouge and Vert. The four

represent limestone, black forests, wine and greenery respectively

It is part of the Aquitaine region of France

It has a population of 400,000

Ryanair and Flybe fly from Stanstead, Bristol and Southampton to Bergerac. In 2001 16,000 passengers flew into Bergerac. In 2004 this figure increased to 200,000

It has 1001 castles

The two most popular town with the Brits are Riberat and Eymet. British population estimates range from 20 per cent to 50 per cent in each.

It is extremely hilly. Make sure the property you're looking at gets the sun all year round. A lot of them are shielded by hills or castles.

Languedoc-Roussillon (Brit Alert: 9 Value Increase: 2)

This is the non-posh south of France. But it's getting posher. The last five years has seen at least a 50 per cent increase in property prices. But things are slowing down according to Mike Monkman from Languedoc Houses. 'Prices have levelled and sellers are more conservative in their expectations,' he says. A detached stone cottage to the north of the region will cost start at around €230,000. In fact this is where to look if you're looking for value for money. Prices go up dramatically closer the sea and the popular medieval town of Pézenas where a three-bedroom apartment will cost you around €140,000. There is a dearth of good quality property at reasonable prices; house-hunters are being shown modern bungalows for astronomical prices. Sadly the increase in property prices has led to a Riviera-style building boom and parts of the region have been wrecked by cheap housing and tacky theme parks. It is the world's biggest vineyard. The climate is Mediterranean and the way of life laid-back. It is one of the healthiest places in Europe to live due to lack of heavy industry and the diet which includes lots of fish, fresh fruit, olive oil and wine. The Languedoc is easy to get to nowadays, with the TGV from Paris to Montpellier. Airports include Montpellier, Nîmes, Perpignan and Carcassonne. The region's capital is Montpellier, also know as Paris by the sea. Chic, lots of culture and great shopping. What's not to like? This is a region for wine and sun lovers. Don't go there if you are mad about punctuality. No one will like you.

Limousin (Brit Alert: 5 Value Increase: 10)

If you're moving to get away from the cold, you need to head south. The south of France has a great ring to it. You could never imagine a bad day living there. It sounds so perfect and in many ways it is. There is plenty of sunshine, amazing countryside; from the rolling meadows of the southwest to the dramatic coastlines of the Mediterranean, olive groves, medieval villages and endless glasses of wine. I hadn't really travelled much in France until we thought about moving to France, and Limousin, in the southwest of the country, was one of the first places I got to know.

Some friends had bought a place there for £20,000. It seemed like a dream. No more mortgage. And they said it looks just like England did 50 years ago. Rolling hills, tall hedges, few houses. There didn't seem to be a downside, so we set off with Olivia (who was then six weeks old) to discover the region.

We left from Burgundy where we had been staying with my aunt and uncle. My aunt is Italian and my uncle is French. They have a house which belonged to his family and was the childhood home of his uncle, the photographer Henri Cartier-Bresson. It is the sort of house you imagine when you think about the French upper classes, lots of high ceilings and old furniture. The kitchen is basic, obviously built with servants in mind. All the beds are antique French. The average height of a French aristocrat must have been not much more than 5 foot 5 inches. I have to sleep diagonally in them. The house is in a medieval village called Noyers-sur-Sereine. The river runs about 100 yards from the house and there is an underground passage linking the two. My uncle's great-great aunt had a long-standing affair with the cardinal of Paris. He used to arrive from Paris by boat and sneak into her bedroom via the secret tunnel. The villagers never understood why this beautiful woman remained single throughout her life.

When he works, my uncle writes books about the history of art. My aunt does something intellectual with films. I had mooted the Limousin idea with them over lunch. We were eating, I recall, asparagus risotto. My aunt is a brilliant cook, and always travels with Italian risotto rice and parmesan.

'It's *la morte civile*,' she said. 'Civil death. There is nothing to do there and the locals are all less intelligent than the cow breed it's named after.'

My uncle nodded in agreement. 'Besides, nothing good ever came of moving somewhere named after cows,' he said.

We had arranged to meet our friends who lived in Limousin in a bar near where they lived. We arrived early in the evening after a long drive through stunning countryside, rolling hills and oak trees. They were right; it looks just like England. We parked the car outside the bar and walked in. As the door opened, a wave of stale smoke hit me. I buried my face in my shawl and clutched the sleeping Olivia closer to my chest. About four rough-looking locals looked up as we walked in.

I suddenly felt very self-conscious. It was a bit like walking into one of those pubs in Yorkshire where nobody talks. Instead, they just stare at you as if they're about to sacrifice you. As soon as our friends arrived, we left the bar. I decided against Limousin without seeing a single house.

The French call Limousin the place that God forgot. Generations have fled the land and sought a new life in the cities. There is even a French verb '*limoger*' which means to send someone to a God-forsaken place. But the Brits, who are mainly agnostic, have no such prejudices. They are beginning to discover the region. They love it for the peace, the countryside, the food and the lack of traffic.

The region is famous for two things; Limoges porcelain and Limousin cows. There are cows everywhere. It is an agricultural region which looks a little like Devon, with its lush green meadows and rolling hills. The roads are windy and single lane. It's just as well there are more cows than cars.

Limousin is made up of three *départements*: Creuse, Haute-Vienne and Corrèze. It has the Dordogne River running through it, rolling hills and even a few English shops. What it doesn't have is hordes of Brits and expensive properties. In fact it doesn't have hordes of anyone. There are only 42 inhabitants per square kilometre compared with an average across England of 376. And even though it is next door to the Dordogne, Limousin is still the cheapest region in France.

In the Corrèze, one of the three *départements* on Limousin, you can buy a three-bedroom house with a garden for €120,000. A farmhouse with some land will cost you €200,000. The problem will be finding one. 'Everyone is after the same thing,' says Melanie van der Meer, an estate agent with the Vallée de la Dordogne agency based in Argentat. 'The Brits all want a property that is old stone and isolated. I try to explain that even if the property is on a road there are unlikely to be many cars going past.'

David Lee moved to a small hamlet close to Beaulieu-sur-Dordogne just over a year ago. Originally from Lichfield in Staffordshire he decided to leave England because he was fed up with it. 'I was sick of the traffic, the vandalism, everything,' he says. 'One day some local kids set fire to the school and I just thought, that's enough.' He spent ten weeks looking all over France and chose Limousin because of the landscape, the fishing and the people. He bought a 200-square metre barn for €47,000 which he intends to convert and live in. The problem is finding the time to do it. 'I am a builder and now have enough work to keep me going for the next two years,' he says. 'I just can't take any more on.' David is living in a caravan next to the barn but moves in with his neighbours from Paris if it gets too cold. 'They are amazing,' he says. 'So hospitable and kind. In fact everyone has been great. I miss my family but I can't see myself going back.' He is planning to convert the barn into a three-bedroom house with an open plan downstairs using straw bails for walls. He will do all the work himself and estimates the materials will cost him around £35,000. 'It will take me about three years,' he says. 'But at the end of it an agent has told me it will be worth €200,000.'

Mike and March Fawcett have been in the region for five years. They bought a bed and breakfast in Beaulieu-sur-Dordogne for £76,000 in September 2000. 'It had been on the market for 18 months when we bought it,' says Mike, a retired Army major. 'I don't think that would be the case now. Everything seems to get snapped up.' They chose the region because it is easy to get back to the UK where they have children and grandchildren. 'I can't believe how undiscovered the region is,' says March. 'Even the French don't seem to know about it.'

But lots of Brits do and more soon will. There are now 14 flights a week to Limousin from the UK. Ryanair predicts that 300,000 Brits will be using the route and 10 per cent of them will be looking to buy property. Even the French press has noticed. *Le Monde* dubbed Limousin 'the new Provence'— not for its olive trees and warm climate, but because it its empty houses are slowly being occupied by Brits.

The new airport at Brive in the Corrèze due to be opened in 2007 is bound to attract one of the low-cost airlines. Brive is just the kind of city the Brits dream about when they think about moving to France. A beautiful old church, cobbled square, masses of shops and cafés with terraces. If you're looking for a property that is likely to increase in value, buy there now and wait for Ryanair to do the rest of the work. You can still pick up a farmhouse ten minutes outside town for around €200,000. 'The Corrèze is an area few people know about, especially compared to the ever popular, and now quite pricey Dordogne, which is right next door. Prices are still reasonable in many areas, but improvements to transport links may well push things up in the next few years—making it a good bet for those looking to buy in the next six months or so,' says David Frere-Smith from French Property Links.

The locals are not unaware of the possibility of cashing in, according to Enrico da Silva Cosme who runs Le Pays Vert estate agency. 'The variations in price can be enormous,' he says. 'The local population see the foreigners buying and so the prices go up. A barn that you could have bought very cheaply three years ago can suddenly cost you 40 per cent more. But it's worth looking around and comparing, some vendors may just be trying it on.'

Jill and Dennis Scorer bought their house in a hamlet above the idyllic village of Saint Merd-de-Lapleau last year. They decided to move to France because they couldn't afford to retire in the UK. They originally thought about moving to Tenerife but opted for France because the houses are cheaper and Dennis, a former long-distance lorry driver, speaks French. 'We looked all around south western France, but fell in love with this region and the people here,' says Jill. 'It is tranquil, beautiful and not over-populated with Brits.'

Jill and Dennis sold their three-bedroom house in Wiltshire for £235,000 and bought a three-bedroom stone farmhouse built in 1799 for €114,000 fully furnished. 'All we had to do was to buy a table,' says Jill. 'And put in double glazing and central heating. But even after we'd done all that we were still below our initial budget of €150,000.'

Jill and Dennis can't imagine ever going back to England. 'We're going back for a wedding in a few weeks' time and I'm dreading it,' says Dennis. 'It's the traffic and the speed of life that gets to me. Here at 5pm there are three cars that go by. That's our rush hour. My only regret is that we didn't do this 20 years ago.'

It is not only retirees that are moving to Limousin. In 2004, 37 Brits registered new businesses in the Haute-Vienne, to the west of the region. One of those is Kevin Marr who moved from Liverpool a year and a half ago. 'I was a plumber back home and didn't see any reason why I couldn't carry on with my trade in France,' he says. 'I work mainly for other Brits at the moment but as my French improves I think I'll get some French clients too.' Kevin moved with his wife and two children to a detached stone and brick cottage close to Bellac which they bought for €120,000. It has three bedrooms and 7000 square metres of land. They sold their terraced house in Liverpool for £215,000. 'We have no mortgage, some money in the bank and a nice life over here,' says Kevin. 'As far as I'm concerned it's a no-brainer.'

It seems he is not alone in thinking so. According to the local social security office there are already 2400 Brits registered in the Haute-Vienne, with another 40 joining every week. According to Anthony Jones from ABC Immobilier property prices are starting to reflect the increased interest. 'A small property to renovate in the Haute-Vienne or the Creuse which would have cost you between £10,000 and £15,000 four years ago will now cost between £30,000 and £45,000,' he says. 'It's simple supply and demand. The amount of people in the UK with that much equity on their homes is enormous so this is where we're seeing the biggest increase.'

There are grants to be had for people wanting to set up farms in the region (you can get more information from www.cr-limousin.fr) as the French government is trying to encourage people to move there.

Lot

What do you do when there are no more stone houses left to buy in the Dordogne? You go across the border to the Lot. The countryside is just as lovely; lush green hills and cliff-lined river valleys. It has plenty of fortified villages and castles, over 400 sites in the region are listed as of historical interest. The capital is Cahors, one of the most beautiful cities in France. And the best news is house prices are actually going down.

'I have just sold a farmhouse that was on the market for €280,000 for €225,000,' says Jean-Jacques Vidaller from Le Tuc Immobilier. 'My message to buyers is not to ignore properties that you think are outside your range as you may be able to negotiate.'

According to Vidaller the annual 15-20 per cent increase the Lot has seen in the last four years is due to English agents, not English buyers. 'They advertise properties in the UK at around 30 per cent more than they are on the market for here,' he says. 'French people see what the houses are selling for and want to get in on the act.'

Carl Schofield from Vilaex International agrees with him. 'The market has slowed down now and prices are back to reasonable levels after a steep rise in 2002,' he says. 'I have seen at least 50 properties with reductions of between 10 and 15 per cent over the past eight months.'

The Lot is not just attracting Brits from across the Channel, but from all over France. Jane Greenwood, an artist, moved to Montcuq from the Côte d'Azur a year and a half ago. 'I left my husband,' she says. 'And the removal man told me that all the women that leave their husbands in Provence end up in the Lot. I thought I may as well try it.' Jane had spent seven years in a village between Cannes and Gras. 'It was just getting wrecked,' she said. 'The fabulous light that all the artists went there for is still there, but Arcadia it is not.'

Jane has bought a small village house which needs doing up. It cost her €73,000 and she predicts she will spend that on it again. 'I'm going to try to limit myself to €50,000 but I probably won't be able to.' She says the most difficult thing about the renovation process has been getting the (male) artisans to do what she wants. 'They don't like being bossed about by a woman,' she says. 'So I hired a man to boss them about. The only problem is he keeps making mistakes.' Jane has rented a shop in the village where she sells fabrics, stencils and pictures. 'I just love it here,' she says. 'It's so pretty, I feel so lucky to be living in this little village surrounded by such beauty. My dream was always to paint landscapes and now within a ten-minute bike ride I can be at any number of stunning sites.'

John and Jane Parris moved to Lachapelle-Auzac in the northern Lot almost ten years ago from Normandy to start working on the then abandoned Souillac Golf Course. They bought an old stone farmhouse which overlooks the Dordogne Valley for £110,000. 'We love the way of life here,' says Jane. 'It is even more relaxed than Normandy. The only downside is it's hard to get a decent curry.'

According to Vidaller, the Lot is attracting a new kind of British buyer, who could go anywhere. 'We are seeing a new kind of Brit moving to the region who don't want to be in Provence,' he says. 'They are middle-class and upwards with serious money to spend. They are all looking for one thing—peace. I am even seeing French people move up from the coast.' They will be joining Brits that have already fallen in love with the rolling hills and benign climate, among them David Essex who lives in a Château south of Villeneuve sur Lot and his son who has a house in Penne d'Agenais. Paul McCartney has also holidayed in the popular village of Montcuq.

Joanna Bastin and her husband Charles, a retired investment banker, bought a house in the pretty medieval village of Tournon d'Agenais ten years ago. 'We had been been living in Monaco and could easily have opted for a retirement home on the Riviera,' says Joanna. 'But we have had a holiday home in the Lot since1989 and love it here. We love the food and the countryside. The people are great. There are a lot of people around one would have thought would have ended up in Provence plus a lot of overspill from the Dordogne.' The property, originally two houses, makes up part of the inner ramparts and dates from 1270. They paid £50,000 but have spent at least four times that on renovating it. The work took three years to complete. 'It was a complete pit,' says Joanna. 'We took nine dump-trucks of rubbish out before we could even begin work.'

The difficulties of renovating a property should not be underestimated according to Michael Groom a self-confessed 'renovation addict' who is on this third wreck in the region. 'People have no idea how difficult it is,' he says. 'And they end up in terrible trouble with shoddy workmanship, workmen not doing their job and so on. Renovating houses in France is not as cheap as people would like to believe.' Michael lives close to Montcuq and Lauzerte with his partner Lauren McMullen, a sports marketing consultant. 'We looked all over France but narrowed our search down to the Lot area and particularly what I call the Golden Triangle here in the Quercy Blanc with its pretty white stone houses,' says Michael. 'We love the peaceful, unspoiled, wooded countryside with its lovely hamlets and historic bastides. And we have excellent access to the Mediterranean, the Pyrenées, the Atlantic and several international airports. In fact I went back to England for a lunch a few weeks ago.'

The bought La Roque, an 18th century farmhouse in April 2003. It had been deserted since the First World War. Michael and Lauren have restored the house which now has three reception rooms, four bedrooms, five bathrooms and a heated saltwater swimming pool. It is set in 10 acres of land. The whole process took about 10 months. 'Michael was here full time,' says Lauren. 'It's just not possible to carry out a project like this if you're not. We've seen neighbours try to and the workmen just sit about all day, who can blame them?' They are now selling La Roque as Michael wants to move onto another project.

According to Carl Schofield, the Lot is attracting Brits looking for a career change and a new way of life. 'When I first moved here the demographic profile was more or less dead,' he says. 'We're now getting much younger people who are looking to integrate and work here.'

Sue and Mike Spring moved to France 11 years ago to run a wine business. 'We wanted to do something different,' says Mike a former manager in the computer software industry. 'We have always been interested in wine so a property with a vineyard was a natural choice.' They chose the Lot because it suited their aims. 'The vineyards we found in the Languedoc were just too big for us,' says Sue, who used to work in recruitment. 'Added to which we knew this region and liked it very much.' They looked for a suitable property for four years while learning French and attending courses in winemaking and vine-growing at Plumpton College of Agriculture. Eventually they found Domaine du Garinet just outside Le Boulvé which is half an hour from Cahors. They paid £160,000 for the two-bedroom house with 40 hectares of land, two and a half hectares of which is vines. They also have one and a quarter hectares of walnut trees and a plum orchard. Sue bakes cakes, shells walnuts, makes walnut oil and prepares prunes which they sell from the domaine and at the local market in Montcuq. Her fig and walnut cakes are particularly popular, as is her marmalade. 'I make 10,000 cakes a year,' she says. 'And during the Seville orange season I spend two solid weeks making marmalade.' The wine business is going well. Last year they produced 10,000 bottles of red (AOC Cahors), 1500 bottles of rosé and 6,000 bottles of white.

'We have no regrets,' says Sue. 'Although it is true that the business does occupy our time more than we had expected. We don't get much in the way of holidays or weekends.'

Midi-Pyrenées (Brit Alert: 7 Value Increase: 7)

The area around Toulouse has seen a dramatic rise in expat residents during the last ten years. When Jill Allcroft moved to a village there 12 years ago, there were only three British families within a 100 kilometre radius of her and she used to have to head home for her annual supply of Branston Pickle. Now there are four English families in her village alone, which only has a population of 300. 'In a way it was a good thing,' she says. 'It forced me to really integrate with the locals and learn French, there just weren't any English people to mix with. Now, that seems an odd thing to say, they're everywhere.'

Jill and her husband Richard stumbled across the area surrounding Toulouse by accident. They were living in Sheffield at the time, and Richard was working as an engineer in Buxton. 'There was an estate agent there who had links with a French agent in this region,' says Jill, who was working as a medical lab technician in a local hospital at the time. 'We came down, saw nine properties in a week and signed on the dotted line. We were in our 30s and decided that if we didn't do it then, we never would.'

Jill and Richard bought a 13th-century stone farmhouse with 45 acres of woodland and meadow near the village of Boussan in the Haute Garonne, south of Toulouse. They paid £55,000 and spent another £60,000 and four years doing it up. The original idea they had was to set up a caravan park, but they found the state restrictions too limiting. 'They seem to dictate everything,' she says. 'From the number of showers you have to have to how much you can charge. The figures just didn't add up.' Richard now has his own building business and Jill runs the farmhouse as a holiday let. She thinks there are several reasons the region has become so popular with the English.

'There are a lot of 50-somethings now who are inheriting money. They've paid off their mortgage and they don't see the point in putting it into stocks and shares. Toulouse is a very accessible city, as well as being very beautiful. It is also smaller than say Bordeaux, which I think is less imposing for people,' she says. 'For rentals it is very well placed for Spain and both coasts and there is no doubt the whole region has been boosted by the cheap airlines. We can now go straight from Newcastle to Toulouse. But I rarely go back. There's not really anything I miss and I can get Branston Pickle here now.'

Driving to Mike and Posy Fallowfield's house just outside Manent-Montané about an hour southwest of Toulouse is almost like driving around the Devon countryside they left behind. The hills are green and rolling. The Devon lanes have been replaced with straight, empty roads, but the skyline could be from Dulverton. Mike and Posy bought their deserted farmhouse in July 2002 for £83,000. They sold their farmhouse in Devon for £585,000. 'The original plan was to let the house and buy a ruin,' says Posy. 'But we couldn't make the money work.' They still ended up with what can only be described as just that, but on a grand scale. Their 17th-century farmhouse stands alone just outside the village. It has 360 degree uninterrupted views, to the south you can see the Pyrenées. The house is large and will eventually have four bedrooms, a study, two sitting rooms, kitchen and a dining room. The only hint of civilisation now among the rubble and dust is an Aga. 'When Mike said we were selling up and moving to France, I said over my dead body.' 'In the end I gave in, but my one stipulation was that we had to have an Aga.'

They moved into a caravan next to the house in March 2003. 'We thought we would be in the caravan for two or three months,' says Mike. 'We're still here and at least another month or so away from being able to move into just one room of the house.'

As with a lot of major property projects, Posy and Mike have found it has taken them much longer than they expected and cost them much more. In addition, Mike fell seriously ill last year and spent three weeks in hospital with a heart problem. 'There was one stage when I was sitting in the caravan, looking at the wreck of a house we had bought, thinking about Mike in hospital and wondering what on earth we had done,' says Posy. 'But we're through the worst now and I have to say the French hospitals were marvellous.'

They chose the region because an old university friend of Mike's lives close by. 'We looked at a lot of rubbish,' says Mike. 'At first we only had a budget of around £30,000 and were shown endless heaps of stones with brambles growing through them.' Once they decided to sell in England, they looked at a few more realistic options and finally settled on the farmhouse. 'We picked this place over the twenty or so others we looked at because the roof was sound and the walls were almost vertical and reasonably intact and we fell for the area,' says Posy. 'You should see some of the others we saw: several shells of farmhouses with collapsed roofs, pretty derelict and depressing, and they all seemed to have a concrete electricity pole right outside the front door. This one was at least lived in at one end!'

The region is easily accessible via several airports. The main and most international one is Toulouse. Depending on where you are outside the city, you have the choice of Bordeaux, Pau, Rodez, Castres, Bergerac and Carcassonne. The TGV line to Paris was recently completed, bringing the journey time down to just under five hours.

According to Kris Misselbrook, an estate agent with Aurignac Immobilier, prices have risen dramatically over the last four years. 'To buy a classic farmhouse, set in a hectare of land, in need of some work and with a barn, you're looking at least at €250,000. Four years ago you could find the same thing for less than half that. It has just snow-balled and I don't see it changing until the economy does.' Misselbrook says he is seeing a trend for people demanding properties at the lower end of the market in the region. 'At least half my enquiries are for properties for under €100,000. My response is well, I've got some nice ruins. For those willing to rebuild a property, there are some stunning timber-framed wrecks for around €85,000, but you'd have to spend at least another €100,000 doing them up.'

Helen Goossens moved to Nérac in the Lot and Garonne, an hour west of Toulouse, in 1993. She left her job as European marketing communications manager for Apple Computers when she discovered she had skin cancer. 'In the end it was nothing too worrying,' she says. 'But it made me realise that it was time to start living life rather than postponing it until my career was over. At the time I was working between 60 and 80 hours a week. So here I am, in my lock keeper's cottage on its own island with my four dogs and six cats.'

Helen found the 19th-century cottage by chance. She travelled a lot in her job and was always reading property magazines. 'I loved reading about houses for sale. One day I stumbled across an advertisement saying 'Are you a fisherman? If so, you will enjoy this lock keeper's cottage on an island.' I'm not a fisherman, but it sounded wonderful, so I called them.' A week later she had seen the cottage and fallen in love with it. 'It was in bad state and the brambles in the garden were taller than me, but I figured I could fix all that,' she says. She bought the cottage for £33,000 and then spent over double that doing it up.

She advises anyone thinking of moving to France to learn to speak French properly. 'It is very nice being part of the expat community,' she says. 'But it is so much nicer being part of the whole community and finding out about the region and the people. Also having the time to make real friends is wonderful.'

A chance meeting with a local clairvoyant gave Helen a new career. 'When she first came to my house, this practically illiterate woman started talking to me in Dutch, Polish, English and German, all languages my late husband spoke,' says Helen. 'I found the story of her life, the struggle to take herself seriously in the beginning, so fascinating that I wrote a book about it.' My friend Carla and I both had a reading with the clairvoyant. It was fascinating, although Carla's reading was much more exciting than mine. She is about to meet a charismatic man from the world of international commerce, while I am, apparently, entering a very calm and tranquil period of my life.

Normandy (Brit Alert: 10 Value Increase: 5)

Those of you who are not mad about the sun can look at the north of France. Northern France has long attracted Brits wanting holiday homes within easy reach. The most popular areas have traditionally been Pas-de-Calais, Normandy and Brittany. The downside here is that the climate is not so very different from England, albeit southern England, although the winters are probably a touch less severe and the summers more reliable. The prices up north are more affordable than down south and if you're looking for a wreck to do up for a modest amount of money, this is where to start.

In Britain, Normandy is renowned for its half-timbered houses, its Camembert cheese and its cider. In France, it is renowned as the home of Madame Bovary and the part of the country where the British live.

'Normandy is fabulous,' says Guillaume de Perthuis, whose family have had a *château* there since the time of William the Conqueror, 'but it is over-run with Britishers. They came in the Normandy landings in June 1944 and haven't gone home.' His mother, the Countess de Perthuis, says that she has fond memories of the Normandy landings, even though the English bombed much of her property. Nowadays she claims not to be bothered by the English buyers, but that is maybe because she spends most of her time in Paris. 'We seldom see English people in our part of Normandy,' says the Countess. 'Perhaps it is because we live in the plain of Caen and the English people stay closer to the coast.'

Normandy has traditionally been popular with the English because it is so near to England's shores. David and Imogen Gardener bought a house there two years ago for that very reason. 'We looked at houses in other parts of France,' says Imogen. 'But I guess psychologically we wanted to be near to England.'

Another major attraction in Normandy is the price of housing. Compared to the south of England, house prices in Normandy are still at least five times cheaper. The area is so large and diverse that prices can vary, but, roughly, you can buy a small cottage in the country for around £25,000; a larger house for £45,000; and a farmhouse with some land for £65,000. Areas closer to Paris are more expensive because of the number of Parisians who want a weekend home. The same price hike applies near the ferry ports, pushed up by English buyers who are prepared to come over every weekend and will pay a premium for less travelling time.

The Gardeners were working for the Caravan Club in East Grinstead when they decided that they wanted a change in lifestyle. 'We thought there must be more to life than working in East Grinstead and living in Eastbourne,' says Imogen. 'Then our employer offered us language classes.

To my surprise, I loved learning French. I nagged my husband that we should move to France, particularly when I looked on the internet and discovered that we could sell our four-bedroom estate house in Eastbourne for this fabulous Normandy long house.'

Their new house is set in two acres of land in la Ferté-Macé, a small village in Orne, one of the least populated *départements* in France. They sold the house in Eastbourne for £180,000. They paid £150,000 for the Normandy house, which includes two self-contained *gîtes* that they manage to rent out most of the year. 'We are never going to be rich, but we are very happy,' says Imogen. 'We are never going back.'

Like 70 per cent of the English buyers of property who are seeking a second home, Mary Davis and her husband James bought in Normandy simply because it is so easy to get backwards and forwards on the ferry. 'We can get from our home in Poole to our house just north of Granville in less than seven hours,' says Mary Davis. 'The longest part of the journey is the boat crossing from Poole to Cherbourg.'

She and her husband bought a farmhouse with another couple over 12 years ago. Seven hours may have been a good journey time 12 years ago, but now you can get from London to the Languedoc in less time, and instead of a chill breeze and a glass of cider you can be enjoying a *pastis* and the Mediterranean sun on your arrival. Nowadays, Ryanair flies from Stansted to Dinard, which will cut some journey times in half.

Unfortunately, no one is able to do anything about the weather. It is a topic that many people try to avoid when talking about Normandy. On the area's official website it only gives the average temperatures and rainfall for the months of March through to October, presumably on the basis that nobody in their right mind would want to stay there any other time. 'It is a shame,' says Imogen Gardener. 'Maybe if we move again, we will go further south.'

Mary Davis says that she would like to spend some time in their house in the winter months, but so far has not managed to pluck up the courage. 'I think it would be difficult in winter,' she says. 'We are quite isolated.'

There are a few English eccentrics who buy in Normandy because of the weather. 'I used to live in the south of France,' says Duncan Green. 'But July and August are too hot for an Englishman.' Green also enjoys the accessibility to England. 'I can get back to my father's home in Somerset in five hours door to door.'

The real attraction here is the escapism. Normandy is very peaceful. Even though it has one of France's most visited tourist sites, Mont St Michel, the coastline is less busy than Brittany's. Older people say that Normandy reminds them of the England of their childhood. Even house prices are about the same as they were in England in the 1950s.

'We paid £30,000 for our farmhouse,' says Mary Davis. 'We immediately invested £10,000 on renovation. We think the value of the house may have gone up a bit, but prices have not gone up anything like they have in England.'

Property experts warn English buyers not to expect much in the way of capital appreciation. There is so much property available that prices are increasing only very slowly. Duncan Green is in the process of selling a four-bedroom house with over an acre of garden with barns, for £80,000. 'Almost anywhere sensible in the south of England and the property would be worth £1 million,' he says.

He recommends the Manche as an area where there are still good rea-sonably priced houses for sale. If you go too far southeast you run into the large number of Parisians who are buying second homes. Most popular of all are the ritzy seaside resorts of Deauville and Trouville, where Parisians come to have fun at the weekend. Just a bit further west is Honfleur, built on the west bank of the Seine. The fishing boats may have gone but the town is full of charming five-storied houses, cobbled streets and the possibility of a cooked English breakfast at every café. 'The English discovered Honfleur a few years ago,' says de Perthuis. 'I feel a bit awkward speaking French there now.'

But you don't need to feel trapped in an English enclave. Even if you want to stay near the coast and have easy access to England, there is over 600 kilometres of coastline to choose from. Administratively Normandy is divid-ed into two rather confusingly named regions: Upper and Lower Normandy. Upper Normandy is the eastern part of the county and not the top part. It includes the *départements* of Seine-Maritime, with its white chalk cliffs and flat fields and Eure, which is full of forests and rivers. Lower Normandy to the west includes Calvados, the scene of the Normandy landings; Orne, home to farms and cider drinkers; and Manche, which is shaped like a thumb with Cherbourg on the tip of the nail.

The area known as Suisse Normande is between southern Calvados and northern Orne. It bears about as much resemblance to Switzerland as Little Venice does to its Italian namesake, but is still perhaps the most charming area for quality houses. This is where you will find many of the half-tim-bered houses made from oak and plaster. They blend into the landscape along with the cows, the trees, and the clouds.

Head even further south and the prices drop dramatically. Here you can buy a cottage that needs renovating for around £15,000. Andy Barr, 44, gave up his job as a criminal lawyer in Tottenham, London four years ago. 'I'd had enough,' he says. 'The work was terrible. One of my friends committed sui-cide, another is in prison and a third is snowed under with legal aid work. Enough was enough. We came to Normandy for a bit of peace and quiet. And we found it. I reckon the nearest night life is in Portsmouth.'

Andy now runs a website which introduces English buyers to properties in Normandy and the *département* to the south, Mayenne. 'Mayenne is good because it is cheaper and more quiet than Normandy,' he says. 'The other bonus is that if you tell people you live in Normandy they want to come and stay with you in the summer. Tell them you live in Mayenne and you'll never hear from them again.' A word of warning about the Mayenne. Some people who settled there a few years ago have had a terrible time, as have several of their friends. In some areas they are not used to foreigners and don't want to get used to them either.

Pays de la Loire (Brit Alert: 5 Value Increase: 7)

Nantes, the capital, is consistently voted the best place to live in France in the French media. It is close to the sea, dynamic and popular with culture vultures due to its many theatre companies. Angers on the Loire is one of the region's prettiest cities where you can sit at a bar in a cobbled street and watch the world go by. The Mayenne (one of the region's départements) has more châteaux per square mile than Paris but is not the welcoming place; some Brits living there say they feel discriminated against. The Vendée, with its 100 miles of sandy beaches is the most visited place in France (by the French) after Provence. Property prices vary; the Mayenne is cheap but the coast is expensive. 'On the coast a four-bedroom farmhouse will cost you around €200,000,' says John Evans from Eclipse Properties. 'Inland you're looking at closer to €150,000. Anything that is good quality is selling very quickly at the moment, there is a lot of demand.' The Pays de la Loire as a whole has been declared a World Heritage Site by UNESCO which calls it a 'cultural landscape of exceptional beauty'. The climate is a bit like Dorset, muggy and rainy but much warmer. This is a region for those who want to go somewhere different. Where you go in the region will depend on what kind of character you are. In cosmopolitan La Baule you can rub shoulders with glamorous Parisians. In the Mayenne you're more likely to rub shoulders with livestock.

Provence (Brit Alert: 10 Value Increase: 3)

This will not suit those of you moving to get away from Brits. It is positively crawling with them, but with good reason. The mixture of mountains and sea is stunning, the light is unrivalled and the night-life wild. Added to which the climate is fabulous. The downside is it will take you hours to get to the beach in the summer time and parts of it have become horribly built up. Prices are pretty steep. And if you're looking for the dream house on the beach at Cap d'Antibes, think again. 'It doesn't exist,' says Bruno Taxy, an agent with Emile Garcin who have offices in London and Provence. For just over €2 million you can buy a four bedroom fisherman's cottage close to the beach at St Tropez. Bruno concedes that properties on the Riviera are often overpriced. A similar property in the Lubéron would be half as much. The capital is Marseille, France's oldest city. The area around the old port is lovely and some of the cobbled back streets are worth exploring. But it's a pretty unromantic place trying to live down its reputation as the drugs capital of France. Aix-en-Provence is a better bet if you're after urban living in Provence. Nice and Cannes have little to recommend them bar shops and the beach, St Tropez is more charming.

Pyrenées

Head southeast from Bordeaux towards the Pyrenées and after three hours you arrive in what is almost a different country. Perpignan is often described as one of the most significant crossroads in France. It has an extraordinary mixture of cultures. It is Catalan, but in France and half an hour from Spain. It is close to the sea, but also to the Pyrenées, making it an ideal spot for ski enthusiasts. It is also only an hour from Toulouse, which gives it international access. There are also Ryanair flights to Rivesaltes, just outside the city.

It took 33-year old Alistair Norman just one weekend to decide to give up his job as a successful IT consultant for David Lloyd's Leisure group and his life in England. 'I saw the view from the terrace of the house,' he says. 'And just knew this was the place for me.'

He is talking about a four-bedroom village house in a village called Lapradelle Puilaurens, half an hour from Perpignan. He came across it by accident, literally. 'I was on a biking tour in the nearby mountains and one of the guys came off so we had to find somewhere to stop and have the bike mended. After I had got over the initial fear of how to explain things to his wife I looked around and realised I had landed in a small piece of paradise.'

Alistair looked at four properties and chose a village house with a magnificent terrace view for £47,000. The house is in the middle of a tiny village, opposite a river. To the right of his house is the old school building and, a little further along, a charming medieval church. Both buildings have bells—the school bell chimes before the church bell and the locals say the right time is somewhere in between the two.

Alistair has already started a company called Upright Tours, aimed at biking enthusiasts. He will organise biking holidays (motor and pushbike) in the region and sell them to clientele in the UK. 'I'll give it two years,' he says. 'If it doesn't work out, I'll come back. At least I will have learnt French and had a great two years away from a stressful job.' Alistair, originally from Exeter, has no worries about maintaining contact with the outside world. 'I'll do it all on the internet, we're just about to get ADSL here in the village. I can't even get that at home in Bradford.'

Margaret and James Hogan moved to Port Vendres on the coast outside Perpignan just over a year ago. Although Margaret is Scottish and James is Irish, they had spent most of their adult life living in London. 'The one thing we were worried about,' says Margaret, 'is that we would miss the theatre, concerts and cultural events. So we chose this region as it's close to

Barcelona, Montpellier and other big cities where we could go and find that sort of thing. What's been extraordinary is that since we moved to France we just haven't wanted to go anywhere.' They bought their village house, a two-bedroom apartment on three floors for £150,000.

'It is hard to find properties here, but it doesn't have a sea view which makes it less attractive to a lot of people,' says James, a writer. Margaret, who was an editor in London and is now taking some time out, says it's ideal for them. 'We have a floor each and one shared floor. There is a granny flat, which is still home to the previous owner's mother, but once she goes we have the option to buy that as well. If we do, it will be more of a house but as things stand, we are quite happy.'

They chose Port Vendres as opposed to the more known towns on the coast such as Collioure and Banyuls-sur-Mer because they wanted to live in a 'real place'. 'I hated the idea of somewhere that just came to life in the summer,' says James. 'Although we knew the region because we used to visit Collioure, it wasn't the sort of place we really wanted to live.' Margaret agrees. 'I really enjoy the day to day life here and even if it can sometimes get a bit much stopping and talking to everyone you meet, you can, if you need to, get the pleasantries over with very quickly. Actually, I'm rarely in a hurry, I am focusing on cultivating my pottering, and I don't mean making pots.'

Margaret and James say there is nothing they miss about England. 'I'm just sorry we weren't in a position to do this much sooner.'

Ian Scott is one person who made the move much earlier than the Hogans; he has been in the region for over 35 years. 'I had just finished art school and was working in an office. I had a house, a car and all that stuff. One day I just thought, hang on a minute; they want the rest of my life for all this. I decided to retire when I was 22. I thought the only people I see selling paintings successfully are old fools so I decided to leave it for a few years, although I kept painting.' He gave up his job as an assistant art editor at the Medici Society and hitchhiked around the world for two years. 'It was all going well until we hit the Sahara with just a tin of sardines and two hard-boiled eggs. It looked quite small on the map. Luckily the locals kept us alive and we managed to get across it.'

After that adventure there was no going back. 'I decided I wanted somewhere with a good climate and political stability. Ian bought a house in a mountainous village outside Perpignan called Llauro for £30,000 in 1974. 'With all its land and outbuildings it's probably worth closer to £250,000 now,' he says. Scott also has two galleries where he exhibits and sells his work. 'Now I'm an old fool and selling paintings. And unknown in four continents.' Ian, who is Scottish, says there is really nothing about Scotland he misses. 'I tend to go back to bury people and that's all,' he says. 'I went back to bury my mother a couple of years ago and found the place dreary.'

According to figures from a local estate agent, around 40 per cent of

Brits who come to the region decide to buy. Laurent Sillon, Sales Manager at JMB Immobilier in Perpignan, describes it as one of the most popular regions in France. 'They love it here,'he says. 'They love the fact that it is close to Spain, the mountains, the sea and that it is not too built up.' According to Sillon, prices have been rising dramatically but they are now stabilising. He says that for £75,000 you can still find a small village house in the villages outside the city itself and a three-bedroom apartment in Perpignan.

Rhône Valley

It is a fact universally acknowledged that Provence is full of Brits. Since the publication of the book A *Year in Provence*, and the subsequent TV series, thousands of them have moved down to buy the house and get the T-shirt. This has affected prices. A Provencal farmhouse will now start at around £450,000. In addition, many Brits feel they want to move to France to mingle with the French, not with their neighbours from Wiltshire. Some have gone further west, towards Toulouse, but there is a closer alternative. The Rhône Valley, which has long been popular with the Swiss and Germans, is now becoming the place to buy if you're a Brit with a budget for the south of France.

The region is relatively undiscovered by the Brits despite the fact that in some villages, such as La Bastide de Virac in the Ardèche, 40 per cent of the 220-strong population is foreign. 'They are German, Belgium and Swiss,' says Diana Little who has lived in the region for three years. 'It is very close to their borders and 30 per cent cheaper than Provence. The British are now starting to discover it.'

Figures from the tourist office back up the theory that Brits are becoming increasingly interested in buying properties in the region. In total around 500,000 British tourists visit the Rhône-Alpes region a year, 75 per cent of them come for the skiing.

'In 2005, for the first time ever, we are seeing more enquiries regarding property than real tourist enquiries. It is hardly surprising. There is so much to offer in the Rhône Valley; the hill-top villages reminiscent of Provence, the vineyards, the local products and heritage,' says Isabelle Faure, head of promotions to Great Britain for the Rhône-Alpes Tourist Board. 'I think all the low cost airlines have made a huge difference in terms of people buying here.'

The Rhône Valley stretches from Lyon to Marseille. If you travel that route today in your house search you will encounter fabulous food, legendary wines, beautiful hilltop villages and dramatic gorges on your way. Any one of the places you pass would be a lovely place to live.

Lyon is where your journey begins. Founded by Julius Caeser in 43 BC, it is France's second city. It has a population of nearly one and half million and a rich cultural heritage as well as being an important industrial and commercial base. Lyon is packed full of important museums and has recently become famous for its painted walls, which are not graffiti but murals celebrating life there. There are 80 walls with various themes throughout the city ranging from the history of cinema to gastronomy, another very important aspect of life in Lyon. Known as the gastronomic capital of France, Lyon is home to 1,200 restaurants serving the best of Lyonnaise cuisine including the local quenelles and *andouillettes* (small tripe sausages). A visit to a concert at the Roman amphitheatre is a must. When you tire of city life, there are several nature reserves within easy reach of Lyon. Just an hour away is the Pilat Nature Reserve where you can go riding or mountain biking. An apartment in the heart of the city will cost you between €70,000 and €100,000. A house four bedroom in the suburbs around €120,000.

Montélimar further down marks the beginning of the Drôme region. The Drôme and the Ardèche are the two most popular regions in with Brits in the whole valley; mainly due to their beauty. The Drôme is home to three of the 100 most beautiful villages in France; Garde Adhémar, Poët-Laval and Montbrun les Baines. Garde Adhémar is one of the most instantly recognisable symbols of the Rhône Valley skyline with its highly placed church with octagonal bell tower.

The Ardèche region is on the other side of the river from the Drôme. Here the Ardèche river has created some of the most dramatic landscapes in the whole of France. The Arc Bridge for example is a bridge on the banks of the Ardèche river carved out by the flowing water below. The Chauvet Grotto, discovered in 1994, and the Ray Pic Waterfall are just some of its other attractions. The Monts d'Ardèche Nature Reserve was created in 2001 and is home to some of the most stunning sights in the region.

If you continue to follow the winding river down towards Marseille, you will come across names that are familiar to wine drinkers everywhere. Gigondas, Vacqueyras and Châteauneuf-du-Pape. The valley is home to around 10,000 wine makers, producing mainly red full bodied wines under the Côte de Rhône wine appellation.

As you would expect for the south of France, prices are not giveaway. Therese Panella, an estate agent with Barjac Immobilier, says some Brits have been put off the region by the prices. 'I had an English family here that were looking for the old stone house, the usual thing the English want,' she says. 'They spent six months looking but in the end had to rethink and go over to a region closer to Toulouse. They could find nothing and that was with a budget of €400,000.' Therese says that apart from the introduction of the euro which immediately put prices up by 25 per cent for the UK buyer, the prices have gone up dramatically due to supply and demand. 'If you're looking for the ruin to do up, forget it,' she says. 'It just doesn't exist any more. They were all sold off to the first wave of foreigners that came along.' Another downside is the wind, the mistral, which flies down the Rhône

Valley at incredible speeds.

You will pay more than €400,000 for a four bedroom old stone farmhouse with a garden in the region. A small town house will set you back around €140,000. 'We get mainly arty Brits, writers or painters down here,' says Therese. 'I think the region suits their temperament.' One English writer with a home there is Geraldene Holt who has written several cookery books and has a herb garden that is open to the public at her home in Saint-Montan.

You end your journey at Marseille, one of the most vibrant and exciting cities in the whole of Europe. The old port is a perfect place for a long lunch after your journey through the Rhône Valley. If you're looking for a city location, Marseille is the ideal place to live; a sunny climate, excellent travel connections and plenty to see and do.

Transport to the Rhône Valley is easy. There are plenty of airports along the coast such as Marseille and Nice. Further north you have Easyjet connections from London to Lyon and Geneva as well as Grenoble. Ryanair flies from London to St Etienne which it calls Lyon on its website but it is in fact 63 kilometres from Lyon. Ryanair also flies to Nîmes. During the winter months you can go Flybe from Southampton and Birmingham to Chambéry/Aix and Thomsonfly from Coventry to Lyon. If you fly to Paris you can take the TGV to Lyon, a journey time of two hours. There is also a TGV to Nîmes and Marseille, journey time is around three hours.

Diana Little has known the Ardèche in the Rhône Valley since she was first married 20 years ago. 'My husband is a geography teacher,' she says. 'And he used to come here on study trips. When we were first married he said that one day we would live here.' Diana's husband Jos is Belgium and so they lived in Brussels for several years, but visited the region regularly on family holidays. 'A few years ago we started to think about coming to live here full time and then a whole series of events contrived to make us do it. My father died when he was 46 and I turned 46. That year I lost three members of my family and I suddenly thought I've got to get on with it if I'm going to do anything different. My advice to anyone is life is short and if you want to do something, don't put it off until tomorrow.'

Diana and Jos found a 15th century silkworm farm that had been converted into bed and breakfast accommodation. It is in the village of La Bastide de Virac, close to the Vallon Pont d'Arc, the beginning of the Ardèche tourist route. 'The views are magnificent,' says Diana. 'We have some of the largest gorges in Europe with panoramic balconies and wonderful opportunities for walks and canoeing.'

They paid over €500,000 for their house which includes six bed and breakfast rooms with en suite bathrooms, private quarters and a vast almost medieval-style dining room. The previous owners had struggled with the business for a few years beforehand so they needed to do quite a lot of work to it.

'I would warn people looking to buy in France that when the French renovate properties they don't always do so to the best possible standards,' says Diana. 'We had terrible problems with electricity and fuses blowing as well as the gas pipes which hadn't been put in correctly.' In addition one of the first things they had to do was to replace the roof at a cost of about €30,000. 'We knew it wasn't in good shape,' says Diana. 'But we didn't think we would have to replace it so early on.' Diana says that although the workmen in the region are professional, they take much longer on a job than is necessary. 'They show up at 8.30 and then even if they have a whole tank of newly mixed cement they drop everything at 12. Then they have to have their siesta so they're not back until 2.30 if you're lucky. Then they go away and the next day they don't show up at all and you find them working down the road on another house.' Diana says the roof took weeks and weeks to complete when it could have been done in one. They also replaced the kitchen which took them three months. 'It's very frustrating, you're living in chaos for much longer than you need to,' she says.

Despite the drawbacks they have no regrets. 'I worked in marketing for 27 years and I suddenly thought, there's got to be more to life than this. There is and it's here in the Ardèche.'

The Best
of the French Coast

The French coast runs for some 5,500 kilometres. The landscape is incredibly varied; there are the sandy beaches of the Languedoc, the rocky shores of Normandy and Brittany, the cliffs of the Riviera and the marshes of the Camargue. Each region has its own traditions, climate, food and culture. To help you choose the right spot for you, I have compiled a guide to the best of the French coast. I start with the North (Bordeaux and up).

La Rochelle

Brits have been buying in the countryside around La Rochelle for years, but they are just starting to discover the city itself. 'The property market in La Rochelle has really taken off since Ryanair started flying there and we are seeing much more interest from Brits than we did a few years ago,' says Langton Highton from the Agence des Iles agency (www.agencedesilesatlantique.com). 'Prices went through a dramatic increase up until around a year ago but look to be stabilising now. For €150,000 you can buy a two-bedroom apartment in the centre of town, and for between €250,000 and €300,000 a villa with a garden.' Flybe has just started flying from Bristol as well.

Weather	7
Accessibility	7
Property Prices	8
Food	7
Scope for value increases	8
Sports	8
Culture	6
Scenic beauty	8
Quality of housing	8
Brit-alert	6

The old port with its medieval twin towers and moored yachts is a heavenly place to stroll around or stop for a coffee. La Rochelle also has the added advantage of being a short drive to the Ile de Ré which is as close to heaven on earth as it is possible to find. Another advantage is that Craig Dennis, masseur to celebrities like Sharon Stone and Jody Foster, has a house in La Rochelle and for a small fee will make you feel like a film star.

Noirmutier

Between La Rochelle and the island of Noirmutier in the Vendée region there isn't much to recommend. The most famous place is les Sables d'Olonne, but sadly this is now just an example of how a coastal town can be wrecked. The main square is rather lovely but the seafront is now so full of modern horrors it's hard to see beyond them and enjoy the splendid beach. It is twinned with Worthing and I think I'd rather go

Weather	7
Accessibility	7
Property Prices	7
Food	7
Scope for value increases	8
Sports	8
Culture	5
Scenic beauty	8
Quality of housing	8
Brit-alert	1

there. Luckily for the inhabitants of Noirmoutier there have been stricter building regulations in place here. The island is idyllic; there is no other word for it. There are two styles of classic Noirmoutier house. One is white-washed with a pink tiled roof, reminiscent of properties in Greece. The other is old stone houses built in the 19th or 20th centuries. Land will cost you €150 per square metre and an old stone house anywhere near Le Bois de la Chaize, the chicest spot on the island, start at €1.5 million. Brits are a rarity. 'I've rarely seen an English person on the island,' says Alexandra Mas whose family has owned a house on the island for the last 40 years. When her grandparents bought the house you could only get to the island by driving there during low tide. Now there is a bridge. The closest airport is Nantes.

Ploumanac'h

This is just what you expect from the pink granite coast in Brittany; wild flowers, wild sea, rocky outposts and dramatic landscape. Ploumanac'h is as good as it gets. Access is easiest by helicopter but failing that you can get the boat from nearby Roscoff to Plymouth. Airports within driving distance include Rennes and Brest. 'Prices in Brittany have risen by 30 per cent over the last three years,' says Chris Slade who runs

Weather	6
Accessibility	5
Property Prices	8
Food	7
Scope for value increases	8
Sports	8
Culture	6
Scenic beauty	9
Quality of housing	8
Brit-alert	1

the website www.ahouseinbrittany.com. 'Far fewer people are now expecting to find something for €25,000.' Just as well. In Ploumanac'h there is nothing you could expect to live in for less than €100,000. The website www.immofrance.com has a four-bedroom property for sale without a sea view for €467,250.

Dinard

Brits have been holidaying in Dinard for more than 100 years. In fact, judging by the amount of old people's homes in the town, that's about the average age of the inhabitants. This is everything you expect from a genteel seaside town. The buildings are solid and attractive, the beach clean and picturesque, the beach huts striped and the grass is groomed. Everything in Dinard seems to be under control, even the boats bob the same way.

Weather	6
Accessibility	7
Property Prices	4
Food	7
Scope for value increases	5
Sports	7
Culture	7
Scenic beauty	9
Quality of housing	8
Brit-alert	6

There are four flowers on the Ville Fleurie sign that greets you. Only 161 towns in France have achieved this maximum accolade. Property is expensive. According to John Orset from the estate agency Guy Hoquet a two-bedroom apartment with a sea view will cost you between €350,000 and €450,000. A villa with a sea-view is anywhere from €1 million. 'But we don't have many Brits buying here any more,' he says. 'They prefer the south-west and the south where there is plenty of sunshine.'

St Malô

St Malô is one of France's most popular tourist destination in Brittany but if you own a home here and visit off season you can enjoy everything it is famous for. This includes the walled city which reminds me of a Victorian infirmary but somehow remains charming and endless beaches with sand and rocks for children to climb all over. The light and views are superb. Houses don't come cheap. The Brits have been

Weather	6
Accessibility	9
Property Prices	4
Food	7
Scope for value increases	5
Sports	8
Culture	8
Scenic beauty	9
Quality of housing	8
Brit-alert	8

buying here for too long. 'An apartment within the city walls with a sea view will cost you around €5,000 per square metre,' says Jean-Francois Fontou from the St Malo-based Hery Immobilier. 'We have just sold a property to some Brits in the centre of Saint-Servan, which is a few minutes walk from St Malo, but really the Brits we see are looking for the countryside more than the coast.'

That may be so, but there is evidence of the British presence all around; some signs offer English breakfast, most of the restaurants have menus in English and there is even a decent curry house.

Cancale

One of the most charming drives in France is the back road that takes you from St Malo to Cancale. There is a view of the sea almost all the way, as well as sweeping green fields, forests and sandy dunes. Cancale is a lively sea-port, famous within France for its oysters. It has been classified a 'Site

Remarquable du Goût' by the Conseil National des Arts Culinaires. This is a place to come if you like seafood.

The demand for property here is more from the locals so it has an authentic feel to it. Prices are around 20 per cent less than in neighbouring St Malo. 'An apartment with a sea-view will cost you around €4,500 per square metre,' says Benoit Jacquet from the Blot Immobilier in Cancales. 'A small house in the centre of town without a sea view starts at €200,000. But there is much less interest here from Brits than in St Malô or Dinard.'

Weather	6
Accessibility	7
Property Prices	7
Food	9
Scope for value increases	7
Sports	7
Culture	7
Scenic beauty	8
Quality of housing	8
Brit-alert	4

Montmartin-sur-Mer

The Normandy coastline stretches eastwards for 375 miles from Mont Saint Michel to the resort of Le Tréport. The first gem along this stretch of France is Montmartin-sur-Mer, a protected town which has yet to be discovered by the masses, even in summertime. The houses are made from local Normandy stone and prices are reasonable. The Cabinet Folliot agency recently sold a large farmhouse for €500,000. 'It's a lovely spot and totally unspoilt,' says Sue Young who runs the website www.yournormandyhome.com. 'This is a place for people who appreciate the natural beauty of Normandy and also like somewhere that is very family-oriented. The beaches here are very safe.'

Weather	6
Accessibility	7
Property Prices	8
Food	7
Scope for value increases	8
Sports	7
Culture	6
Scenic beauty	8
Quality of housing	8
Brit-alert	4

Access to Montmartin is possible via boat, train or plane. Cherbourg is a short drive away as are Coutances and Granville where you can catch a train. The closest large airport is Rennes.

Barfleur

Barfleur is said to be the prettiest village in France. I haven't been to all of them so can't confirm this, but it is stunning and certainly up there among the best I've seen. This historical fishing village at the end of the Cotentin peninsula with its grey granite houses and slate roofs has an active fishing port that lends it an air of authenticity other seaside resorts lack. It was the favourite port of the nobles after 1066 as they travelled back and forth between the two countries. Properties come up

Weather	6
Accessibility	8
Property Prices	8
Food	7
Scope for value increases	8
Sports	7
Culture	6
Scenic beauty	8
Quality of housing	8
Brit-alert	4

rarely in the main village and when they do normally get snapped up very quickly.

Karen La Rosa who works for the Agence Gimazane Immobilier in Barfleur says the last property she sold on the port was to some Brits and it went within 48 hours. 'I could have sold it a dozen times,' she says. 'It was a semi-detached property with three bedrooms which went for €230,000 two years ago.' Prices have increased by around 16 per cent over the last two years according to La Rosa who has a property on her books now 50 yards from the port with three bedrooms for €300,000. 'But I don't expect it will be sitting around for long,' she says.

Access to Barfleur is extremely easy if you live in Poole or Portsmouth as Cherbourg is half an hour's drive. From the end of May Flybe will fly to Cherbourg times a week from Southampton.

St Tropez

No investigation of the French coast would be complete without St Tropez where Brigitte Bardot pranced on the beach in a bikini and a legend was born. Despite the fact that it is the most famous place on the French coast, St Tropez retains some of its old style charm. Unlike other Riviera towns, it still has a village feel to it in parts. According to Bernard Desterac from the estate agency Goldo International

Weather	8
Accessibility	7
Property Prices	1
Food	8
Scope for value increases	4
Sports	8
Culture	4
Scenic beauty	8
Quality of housing	7
Brit-alert	7

prices have increased dramatically in and around St Tropez since 1998 when the pound was at its strongest against the franc. 'It was the arrival of British people which originally pushed the prices up,' he says. 'We have seen increases of as much as six times in some areas within seven years. Now of course the prices are being sustained by a Russian clientele.' Basic villas in or around St Tropez start at €2 million. If you want a place on the water's edge you'll pay between €10 and €20 million.

Sanary-Sur-Mer

Sanary-Sur-Mer probably hasn't changed that much since writers Sybille Bedford and Aldous Huxley hung out there in the 1930s. It has escaped much of the British influx to France as it was traditionally a town full of Germans. Not of the 'first on the sun-lounger' type, but the literary kind. During Hitler's ascent, Sanary was the capital of German literature in exile. It is extremely accessible, just off the motorway and

Weather	8
Accessibility	9
Property Prices	4
Food	8
Scope for value increases	6
Sports	7
Culture	7
Scenic beauty	8
Quality of housing	7
Brit-alert	1

within easy reach of airports at Marseille, Toulon and Nice. According to Christian Gambarutti who runs the Agence Gambarutti in Sanary the Brits prefer to be in British ghettos like Le Lavandou, a few miles up the road towards St Tropez. 'The handful that has bought here has chosen properties around the expensive area of Portisol,' he says. 'It's very pretty but if you buy on the wrong side you can't open your windows when the mistral is in full force.' A decent sized house in Sanary will cost you around £500,000. A small apartment with a sea view will start at £200,000. It is not a cheap place to buy property but in my opinion it is the most charming and unspoilt town on the French coast. Though like anywhere in Provence, it is best avoided in August.

Cassis

Cassis, or Cassi as the locals pronounce it, is almost as charming as Sanary and shares, according to a local restaurateur, a great literary tradition. 'We have lots of intellectuals here,' he told me. 'Joanna Trollope for example.' Moving swiftly on, Cassis has one big disadvantage. Rather like St Tropez, you can only get reach it from one tiny windy road, so getting to and from town during July and August becomes difficult

Weather	8
Accessibility	6
Property Prices	4
Food	8
Scope for value increases	8
Sports	7
Culture	7
Scenic beauty	8
Quality of housing	7
Brit-alert ('intellectuals')	4

without a helicopter. But it has the same charming old-style port as Sanary (bar the horrible tourist information office which one wonders how they ever got permission to build). Traditional fishing boats mix with the luxury yachts and the waves crash against the lighthouse. Prices are a little less than Sanary due to the road issue. Villas in and around Cassis start at around £400,000, an apartment in town with a sea view will set you back around £150,000.

Sète

Thierry Cazin who runs the Abessan estate agency in the Languedoc, says the coastal town of Sète in the Languedoc is as good an investment as you're likely to find on the French coast. 'It is easily accessible, only 25 minutes from Montpellier airport, has a very pretty centre and sandy beaches, it is perfect for second home owners,' he says. Sète is France's principal fishing port on the Mediterranean so if it is an

Weather	8
Accessibility	8
Property Prices	6
Food	8
Scope for value increases	6
Sports	7
Culture	5
Scenic beauty	7
Quality of housing	7
Brit-alert	7

authentic town you're looking for, this could be it. There is nothing poncy about Sète. It is not as picture perfect as Sanary or Cassis, but it is has a rustic charm which rubs off on most visitors. Locals call it the Venice of the Languedoc, which is an exaggeration, even if there is plenty of water. The best place to buy in Sète is on the Mont Saint-Clair which rises 183 metres above the town with views towards the Mediterranean, the Pyrenees, the Cevennes and the Thau lagoon. Property prices on the peak are around 20 per cent higher than they are in the town. Cazin has a five-bedroom villa for sale with a living space of 210 square metres and a garden of over 2000 square metres for £555,000. Agde and Cap d'Agde are other coastal towns in the Languedoc. They should be avoided. Unless you like house hunting in the nude, in which case head for the nudist colony at Cap d'Agde where you can pick up a small apartment for less than €80,000, among other things.

Marseillan Ville

Just down the road from Sète is Marseillan Ville. It looks like St Tropez probably looked before Brigitte Bardot decided to grace the beach there. It is staggeringly pretty, with one of the most unspoiled ports in France. You can while away many an afternoon at the Château du Port restaurant, drinking wine and watching the boats go by. Do not confuse it with Marseillan Plage, which is worse than Margate. There is a beauti-

Weather	8
Accessibility	7
Property Prices	8
Food	8
Scope for value increases	8
Sports	7
Culture	6
Scenic beauty	8
Quality of housing	7
Brit-alert	8

ful stretch of beach that goes on for seven kilometres, all the way to Sète. Marseillan is extremely easy to get to as its only 40 minutes away from Montpellier airport. There is also a nearby TGV station at Agde. 'It's the perfect place to buy a holiday home,' says Alex Charles who runs www.creme-de-languedoc, a website dedicated to the region. 'And with effective marketing you can easily rent property out. Expect to pay around €160,000 for a two-bedroom apartment and €200,000 for a three-bedroom villa.'

Collioure

Collioure in French Catalonia is known as the city of painters and attracted some of the best, including Matisse who invented modern painting there in 1907. There is evidence of painters all around; from the romantic Les Templiers bar and hotel where painters exchange their goods for beer to the Fauvism walk along the coast. Collioure is relatively easy to get to, with regular flights to Perpignan and Gerona just over the border in Spain. 'The Collioure real estate market remains bouyant with a strong

Weather	8
Accessibility	7
Property Prices	7
Food	7
Scope for value increases	6
Sports	5
Culture	7
Scenic beauty	8
Quality of housing	7
Brit-alert	7

demand for correctly priced properties, ' says Neil Hitchen from the property website www.colliourepoperty.com. ?Demand is truly international with French , Scandanavian , Irish and of course British buyers. Prices start at around €120,000 for a studio and from €150,000 for a one-bedroom flat. You'll pay around €230,000 for a two-bedroom flat with garden in the old town. '

Biarritz and St Jean-de-Luz

Old world charm and exclusive designer shops meet in Biarritz to create a luxurious and cosmopolitan environment which is reflected in the property prices. Apartments in town with a sea view start at €6,000 a square metre. A small modern house without a sea view that needs renovating will cost you at least £250,000. But Biarritz is expensive with good reason. It is a magnificent town, reminiscent of a grander ver-

Weather	7
Accessibility	9
Property Prices	2
Food	8
Scope for value increases	3
Sports	10
Culture	8
Scenic beauty	8
Quality of housing	9
Brit-alert	6

sion of Brighton in the nineteenth century with glorious buildings and grand walkways. The Atlantic Ocean crashes onto the beach in the middle of town and you can watch the surfers do battle with the waves from any number of bars along the front. 'I get a lot of clients from London,' says Julia Troccaz, who runs a property website called www.beyondbiarritz.com. 'They are mainly outdoor types who come here for the surfing, golf and skiing.' If you can't afford a house within sound of the surf go half an hour inland where property is half the price. Alternatively rent room 702 in the Hotel Windsor and go for the weekend. It is a basic room but the view is one of the best along the French coast.

A few miles down the road is St Jean-de-Luz. With its half-timbered chalet-style houses it looks like a ski resort that's been washed up on the beach. There is a horseshoe-shaped bay where the water is calmer than in Biarritz so better for children. Much of the centre of town is pedestrianised and the streets are lined with plane trees that provide shade in the summer. Property prices are not much lower than in neighbouring Biarritz.

Arcachon

If you like sandy beaches this is the place for you. Head for the highest sand dune in Europe the Dune de Pyla. On a windy day as you clamber up to the top you can feel like an extra in Lawrence of Arabia. The view from the peak is breathtaking. Some property in Arcachon is marginally less expensive than it is in Biarritz. Possibly because you don't have designer shops or the crashing

Weather	7
Accessibility	7
Property Prices	7
Food	8
Scope for value increases	6
Sports	9
Culture	5
Scenic beauty	7
Quality of housing	8
Brit-alert	5

waves of the Atlantic as it is on an oyster-shaped bay. But it has plenty to recommend it. A beach in the middle of town, two piers and plenty of good restaurants. Villas in and around the town start at €450,000 for a 100 square metres of living space with little or practically no garden. For a large house with a sea view you're going to pay at least €1 million. According to Caroline Berg at CBI Immobilier prices have been rising steadily for the past six years and will continue to do so. 'People are prepared to pay almost anything for the right property,' she says. She says there is increasing interest from Brits in the Atlantic coast of France. 'They used to buy old farms inland, but now they're beginning to be interested in the coast.' Some people will suggest you head for Hossegor, down the coast towards Biarritz for the great outdoors. Don't. It is an ugly little place with a beach surrounded by housing estates. The surf may be great, but for most people that's not enough. Although I guess if you spend most of the day with your head under water it's immaterial what your surroundings look like.

For those of you looking for a property with a difference, why not try Cap d'Agde, Europe's largest nudist colony. Every summer around 250,000 people descend on the grim concrete holiday village for the sole purpose of getting their kit off. When I heard it was a mere half an hour away from my house, I felt it my duty to investigate.

I enjoy a skinny dip as much as the next person, but if there's anything likely to put you off nudism for the rest of your life, it's a visit to Cap d'Agde. The whole place is crawling with bodies that saw better days in the 1950s. I run across Barbara and Henry from Staffordshire on the beach. Now they are, putting it kindly, edging towards advanced middle age. But compared with some of the specimens on display they look like Greek gods.

'I'm really not mad about it,' says Barbara. 'But Henry likes it here. This is the third time we've been.'

'I love the freedom,' says Henry, carefully shielding his private parts with a copy of the Daily Mail. 'I went to my first naturist beach when I was 20 and have been hooked ever since.' He admits their friends and family don't know they come here.

Richard, who prefers not to give his last name, bought an apartment six years ago for £54,000. 'It has two bedrooms, a sitting room and a dining room, but you can sleep six,' he says. 'I live here full time but am not as dedicated as some of the other naturists who walk around naked when it's minus two outside.'

Property in Cap d'Agde is cheap and the rental market thriving. You can pick up a studio which sleeps six with a view of the beach (naked oldies included) for €148,000. This can be rented out for around €900 a week during the high season. According to Philippe at Agence René Oltra, there is always rental demand. 'There are more and more English coming here,' he says. 'They love the sea, the light and the freedom. If you have a nice studio with a view of the sea you will always be able to rent it out.'

Some Brits who own property have got over the delicate issue of housing non-naturist relatives by buying an apartment outside the compound as well as inside. Graham and Sheila from Hampshire have two holiday homes here. 'We come down with all the family for three weeks in July,' says Sheila. 'Some of them prefer the non-nudist beaches so they stay in our apartment in the actual town. We rent them both out through an agency the rest of the time and the whole thing more than pays for itself.'

Those who have bought outside the naturist compound are keen to stress that Cap d'Agde has much to offer apart from sun-tanned bottoms. 'It is a lovely resort to visit all year round, full of oleander and palm trees,' says Sheryl Simmons who bought a property on the Richelieu beach earlier this year with her husband Bob. 'Our apartment is only a short walk from the international golf course.'

The only people who are allowed to keep their clothes on the naturist village are the workers. In the post office I meet Stéphanie, Pierre and Carol. Pierre was working in a post office up north but was told it was either relocate to Cap d'Agde or go on the dole. 'I chose Cap d'Agde, although I tried to tell them I was very shy and upset by nudity,' he says grinning broadly. Carol says in the five years she has been there she has only seen one good-looking man. 'Luckily the counter is quite high,' she says. 'Even though I grew up in Cap d'Agde I find it all a bit much.' Stéphanie says the black men are usually better looking. 'The average age here is about 55,' she says. 'At first I found it terribly off-putting, but you get used to it pretty quickly.'

I wander around the beach fully clothed looking for naked people to chat to. I am constantly aware that I am breaking one of the laws of the village. 'Total nudism is obligatory within the village and on the beach, as soon as climatic conditions permit it,' say the regulations. Feeling horribly conspicuous I retreat to the first aid tent. I meet Jean-Louis, a lifeguard. He has worked on the beach for five years and would not look out of place in Baywatch. He tells me he deals mainly with sunburn. I am tempted to ask him where the sore spots are. He expertly puts a plaster on a blister I have got from wandering around all day. Maybe that's why no one wears shoes. As I leave he smiles charmingly. Typical. The only man I would like to have seen naked is fully clothed.

Buying Tips

When I moved to France I spoke no French, knew little about the county I was moving to and had no guarantee of an income. Looking back on it, I must have been deranged. Any number of things could have gone horribly wrong. Would I do it differently if I did it again? You bet. Here are ten top tips for a successful move:

1. Accessibility
If you are not going to move to France full time you need to think seriously about how you are going to get backwards and forwards, as well as how your tenants are going to get to your house if you're thinking of letting it out. Beware of buying a property close to a small airport where only one discount airline operates. What happens if it goes bust? Try to find somewhere with several options. The ideal is a mixture of a small airport, the TGV and an international airport not more than an hour's drive away. Being in the middle of nowhere is all very lovely, but not when it's a fifteen hour car journey from London.

2. Visit the Mairie
Before you buy, go the local mayor's office and ask questions about the property and surrounding area. You do not want to arrive with all your belongings three months later to find a wind farm in your back garden. There will be plans of the house and countryside around which will show if the land is constructible or not and the mayor's office will also be aware of any major projects in the pipeline. They are not, however, under any legal obligation to tell you, so you may want to ask around as well. In the countryside, wind farms and rubbish dumps (*déchetterie*) are the main worries, along with major roads and airports of course.

3. Paperwork
Photocopy every bit of official-looking paper you have at least ten times

before you move. Get copies of your birth certificate with your parents on it as well (I am not joking). Get marriage certificates, national health cards and birth certificates for you and your children translated by an officially approved translator (you can get a list from the French consulate). I found in my struggle to get onto the French system that shoving bits of stamped and official looking paper under people's noses worked better than anything else.

Location, location, location

George and Tina bought a crumbling manor house in the middle of nowhere outside a village called Grazay in the Mayenne (Pays de la Loire). They picked it up for hardly any money and did it up themselves. George is a builder. They worked on it for almost two years, and spent their life savings on it. Once the work and their savings were finished, they decided to try and find jobs. George went all over the region, dropping off leaflets and talking to people. No one wanted to employ him. Tina was a hairdresser in the UK, but as she speaks hardly any French she couldn't get work here. Finally, George went to Spain where he got work through a friend, and Tina went back to England, where she is living with her mother. The house is up for sale but they have had to drop the price dramatically. 'It's just not the sort of region where anyone is going to spend €350,000 on a house, even if it is beautifully done up and has ten bedrooms,' says George. 'We really didn't think it through. I never imagined I wouldn't be able to get work. I have to say I feel there is a certain amount of xenophobia involved.'

Although George is keen to stay abroad, Tina has no desire to leave England again. 'At least I know what's what here,' she says. 'It was all meant to be a bit of an adventure, but I felt terrified by the end of it. They all seemed to hate us and I'm sure our cat, which just disappeared one day, was picked up and thrown in a well.'

---

4. Education

You will need to decide before you move whether you want your children to go into the French or the international system. The French system is very academic and extremely tough for children who have no French to integrate into. Teachers I have spoken to say it takes about three terms for a child of around 8 with no French to acclimatise. The upside is that the educational levels are high, discipline is generally speaking excellent and it is free. If you are going to go for the state system then check out the school in your area before you decide to buy. According to a French teacher friend of mine, you should avoid those in the ZEPs (*zone d'éducation prioritaire*). They are usually in suburbs and have a lot of problem children. The French 'private' sector is also an option. The French private schools are state subsidised and great value. They tend to be religious schools and the main difference is that the teachers don't go on strike as much as the state schools. There are also around 30 international schools in France, some of which offer an English curriculum. These are expensive; usually around €10,000 in fees and €6,000 on top of that if you want your children to board or live with host families.

5. Location

By this I don't just mean where in the France, I mean the position of the house as well. If you love the evening sun and go to sleep imagining you and your friends enjoying a glass of wine on the terrace bathed in balmy evening sunlight, then make sure the terrace gets the evening sun. Also look carefully at the position of the pool (or proposed pool). Does that get the sun all day long? Check out the selected location at ALL times of the year. Some places are very hot in the summer but suffer from unexpected cold and wet in winter, as well as horrendous winds. Some places are a dream in the winter and a mass of tourists and the related activity in the summer (fun fairs, clubs which are open all night in summer but are virtually invisible in the winter).

6. What will you do?

Do not assume that because you have a successful career back home, you will be able to replicate it in France. In most instances your UK qualifications will not be valid, even if you speak fluent French and have a job, such as teaching, that is transferable. If you want to set up your own business, you have the French bureaucracy to deal with and remember that growth will be limited due to the punishing social charges here. If you employ anyone you will pay half their salary again in social security contributions and tax. If you have come out to semi-retire and live off the income of a gite then you need to be sure you have a good business plan. There are now five gites for every person looking. If as a couple you were both used to working full time you might find it a bit of a shock seeing so much of each other. 'I am so fed up with him hanging around the house, I am trying to encourage him to build a garden shed,' writes a reader who has moved to Limousin with her husband, a former London cabbie.

7. Culture and Lifestyle

If you are moving from Islington to deepest Mayenne, be realistic. How will you cope with having to drive for 40 minutes to the supermarket? There is no equivalent of Upper Street. Eating out will be followed by a long drive home. Are you happy to watch George Clooney in French? In the provinces they dub everything. Maybe you should consider living at least close to a reasonably cosmopolitan city? People tend to get carried away by the dream of living in splendid isolation, but don't realise how terrifyingly lonely it can be.

> Capital Gains
>
> If you are selling a house in the UK to move to France, the ideal thing is to become a resident first. You will then not have to pay capital gains tax in France on your UK property. In order to do this, you must establish residence in France in the tax year prior to the one you sell in. To establish residency you need to spend more than 183 days a year in France. And you must not spend more than 90 days in the UK. You have to be careful, though, that the Inland Revenue does not use your UK property to challenge your French tax status. However, if you rent out your property this can be avoided.

Especially if the locals are not friendly. Pick somewhere that is used to foreigners, such as Provence.

8. Legal Advice

When we bought our house here we used the same lawyer as the vendors. This is common practice but is not very sensible. If you have a problem with the purchase you will need independent legal advice. You should also beware of agents offering legal advice packages, they are costly and I have had countless letters of complaints about them. 'There are reported cases of lawyers deliberately ignoring or failing to investigate matters which could adversely affect the best interests of the buyer,' says Stephen Smith of Stephen Smith (France) Ltd. 'Hence the need to instruct independent bilingual lawyers who do not rely on estate agents for their living.'

9. Integration

Learning French is an obvious tip. But it is amazing how many people don't bother. There is an increased animosity towards Brits that just point and shout, so get your phrase books out and make an effort. I have heard a few terms of endearments recently to add to *les rosbifs*. *Les goddams* and *les ****-offs*. I think the fact that a lot of Brits come over expecting some sort of colonial lifestyle has a lot to do with the growing resentment.

10. Healthcare

Prepare as much as you can before you leave the UK. There are lots of forms you can get that will make getting onto the system in France a lot easier. Start off with the E 1 11, which at least covers you for the short term but find out from the UK health authorities what you need.

On the fiscal and administrative side, my top tips are as follows:

1. *Obtain a precise costing for renovation in advance of buying:*

Too many people assume that because the price of property is cheaper in many locations than in the UK, renovation of an old property will also be less costly. This is almost always NOT the case and material and labour costs can be significantly higher than expected, and this can break the budget you have set for the property and the work.

2. *House size and income*:
Remember that if you are buying for long term retirement the big house at the top of the hill may look everything you ever dreamed of now, but in ten years' time you may regret that it is not more suited to more limited mobility. Too many people buy the most expensive home they think affordable and believe that the cost of living will remain constant—it does not. Being over-housed and under-capitalised is a common mistake a few years down the line. Jane Austen said 'Nothing in life is as comforting as an adequate income.' Make sure your income is adequate in the long term. Make sure that whatever it is that brings you an income at home, can do so abroad. Many UK qualifications won't be valid in France, for example.

3. *Tax matters*:
Do not think that what works in tax planning in the UK will also work in the country you are moving to: most frequently the opposite is the case. You must take advice from an independent qualified adviser who understands and has experience in both UK tax matters and those of the country you are moving to, or you could end up paying more tax than is necessary. There is nothing quite as complicated as the French tax system, so you need to find out what applies for your specific circumstances. There are several tax specialists and lawyers that can help you, such as Russell Cooke and Blevins Franks. However, there are a few tips you should be aware of. For example, in most cases, when you sell your house in the UK, once you are a resident in France, you will not have to pay capital gains tax on it.

4. *Pension matters*:
Get advice from a pensions adviser who knows the rules in the place you are moving to, as in most non UK locations the rules are very different. For example, the UK concession that allows you to take part of your pension fund as tax free cash is almost always taxable income in the new country. You can avoid this risk if you act early to establish your fund in a manner designed to avoid it.

5. *Investment arrangements*:
What you needed from your investments before you relocated abroad may not be suitable once you have arrived. There are many investments that are tax favoured (PEP's, ISA's, TESSA's etc) in the UK but which are fully taxable in the new country. You will need to rethink what you want from your

Viagers

An interesting way to plan ahead is to buy a property in France is through a *viagers*. You pay a deposit of 30 or 40 per cent of the purchase price and an annual rent as an annuity until the seller dies. The annuity at the moment is 8.5 per cent of the agreed purchase price a year. 'The advantages for the buyer are that they can buy now before prices increase,' according to Guy Medd from Gascony Homes. 'In addition, the seller has to maintain the property to an agreed standard. Finally, it is like an interest-free loan once you have paid the capital up front.' The obvious disadvantage is that you're gambling on the seller's health. André-François Raffray probably thought he'd got the deal of the century when he signed a viagers with Jeanne Calment who was 80 at the time. He agreed to pay her FF500 a month for her apartment until she died. He ended up giving her twice the market value for it before he died in 1995. She died aged 122, two years after him, and still holds the record as the world's oldest known woman.

investments both in the short and longer term, and to receive advice from an independent adviser who knows what the investment tax breaks are in your new country.

Your Move

Utilities

There are lots of things you can organise in advance of your move to make life easier when you get to France. For example, most agents will help you have a phone line connected and also sort out electricity and gas with the local EDF (Electricité de France) and GDF (Gaz de France) branches. If your agent can't help you, you can contact your local utility direct via website www.edf.fr.

Phone

The easiest thing if you want to get a phone number sorted out before you move is to go onto www.francetelecom.com/en/worldwide/europe/focus and contact a France Telecom representative there. Cordelia, a friend of mine who recently bought a house close by, was extremely impressed with the

To move all our belongings to France seemed to me incredibly expensive. We were given quotes from removal companies that ran into thousands of pounds. A cheaper alternative is to find an antique dealer who is UK-based and goes to France regularly to buy furniture. They often travel to the Continent with empty lorries, which they then fill with French antiques to be sold in the UK.

In the end we found a couple of young lads willing to make the journey, along with Max the cat. They ended up staying for a few weeks, helping us to sort out the house. Rather brilliantly, I was able to change my mind about where things were to go about a million times and because I was feeding them and providing litres of local wine, they couldn't complain.

When we moved to France five years ago, Max, the cat, travelled down in the cabin of the lorry that was transporting our furniture. Although the driver said they got on well, Max was grumpy for a month, living in a Sussex trug and refusing to come out. I blame the driver's chain-smoking and appalling taste in music. If I were to move Max again, I would look at alternatives.

Before the journey, Max and I had to jump through a few bureaucratic hoops. To take an animal in and out of the UK without quarantine, it must be registered with the Pet Travel Scheme (PETS) run by the Department for Environment, Food and Rural Affairs (Defra). The scheme issues pet passports to animals once they have been fitted with a microchip, vaccinated against rabies, had a blood test and been issued with a certificate to show they have been treated for tapeworm and ticks.

When returning to the UK, pets must have a French vet's certificate showing that they have received treatment for fleas, ticks and worms within 24-48 hours of the journey.

The PETS scheme also has approved routes, so Defra can keep tabs on animals in transit. My favourite way to travel to and from France is by train, but, sadly, Eurostar isn't on Defra's list.

'Britain is a pet-mad nation,' says Lesley Retallack, head of press and events at Eurostar, 'but we have to weigh that up with the international profile of our passengers, who are not keen on travelling with animals.'

Eurotunnel will let you take your pet in your car and even has pet-exercising areas at its Folkestone and Calais terminals. It prefers you to put cats in a container, but dogs don't need one. And if you decide not to come back, your pet's travel is free. The return leg, however, costs £30.

On boats, there are several options. Speed Ferries charges £15 per crossing for a pet, and you must ensure that it stays in the car during the trip. Brittany Ferries allows a maximum of two pets per passenger and charges £30 return per animal.

Pets can fly with British Airways. The fare is based on the animal's weight. For a flight from London to Nice, for example, the cost is £8.22 per kg, plus a £80 handling fee, so the journey would cost about £360 for an average-sized labrador. As with unaccompanied children, unaccompanied pets cost more.

Within France, if you want to travel on SNCF with your pet, you can (assuming the train staff are not on strike). But there are strict guidelines. If your pet weighs less than 6kg, it can travel in a box or bag measuring no more than 45cm x 30cm x 35cm for only €5 (£3.50).

service. 'They found someone in the nearest France Telecom office to us who spoke English. She took our details and then gave us our new phone number. The whole thing took about 15 minutes. We immediately phoned the number and imagined the phone ringing in the lovely house we had just bought.' The lady even arranged for them to have the French equivalent of call waiting (called '*Top Message*').

Bank account

Before you do all these things, though, you need a French bank account. You should probably think about opening one as soon as you start looking for a house. Go to the bank of your choice with your passport, marriage certificate if you want a joint account, and proof of your UK address like a phone or electricity bill. You can also open an account from the UK. Several of the large French banks have branches in London. Crédit Lyonnais, for example has a branch in the City (www.creditlyonnais.fr). You can call them on 020 7588 4000. You can also go to a website specifically designed for British clients and run by Crédit Agricole, www.britline.com. This tells you how to open an account and gives you all sorts of useful information.

The word for current account in French is a *compte chèque*. One of the most notable differences between the banking systems in the UK and France is that it is illegal to write a cheque in France if you don't have the funds to cover it. If you do so, you are given 30 days to rectify the situation, after which a block will be put on your account for one year. During this time you are banned from writing cheques. In addition, your details are kept on a central list with the Banque de France, and if you try to open another account the police are informed. We have just discovered a brilliant overdraft facility which gives you up to an additional €2000 automatically as and when you need it. It's called *Compte Open* and is available with Crédit Agricole du Midi.

RIB

You'll find that in France it's impossible to do a lot of things without a *Relevé d'Identité Bancaire* known as a RIB. Even when you register at the social security office you need one, so they can take your contributions out and pay any refunds for treatment in. It's a small piece of paper you'll find in your cheque book, with your bank details on. You also use RIBs to set up standing orders.

Birth Certificates

France is a country full of bits of paper. I sometimes wonder how it doesn't sink with the weight of them all clogging up bureaucrats' offices all over the

It is allowed out of its box, but only on a lead. If the animal weighs more than 6kg, it must be muzzled, on a lead and pay half the cost of a second-class ticket-although I assume it's not allowed to take a seat. Obviously, these restrictions do not apply to guide dogs.

For those of you moving out to France with your horses to escape the hunting ban, there are plenty of companies that will move them for you. John Parker International, for example, has been moving horses for more than 25 years. 'We are moving horses to France every week,' John Parker says. 'There is steadily increasing demand.'

country. When you move here, you will need not only your birth certificate but your birth certificate with BOTH parents' names. You will also need your marriage certificate if you are married, along with countless copies of your passport and any other official document you ever owned. These will all have to be translated by an officially recognised translator. They are very easy to find through the British consulate in Paris (+33 (1) 44 51 31 00, www.amb-grandebretagne.co.uk) or the French embassy in London, if you want to get them done before you move. You should take at least 20 photo-copies of everything, so you have them to hand.

The Buying Process

Unlike English law, French law does not recognise the concept of subject to contract. An offer on a property should not be made unless you are absolutely certain you want to buy it. Before the offer is made you should consider all the conditions that you wish to include in the contract. We included a clause saying the purchase was contingent on us being able to raise the financing to buy the house as well as the findings of the land search being satisfactory (in other words that there were no plans for wind-farms, motorways and so forth, close to the house).

The next step is to sign either a *Promesse de Vente* or a *Compromis de Vente*. This may be prepared either by the *notaire* (a French lawyer who deals with property transactions) or the agent.

In many cases, only the vendor's *notaire* is inserted in the contract. A buyer should not automatically agree to this, and should consider instructing his own *notaire*. Nonetheless, we were told it would make things easier if we used the same *notaire*. It is the purchaser who pays the *notaire's* fees. If there are two *notaires* involved, there is no extra cost to the purchaser as the notaire's fees are fixed by law and the fee will be shared.

Contracts are signed early on in France and contain 'Conditions Suspensives'. These are the conditions mentioned above and must be satisfied before completion can take place. Until the conditions have been fulfilled, completion of the contract is not possible. If any of the *Conditions Suspensives* are not satisfied, the contract is deemed to be null and void and the purchaser is entitled to the return of his deposit.

These conditions are important and need to be checked carefully. In particular, the contract may need to be amended to take into account the fact that a mortgage is needed to finance the purchase. This clause cannot be added at a later date. The drafting of the contract is very important and a pre-printed form can *never* replace professional advice.

French contracts are also usually conditional upon rights of pre-emption, in other words, that nobody with a right to buy the property does so. A

Before you buy a house you should check the classified zone of the particular piece of land or house you are buying. If it is an area designated for development you may find yourself pre-empted by the local mayor. Tim and Cordelia Simmonds recently bought a small village house with some adjoining land close to Perpignan. Before they signed the *Compromis de Vente* (the initial contract to buy) they were told by their lawyer that the mayor had a pre-emption right on the land just outside their house, where they were planning to build a swimming pool. He advised them to insert a clause in the contract stating that the property could only be sold as a whole entity. 'This meant the mayor would have to fork out for the house as well if he wanted to pre-empt us,' says Cordelia. 'It also means we are protected when we sell it.'

In France 90 per cent of all property is subject to pre-emption rights. This means the mayor of the local council has to provide a certificate of pre-emption before you can sign the final *Acte de Vente* (act of sale). Just 18 days before they were due to move into their dream chalet in a small French ski resort close to Geneva with their two young children, keen skiers Ian and Gill Edwards were told there was a problem. 'The house was sold, the removal was booked, the children registered at the local school and nursery,' says Ian. 'Then we had a call from the *notaire* to say that the council was buying the chalet.'

They went to France immediately to meet the mayor, and to see if the situation could be resolved. 'We found we had no rights,' says Ian. 'The chalet was needed for the local lift company.'

Gill admits that their first reaction was shock. 'We felt very frustrated and extremely disappointed. We had understood that any chance of pre-emption was extremely remote, and would normally happen within the two months following the exchange, which was signed in the February. Pre-emption took place seven months later in October, by which time clients had reserved, contracts had been signed and workmen engaged for the realisation of our long-held dream. We understand and see the reasoning behind the decision, it was the incredibly late timing of it which caused the major frustration. We were extremely unlucky.'

Ian and Gill are now waiting for a new-build in the village to be

strange quirk in French law is that it gives certain parties—such as the local mayor—the right to buy in place of the purchaser. If the right is exercised, the deposit will be returned to the purchaser. I have watched countless friends go through the nail-biting experience of waiting to see if the commune wants to exercise its right to buy their house. So far, it has never happened.

The purchaser of a residential property is given a seven days' cooling-off period after signing the *Promesse de Vente*, during which he can withdraw from the contract without penalties.

Following signature of the contract, searches are made. The *notaire* will obtain the equivalent of a Land Registry search from the *Conservation des Hypothèques*. This search will disclose any restrictions on the vendor's right to convey title and the existence of charges.

In addition, either a *Note d'Urbanisme* or a *Certificat d'Urbanisme* is obtained. This is a document from the local authority which declares the existing use of the land and administrative restrictions or requirements which apply. The *Certificat* may also give information on whether building is allowed, the density and other details of development. If the *Certificat d'Urbanisme* is positive, planning permission—*Permis de Construire*, will normally be granted.

Roads along your property

Sarah and John Palmer bought a house near Aix-en-Provence four years ago. It is in the middle of a village, on the main road. 'It didn't occur to us that this might cause us problems in the future,' says Sarah. Six months ago, they had a letter from the mayor informing them that the road was going to be widened and that three metres would be taken off their garden to carry out the project. 'We have tried to fight it,' says John. 'But apparently there is nothing we can do.' The Palmers will lose a significant amount of their garden, which is small in any case. 'Luckily the swimming-pool is at the other end from where they want to chop up the garden,' says Sarah. The Palmers will not be paid for the land, as the mayor has a legal right to the land in the interests of the community. In some instances the land owners might be paid compensation but not where the alignment is of fairly limited effect. Before you buy, check whether your land is close to a road that could be upgraded, straightened or enlarged. This is called alignment and your lawyer should be able to obtain a something called a certificate of alignment stating your property is exempt. However, be aware that the situation may change in the future.

completed. The whole experience has not put them off living in France. 'We have had so much support, not only from the removal company Britannia Beckwith of Brighton, but from both French and English friends in the village, whose advice and help in putting us up has been absolutely invaluable.'

Once all these issues have been satisfied, the final completion deed, called the *Acte de Vente*, is drafted by the *notaire*.

The signing of the *Acte de Vente*, the final deed of sale, has to take place before a *notaire*. The expenses, the *Droits d'Enregistrement* and the legal fees are also paid at the signature of the *Acte de Vente* by the purchaser.

Bear in mind that a local council may decide to exercise its *pre-emption* right on the sale of your house. It does not have to come up with the money for six months. In the meantime, you keep the right to occupy the property. The council can purchase the property at a lower price than the market value, in which case you may:
— withdraw from the sale and keep the property;
— stick to your price and let a judge fix the amount the council has to buy it for. Remember, pre-emption rights can also be exercised by the tenant of a property.

Harriet and Lance Kenny had never heard of Safer until they tried to buy a house in southwest France. The notaire wrote to Safer which has a time limit of two months to state its interest in the property. It did not do so and so the notaire prepared a conveyance deed which stated that Safer had waived its rights. Harriet and Lance completed their purchase.

They moved to France and their three children started school there. Six weeks after they moved in they received a letter from Safer advising that it had decided to buy the property and that it had in fact confirmed its intention to the notaire within the two month period. The notaire denies this. The outcome is that the Kennys will have to find somewhere else to live within six months

According to the Law Society a growing number of Brits are falling foul of the law when buying properties in France. There are several issues you should be aware of as a buyer. The first and possibly most important is to take proper legal advice.

There are several companies offering complete house-purchasing packages, including legal advice. These need to be checked out carefully. One reader wrote to me saying she had paid several thousand

These fees include the *notaire's* fees, stamp duty and registration fees. Where the property is more than five years old, these will amount to approximately 6.5 per cent of the purchase price. These are payable in addition to the purchase price.

For newly built properties, French VAT (TVA). at the rate of 19.6 per cent is usually included in the price as well as *notaire's* fees and taxes of approximately 2 to 3 per cent of the purchase price.

If you do not wish to or are unable to attend completion in person you can appoint an attorney to execute the *Acte de Vente* on your behalf using a Power of Attorney or *Procuration*. This document must be drawn in French, signed before a Notary Public and forwarded to the Foreign &

---

pounds for a legal package from one of the biggest UK agents operating in all over France, only to find they had got the completion date wrong and she couldn't move into her home when she had planned. She has been given £500 compensation, but it is nothing compared to what she paid for the service in the first place and the trouble their mistake has caused. Before opting for a package, check if the agency's staff has French conveyancing experience and tax qualifications. 'The agency should also have a *carte professionelle*, which enables them to work as registered agents in France,' says Phil Turnbull who runs an interpreting service for Brits in France. 'People generally don't use a UK professional without checking credentials, why do so in France?'

According to Dawn Alderson, solicitor with Russell Cooke Solicitors, you should also be aware that the conveyancing system in France is very different. 'I have had calls from clients in campsites, surrounded by all their belongings,' she says. 'They took the completion date to mean the same as it does in the UK. In France it is an approximate date and not set in stone like it is here.'

Finally, make sure there are no obligations on the property. Friends of mine bought a place recently and found there is an ancient right for an aged relation of the previous owner, living in an old people's home nearby, to move in if he ever wants to. A year on he hasn't shown up. But I don't know what they will do if he ever decides he's had enough of the old people's home and arrives on their doorstep with a suitcase.

Property is considered untouchable in France and a *compulsory purchase order* can only deprive someone of their property in case of public necessity (road construction, extension of an airport etc). Compensation will have to be paid.

Commonwealth Office where a Certificate—*l'Apostille*—is annexed to give legal effect in France.

You may find the *Acte de Vente*, a document many pages long in French legal jargon, bewildering. An independent advisor can review this document and explain the procedure to you in your own language and in terms you can understand.

NB! For exact and up-to-date information and help on legal issues always contact a legal professional first.

Apart from the fromalities. There are some fundamental questions you need to ask yourself before you rent out your property.
    First, why do you want to rent it out? Is it to make money or is it to cover your costs?
    Second, how often do you want to be there yourself? Do you want to go there on certain dates, ie peak times when the rates are highest?
    Third, what sort of person do you want to stay in your home? Will you accept children and/or pets?
    The answers to these questions will determine how you should furnish and equip your property. You should probably in all cases go for good quality, robust furniture that can be easily cleaned and is low maintenance. Bear in mind that items like dishwashers and washing machines are essential. White tiles in the kitchen are not a good idea. You should sleep in all beds of your home to make sure the bedrooms are comfortable. Wooden or tiled

---

Rental tips

1. Do think carefully about location if you're buying to rent. Easy access to the UK is essential.
2. Talk to an agent before you buy and find out what you could realistically get for your house.
3. Get legal advice on the rental contract, or at least run your contract by an experienced agent.
4. If you're not going to be there, make sure you have someone on-site who can look after the property and guests for you.
5. Don't be tempted to overcharge. Guests will take it out on your house.
6. Get a hefty deposit.
7. Remove the phone, unless you have discussed it with the tenants beforehand.
8. Don't go for a cream colour scheme.
9. Do use a local, reputable agent, at least if you're not going to be there.

Agents

Agents can earn up to 25 per cent of the rental income in France, depending on how long the rental period is and how much they do. At the most basic level, there are companies which simply advertise your property and take the money for it. The fee for this service is normally 15 per cent. A good agent should see tenants in and out and arrange for cleaning staff. It may be well worth the cost but you should be clear from the outset exactly what the agent will do for his or her commission. The following questions should be asked:

* Will they pay to advertise the property?
* Will they guarantee a minimum level of bookings?
* Will they vet potential guests?
* Will they inspect the property before and after each booking and check the inventory?
* Will they welcome guests and show them around the property?
* Will they organise repairs and maintenance?
* Are they available 24 hours in case of emergencies?

To find agents or local property-management people the best thing is to talk to other property owners in the area. Whatever else, though, make sure they speak English as a lot of guests won't speak French.

floors with washable rugs and throws for soft furnishings are a good idea. *Do not put carpets in the bathrooms.* You should allocate a storage area or

Self management

If you are planning to advertise your house yourself, you will need a house manager, someone on-site who can deal with the plumbing if it breaks down, who can see the clients in and out, and arrange for the cleaning staff to come in once they've left. A house manager will cost anywhere between €100 and €400 per month.

Leaving the keys with a neighbour is really not an option. It won't make you popular and if anything goes wrong, there is no one there to deal with it.

According to Tony Tidswell, who runs www.rentalsfrance.com, you should be ploughing at least half your turnover into marketing the property. 'There is such a lot of competition now,' he says. 'If you don't have your house on several sites and come up with a nice-looking brochure chances are it won't get rented out.'

Advertising

★ You can just advertise the property on a holiday home website. The key to this is to make sure your advertisement is spot-on. The copy you write should be engaging and readable. Normally you have room for between 500 and 1000 words, but you must tell potential tenants the most important things first, as they often won't read the whole thing.

★ 'Think of your advertisement as a pyramid,' says Speller. 'With the key points at the top and more details as you go down. The headline should give a short well-crafted summary including the type of property and its most important selling features.' The sentences should be clear and concise. Remember that some people reading the advertisement may not be English so don't use colloquialisms or abbreviations.

★ The Internet is a visual medium and your choice of photograph is absolutely crucial. It is the most important selling tool in the whole advertisement. Only use clear, well-lit, bright photographs taken on a sunny day. Try to include both interior and exterior shots, people like to have an idea of the décor and style of a place.

cupboard for your personal items, but try to leave a few things like vases out so the place doesn't look too impersonal.

Before your first guests arrive, you should prepare an inventory and a guest manual. This should contain relevant information about the property and the area such as information on the local town, leisure activities, house rules and how things work, who to contact in emergencies, as well as a contact number for someone who can sort out plumbing and electricity problems, and so on.

Also, before they arrive, make sure everything is as perfect as it can be. First impressions are vital. Make sure essential supplies, such as loo rolls, soap and kitchen paper, are available. Kitchen cupboards should have the

If you're worried about falling foul of the French authorities when employing staff for cash, there is a simple new system you can use. It is called the cheque emploi service and enables you to use cheques to hire occasional help such as nannies, gardeners, cooks and cleaners. You get a special chequebook from your local bank after filling in a form that means the CNCESU (Centre Nationale du Cheque Emploi Service Universel) automatically deducts any social charges from your bank account. For more information, call 0820 002 378 from within France, or go to www.cesu.urssaf.fr/cesweb/home.jsp

Rates

* You should make sure your rental rates are easy to understand and, although there will obviously be differences between seasons, try to keep them to a minimum.
* If getting your bookings early is important to you, you will need to quote lower rates. If you are prepared to take a bit of a risk and wait, you can go for higher ones.
* 'The pattern of holiday bookings has drastically changed over the last few years,' says Marcelle Speller from www.holidayrentals.com. 'People are no longer just booking four weeks in the summer. They book holidays over Easter, half term, they book long weekends. It is no longer the case that if you're not fully booked in January for the summer you should panic. People are more flexible now and will book much closer to the time of travel.'
* Bear in mind with weekend bookings that the changeover will cost you as much as it would if someone had stayed for a week, so you may want to factor in the cost of cleaning at least into the rent you quote for shorter periods.
* Make sure your contact details are correct. There is nothing more annoying than not getting through—people will rarely try more than once.
* When you get an enquiry, reply straight away. Some wonders even use instant messaging now and reply within minutes.

basics like tea, coffee, sugar and UHT milk. If the property has been let out for more than a week, it is normal to provide a cleaner and a change of linen at the end of the first week. If at all possible have someone take the key from the guests and say goodbye at the end of their stay.

Keep a track of anything you spend on the house so you can offset the costs against tax. You must also let your insurance company know when you decide to rent out your property; your premium will probably increase, but if something happens and you haven't informed them, they won't pay up.

The cheapest option for renting out is to go for a website like www.frenchconnections.co.uk, www.frenchcountry.co.uk, www.holi-

If you are away from your property during July and August and you inform the municipal police (gendarmerie), they will patrol and check things in your absence.

You need to leave a contact number and address with them. The service applies to rural and urban areas and is called Operation Tranquillite Vacances.

Pool tips
* New pools should come with a 10-year guarantee. Make sure your installer provides you with this. If it is a big name company, get something in writing from head office before signing or paying.
* Be careful in rocky or mountainous regions that might have porous or seismic ground. Pools can move and leak, which can cost a fortune in water and repair bills. Installers are not obliged to check this. Get an engineer involved if you're at all unsure.
* A pool maintenance man will cost around £50 per week.
* Don't put too much chlorine in or your hair will turn green.
* When buying a property without a pool, do make sure you have the required minimum amount of land to build one.
* Check out the law regarding fences and nets.

dayfrance.com, or www.holiday-rentals.com. You will pay an annual fee of between £100 and £190 for an advertisement with pictures, depending on how much space you want. The potential tenants contact the owner direct and the rest is up to you. This option is really only viable if the owner is on-site.

Holiday letting companies like Bowhills can also be useful. But owners should make sure there is an agent nearby. As far as using an estate agent goes, the fees vary. An owner can expect to pay at least 20 per cent. However, it can be well worth it if the clients turn out to be tricky. On the Riviera, www.francenetvillas.com offers a personalised service.

If you are buying to rent, bear in mind that house prices vary enormously across France. The south is more expensive than the rest of the country, and the Riviera the most exclusive. In the Languedoc, you can buy a tiny village house for around £35,000. On the Côte d'Azur, that will get you a garage. For a five-bedroom family house with pool, depending on location and views, you will pay between £200,000 and £400,000 in the Languedoc. Along the Riviera a similar property with a sea view would be around £1 million. In terms of living costs, the Languedoc is a lot cheaper than the Riviera. Cleaning staff cost around £6 an hour as opposed to £8 an hour. You can get a cook for £15 an hour, on the Riviera you will pay up to £40 an hour. Pool maintenance is around £240 per month, on the Riviera it is £300. The property tax (taxe foncière) depends on the size of your house, but for a five-bedroom house in the Languedoc expect to pay around £800 a year. On the Riviera a similar sized house with a sea view will cost about £3,000 a year. Insurance for a five-bedroom property will cost you up to £350 a year in the Languedoc. On the Riviera it is around £400-£500.

Work

If you are living and working in France, you will be liable to pay tax in France on your earnings. In addition, you will also have to pay social charges and healthcare charges on your French earnings.

If you are employed in France, your employer will deduct all social security contributions at source. These include contributions to the healthcare system, unemployment insurance and old-age pension, and are usually around 18 per cent of your gross income. Employers do not deduct tax at source, so you will need to keep aside a portion of your income to pay your tax bill at the end of the year.

If you live in France and want to be covered you need to join the Régime Obligatoire (RO) and contribute to the Sécurité Sociale. This entitles you and your dependants to medical treatment. Once you are registered, you will be given a magical thing called a Carte Vitale, which you hand over to doctors (for automatic reimbursement) and chemists instead of money.

The contribution you make to the social security system will depend on what you earn but is usually around 22 per cent of taxable income. If you are employed, your employer will pay this automatically. If you are self-employed you need to register at your local Caisse Primaire d'Assurance Maladie (CPAM). The Sécurité Sociale will cover between 75 per cent and 90 per cent of treatment and 40 per cent to 70 per cent of medicines. The patient is liable for the remainder unless the illness is critical. We have a private insurance company (called a mutuelle or complémentaire) which covers this portion and costs us around £60 per month for the whole family. The mutuelle pays the difference between the state's contribution and 100 per cent. There are several companies that offer the service in France and the premium will depend on what level of cover you chose. For example, you may want to have cover for eyes and teeth. You can also opt for cover from a mutuelle at over 100 per cent which will then help to offset the cost of a private room or hospital.

If you're retired, you will need to get an E121 form from the NHS. This will entitle you to the same healthcare as a French pensioner.

If you're moving to France contact the Centre for Non-Residents in Newcastle (on 0191 225 4811). Get as many forms as possible. I found having lots of bits of paper helped during my year-long struggle to get us registered. And there was a brilliant form that covered me for childbirth (fairly essential as I was eight months pregnant when we left England). It is called an E112. An E104 is also useful. It is a record of UK National Insurance contributions and could help you to register here. If you're planning to claim unemployment benefit you will need an E301. If you are self-employed you should get an E101. For those of you with holiday homes, the most practical thing is still the E111, which is a simple form you fill in at the post office. This way you have to pay for healthcare up front, but you get refunded from the NHS once you get home. The list of E-forms is practically endless and you should call the above number to see which ones you need.

The way to get registered is to go to your local CPAM with the form that is relevant to you, which you have already organised from the centre for non-residents in Newcastle. At my CPAM there is an international department called the Conventions Internationales. You should also take along your birth certificate (with both parents on-no I'm not joking), as well the birth certificates of any children, your marriage certificate if you're married and proof of income and tax paid if possible. If you're employed, salary slips will do. If you're self-employed you will need your accounts or at least some written proof of what you earn.

If you live in France but work for a UK company and your duties are carried out wholly in the UK, you are liable to pay tax in the UK on your earnings. France will not tax this income directly, but will take it into account when calculating the tax rates to apply to any other income arising in France (*taux effectif*). This method of double taxation relief is likely to change when the new 2004 UK/France Tax Treaty will come into force after ratification by both countries.

If you live in France but work partly in France and partly in the UK for a UK company, you need to split your earnings between the UK and France on a time apportioned basis. The portion of your earnings relating to your UK duties will be taxed in the UK, and taken into account in France for the *taux effectif*, as described above. The portion relating to French earnings will be directly taxed in France.

If you are self-employed in France, different taxation regimes apply, and the correct regime will depend on the nature of the activity carried out, and whether your profits are classed as 'commercial' or 'non commercial'.

Commercial profits (Bénéfices industriels et commerciaux—BIC)
Income from trading activities is taxable under this heading. Where your gross annual income is below €27,000, your profits will be taxed under the *Micro-BIC* regime. This allows you to deduct a flat 52 per cent for expenses, so only 48 per cent of your income is taxable.

Non commercial profits (Bénéfices non commerciaux)
This regime would apply to income earned from 'intellectual activities' and would apply to teachers, doctors, lawyers, accountants, architects etc. There is a *Micro* regime which applies where your gross annual income is below €27,000. The *Micro* regime allows you to deduct a flat 37 per cent for expenses, i.e. only 63 per cent is taxable.

The disadvantage of the *Micro* regimes is that they will always show a fixed profit. So, if your expenses are higher than the 52 per cent or 37 per cent flat deductions, you may choose to opt into a 'real' regime, which allows you to deduct actual expenses incurred, although you are required to prepare accounts which must be approved by the French tax authorities. The cost of preparing formal accounts under the latter regime should be taken into account when deciding which regime you elect to be taxed under.

In addition to tax, France levies social charges and healthcare charges on all earnings, whether from employment or self-employment.

Social Charges
These charges go towards funding the social security system in France. You will usually pay at a rate of 8 per cent on your earnings. In general, it is the gross amount of income received that is subject to the social charges, although for earned income you get a 5 per cent deduction for expenses, so the social charges are applied to 95 per cent of earned income. If your income relates to duties performed in the UK, you may be exempt from paying these charges on your UK earnings.

Healthcare Charges
Healthcare charges are payable on your net taxable income at a rate of 8 per

cent above a threshold of €6,721. Again, if your earnings arise in the UK, you may be exempt from the healthcare charges on your UK earnings.

This is a brief summary of what are complicated issues. I would recommend you always seek professional advice by a qualified practitioner in relation to your individual circumstances.

Language

Many of my friends have used the Michel Thomas CD set. This is for beginners and costs around £60. It is published by Hodder & Stoughton. He maintains that you can learn without writing anything down or trying to remember it. On the CD you listen to him teaching two 'pupils', one of whom is so stupid you wonder how she ever found her way to the recording studio. But I suspect she's there to make us feel better. You can always tell his disciples, as they are very good on the word *confortable*, which he pronounces confortaaaaable.

There are hundreds of websites offering French courses. One of the most user-friendly is the BBC one. The address is www.bbc.co.uk/languages/french/index.shtml. It is free, easy to navigate, and has lots of different areas depending on what you're after. For example, you can take a train, go for a drink with a friend or practice your grammar. It seems especially geared towards the beginner, but there is a fast-track section for those with some French.

If you have Sky Digital you can tune into the French TV 5 on channel 825 before you get here and become an expert on French culture, as well as language.

The Laura K Lawless site (www.french.about.com) is great, lots of resources you can use to learn French from your armchair. She sends you a French lesson every day, and when I have the time to look at it, I find it extremely useful.

The *Alliance Française* organises courses all over the world and can be contacted at www.alliancefr.org.

There are also several websites offering CD-ROMs for sale either combined with online teaching or alone. The most popular is probably www.linguaphone.co.uk. The tapes or CDs are expensive, for example, £250 for a French course that promises to take you from beginner to expert.

A company called Learn Direct at www.ad.uk.doubleclick.net also offers CD-ROMs and an online French course. Unfortunately neither are available

A free language course

One of the most maddening things about moving to France is the amount of bureaucracy you will be exposed to. It took me about 20 visits to the social security office in Béziers to get the family registered on the health system. Bureaucracy plays a central role in your life in France in more or less everything, from registering your car to enrolling your children at school. What you should do is to treat these bureaucratic battles as a free French lesson. That way they won't seem like a waste of time.

to buyers outside the UK, so it's only of use if you're still based there.

For a live teacher you could go to an intensive course in London at BSL Interlenguas (www.interlenguas.co.uk, 020 7263 7589) but it would set you back £575 per day. I think this must be more geared to business people. They also offer a ten-day course for £5,500.

In France you can have a week's intensive language learning for £275 with www.languagesabroad.co.uk. They have centres all over the country and provide all manner of courses.

Along similar lines to Michel Thomas, there is the Rosetta Stone learning method. It calls itself a 'dynamic immersion method' and claims you will learn naturally without writing or memorising. They kindly sent me a course to test, suggesting I chose a language I know nothing about in order to assess how effective it is. I chose Russian and can now say lots of useful things like the boy and the dog, the boy on the aeroplane and the girl in the boat. I highly recommend it to people who have a visual memory. It is an active way of learning in that you have to pick the picture you think the person is describing, and quite a challenge to improve your marks every time. The website is www.therosettastone.co.uk. There are two levels for French CD-ROMs, level one is £149.00 and level two is £169.00.

But don't despair if the language issue gets on top of you and progress is slow. According to a recent survey of French adults aged between 18 and 65, 12 per cent of them find writing, reading and understanding simple texts in their native language difficult.

Vive la Différence!

───── Frequently Asked Questions

Some people who think about moving to France are terrified by how different it is. The fact that you can't leave your property to whomever you like is hard to grasp for an Anglo-Saxon. The banks being closed every Monday seems crazy until you get used to it. I have found that a number of the same issues come up all the time so have decided to put them all together in one place.

Capital Gains Tax

Capital gains tax is paid when you make a profit on a property which is not your principal home. For non-residents of France, capital gains tax due on property sales for a non-EU resident is 33.33 per cent and for an EU resident it is 16 per cent. There is no relief on this for the first five years of ownership—after that it reduces by 10 per cent each year down to zero after 15 years. You can offset building work done by a registered French builder but you have to produce proof that the account was paid. 'Alternatively, a fixed allowance of 15 per cent of the acquisition price from the 5th year of ownership may be deducted,' says Dawn Alderson, of Russell-Cooke solicitors. 'The outstanding tax will then be paid directly by the notaire on your behalf.' I want to make it clear that UK residents will still have to declare the sale of any property in the UK for UK capital gains tax purposes. An allowance or credit given will be given for the tax already paid in France. No capital gains tax is due for properties under €15,000. For French residents selling their second home an additional 11 per cent social taxes are due on top of the 16 per cent. If you are non-resident you are potentially exempt providing you have been a resident at some stage for at least two years and that the property has not been rented since January 1st of the year pervious to the sale.

Taxe d'habitation and taxe foncière

There are two types of local taxes relating to homes: *taxe d'habitation* (res-

Renting out your second home—a case study

Tom, a friend of mine in our nearest village, owns a three-bedroom house, which he bought for £100,000 several years ago. He rents it out for July and August, as well as some weekends off-season, and sometimes for half term. His average rental income a year is about £10,000. During the peak season he gets £1000 a week. Out of this come his local taxes, both the *taxe foncière* (property tax) and *taxe d'habitation* (residential tax). The total combined is £1500 a year. The amount you pay is calculated according to how much land and property you own but also differs between local authorities. On top of this, Tom has to pay income tax on the rent. The standard rate for non-residents on their rental income is 25 per cent on the profits, which the revenue calculates as 28 per cent of gross income. In other words, they give you 72 per cent relief for expenses such as maintenance and repairs. The gross income should also be declared in the UK and you will get a credit for the tax paid in France. After taxes Tom's profit is around £6500.

'That sounds great,' says Pat Bellis, of Riviera Search International. 'But he hasn't even started to pay for all the maintenance costs. These include a gardener, a cleaner, a pool man, the cost of water, fuel, electricity and so forth.'

The cost of employing people in France is astronomical. As an employer, you can end up paying 45 per cent on top of their salary for social charges. And employing people for cash is not an option, according to Dawn Alderson of Russell-Cooke Solicitors. 'It is totally illegal,' she says. 'And the authorities take a very dim view. It's a complete no-no, which could see you end up in court.'

Most of us don't have big enough houses to employ full-time staff, so what are the options for casual labour, if cash is out of the question?

First, and easiest, use a company or a sole trader registered in France, who will invoice you as a business complete with a *Siret* number, which proves the company or entity is properly registered.

Second, talk to your bank about setting up a *chèque-emploi-service* through which you can legally pay a casual worker via your bank account. This is a scheme within the French system to allow people to employ cleaners and gardeners cheaply and easily.

Third, draw up an employment contract whereby you, the employer, would have to issue pay-slips and also be responsible for the employees' social security contributions. This would also mean you need an accountant to with the pay-slips and so forth.

Tom uses self-employed gardeners and cleaning staff. The

idential tax) and *taxe foncière* (property tax, similar to council tax in the UK). Residential tax is payable by anyone living in a property in France, property tax is paid only by the owner of the property. Both taxes are payable on main or second homes and whether you are a French resident or not. If your property is 'habitable' (i.e. furnished) on January 1st of any given year, you are liable for tax for that year. The amount of tax you pay will usually be based on the rental value of the property for the previous year, as well as the living area and factors like whether or not you have central heating, a swimming pool, location and so on.

Wealth Tax

If you are living in France, wealth tax is usually assessed on your worldwide assets. The tax is payable on assets over €732,000 (£505,000) and rates start at 0.55 per cent and increase on a sliding scale. If you have assets above €15,255,000 (£10,500,000) the rate goes up to 1.8 per cent.

The new 2004 UK/France Tax Treaty, which will come into force after ratification by both governments, provides substantial relief from French wealth tax for UK nationals (who are not French nationals). For the five years after becoming a resident of France, your wealth tax will be based on assets in France only; all other assets will be ignored. In the sixth year following French tax residence, wealth tax would then be payable on worldwide assets. Therefore, once the Treaty is ratified, you should try to arrive at the beginning of a tax year, rather than the end of the previous tax year, in order to stretch out the five year exemption time period.

Tax on rental income

It does not matter where you live, or where you collect any rental for your home in France, or where your personal tax is paid. If the house you are renting out is in France, all income from it is considered as being earned in France and tax *must* be declared on this income in France. Tax must be paid here, even if you declare and pay tax in another country.

If you are already making a tax declaration in France you can add the property income to your declaration, deduct all relevant expenses and you are liable to tax at 25 per cent on the balance. If relevant expenses are greater than your income, no tax is due.

If you do not already make a declaration, the simplest system is a *regime micro* for your property. Under this scheme, you are only liable for tax on 30 per cent of the income; they allow you the balance as expenses. You pay tax at 25 per cent on 30 per cent.

In addition there may be local tourism and occupancy taxes. Your local *mairie* or *prefecture* can help with this information. These taxes are usually payable per bed, usually around one euro per night.

You are not likely to face double taxation if you have paid your taxes in France and then take the balance back home.

gardeners get £10 an hour and the cleaners get £6. In 2003 he spent £1,600 on both. His total profit is now £4,900. And he has still to pay for fuel (around £400 a year), electricity (another £600 a year), pool maintenance (on average £500 a year) and water, which is £700 a year. All these costs obviously vary according to the region you are in and how big your property is. Another thing to factor in is the changing rentals market. 'Gone are the days when people just went away in the summer for three weeks,' says Marcelle Spelling, Director and Co-Founder of holidayfrance.com 'Now they come for the weekend, for short breaks and so forth. But as a landlord you have to remember that the changeover costs the same whether they have been there for two weeks or two days.'

In addition to the costs of maintaining the property, Tom also pays to advertise it on the Internet with www.rentalsfrance.com. The amount varies, if he doesn't get any bookings, he pays nothing. If he does, he pays 10 per cent of the rental income up to a ceiling of £195. Another 15 per cent of his rental income goes to a local lady who sees the guests in and out and is on hand to deal with any problems. His profit is now down to £1,020. And that's before he's paid the mortgage.

Inheritance laws

This is a huge topic as the French inheritance laws are incredibly complicated and very different to the English ones. Even if you die in England, your French property will be subject to the rules of French succession law. In France you cannot disinherit your children. You are not free to dispose of your estate as you wish. Certain members of your family, such as children and parents (but not spouses), have an absolute right to inherit certain parts of your assets. Percentages vary according to the number of children, but where there are children and/or parents, a will that leaves everything to the other spouse will not be upheld. If you have one child half the [French] estate goes to that child. If you have two, two thirds of the estate are shared equally between the two children. If there are three or more children, three-quarters of the estate is shared equally between them.

One of the major problems is protection of the surviving spouse. Under French law he or she is only entitled to one quarter of the estate if children from a previous marriage involved. If there are only children in common involved, the spouse is entitled to a life interest in the whole of the property, which means he or she can live there for the remainder of his or her lifetime. However, the property cannot be sold without the approval of the children.

This is a complicated issue and you should always take legal advice about your personal circumstances, but here are three examples to guide you.

A married couple—one of the partners has children
'I'm married to a man who has three children,' says Linda Lewis. 'I have none. We live in a house with no mortgage, which is in my name only as I alone paid for it. I want to know whether, in France, women can own property independently of their husbands as I don't want to be in the position of finding myself widowed and having to 'hand over' a share of my home to other people's children.'

The answer is that, as the property was purchased solely in Linda's name, it will not fall into her husband's estate and his children will have no rights over the property. If Linda had children, under French law on her death a percentage of the property would be divided between them.

According to Dawn Alderson, solicitor with Russell-Cooke, there are other issues Linda should be aware of. 'If Linda and her husband move to France, it would not only be the house which could be subject to French rules and rights for children,' she says. 'It would also be the couples' investments and other assets worldwide with the exception of any immovable property outside of France. This is because in all likelihood, they will be considered to be domiciled in France very shortly after taking up residence. Linda should bear in mind the question of who is paying for the property. If the funds are in her sole name at the present time, there is no problem if she purchases the property in her sole name. Should the funds belong to both her and her husband, we would need to ensure that the money for the purchase is in actual fact paid from her own assets and is not made from a jointly owned account.'

A married couple—have children together and one has a child from a previous marriage/relationship
To make things easier, I will take the example of a father who has one child from his first wife, and two children from his second and current marriage. (It is worth noting that French law now considers children from non-married couples in the same way as children from married couples in terms of succession rights on their parents' estate.)

On the first death:
Scenario A: Should the father be the first spouse to die, the three children will equally have reserved rights in respect of his share, i.e. in this case, each child receives a quarter outright and the wife may by will receive one quarter outright also. If a valid will has been made and the spouse was given the maximum available portion, she could choose to inherit either a one quarter share and a life interest in the three quarters or a life interest in the whole.

Scenario B: Should the wife be the first spouse to die, then only her two children inherit her share as the third child has no parental connection with her. In this case, the two children would inherit each one third of her share and the spouse the remaining third by will. Again, the surviving spouse could receive a life interest in the whole property if a will had been made and the interest would be owned by the two children or the spouse could receive a quarter outright and three quarters in life interest. (Please note inheritance tax is payable by the beneficiary depending on the amount.)

On the second death:

If a life interest had been selected by the surviving spouse, this will obviously be extinguished and the children (three of them in scenario A, or two of them in scenario B) would become automatically owner of the whole property.

An unmarried couple without children

The parents are also reserved heirs. If the deceased spouse had one parent, this parent is entitled to one quarter of his son's or daughter's estate and the surviving spouse can inherit the remainder by will.

If the deceased has both his parents, each parent is entitled to one quarter, and the surviving spouse to one half of the property. If no parents are alive, the property can be freely given between the spouses by will, subject to the payment of inheritance tax.

Inheritance Tax

The French take the view that all the worldwide income and assets of a resident are taxable. The system is under review at the moment, but currently this is how things stand. Inheritance taxes paid in France range from five to 60 per cent depending on the value of your estate and how closely your heirs are related to you. The amount of tax each child has to pay will be based on the sum inherited less an abatement of €46,000 each. The rate of tax for a spouse is based on the net sum less €76,000. The maximum tax rate for close relations is 40 per cent. For more distant relatives like brothers and sisters the rate of tax is 45 per cent and the nil band is only €100.

French law regards unmarried couples as unrelated to each other so the surviving partner has to pay inheritance tax at 60 per cent, except for the allowance of €100. Cordelia and Tim aren't married and have two children together. They decided to buy the house only in Cordelia's name to avoid the inheritance tax. In addition, both her parents are dead so there are no inheritance issues there.

So-called *donations* are an alternative way to pass money or property to children or grandchildren. Under this scheme, each parent can give €50,000 every 10 years and each grandparent can give €30,000 every 10 years. To do this you don't need to involve a lawyer or *notaire*, just ask for a form from your local tax office.

You can give part of a house or flat to a child, up to €46,000 for each parent every 10 years and renew the operation for the following 10 years until the whole property is the child's. But this involves an official *acte* with a lawyer, with the corresponding expenses.

The French government is currently drafting a new law which will revise and hopefully simplify successions although this is just in its first stage yet. The position currently is (but check whether it has changed):

—exemption for children & parents: €50,000
—exemption for spouses unchanged
—an additional global exemption of €50,000 (shared between the children and surviving spouse in proportion to their respective rights if the Estate is shared between them)
—exemption for brothers & sisters: €1,500
—exemption for person related by a PACS: €57,000
—exemption for non related persons: €1,500

Legal costs on house purchases

It was close to the end of the purchase process of our house that we were suddenly presented with a bill for £25,000 that we had no idea we would get. This was for the legal (*notaire's* fees) and taxes. As a rule, this sum is normally between 6.5 per cent and 8 per cent of the purchase price, and it is worth working out what the property will cost you, including all taxes before you decide to buy it. Of this amount, the *notaire* actually only takes between 1.5 and 2 per cent, the rest is taxes.

Who is responsible for the agent's commission?

This is something you need to know in advance, because the agent's commission in France is huge compared with the UK, it starts at 6 per cent and can go up to about 10 per cent. It is usual practice for the vendor of a French property to settle the agencycommission, although they will normally just factor it into the price. However, in some cases it depends on the negotiations. You should ensure that the price you agree is clearly stated inclusive or exclusive of commission and that the vendor is responsible for this.

Is it possible to obtain a survey of the property?

Yes, although this is not usual practice in France, you can instruct an architect or a UK-trained surveyor to carry out a survey on your behalf. This can be arranged through a law firm, see for example www.frenchproperty law.co.uk.

How long does the transaction take to be completed?

It varies from one case to the other and is normally something you agree with the vendor. In our case, we signed the *Compromis de Vente* (agreement to buy) in May and the owners said they wanted one last summer here so we agreed that we would take possession on September 1st. From the moment the *Compromis de Vente* is signed and the cooling-off period has expired, a three month delay is the norm. However, if the local searches or other paperwork have not been received by that time, the process will take longer.

St Tropez tax

Sha Starr and her husband bought a house in the Var two years ago. It had originally been on the market for €404,000 but as it had not sold the price was reduced to €350,000. The Starrs carried out a lot of work on the property. Eighteen months later they received a letter from the St Tropez tax office saying the villa was valued at €690,000. 'It was by then,' says Sha. 'But partly due to all the work we had done.' They were told that they not only owed them tax on the difference between what they paid and its worth, but also 18 months interest on the money. The Starrs employed an expert to argue the case on their behalf at a cost of €1500. He and the tax office came to a compromise and valued the property at €450,000. The Starrs will have to pay a lump sum of €5,000 plus 18 months back tax. 'The tax office felt that as we had bought the house cheaply they wanted a cut,' says Sha. 'Obviously in France a property is not worth what somebody will pay for it, but what the tax office thinks its worth.'

Unaccompanied minors

BA recently introduced a fee of about £30 each way for each child if they fly unaccompanied. Air France rather cleverly hides the fee in the fare, so effectively you don't get a child discount, consequently the fares are no cheaper than BA. On Ryan Air children are charged full fare after 23 months but cannot fly alone until they are 14. There is no service for unaccompanied minors. Children under the age of 12 cannot travel alone on Eurostar, but between the ages of 12 and 16 they can, as long as they have a letter of consent from a guardian. On Eurostar children go free up until the age of four and child fares from London to Paris start at £25.

Alcoholics Anonymous

A great friend of mine who lives close by recently called me with an unusual request. 'I have some people coming to stay,' she said. 'And one of them needs an AA meeting while he's here.' 'It seems to me we might all need them one day so we may as well find out where they are,' she added.

The French equivalent, *Alcooliques Anonymes*, has an excellent website where they list meetings taking place in every region in France, as well as meetings held in English. Just go to www.alcooliques-anonymes.fr click on Les Groupes and there is a link to the list of all the meetings you could ever need. The main contact number is in Paris +33 1 48064368.

Carte de Sejour

When we first moved here it was obligatory for us to have a *carte de sejour*. I found it one of the most difficult things to get hold of, requiring several visits the *mairie* with hundreds of bits of paper. I am overjoyed that no EU member will ever have to go through the process, as it has been made obsolete. 'The *carte de sejour* contravened the rights of free movement to member states within the community,' says Dawn Alderson, solicitor with Russell-Cooke. 'It is no longer required for EU residents who wish to reside in France, but in some cases may be needed to carry out an economic activity.' It is still a requirement for non-EU nationals (bar Swiss nationals) who wish to become resident in France. There are no plans for anything to replace it for EU nationals.

Land Grab

Several readers have written to me asking whether or not the land grab policy in France is a contravention of the EU law on human rights. 'International law clearly states that no government or public authority can deprive you of your property, unless: (a) the law of that country states that it can; and (b) it is in the public interest to do so,' says Stephen Smith, a bilingual lawyer specialising in French property and tax with Stephen Smith France Ltd. 'But the European Court of Human Rights cannot get involved unless you have exhausted all the domestic possibilities in France. In other words, you must first go through the hierarchy of French courts with your French barrister and other legal team up to supreme court level, and also lobby the French government for redress. All of this can take years and be very expensive.'

According to another lawyer friend who wishes to remain anonymous, local mayors can get away with pretty much anything they want. 'They make up their own definitions when it comes to what is and what isn't in the public interest,' she says. 'I would strongly advise anyone against litigating. It is rare that the man or woman in the street wins against the French powerful French administration.'

No claims bonuses in France

Direct Assurance, a leading internet based car insurer, told a reader with a five year no-claims bonus that French insurance companies do not accept bonuses from overseas insurance companies. This is not the case. However, by the time said reader had discovered his mistake he had already paid the premium. When he tried to cancel the contract the company only returned two-thirds of the premium along with a letter explaining that Direct Assurance, and not all French insurers, does not accept overseas no-claims bonuses. A spokesman from Direct Assurance confirmed that their policy is to only accept no-claims bonuses from France. Most French insurers do accept no-claims bonuses from abroad, so it's worth shopping around, especially as car insurance in France is so much more expensive here than in the UK.

Train tickets

If you call SNCF and ask to change or refund a train ticket they will tell you that there is no other option but to go to a station in person and do it before the train you were booked on is due to leave. This is not so. In some cases you can change it online and if you can't do that call the normal SNCF number (3635) and key # 33 as soon as the menu begins. You will need your ticket with you to key in all sorts of codes from it but you can cancel the reservation via an automated service. If you do cancel a reservation on the internet or the phone you need to take the ticket to any station within three months to secure the refund. But at least the pressure is off to appear in person before the ticket is rendered invalid.

Cheap calls

There is a company which allows you to call abroad for local rates. All you need to do is to dial an access number before the number you want and you can talk to anywhere from Manchester to Mumbai for a few centimes a minute. For more details go to www.telerabais.fr for example.

Tax on rental income

Income from letting French property must be declared to the French tax authorities by 30 April in each year. The onus is on the tax payer to obtain, and submit the French tax returns which French tax law obliges him to make. 'Even if the property was only occupied for three days and the owners were paid a bottle of whiskey in recognition, this technically would be classed as income and declarable to the French tax authorities,' says Stephen Smith from Stephen Smith France Ltd. 'Do not forget that UK domiciled owners of French property must also declare their French source rental income to the UK Inland Revenue. They can claim a credit for any French tax paid and will only be taxed again to the extent that their liability to UK Income Tax exceeds the rate at which they were charged in France. Such is the nature of the various allowances and deductions that many people do not pay any French income tax at all.' The standard rate is 72 per cent for deduction of expenses. In other words 28 per cent of your income is taxable if less than an annual €76,300.

Conservatory question

Do you need planning permission for a conservatory?. The answer is that if it's less than 20 metres squared you don't. But you do need a *déclaration* or *permis de travaux* which you can get from your local mayor's office and which can take up to a month to arrive. You need to take along pictures and plans to your mayor and they will open a dossier. One thing to remember is not to ask for a *conservatoire*, which means a music school. In French, rather confusingly, the word for conservatory is *véranda*. For more information go to www.travaux.com/dossier/ veranda

Intensive French lessons

'We are moving to Limousin in September,' said Claire Donald from Surrey. 'Our daughter, now aged 11, will be starting in a local school. Is there anywhere I can send her before then for an intensive language course?' There are lots of courses on offer, mainly in France. The Accord Language School in Paris for example runs a camp for teenagers and courses for children aged six to 12. See www.french-paris.com for more information. Lines operates in the Trois Vallés and runs courses throughout the summer. For more information go to www.lines.ac. If you can't send her to France for the summer then the best thing would be to get a French au pair to come and live with you and speak only French to the whole family between now and September. Could even work out cheaper than the language course and you all get to benefit.

Counselling in France

There is a website, www.counsellingfrance.com, which lists English-speaking counsellors who provide either online or face-to-face support. There is also a cancer support section.

Bouncing cheques

A little known fact about France is that it is illegal to bounce a cheque. If you do bounce a cheque you are given five days to rectify the situation. Should you fail to do so, you are then banned from having a bank account for five years. This has just happened to a friend of mine with a house close by. She wrote a cheque for €750 unaware of the fact that there was no money in her account. Of course by the time the warning letter from the bank was forwarded to her UK address it was too late to do anything about it, although I am told by another cheque-bouncing friend that if you phone the bank and weep that helps. Should that fail you can appeal against the ban, put lots of money into your account and ask the victim of your bounced cheque to write to say he or she has received the funds owed.

Insurance worries

If you're planning to lock your French home up for the winter it is worth checking with your insurance company that you are still covered for eventual break-ins, flooding or other disasters. 'If your house is unoccupied for more than 30 days you need to notify your insurers of arrangements you have made to safeguard the property like a neighbour checking on it regularly,' says Robin Innes, senior manager of FLG Insurance Brokers. 'In fact it is important to have someone on the ground as many policies state that a burglary or burst pipe has to be reported within two days or your claim will not be paid.' It may not be just the fact that you're away that means you can't claim. Dave and Jan Denholm found that repairs to their roof after damage caused by strong winds were not covered by their insurer at all. 'Groupama told us that as the damage was caused by natural events we weren't covered,' says Dave.

End of Notaire Monopoly
The European Competition authorities are looking into the monopoly French notaires have on all property purchases. At the moment, notaires need to be of French nationality and any property purchase involves giving them a percentage which is set by the government. The EU is pushing for a liberalisation of the market. But according to Dawn Alderson from Russell Cooke Associates it will not necessarily mean buying property will get cheaper. 'What you have to remember is that at the moment notaires take a percentage of the purchase price,' she says. 'This is bad news if you are buying a very expensive property but if you are buying for around £200,000 say then you will almost certainly get better value from a notaire than you would a lawyer.' In addition if you share the same notaire with the vendor, you split the cost. Although some would say this isn't a good idea as the notaire will not necessarily be working in your best interests if he or she is working for two clients.

Breakdown cover
If you are resident in the UK and your vehicle is UK-registered and insured then you can get AA cover in France from £10.90 a day. For more information call 0800 0852840 or go to www.theaa.com and click on European Breakdown. If your vehicle is French-registered and insured you need to get something called Europ Assistance from a France-based company like Bacchus Insurance. For more information please call 0033 (0) 5 45 82 42 93 or email info@bacchus-insurance.com.

Removal brokers
A friend of mine who recently moved from London to France says he saved himself more than one thousand pounds by using a removal broker. These are people who take all the details of your move and then find the company that offers you the best price. ET Brokers, the company my friend used, charged him £35.25 for the service. Their website is www.etbrokers-removals.com and telephone number 0044 (0) 870 800 3880.

Train tickets

If you call SNCF and ask to change or refund a train ticket they will tell you that there is no other option but to go to a station in person and do it before the train you were booked on is due to leave. This is not so. In some cases you can change it online and if you can't do that call the normal SNCF number (3635) and tap # 33 as soon as the menu begins. You will need your ticket with you to key in all sorts of codes from it but you can cancel the reservation via an automated service. If you do cancel a reservation on the internet or the phone you need to take the ticket to any station within three months to secure the refund. But at least the pressure is off to appear in person before the ticket is rendered invalid.

Missing bits

Beware of bits missing from packets when you buy anything in France. I recently got a mobile phone home to find the battery missing. I phoned the shop I bought it from, a mere three-hour drive from my home, and was told I would have to come back to collect another one. A friend of mine recently bought a shower-kit from a shop in Montpellier only to find the shower head was missing. He called the shop and was told it was up to him to come back and pick up another one. As he didn't see what other option he had he did just that. He was amazed when the sales assistant calmly opened another packet containing the identical shower-kit in front of him and removed the head from it to give to him. 'I realised that was what must have happened to mine,' he told me. You have been warned.

Changes to E111

The E111, the form you get from the post office which entitles you to free or reduced cost healthcare cover in European Union countries, is changing. The main difference is that the new form will be issued on an individual and not a family basis. However one family member can complete the form on behalf of spouse and children. You will still be able to get the form from the post office.
www.dh.gov.uk/PolicyAndGuidance/HealthAdviceForTravellers/fs/en

Land regret

'A neighbour of mine has just signed a *compromis de vente* to sell a piece of land he owns adjoining our house,' says Anthony with a holiday home in the Var. 'I want to buy the land and as I am a cash buyer he is keen to sell to me. Sadly he didn't know how to get hold of me and the previous transaction went through while I was in England. Can he get out of it?' According to Stephen Smith from Stephen Smith France Ltd, it is possible, but the vendor may need to pay a fine. 'Most properly drawn *compromis* include a clause whereby if the vendor withdraws for any reason she or he must pay damages of typically 10 per cent of the agreed purchase price,' he says. It is also worth noting that in France you can go to your local *notaire* (notary) and sign an agreement for right of first refusal on land adjoining your property.

Priorité a droite

This quirky French driving law causes much confusion among Brits living here and probably a few accidents. It seems ridiculous, but there are places where if you are driving along a main road people coming from the right (where there is no give way or stop sign) have priority. Just to keep you on your toes, this isn't always clearly indicated so you can be going along quite happily when cars suddenly appear from nowhere forcing you off the road. Anyone wanting to know more can buy the French equivalent of the Highway Code, the Code Rousseau.

France Telecom helpline

When you want to shout at someone from France Telecom it is now possible do so in English. The French telecoms operator has opened a helpline to cater for non-French speakers living in France. The number is 0800 364 775 from France or +33 1 55 78 60 56 from abroad. The helpline is open Monday to Friday 8.30am to 8pm. You can also fax them on +33 1 55 78 62 70.

Easy Move

If you're moving house within France there is a website developed by the snappily named *Agence pour le developpement de l'administration électronique* (ADAE) to make your life easier. Go onto www.changement-adresse.gouv.fr, enter your old and new address as well as your social security number and the site will pass the information on to the various administrative authorities including tax, social security and unemployment.

Lost and found

What to do with lost animals?' If the animal has a tattoo (usually found in the ears) then call the *Fichier National Canin* on 0149375454 (for cats the number is 0155010808). The animal may also have a microchip, but you need to take it to a vet for scanning. Failing both of the above, contact your local mayor's office to see if anyone has reported the animal missing. You should also notify the local police. If you don't want to keep the animal, the mayor will put you in touch with the local pound or you can look in the yellow pages for an animal refuge (not as prolific in France as they are in the UK).

Retiring made cheap?

'A friend told me recently that as a retired gentleman he did not need to pay *taxe d'habitation* on my property.. Sadly, it's not true. Gentleman or not, you need to pay it, as does almost everyone else in France. The only exceptions are the disabled, those on state welfare or those living off an income below a certain level.

French tax haven?

There is a simple savings structure in France called Assurance Vie which entitles you to leave your money, tax free, to whomever you wish. This means you can not only save huge amounts of tax but also avoid the stringent inheritance laws here. 'This is particularly useful for foreigners who have retired here,' says Stephen Langton, Montpellier Partner of Blevins Franks International. 'If you name the beneficiaries of the Assurance Vie, then in the event of your death, each of them will be entitled to €152,000 free of French inheritance tax. However, if you set up the Assurance Vie before becoming a French resident there is no limit to the amount beneficiaries can inherit tax free.'

Under the proposals contained in the latest France/UK Double Tax Treaty, if a British national sets up the Assurance Vie outside France, in Luxembourg for example, then the assets invested within it will be free of French wealth tax for five years.

Notary fees

You should expect to pay around 6.5 per cent in notaire's fees on properties over five years old which will include taxes. Out of the 6.5 per cent the notaire's fee is actually only 0.825 per cent, the rest is taxes and land search fees. If the property is less than five years old then the French VAT of 19.6 per cent is payable and the notaire's fees are reduced. If your property is less than €16,700 then the percentage of notaire's fees will be higher.

Grumpy ghosts

If you're thinking of moving to France you should be aware that it is not only your living neighbours that can make life difficult for you. Richard Hoblyn, a stockbroker from Sussex, bought a farmhouse 20 kilometres south of Limoges last year. 'The house is definitely haunted,' he says. 'Windows and doors keep opening and shutting and we've had knives flying across the kitchen.' According to the locals it's to be expected as the place hasn't been lived in for over 30 years. 'I wonder if the ghost is rebelling against English-speaking inhabitants,' says Richard. He plans to call in the Catholic Church. In France each diocese has someone authorised to carry out exorcisms, your local church or mayor's office will know how to contact them. The exorcist at Notre Dame in Paris has his own little cabin if you want to pay him a visit.

Seven-day warning

A company called Laugil approached me a few months ago selling a water-softening system. I was told by the salesman that our water was too hard for the baby's skin, bad for our pipes, ruinous for the kettle and so on. He said I could try the system (a combination of filter and salt) and then send it back if I didn't like it. I foolishly agreed to sign a contract for monthly payments. It seemed the most effective way of getting the man out of the house. My husband said the water now tasted bitter and demanded we get the thing taken away. I noticed no change in the quality of water. 'You have to wait,' a spokesman from Laugil told me. 'Once it all settles down it will be fine. Give it a couple of weeks and then you can send it back.' I waited another two weeks and called again. 'You can't send it back now,' I was told. 'It's more than seven days ago since you signed the contract.' Not only do I now have an expensive, ineffective water filter and a grumpy husband, but I am locked into a maintenance contract with the company for new filters and so on. According to Dawn Alderson, solicitor with Russell Cooke solicitors, I should have terminated the contract within seven days and then I would have been free to negotiate the return of the system. 'If in doubt you should always take advantage of your right to terminate a contract during the cancellation period by giving notice in writing, always by letter with acknowledgment of receipt,' she says. 'You can then negotiate with the seller at leisure.' The seven-day cooling off period applies to contracts in France where sales are made by correspondence (telephone, minitel, internet) or for sales made to you in your home or place of work.

Children learning French
A company called Petit Pont uses interactive CD roms, audio CDs and books to teach children French (www.petitpont.com.) You could also find out if there are French nursery schools or French classes for children in your area. Or hire a French au pair and ask her to speak French to all of you.

Obliged to sell
Those of you selling your house in France should be aware that if you get an offer for the asking price, you could be legally bound to accept it under terms of the standard contract (called a *mandat de vente*) you have signed with your agent. If you refuse, you could be liable to pay the agent's commission, normally around 6 per cent of the price. You should check your contract has no clause stating your obligation to sell before you sign it.

Naming of babies
The French have ended the use of the patronym whereby a new-born child automatically bears its father's name. From January 2005 babies born to married couples in France are no longer required to bear their father's surname. They can be given their mother's surname, or their father's, or a hyphenated mix of the two. However subsequent siblings should carry the same surname.

Insurance notice
A friend from the Mayenne saying that she is being pursued for unpaid premiums by her French house insurer. She wrote to the company to cancel the policy before signing up for a cheaper one. However, she failed to send her letter by registered post. When cancelling any insurance policy in France be it car or home you have to give two months' written notice and send this notice by registered post

Pools

Pool owners should install one of the following:

1. A fence or a wall. This should stand 1.1 metre high from the ground and have a self-closing gate. It should be a minimum of one metre from the edge of the pool. The maximum is determined by whether the fence is still deemed to be effective, but it is probably not more than 10 metres. It should prevent a child under the age of five from having access to the pool.

According to Tim Hammond, director, at Safer Pools, a network of 30 individual pool companies throughout France, this solution is the safest of all the devices. 'Because of the gate, the child cannot get in if the pool is unsupervised. The other advantages of a fence are that it will be accepted by all the insurance companies as a safety device, and also can take it down in ten minutes when the property isn't let or you're there on your own,' he says. With Safer Pools, a standard-size pool of ten by five metres costs around £1500 to fence plus £250 for the gate and another £250 for installation.

2. A cover. This is more expensive than the fence, but can replace both your existing winter and summer covers. They cost around £2800 plus an installation fee of £200. The disadvantage is that when the cover is off, you are not insured, so if your tenants decide to leave the cover off and someone drowns you could still be liable. Nets have not yet been approved but may gain approval at a later stage.

For more information:
www.equipement.gouv.fr
www.saferpools.co.uk, contact@saferpools.co.uk
Hotline   (calls from the UK)0871 711 3371
                   (calls from France)06 62 28 04 79

3. An alarm. The alarm sets off a 150-decibel siren in the house and by the pool, as well as flashing lights. It costs £600 and installation around £70. But these are not considered sufficient if there isn't a permanent presence on the site.

4. A telescopic enclosure vaulting over the pool. This costs £8,000 or more. However, it does have the added advantage that you can swim all year round.

Hammond says people have been so confused by the law and its specifications that some have chosen to sell up and move back home rather than deal with it.

'Everyone will have to do something come 2006,' says Hammond. 'But there are questions as to how they will enforce the law.' As it is a law of the senate, it means it can be enforced locally. 'I don't think they will be too active about it initially,' says Hammond. 'But they will make an example of cases when accidents happen.' The punishment is a fine of £30,000, enough to buy several pool enclosures. As the mother of three young children, I am well aware of the risks of a pool, but can there really be a substitute for keeping your eye on the children at all times? Research from some states in America suggest that such legislation adds to the number of deaths by drowning, because parents stop supervising the pool area. For more information go to www.afnor.fr. There you can buy a technical sheet containing the full details of each category from the official French organization in charge of the norms.

Cynics who remember the furore when France introduced a ban on smoking in 1992 in public places will take heart from the fact that nobody has yet been prosecuted under the tobacco law. I might well decide to cover my pool, but I'd like to be able to decide when and how I do it myself.

Whatever next? A law telling me I have to wear a swimming costume?

Leaseback Schemes

One of the most popular ways to sell new developments in France is through a leaseback scheme. Potential buyers get a free holiday home, while making a sound investment and getting a return on their investment.

This is how it works. The purchaser buys the freehold of the property and then leases it back to a developer or rental company. The owner is guaranteed a rental income, usually between 3 per cent and 7 per cent of the initial investment. At the end of the lease period the property is returned to the purchaser. The big advantage with leaseback is that the government refunds the VAT (19.6 per cent), providing that the lease runs for 20 years and you don't sell within that time. However, you usually have the option to use the property for three to six weeks a year at no cost.

So far, there seems to be no downside. You get a guaranteed return on your capital, the property is increasing in value, the developer takes care of all the rentals, you get to go there for your holidays and at the end of 20 years you can move in.

'For us it seemed like the ideal solution,' says Grant Hitchin, who was looking to buy a place via the leaseback scheme at the beginning of this year. They were considering an apartment just outside Paris for £35,000. 'My wife and I knew we wanted to retire in France and this way we could buy something now while prices were still affordable. The government VAT refund was our deposit, the monthly return was more than our mortgage would cost, and we could use the place for holidays.' Grant was about to sign up for a development in Paris when he came across a web site called www.frenchpropertydigest.com whilst surfing the web one evening. 'There was a huge amount of information on leaseback and after I'd read it, I decided to forget the whole thing.'

Tony Tidswell, who runs the site, is concerned that potential investors are being led astray by the leaseback scheme. 'It seems like a great idea,' he says. 'But having studied the leases these management companies are asking people to sign, I am seriously worried about what people are letting themselves in for. They may find that there are heavy penalties for opting out of the leaseback agreement and that they never actually have control of their property.'

The law stipulates that the management company has the right to renew the nine-year agreement automatically and that the purchaser is not able to cancel the lease without paying a huge indemnity and refunding the VAT on the purchase price.

'These schemes are moving towards deception in the way they are marketed by some web sites and agents,' says Tidswell. 'They are telling buyers they can get a house for no cash up front, which looks very attractive. But when you go into the small print, it can be a very different story. What people end up with is a steady return on their investment, but not much more. In some cases it can be described as an investment plan and not a property deal.'

According to Dawn Alderson, solicitor with Russell-Cooke Solicitors, leaseback schemes are not suitable for the average purchaser. 'What you have is a commercial-lease situation, which for the right investor is fine. But it is not geared towards the individual looking for a home. In that situation it can be a very dangerous thing to get involved in.' Alderson points out that the VAT refund is contingent upon the management ensuring that the development remains classified as a *Résidence de Tourisme* during the 20 year period. 'What happens if the management company doesn't fulfill these criteria, or simply goes bust? They lose you the VAT refund and it's a situation you can't possibly control.'

Leaseback checklist

* What is written into the lease agreement after the first nine years?
* What are the terms of the renewal or cancellation?
* Is the renewal automatic and will you have to pay a penalty if you do not renew it.
* How much does the management company charge for upkeep of the property?
* Are there any penalties, either in the purchase or the leasing contract if you want to sell?
* Are you free to sell to whomever you chose and free to advertise the sale openly?
* What happens if the management company goes into liquidation?
* Can another company take over the property and if so will you have the same contractual terms?
* As well as contractual issues, you should check whether there are any other factors that could affect the resale value such as proximity to flooding or strong winds.

Web sites selling leaseback schemes describe it as a 'buy-to-let with a free holiday.' In their frequently asked questions, they maintain that after nine years the choice is yours as to what to do with the property. In fact, the lease has to be renewed legally so you do not have the choice. In other words, even if the management company has said they will hand over the property to you, they do not have the legal right to do so. Some management companies get round this by setting up shell management companies that give you a lease that looks like you can opt out but that can in fact be wound up and replaced with another at the time of renewal.

Before signing anything, you need to go through the lease and check the points listed in the box. You would also be well advised to see a solicitor. If you do sign and regret it, there is a seven-day cooling off period, but you should send your letter of cancellation by international courier. There have been cases where the management company have simply ignored the registered letter or maintained it arrived outside the seven-day period. 'Leaseback is getting as bad a name as timeshare,' says an English estate agent based near Paris who does not wish to be named. 'I certainly won't be recommending any of my clients get involved with it.'

Having a Baby

I moved to France when I was seven months pregnant. I knew nothing about giving birth here, I didn't even speak the language. I had already had one baby in England, at a natural birthing centre, with no drugs and no doctors. It had been a good experience and I was keen to repeat it. As it turned out, for my first birth here I was fully drugged and had a Caesarean. Here are things I wish I had known earlier.

Covering the costs

If you haven't yet left the UK the first thing to do is to get hold of an E112 available from the NHS international services (number below). This entitles you to medical care abroad for a pre-existing medical condition, such as pregnancy. It was a passport to free scans, x-rays, consultations and ultimately childbirth and postnatal care. The only thing it didn't cover was the £20 a day I had to pay to be in a private room. If you are moving permanently, you should also look into getting an E104 which is a statement of all your contributions in the UK, and will mean you can transfer onto the French system. You can get this statement from the Department of Health (number listed below).

All costs should be reimbursed, you just have to fill in the *Feuille de Soins* (a piece of paper, normally brown, which details the care you have had and the cost) and send it off to your local CPAM (*Caisse Primaire d'Assurance Maladie*).

If you live in France and are already on the French system, your costs should be covered automatically. It may be worth signing up for a private insurance (called a *complémentaire*) company to cover anything the social security doesn't cover for the full 100 per cent. I was able to sign up for one even though I was already pregnant.

Prenatal care

If you get pregnant in France and you want to have a baby within the French

Useful baby vocabulary

amniocentesis	l'amniocentèse
baby	le nourrisson/le bébé
birth/delivery	l'accouchement
breastfeeding	allaitement maternel
breech	une présentation par le siège
formula milk	le lait en poudre
forceps delivery	l'accouchement au forceps
maternity	la maternité
maternity benefit	l'allocation de maternité
maternity leave	le congé de maternité
pregnant	enceinte
pregnancy test	un test de grossesse
prenatal	prénatal
postnatal	post-natal
postnatal depression	la dépression post-natale
she is three months pregnant	elle est enceinte de trois mois
she's overdue	elle a dépassé le terme
shit, it's twins	merde, c'est des jumeaux
the baby was two weeks overdue	le bébé avait deux semaines de retard
to get pregnant	tomber enceinte
twins	des jumeaux
when is it due?	c'est prévu pour quand?

social security system, the first thing to do is to go to your doctor and fill in a '*Déclaration de Grossesse*'. This will normally take place towards the end of the third month of pregnancy and gets sent around to the various authorities and means your pregnancy is registered. The doctor you go to is up to you, but they must be agreed by the social security (*conventionné*). My local doctor recommended a gynaecologist to me who carried out all my monthly checks. This includes monthly blood tests to check for toxoplasmosis, measles etc. You take the blood tests to a laboratory of your choice, to find one look under *Laboratoires d'analyses de biologie médicale* in the yellow pages. During my first pregnancy in France they sent a nurse to take blood samples at my house to ascertain my blood group.

You will also have several scans during your pregnancy. Very early on they will be able to determine the sex, and if you don't want to know you should tell them. Most people in France find out, if they don't, they call the baby '*un bébé surprise*'. If you are over 35 you will be offered an amniocentesis to determine any genetic disorders. When I had mine they left the results of it (all fine) and the sex of my baby on the answering machine (which I didn't want to know). Towards the latter stages of pregnancy you will also have to meet the anesthetist who will talk to you about the kind of pain relief you are likely to require. Epidurals are freely available and having given birth without one, I thoroughly recommend them. In fact, the French are not big on natural childbirth, when I arrived with my ideas of a drug-free labour they all looked at me as if I was deranged. I know of only one woman here who has given birth at home, with the help of a midwife.

Midwife

A midwife is called a *sage-femme* (literally, a wise woman). Once your pregnancy declaration is in the system, you will have a letter from your local midwife inviting you to attend a course. Although this was my third baby, I went along. Not so much because I wanted to learn how to give birth, but partly to have a contact to call if I had any worries. Also it was a very good French lesson.

Giving birth

You will give birth in a clinic or a hospital and are liable to pay only for extras, like having a single room, TV and phone. The average stay is five days. I loved my time at the *Clinique Champeau* in Béziers. I remember the first time being amazed when a lady in a white coat came in to tell me the day's menu and ask me if there was anything I didn't eat. Don't forget to bring all your social security papers with you to the birth, the whole system thrives on bureaucracy and the first thing they ask you for, as you come panting into the clinic, is your social security status.

Both my births in France were relatively pleasant experiences. The first one was more like surgery than childbirth, but all involved did their jobs admirably. The second one was overseen by the midwives at the clinic, one of whom fought the obstetrician in charge to save me from a second Caesarean. My son arrived just as he was getting the operating theatre ready. I am eternally grateful to the midwife, the whole birth experience and the recovery was the best of all three.

Admin for the child

The admin for the baby starts as soon as s/he is born. You are legally obliged to register the birth of your child within three days at the local mayor's office, so you'd better have a name ready. When my husband went to register Beatrice (our second daughter) at the Béziers *mairie* he was told that one of the reasons for the registration was to make sure the child wlasn't given a ridiculous name. He asked who decides whether the name is ridiculous. Apparently it is whoever happens to be dealing with your registration. He thought briefly about Kylie Budgerigar or Gianluca Vialli, but decided to stick with Beatrice.

At hospital you will be given a *Carnet de Santé* for your baby. This is a book that contains his or her health records, things like vaccinations, and check-ups. Your baby will have a check-up once a month by the doctor of your choice. Your child has to have certain inoculations (like TB) in order to go to a crèche or school. You will be sent reminders when it is time for your child to have inoculations, once they are pre-school age. For the baby, the hospital should give you a list of timings.

Nationality

When both parents are foreigners (say British), the baby takes on their nationality. When the child is 13, providing s/he has lived here for at least five years, the parents can ask for French nationality on his or her behalf. When the child is 16 s/he can ask for French nationality him or herself, providing again s/he has lived here at least five years. At 18 the child becomes automatically French, but keeps his or her British nationality.

Postnatal care

The baby will leave hospital along with a whole medicine cabinet of vitamins, fluoride and creams in case of nappy rash. You will also be given some ghastly red stuff to treat the umbilical cord sore with. It dries it so it falls off more quickly.

Benefits and maternity/paternity leave

If you have fewer than two children you are entitled to 16 weeks' maternity leave (six before childbirth and 10 after it). If you have more than two chil-

---

Useful associations and addresses

NHS International Services Team +44 191 225 4811; Department of Health +44 20 7210 4850

Caisse d'allocations familiales (www.caf.fr), the government body responsible for paying out. There is one in every city, contact them for more information on your rights.

Protection maternelle et infantile, a service provided by the *Conseil Général* where social workers, midwives, doctors and paediatricians answer your questions. Look for your local branch on the Internet.

Mouvement français pour le planning familial (www.planning-familial.org), the French family planning organisation with 67 branches throughout the country. Information on contraception, abortion, sexual violence, etc. Information is confidential and free.

Centre d'information et de documentation femmes et familles (www.infofemmes.com), +33 1 42171200. Advice on women's rights, legal help and so on. Advice is free and confidential.

dren, this goes up to 26 weeks (eight before childbirth and 18 after it). Fathers are entitled to a leave of 11 consecutive days, to be taken within four months of the birth.

In order to be eligible for family allowance you have to provide the CAF (*Caisse d'allocations familiales* www.caf.fr) with the *Déclaration de Grossesse* within the first 14 weeks of pregnancy. Allowances depend on your personal circumstances and you should contact your local CAF for more information. However, the most frequently provided ones are:

? *L'Allocation pour jeune enfant* (APE) which is generally given to those on low incomes. It starts from the fifth month of pregnancy and goes on until the child's third birthday.

? *Allocations familiales.* If you have two or more children you are entitled to this allowance which does not depend on your income.

Planning Permission

Planning permission is required in France for any new construction (subject to certain exemptions) or any proposal which changes the architecture of an existing property, its dimensions, its drainage or the layout of the surrounding area. It is also required for a change of use e.g. conversion of a barn into a dwelling.

Work on an existing building also requires planning permission where it affects the volume of the building or creates supplementary levels.

Certain categories of construction are exempt from planning permission and are instead subject to a *déclaration préalable* (prior declaration) from the mayor These are works such as terraces, with certain restrictions, and the creation of a balcony or veranda, again within certain restrictions on size. A *déclaration préalable* is also required prior to re-facing work being carried out, for instance.

The *déclaration préalable* is a simplified system whereby the application *dossier* is completed on a standard form and submitted with appropriate plans. The employment of an architect is not obligatory. The form is filed at the *mairie* and, if following the publicity the authorities remain silent for a period of one month, their tacit agreement is deemed to have been given. However, for certain buildings, e.g. historic monuments, the period is increased to two months.

If a full planning permission is required, a formal application *dossier* should be prepared, with comprehensive plans drawn up by an architect. The architect's involvement is obligatory, unless an individual wishes to build or modify a construction for their own use (as long as it is not agricultural) and the habitable surface area does not exceed 170m² (current rules).

After the planning application is filed with the local *mairie*, it will again be publicised. The normal period for consideration of the file is two months, but this can be increased for certain types of building, such as those classified as historic monuments. Once planning permission has been obtained, it can still be appealed by third parties within a period of two months from the date of granting permission.

The situation is complex and professional advice should always be taken prior to proceeding. Once the permission is obtained, building work must commence within a period of two years. Following completion of the works, a letter must be sent to the *mairie* confirming that the works have been completed (*Déclaration d'Achèvement des Travaux*) and the *Certificat de Conformité* (certificate of conformity) is requested which, if granted by the *mairie*, will confirm that the works were carried out in accordance with their permission.

Bear in mind that planning regulations vary from region to region. You should check with you local *Service de l'urbanisme* at the *mairie*, or go to www.vivremamaison.com or www.equipement.gouv.fr.

Le Troisième Age

For those contemplating retirement to France it is comforting to know that the French healthcare system is among the best in the world, and that it also covers dental care, which is increasingly difficult to find in the UK under the National Health Service. Furthermore, those of retirement age in receipt of a state pension do not have to make social security contributions to the service. It is essential however, before leaving the UK, to obtain form E121 from the Department of Work and Pensions, Tyneview Park, Newcastle upon Tyne, NE98 1BA. This needs to be filled in and taken to your local *Caisse Primaire d'Assurance Maladie* (CPAM) to get on to the French system.

The most striking difference between the healthcare services of the two countries is that in France payment is made in full, following treatment and then reimbursed. Normally 70 per cent of the cost of treatment, which includes some acupuncture and homeopathy treatment, is reimbursed, and the balance can be funded by additional private medical insurance. While you are not required to register with a particular doctor and can obtain medical assistance from any doctor or specialist in France at any time, it obviously makes sense to find a doctor and dentist near where you live. Also bear in mind that many French doctors do not speak English, so brushing up on your medical vocabulary might be useful.

When choosing a doctor or dentist it is important to verify that he or she is approved by social security (*conventionné*), otherwise you will not be reimbursed any costs. You can obtain a list of doctors registered with social security from your local social security office.

In order to be reimbursed, you need a *Carte Vitale* which you will get from your social security office once you're on the system. You give this to the doctor following treatment and your bank account will automatically be reimbursed.

Prescribed medicines are also covered by the system, and are reimbursed on a sliding scale up to 100 per cent, depending upon how essential they are. In every case payment has to be made in full following treatment, and the costs are reimbursed.

Emergencies are covered by the *Service d'Aide Médicale d'Urgence* (SAMU). Dial 15 for your nearest unit. It provides ambulance services manned by trained staff with cardiac and resuscitation equipment. Payment is made and reimbursed in the normal way.

There are both private and public hospitals in France. Most private hospitals specialise in some particular type of treatment. The cost of treatment in private hospitals is normally higher than in public hospitals, although some may have an agreement with social security and operate in the same way as public hospitals. Admission to hospital is normally subject to a recommendation by your doctor, except of course in the case of emergency treatment. In the case of life threatening conditions, reimbursement is normally made in full.

It is worth bearing in mind that the French healthcare service is heavily indebted and costs are out of control. At some point in the future one must imagine that this issue will be addressed and means will need to be found for greater contributions to support it.

French taxation considerations for pensioners

Anyone contemplating retirement to France and therefore becoming subject to French taxation and succession law needs to consider carefully in advance three aspects, namely income tax, wealth tax and inheritance tax. These need all to be thought through before becoming domiciled in France as some of the tax advantages available can only be accessed *before* becoming a French tax resident. Professional advice should be sought if the sums concerned are significant. Anyone living in France is legally required to file an annual tax return stating their worldwide income. Even residents that have no income are required to file a blank return. You should also bear in mind that if your worldwide assets and income add up to more than €720,000 you may be liable for wealth tax.

1) Income Tax

There is a sliding scale for Income tax, as in the U.K. and although the top band is 48.09 per cent, most families will pay less in France especially if their prime source of income is a pension. French income tax is calculated on the basis of 'parts', which in fact equates to a family member. A retired couple would therefore consist of two 'parts'. Any income is split equally, taxed at that rate, and multiplied by two. A retired couple would therefore normally pay less income tax than in the U.K.

Most pension income, whether it be from a personal pension plan or UK state pension, is only taxed on a portion of its value, normally 72 per cent due to allowances. Furthermore pensions are exempt from French social charges, normally 8 to 10 per cent. However investment income, bank interest and Premium Bond winnings would be taxed at an additional 10 per cent to your French income tax band. It follows therefore that Premium Bonds are not a tax efficient vehicle for French residents.

There is however another form of investment, life insurance investment bonds (*Assurance Vie*), which are very tax efficient as the growth within the bond is tax free, and if income is taken, a large part of it is considered as return of capital and is tax free. Specialist advice should be taken on these investments.

2) Wealth Tax

This is levied annually on a sliding scale on wealth above €720,000 on all assets whether in France or elsewhere. The value of a French home is discounted by 20 per cent for wealth tax purposes and there are exemptions for fine art, antiques and 'collectors items'. The rates start at 0.55 per cent between €720,000 and €1,160,000.

However the funds in a personal pension plan written in trust are not considered part of your assets for Wealth Tax purposes, although of course the income is taxable as above.

3) Inheritance Tax.

This is a complicated subject, not least because French succession law divides an individual's assets into a disposable portion, and a reserved portion. The reserved portion must go to a protected heir, normally the child or children. A spouse is not considered to be a protected heir and therefore arrangements have to be made to ensure that a surviving spouse is taken care of. A French will is essential. This can be as simple as a hand written note along the following lines:

Je soussigné [e] [full names] *révoque tous testaments antérieurs. Je déclare en décès vouloir laisser tous mes biens mobiliers et immobiliers m'appartenant en France et en Angleterre à mon épouse* [full names + maiden name] *et en cas de son décès avant moi à* [full names and relationship] *habitant* [address]

Fait ce jour [date] *à* [place]
[Signed]
[Print full name]

You can either pay your lawyer or *notaire* to keep a copy of this or just put it somewhere safe at home. Please note though it must be hand written.

Inheritance tax regulations are completely different from the U.K. While at first they appear draconian, for example inheritance tax is chargeable between spouses above a basic allowance of €76,000, and legacies to stepchildren are charged at 60 per cent above a basic allowance of €1500, there are a number of ways of mitigating these taxes. The life insurance investment bonds (*Assurance Vie*) mentioned above allow you to pass €152,500 to each beneficiary, free from French inheritance tax. There is no limit to the amounts that can be gifted to each beneficiary in this way if the investments are made before becoming tax resident in France. Furthermore this type of investment is not subject to French Succession law so you are at liberty to leave money to whomsoever you wish within certain limits. These investments also offer certain guarantees that protect your capital and as a result are not very exciting, but they make 4 to 5 per cent at present, and pensioners are usually interested in safety rather than the excitement of the market for most of their funds.

It is perfectly possible to reduce your liability to the three main taxes levied in France within the law and maintain a good standard of living provided you plan well ahead and seek advice before moving to France. In that way there will be no surprises, and you will not be subject to unexpected tax demands which can blight a happy retirement.

The 22 Regions of France

The last time I was in London, I took a cab from Sloane Street to Wandsworth. 'England's going to the dogs,' said my East End cabbie. 'Too many immigrants. I bet you was the only English person in Sloane Street.'

I was too scared of being thrown out of the cab to tell him I am, in fact, half-Swedish, half-Italian.

'I'm moving to France,' he continued as he swung into the Wandsworth Bridge Road.

'Oh really,' I said. 'Whereabouts will you go?'

'Dunno, probably Limousin.'

My first thought was-thank God, nowhere near me. My second was, how would one decide?

France is so diverse it could almost be a continent. It is the largest country in the EU and with a population density of 49 people per square kilometre compared with 361 in the UK it is far less populated than most EU countries. It is divided into 22 regions and 96 numbered départements, which are the equivalent of British counties. The departments are subdivided into communes, which also have their own authorities (run by the mayor) like British town or parish councils.

There are four main climatic zones in France. The Continental zone, which is characterised by warm summers but heavy rainfall and cold winters. This zone includes the northeastern corner of France as well as the Auvergne, Burgundy and the Rhône Valley. The average winter temperature is 9 degrees and 24 in the summer. The Mediterranean zone comprises the south and southeast corner, including the Languedoc-Roussillon, the Riviera and Provence. The climate in this zone is hot and dry. The winters are generally fairly warm (although it has snowed twice since we moved here) and rainfall is unpredictable. When it does rain it really pours and we are often stranded as our house is in between two rivers. In the winter, temperatures are on average around 11 degrees. The Oceanic zone affects the regions from the Loire to the Basque and is characterised by warm summers and mild winters with heavy rainfall, with average temperatures of 8 degrees in the winter and 24 in the summer. Finally, the Mountain zone which affects the Alps, the Pyrenees and the Massif Central. In this zone you can expect cool summers and very cold winters. The average temperature in the winter is 3 degrees and in the summer 25.

Alsace
Area:
8,280 km²
Population:
Around 1,700,000
Climate:
Continental and wet
Capital City:
Strasbourg
Departments:
Bas-Rhin, Haut-Rhin
*Miles from V&A Museum in
London to Strasbourg*:
460
Estimated driving time:
6 hours
Cost of tolls:
£26.50

Where is it?
On the German border in the north-east of France. Lots of flights from London to Strasbourg where the Council of Europe and the European Parliament sits.

History:
Was incorporated into France in 1681 by Louis XIV but re-absorbed into Germany after the Prussian victory of 1870. Then back to France in 1918. The Alsatian or Allemanic language can still be heard in some villages but less and less.

What do they eat?
Choucroute was invented here, sauerkraut with smoked ham, sausages and potatoes. The term *à l'alsacienne* means with sauerkraut.

What do they drink?
There are seven Alsace wines: six whites and one rosé, all named after the grapes they are made from.

Gewurztraminer, Muscat, Pinot Blanc, Pinot Noir, Riesling, Sylvaner, Edelzwicker and Tokay Pinot Gris. The Alsatians are also big on beer, Kronenbourg being the best known.

What do you do there?
Go shopping across the border in Germany where everything is cheaper. Ski, walk in the mountains, fish and ride horses. Walk in the lovely countryside.

Who lives there?
The Alsatians, a population that sees itself as neither French nor German. They say '*à l'intérieur*' when they mean the rest of France and will not hesitate to speak of the Boches when speaking of the Germans. They have a very strong identity. Far more reliable than the French (Geneviève, my cleaning lady is Alsatian and shows up for work ten minutes early) and much more Germanic in outlook.

What does it cost?
A lot. The classic Alsace house is half-timbered, gabled and expensive. You will pay around £80,000 for a two-bedroom apartment.

Why is it hot?
A rich region. Close to Paris, good connections with major German cities. The upper Vosges mountains. Pretty villages. Beautiful countryside.

Why is it not?
Bad crime rate in the major cities of Strasbourg and Mulhouse. Not much to do if you don't like sauerkraut or wine that comes in funny shaped bottles. Also very hard to adapt at

first, according to friends who have tried it.

Aquitaine
Area:
41,308 km²
Population:
Around 2,880,000
Climate:
Continental
Capital City:
Bordeaux
Departments:
Dordogne, Gironde, Landes, Lot-et-Garonne, Pyrénées-Atlantiques
Miles from V&A Museum in London to Bordeaux:
493
Estimated driving time:
10 hours 50 minutes
Cost of tolls:
£20.18
Where is it?
In the far south-west on the Atlantic coast.
History:
Was the capital of the Dukes of Aquitaine in the 11th century. The Brits bought so much wine the capital of Bordeaux became very rich.
What do they eat?
Truffles, *foie gras*, duck, pâté, snails and walnuts. The Périgord (the French name for the Dordogne) is known for its truffles, apricots and strawberries.
What do they drink?
Wine, wine and yet more wine. This is the world's most famous and prestigious wine-growing region. The vineyards of Bordeaux produce Margaux, Médoc, Sauterne and Saint-Emilion wines among others.
What do you do there?
Drink, eat, swim, surf. The region covers a vast area, stretching from the borders of the Massif Central to the Spanish border and the Pyrénées, so there is a lot of potential.
Who lives there?
Basque region separatists, although they are now very peaceful, wine makers, wine sellers, wine snobs, in fact, every kind of wine buff you can imagine. Bordeaux itself has a reputation as one of the least friendly places in France. The population is said to be more closed than the rest of France. However, closer to Spain, in the Pyrenées-Atlantiques it is a different story. The Dordogne is almost synonymous with Brits, it was the first area to be invaded by British second-home owners. The place is crawling with them.
What does it cost?
In the city of Bordeaux prices are rising as the major overhaul in the centre comes to an end. Wine-growing land is hugely expensive. In the Dordogne there isn't much left to buy and a tumble-down barn could cost you more than a *château* in Limousin.
Why is it hot?
A great quality of life if you can afford all the best the region has to offer. The wine industry dominates, so it helps to be involved in that. Bordeaux itself is a major centre of commerce and communications, so

travel almost anywhere is easy.

Why is it not?

Don't move to Bordeaux if you're not into wine, you'll find that's almost the only thing anyone talks about. Don't move to Biarritz if you can't surf.

Auvergne

Area:

26,013 km²

Population:

Around 1,315,000

Climate:

Mountain/Continental

Capital City:

Clermont-Ferrand

Departments:

Allier, Cantal, Haute-Loire, Puy-de-Dôme

Miles from V&A Museum in London to Clermont-Ferrand:

517

Estimated driving time:

8 hours 40 minutes

Cost of tolls:

£33.08

Where is it?

In the middle of the country. Some might say in the middle of nowhere. Clermont-Ferrand is the half-way point of a drive from England to the south of France.

History:

Rebels. A tough people, historically opposed to the government. The Auvergne has been inhabited since the Celts in 400 BC. Was once an important wine region but phylloxera wiped out the industry in the 19th Century.

What do they eat?

Cheese. This is where Cantal and Salers come from, as well as Saint-Nectaire and Bleu d'Auvergne. Staple dishes include anything *à l'auvergnate* which means with cabbage, bacon and sausage. The *potée auvergnate* is a typical local dish, a hot pot of vegetables and pork.

What do they drink?

Anything to keep warm.

What do you do there?

Walk, hike, swim, hang glide and enjoy the dramatic landscape.

Who lives there?

Not a lot of people, as a lot of it is above 3,000 feet and largely uninhabited. The ones that are there are rugged, independent and quite poor.

What does it cost?

Cheap. The image is of a poverty-stricken region with dire housing. There really isn't a market in holiday homes, but you could start a trend. With £10,000 you could still buy a derelict place, and it's one of the few places in France where you can still do that.

Why is it hot?

The volcanoes. Apart from that, er, well, some French would describe it as a place to leave, not to go to. If you like countryside and lots of space, it's for you. Masses of outdoor activities including skiing, rafting, biking, hiking and hang-gliding. Also some wonderful Romanesque churches and medieval castles.

Why is it not?

Remote, cold. Apart from on top of the volcanoes of course.

Brittany (Bretagne)
Area:
27,506 km²
Population:
Around 2,860,000
Climate:
Oceanic
Capital City:
Rennes
Departments:
Côtes d'Armor, Finistère, Ille-et-Vilaine, Morbihan
Miles from V&A Museum in London to Rennes:
124
Estimated driving time:
8 hours 41 minutes
Cost of tolls:
None
Where is it?
The far north-western corner.
History:
Brits have been emigrating here since the end of the Roman Empire. It became fully French in 1532, prior to that it was an independent dukedom that generally avoided the Anglo-French wars. If you speak Welsh or Cornish then you will understand a lot of the Breton language which is still spoken, although it has been suppressed by Paris. There is a move to resurrect this Celtic language, parents can now send their children to Breton schools.
What do they eat?
Legendary seafood (the official *plateau de fruits de mer* is expected to have at least six different shell-fish), lamb and artichokes. For the French the region is symbolised by crêpes, every crêperie in France calls itself Bretonne.
What do they drink?
Cider. Brittany was once full of vineyards but they were torn up in the 16th century and replaced with orchards. Cider goes very well with crêpes.
What do you do there?
750 miles of coastline so lots of water activities. For history fans there are lots of megaliths, museums, *châteaux* and medieval towns. The Gulf of Morbihan on the southern shore is stunning, dotted with tiny islands and the Ile aux Moines with its fairy-tale woods. Further inland is the medieval forest where the Knights of the round table sought the holy grail.
Who lives there?
Lots of Brits with second homes. The locals are used to us by now. We even had the same name, Great Britain is *Grande Bretagne* and Brittany is *Petite Bretagne*. But Mark, one Breton friend of mine, says he is appalled by the fact that there are now British villages. 'We don't really like foreigners,' he says. 'And by that we mean people from other parts of France as well.' Watch out—there are some members of the Breton liberation front left, though it has almost died out now. They famously (accidentally) killed a McDonald's worker in 1999 when they bombed it.
What does it cost?
Around 20 per cent of homes are

second homes but prices are still very reasonable.

Why is it hot?

Proximity to home, coastline, countryside.

Why is it not?

Rain. In the winter you might as well have stayed in England and saved yourself the crossing.

Burgundy (Bourgogne)

Area:

31,582 km²

Population:

Around 1,624,000

Climate:

Continental

Capital City:

Dijon

Departments:

Côte d'Or, Nièvre, Saône-et-Loire, Yonne

Miles from V&A Museum in London to Dijon:

430

Estimated driving time:

7 hours 30 minutes

Cost of tolls:

£24.83

Where is it?

The northeast of France, a good place to stop off on your way to the ski slopes.

History:

An independent kingdom for 600 years, there is a wealth of historic towns and beautiful *châteaux*.

What do they eat?

Boeuf Bourguignon, in fact anything *à la bourguignonne* (cooked in red wine sauce with mushrooms, shallots and bacon bits), *foie gras*, coq au vin and extremely garlicky snails cooked for hours in Chardonnay. In fact anything likely to raise your cholesterol levels and give you bad breath. If you don't like the taste of anything you can just cover it with Dijon mustard.

What do they drink?

Wine, wine, wine. But the good stuff doesn't come cheap. Home to Chambertin, Pommard, Meursault, Chablis and Pouilly-Fuissé.

What do you do there?

The medieval city of Vézelay from where Richard Lionheart launched the Third Crusade. The Musée des Beaux-Arts in Dijon is sometimes called 'Le Petit Louvre' due to its extraordinary collections ranging from medieval art to Impressionist.

Who lives there?

My aunt and uncle. Winemakers. Mustard makers. Brits who like the countryside because it looks just like England. Rich Parisians with weekend cottages. Don't forget Burgundy was an independent kingdom for 600 years. They are very proud of their heritage, cuisine, wine and so on. But the locals I have met are friendly

What does it cost?

Not cheap, but you can find bargains if you're prepared to live very rurally. Prices rise closer to Paris and the TGV

Why is it hot?

Gorgeous countryside. Easy trip to Paris with the TGV, also excellent motorways with easy access to Lyon and beyond. Lots of lovely rivers and canals. No real industry so very unspoiled.

Why is it not?

Can get very cold in the winter. Some parts are isolated.

Champagne-Ardenne

Area:

26,605 km²

Population:

Around 1,352,000

Climate:

Continental

Capital City:

Reims

Departments:

Ardennes, Aube, Marne, Haute-Marne

Miles from V&A Museum in London to Reims:

245

Estimated driving time:

4 hours 51 minutes

Cost of tolls:

£11.58

Where is it?

Right up in the north east, borders Belgium.

History:

The founder of champagne, a 17th-century monk called Dom Perignon came from the region. He tried adding yeast to bottles of fermenting wine and ended up with champagne. However, it was not until the 19th century that large-scale production got under way. This was largely because they developed glass bottles strong enough to hold the exploding wine. Twenty-six of France's kings were crowned here.

What do they eat?

Not one of France's gastronomic regions, the most notable local dishes are pig's trotters and white sausage. There are some fine cheeses such as Grand Condé and Rocroi.

What do they drink?

Champagne, the wine of kings and the king of wine.

What do you do there?

Celebrate. Make, sell, drink, grow champagne. If you're not into champagne you would go walking or boating. There are 650 kilometres of waterways and lakes.

Who lives there?

Champagne makers. Heidsieck, Moët et Chandon, Taittinger, Veuve-Clicquot. This isn't really a tourist destination so not many second home owners.

What does it cost?

Not much at all, as long as you're not trying to buy wine-growing land.

Why is it hot?

Close to the Channel, cheap houses, lovely countryside and lots of champagne.

Why is it not?

Champagne can give you a hangover. The *Climate* is wet and humid.

Corsica

Area:

8,681 km²

Population:

Around 260,700

Climate:

Mediterranean

Capital City:

Ajaccio

Departments:
Corse-du-Sud, Haute-Corse
Miles from V&A Museum in London to Ajaccio:
Don't even think about it, get on a plane. Or, if you happen to be in the south of France, a ferry from Nice, Toulon or Marseille.
Where is it?
In the middle of the sea, 100 miles south of the French Riviera, 50 miles from the Italian coastline and eight miles from Sardinia.
History:
Has not been independent since Roman times. France bought the island in 1768 from the Italians. Napoleon Bonaparte was born in Ajacco in 1769. Christopher Columbus was also Corsican.
What do they eat?
All kinds of fruit. The local cuisine is strongly flavoured with wild herbs. The national dish is stewed goat but all sorts of game is popular as well. Sea fish and shell fish, a must.
What do they drink?
A white muscat aperitif from Cap Corse. The island also produces some wines: Santa Barba and Fiumicicoli, to name two. Also a strong liquor made out of myrtles.
What do you do there?
There is no industry, the only income comes from the tourist trade. If you're on holiday you swim, walk, eat and pick fruit.
Who lives there?
Corsicans, who speak a dialect that is more similar to Italian than French. Lots of Italians with summer homes, they are generally more welcome than the French.
What does it cost?
Expensive. Anything by the sea is sold at a huge premium. The cost of living is much higher than mainland France.
Why is it hot?
A stunning island. Nicknamed Island of Beauty. 600 miles of coastline. People's hospitality (as long as they're not members of the FLNC, the Corsican liberation movement).
Why is it not?
Corsicans are prone to using dynamite to blow up non-Corsican residents' houses. It is also quite inaccessible.

Franche Comté
Area:
16,202 km²
Population:
Around 1,084,000
Climate:
Continental
Capital City:
Besançon
Departments:
Haute-Saône, Doubs, Jura, Territoire de Belfort
Miles from V&A Museum in London to Besançon:
451
Estimated driving time:
8 hours 31 minutes
Cost of tolls:
£22.82
Where is it?
Good question. My French friend Alex didn't even know, neither did

Caroline, another French friend. On the eastern border with Switzerland.

History:

Became part of France in 1678 when Louis XIV annexed it. The city of Belfort has a rich history: it was part of the Habsburg empire in the 14th century, later on it was ruled by the princes of Monaco, then became part of Alsace under German rule in 1871.

What do they eat?

Meat—Franche-Comté is known for its charcuterie, particularly smoked beef, sausages and hams. The local cheese, Comté, is said to be the most popular in France.

What do they drink?

Wine, mainly white, there are four AOC areas in Jura.

What do you do there?

In Besançon they make clocks. You are next door to Switzerland, there is lots of skiing, fishing, walking and white-water rafting.

Who lives there?

Not many foreigners, as it is very remote. Clockmakers and people who like the Swiss influence. Also pipe-makers.

What does it cost?

Building land is very cheap and there are plenty of timber-framed farm-houses for not much money.

Why is it hot?

Good if you don't ever want to see another English person and you like lederhosen. Also wonderful country-side, more than half the region is covered with forest.

Why is it not?

No TGV or plane links, very tough to get to. Freezing in the winter. My friend Caroline calls it '*une region paumée*', a godforsaken place.

Languedoc-Roussillon

Area:

27,447 km²

Population:

Around 2,445,000

Climate:

Mediterranean

Capital City:

Montpellier

Departments:

Aude, Gard, Hérault, Lozère, Pyrénées-Orientales

Miles from V&A Museum in London to Montpellier:

729

Estimated driving time:

11 hours 30 minutes

Cost of tolls:

£44.39

Where is it?

Down south, between Provence and the Spanish border.

History:

Greeks. Romans. Cathar massacres. The region is full of castles, abbeys and cathedrals to visit. Canal du Midi, one of the world's first great engineering projects. One of Europe's most famous 'medieval' towns is Carcassonne, where crusaders slew heretics. Spanish refugees fled here after the civil war.

Who lives there?

Local wine making population and *pied noir* refugees from Algeria. Other immigrants from North Africa (accused World Trade Center conspirator Mohammed Moussawi is from Montpellier.) Recently invaded by northern Europeans seeking sunshine and cheaper houses than in next door Provence.

What do they eat?

Mediterranean food—fish, seafood, fresh fruit and vegetables, olive oil, anchovies, olives.

What do they drink?

Fantastic wines—this is the world's largest vineyard. My favourites are wines from Domaines Paul Mas, Canteperdrix (in my village), St Martin de la Garrigue Domaine Sainte Rose and Seigneurie de Peyrat.

What does it cost?

Has been one of the best values in Europe; prices rocketing in past three years. The brave willing to take on rehab projects can still find bargains. £150,000—two to three bedroom village or town house. £350,000—isolated farmhouse that needs renovating. £1 million—château, vineyard.

Why is it hot?

Location, it is easy to get anywhere. Montpellier, one of the fastest-growing cities in Europe, is being run by a visionary socialist dictator. Many successful, young, dynamic types are leaving the north to move down. Not just Brits but Swedes, Germans, Dutch and so on. There is a vibrant social and working scene that didn't exist five years ago. *L'Express* rates it as the best place to live in France. Furthermore, Spanish influence such as bullfighting and obligatory siestas in the summer. Cap d'Agde is Europe's largest nudist colony. A must-see.

Why is it not?

Worst drivers in France with highest fatal accident rate. Savage dogs, vicious wild pigs, scorpions, killer wasps. And my daughters. Scary.

Limousin
Area:
16,942 km²
Population:
Around 717,600
Climate:
Cool
Capital City:
Limoges
Departments:
Corrèze, Creuse, Haute-Vienne
Miles from V&A Museum in London to Limoges:
499
Estimated driving time:
8 hours 30 minutes
Cost of tolls:
£23.10
Where is it?
The Massif Central, south west.
History:
Lots of museums in Limoges dedicated to the city's illustrious porcelain making past. Became part of France in 1607 under Henry IV. A stronghold in the Anglo-Angevin wars.

What do they eat?

The region is famous for its Limousin cows, some say they live better than the locals do. The local cuisine is often described as simple and filling. Lots of beef and chestnuts.

What do they drink?

Wine, Ricard, Pernod, the usual.

What do you do there?

Lots of outdoor activities. Limoges is world-famous for its porcelain, but even that can get boring after a few visits. This is France at its most rural and remote. Seen as a gateway between the industrialised north and laid-back south. Some cultural and gastronomic festivals during the tourist season. The painter Auguste Renoir came from Limoges, but other than that the region is rather lacking in the cultural tradition of the rest of the country. Jacques Chirac is from Sarran in Corrèze.

Who lives there?

Lots of tough, dour farmers. Walking into a bar can sometimes feel like wandering into a pub in deepest, darkest Yorkshire where everyone stares at you but no one talks to you.

What does it cost?

About the lowest in France.

Why is it hot?

Looks just like rural England did 50 years ago, stunning countryside, rolling hills. Lakes, rivers, chestnut forests and wide open spaces. This is a place for those who love a rural life. Sparsely populated.

Why is it not?

Slightly removed from the rest of the world, let alone the rest of France. A bit of a cultural desert. And personally I am not remotely interested in porcelain. During World War I, Marshal Joffre sent an incompetent general to Limoges. As a result there is a French verb—*limoger*—which literally means demoted or sent to some god-forsaken post.

Centre/Val de Loire

Area:

39,151 km²

Population:

Around 2,443,000

Climate:

Continental

Capital City:

Orléans

Departments:

Cher, Eure-et-Loire, Indre, Indre-et-Loire, Loiret, Loir-et-Cher

Miles from V&A Museum in London to Orléans:

338

Estimated driving time:

6 hours 18 minutes

Cost of tolls:

£17.89

Where is it?

Near the middle, slightly to the west of Paris.

History:

Known to the Brits as the Loire Valley, evidence of the struggle to get rid of the English in the 15th century is everywhere in the form of fortresses and castles. It was known as the playground for the aristocracy and the result is hordes of splendid *châteaux* to visit.

Who lives there?

Lots of fruit farmers and winemakers. Lots of Parisians with second homes.

What do they eat?

A fertile region which produces more cereal than anywhere else in France. Also big soft fruit producers. Home to the most popular French pudding, the Tarte Tatin, invented by the Tatin sisters in Lamotte-Beuvron.

What do they drink?

No fewer than 22 AOC wines including Sancerre, Vouvray and Valençay.

What do you do there?

Visit *châteaux* and cathedrals. The cathedral at Chartres is a world heritage site.

What does it cost?

Expensive as the regional capital is only an hour from Paris. Almost 20 per cent of properties are second homes, but prices are not unreasonable.

Why is it hot?

Lots of culture, *châteaux* and rivers.

Why is it not?

Flat landscape. And after visiting 10 *châteaux*, you'll probably have had enough.

Pays de la Loire

Area:

23,081 km²

Population:

Around 3,155,000

Climate:

Oceanic

Capital City:

Nantes

Departments:

Loire-Antlantica, Maine-et-Loire, Mayenne, Sarthe, Vendée

Miles from V&A Museum in London to Nantes:

306

Estimated driving time:

9 hours

Cost of tolls:

None

History:

Always popular with kings and noblemen. Nantes was the traditional seat of the Dukes of Brittany. In fact, it was part of Brittany until 1962. Traditionally royalist, they defended the king during the revolution.

Who lives there?

Lots of young dynamic people in Nantes, as well as students. Lots of culture vultures—this is the home to several celebrated theatre companies including the Royal de Luxe.

What do they eat?

Mogette—white *haricot verts* basically. According to my friend Alex who comes from here they eat them in sandwiches. Fish, seafood (lots of baby eels), Port Salut from the Mayenne.

What do they drink?

Muscadet wines, Saumur Brut, a white sparkling wine, pudding wines from the Côteaux du Layon, wines from the Fiefs Vendéens.

What do you do there?

Alex tells me that Vendée is the second most visited region in France after Provence. There are fine sandy beaches and two beautiful islands off the coast; the Ile d'Yeu and the Ile de Noirmoutier. Lots of water sports, as well as golf and walking. Also, lots of castles to visit: the Mayenne is reputed to have more *châteaux* per square mile than anywhere else outside Paris. Nantes is a very popular and dynamic city.

What does it cost?

Along the coast about 20 per cent of properties are second homes. Prices vary. Nantes, one of the most popular cities in France, can be quite expensive. The Mayenne is much cheaper.

Why is it hot?

According to my friend Jacques Kuhnlé, the locals are very friendly. 'In Angers, one driver saw I was looking for my way around and spontaneously showed me the way. One lady I asked about a good not too expensive restaurant went out of her way to take me to one.' Alex says the locals can be cold at first but are very loyal once they get to know you. Parts of the region (Nantes and Vendée) are often voted the best place to live in France.

Why is it not?

The Mayenne is not reputed to be the most welcoming region in France, as you will have gathered from stories in this book. Very agricultural, more closed.

Lorraine
Area:
23,547 km²
Population:
Around 2,311,700
Climate:
Continental
Capital City:
Metz
Departments:
Meurthe-et-Moselle, Meuse, Moselle, Vosges
Miles from V&A Museum in London to Metz:
361
Estimated driving time:
6 hours 26 minutes
Cost of tolls:
Nothing if you go from Calais to Lille and then into Belgium through Charleroi, Namur then south to Luxemburg where petrol is much cheaper. Otherwise £19.35.

Where is it?

North east, next to Germany.

History:

Traditionally a coal exporting region but the coal mines are now closed.

Who lives there?

Farmers, ex miners. Has a fairly grim image.

What do they drink?

Moselle white wine, Gris de Toul

What do they eat?

quiche lorraine, tarte aux mirabelles, Munster cheese. This is dairy-farming country so lots of dairy products.

What do you do there?

Go to Metz and Nancy where there is plenty going on. There is a '*festival du film italien*' in Villerupt where the greatest film directors meet. First world war monuments in and around Verdun. You can visit the ligne Maginot fortifications.

What does it cost?

Going up because of Germans, Belgians and Dutch buying houses.

Why is it hot?
Both rural countryside and mountains, skiing in the Vosges.
Why is it not?
Cold wet Climate. Locals rather cold too, but reliable. More friendly in the industrial areas where the first waves of immigrants settled.

Nord/Pas-de-Calais
Area:
12,414 km²
Population:
Around 4,000,000
Climate:
Oceanic/Rainy
Capital City:
Lille
Departments:
Nord, Pas-de-Calais
Miles from V&A Museum in London to Lille:
145
Estimated driving time:
3 hours 37 minutes
Cost of tolls:
None
Where is it?
The very north, next to Belgium
History:
Came under French rule in 1668. Prior to that, a borderland between Flanders and France.
Who lives there?
Big drinkers and party animals. 'These people are renowned for liking the good life,' says my Breton friend Mark. 'They love to party and are always very welcoming.'
What do they eat?
Distinctly Flemish: *moules frites*, fried chicory, meat in aspic.
What do they drink?
Beer, beer and more beer.
What do you do there?
Play golf at Le Touquet, one of the best courses in France. If you're looking for a job, this is where all the home shopping catalogues have their headquarters, a huge industry in France. The locals also have a reputation for partying and enjoying bar life.
What does it cost?
Quite reasonable prices, has been largely overlooked by people getting off the boats at Calais and driving through it. On the coast prices go up.
Why is it hot?
Very easy to get to from London, only two hours by trains to Lille. Lille is a fantastically dynamic city with lots going on. Also very close to Paris and Brussels. The Carnival of Dunkirk. Very nice people with a reputation for being calmer than your average French person due to the Flemish influence.
Why is it not?
Cold in the winter. One of France's most industrialised regions. Also very flat.

Lower Normandy
Area:
17,589 km²
Population:
Around 1,416,000
Climate:
Oceanic, like southern England really, but with more reliable sum-

mers.

Capital City:
Caen

Departments:
Calvados, Manche, Orne

Miles from V&A Museum in London to Caen:
86

Estimated driving time:
6 hours 50 minutes

Cost of tolls:
None

History:
Strong ties with Britain and North America. The resorts of Trouville and Deauville made famous by the Emperor Napoleon in the 19th century. Still frequented by rich Parisians. The birthplace of William the Conqueror.

Who lives there?
See below

What do they eat?
Fresh fish, duck, fruit, Camembert, Livarot and Pont l'Evêque cheeses. Lots of cream and butter with everything. Sea food.

What do they drink?
Calvados. Strong, dangerous and far too easy to drink.

What do you do there?
Visit the Bayeux Tapestry. Mont Saint Michel, one of the seven wonders of the world.

What does it cost?
Not bad at all, although the coastal properties sell at a premium.

Why is it hot?
Close to England if you're only planning to come for holidays. Combined with Upper Normandy it

has almost 400 miles of seaside with cliffs, pebbly and sandy beaches. Inland wonderful forests and streams. Lots of beautiful orchards to lie and dream in.

Why is it not?
Cold in the winter.

Upper Normandy

Area:
12,258 km²

Population:
Around 1,781,5000

Climate:
Oceanic

Capital City:
Rouen

Departments:
Eure, Seine-Maritime

Miles from V&A Museum in London to Rouen:
114

Estimated driving time:
4 hours 30 minutes

Cost of tolls:
None

History:
Rich history with links to England. Big connection with writers and artists inspired by its countryside while still being close to Paris. Monet grew up at Le Havre.

Who lives there?
Mainly Parisians with second homes. But the locals at least have a reputation for being friendly.

What do they eat?
As above.

What do they drink?
More Calvados.

What do you do there?

Visit Claude Monet's garden at Giverny.
What does it cost?
As above.
Why is it hot?
Seriously close to London and Paris. Rolling pastures and half-timbered houses.
Why is it not?
Cold in the winter. Not a good place for a bored housewife. Look what happened to Emma Bovary.

Paris and Ile de France
Area:
12,072km²
Population:
Around 11,028,000
Climate:
Temperate
Capital City:
Paris
Departments:
Paris, Essonne, Hauts-de-Seine, Seine-et-Marne, Seine-Saint-Denis, Val-de-Marne, Val-d'Oise, Yvelines
Miles from V&A Museum in London to Paris:
254 Miles
Estimated driving time:
2 hours 34 minutes
Cost of tolls:
£12.14
Where is it?
North, in the middle.
History:
Paris became significant in 987 AD. It became the centre of the French state when Hugues Capet crowned himself king in the 10th century, because it was the only region under his control.
Who lives there?
People from all over the world. And of course from all over France, although my French friend Mark says you go to Paris 'as a last resort if you can't get a job anywhere else'. Mind you, he lives in Exeter, so can we trust his judgement?
What do they eat?
Steak and frites. Eat them in a brasserie on a leafy boulevard.
What do they drink?
Anything you like, you can enjoy the best of France here.
What do you do there?
Where do I start?
Notre Dame, the Eiffel Tower, you know it all by now. If it's your first visit take a walk though the elegant streets and soak up the atmosphere. Outside the city you have splendid countryside and of course Versailles.
What does it cost?
Very expensive in the centre of town and houses rarely come on the market. The best you could hope for would be an apartment.
Why is it hot?
Only the most beautiful city in the world, and one of the most pleasant to live in according to polls in newspapers. The surrounding area is beautiful as well.
Why is it not?
Parisians have a reputation for being incredibly unfriendly. I once overheard a foreigner asking saying to a chic Parisian lady:
'I'm looking for the rue d'Anjou.'
'Well, I hope you find it,' was her

response.

Picardy
Area:
19,399km²
Population:
Around 1,863,500
Climate:
Continental
Capital City:
Amiens
Departments:
Aisne, Oise, Somme
Miles from V&A Museum in London to Amiens:
172
Estimated driving time:
3 hours 55 minutes
Cost of tolls:
£6.59
Where is it?
Between Calais and Paris.
History:
The Battle of the Somme, one of the most poignant names in history. Around 1,353,000 died trying to win some land from the Germans. Also the birthplace of France in 486 when Clovis made Soissons the first capital of the Franks. Later, in 987, Hugues Capet was crowned King of France at Noyon. Amiens has an amazing architectural heritage.
Who lives there?
Who knows? Certainly none of the French people I asked. None of them had ever been there, although they all said Amiens was a nice city.
What do they eat?
Fresh food from market gardens, smoked river eel, cheese, waterfowl and lamb.
What do they drink?
Cider and beer.
What do you do there?
Amiens is known as the Venice of the North (along with Amsterdam) due to its lakes, watergardens and rivers which you can explore in punts. Major literary festivals. There are also 70 kilometres of dunes, cliffs and beaches.
What does it cost?
Not too much, it has been largely ignored by foreign home owners.
Why is it hot?
Very close to England and Paris, lovely countryside, marvellous Gothic cathedrals.
Why is it not?
Wet and flat.

Poitou and Charentes
Area:
25,810 km²
Population:
Around 1,622,800
Climate:
Continental
Capital City:
Poitiers
Departments:
Charente-Maritime, Deux-Sèvres, Vienne.
Miles from V&A Museum in London to Poitiers:
341
Estimated driving time:
8 hours 54 minutes
Cost of tolls:
£7.56
Where is it?
West, between the Loire Valley and

Bordeaux.

History:

Scene of a great English victory in the 100 Years' War in 1356. Also the seat of the Dukes of Aquitaine. Parthenay was on one of the main routes of the pilgrimage to Santiago de Compostela so has a lot of Romanesque churches.

Who lives there?

Insurance brokers. Farmers. This is the middle of nowhere. Not much else to report.

What do they eat?

Fish, lots of oysters, seafood.

What do they drink?

Cognac. This is the centre of the brandy industry.

What do you do there?

Visit Futuroscope, a virtual reality theme park. Also the largest national park and wetland on the western side of France, the Marais Poitevin. If you work in insurance, you could easily get a job in Niort which is the centre of the French insurance industry. Or you could make slippers, a product the region is famous for. Lively resorts such as La Rochelle, Royan and the islands of Oléron, Aix and Ré. Music festival at La Rochelle.

What does it cost?

Getting expensive, especially the area bordering the Dordogne.

Why is it hot?

Supposedly as sunny as Provence on the coast, 2250 hours a year, accord-ing to the tourist office. Good place to live if you like Cognac. Not much rain at all.

Why is it not?

The marshlands, to be avoided.

Provence Alpes/Côte d'Azur

Area:

31,400 km²

Population:

Around 4,452,000

Climate:

Mediterranean in some parts, dry summers overall, humid winters fur-ther inland.

Capital City:

Marseille

Departments:

Alpes-de-Haute-Provence, Hautes-Alpes, Vaucluse, Bouches-du-Rhône, Var, Alpes-Maritimes.

Miles from V&A Museum in London to Marseille:

734

Estimated driving time:

11 hours 39 minutes

Cost of tolls:

£44.11

Where is it?

Down in the south, between the sea and the Alps, pretty convenient.

History:

Marseille is France's oldest city, founded by the Greeks in the 5th Century BC. It was Roman from 49 BC and then under the counts and kings of Provence in the Middle Ages. It became French in 1481. A gateway to North Africa, it has become home to large numbers of immigrants. It has nothing at all in common with the expensive resorts of the Côte d'Azur, which were so popular with the Victorians, the first tourists to visit the region.

What do they eat?

Lots of extremely healthy food; olive oil, fresh vegetables and fruit, fish, *aioli* (garlic mayonnaise), Salade Niçoise, and fish soup (*bouillabaisse*). The Camargue, wild horse and cowboy country, is France's rice-growing region.

What do they drink?

Rosé de Provence, pastis (especially in Marseille), lots of excellent Rhône wines like those made by Jean-Luc Colombo.

What do you do there?

Depending on where you are; pose, eat, drink, chat to celebrities.

Who lives there?

George Michael, Michael Schumacher, Posh and Becks, Elton John, lots of other foreigners as well as some locals although they are becoming a rarity.

What does it cost?

A lot, the prices are equivalent to Paris. Expect to pay €145,000 for a 2 bedroom flat in an old village house in the Var.

Why is it hot?

The place to be. International hotspots like Nikki Beach in St Tropez make this coast the one to be seen on. The rich and famous have been coming here for years. The landscape is stunning, a mix of mountains and coastline.

Why is it not?

Very expensive and built up. Terribly crowded in the summer, it can take you half an hour to get two kilometres in a car. 'Lazy noisy people' according to an anonymous French friend. Danger of running into Elton John.

Midi-Pyrenées

Area:

45,348 km²

Population:

Around 2,505,900

Climate:

Continental hot

Capital City:

Toulouse

Departments:

Ariège, Aveyron, Gers, Haute-Garonne, Lot, Hautes-Pyrenées, Tarn, Tarn-et-Garonne

Miles from V&A Museum in London to Toulouse:

677

Estimated driving time:

10 hours 50 minutes

Cost of tolls:

£31.56

What do they eat?

Celebrated cuisine including *foie gras*, roquefort cheese and the infamous cassoulet which my husband says is a little bit like running across a ploughed field. You start well, but get bogged down towards the end.

What do they drink?

Great local wines including the wonderfully robust Cahors, Fronton and Gaillac. Armagnac is made here.

What do you do there?

Toulouse is a fantastic city with lots going on. It is renowned for its Asian cuisine, something Brits often miss over here. The region is one of the largest in the country and has a landscape of ancient towns, villages, castles, Romanesque churches and colourful history.

Who lives there?

This is *La France Profonde* and expats are not around every corner. Locals have a reputation for being laid-back and good fun. Lots of industry in and around Toulouse, especially in the aerospace sector.

Prices:

The last five years have seen increases. There are still bargains to be had in rural areas.

Why is it hot?

A truly French experience. Easy access to the rest of the world and France via the TGV or airport at Toulouse. An IKEA that is easy to find just outside the city, delivery of Swedish meatballs every Tuesday.

Why is it not?

Bloody cold in the winter. In fact, I was there in April one year and it hailed.

Rhône-Alpes

Area:

43,798 km²

Population:

Around 5,608,200

Climate:

Continental

Capital City:

Lyon

Departments:

Ain, Ardèche, Drôme, Isère, Loire, Rhône, Savoie, Haute-Savoie

Miles from V&A Museum in London to Lyon:

540

Estimated driving time:

8 hours 58 minutes

Cost of tolls:

£30.52

Where is it?

South east, just above Provence.

History:

Gallo-Roman remains, Romanesque art, Renaissance and Medieval sites.

Who lives there?

People with serious jobs in industry, gastronomical enthusiasts and wine makers. The locals are said to be welcoming and full of nice people.

What do they eat?

Anything you want, Lyon has more restaurants per capita than anywhere else in France. Local food predominantly dairy and meat based. Specialities include *quenelles*, fish or meat dumplings. Lyon is also known for its calf's and sheep's feet. Bresse chicken is a must, patriotic chickens with blue legs, white feathers and red crests.

What do they drink?

Beaujolais, Côte du Rhône and rather more expensive Châteauneuf du Pape.

What do you do there?

This is a vast region with much to offer. Lyon is very industrialised, over 80 per cent of the population is involved in some kind of industry. In terms of holidays, you eat, drink, eat some more then maybe visit one of the famous sites like the Gorges de l'Ardèche.

What does it cost?

The prices vary enormously. The Ardèche is particularly popular with

Brits but there are still some bargains to be had.

Why is it hot?

So much to do, so much variety,
Lyon is now France's second largest
city. The countryside is marvellous,
endless lavender fields, lakes, and
Mont Blanc, Europe's highest peak.

Why is it not?

The spaghetti junction around Lyon.
You haven't lived until you've got
lost there. Also the industry. Lyon is
not a place to come to live the
French rural idyll.

Useful Addresses

Places to stay
Peter and Lizie Wildman www.holi-day-rentals.com/ index.cfm/property/10037.cfm
Jill Allcroft www.holiday-rentals.com/index.cfm/ property/7257, www.esbayles.com
Alan and Penny Hastings-Jones tel: +33 (0) 4 67 24 78 99
Fiona and Bruno De Wulf, Château de Créancey, www.creancey.com
Gavin and Angela Quinney, Château Bauduc, www.bauduc.com
Fiona Cantwell and Tony Archibold, Château de Marcenac, www.chateaumarcenac.com, fiona@chateaumarcenac.com

Advice and Professionals
Dawn Alderson, solicitor and avocat, partner with Russell Cooke Solicitors, aldersond@russell-cooke.co.uk, tel: +44 (0) 20 8789 9111
Bill Blevins, Blevins Franks International, www.blevinsfranks.com, tel: +44 (0) 20 7336 1116
Tony Tidswell, www.frenchproper-tydigest.comwww.1stvacations.com
Marcelle Speller, www.Holiday-Rentals.com, marcelle@holiday-rentals.com, tel: +44 (0) 20 8743 5577, fax: +44 (0) 20 8740 3863
Richaed Allcroft allcroftrchrd@aol.com (builder)
Kris Misselbrook www.french-property.com/aurignac, tel: +33 (0) 5 61 98 86 92
Paul Beaufils, www.buyahousein-france.com
Jeffrey Quirk, JQ International, tel: +33 (0) 6 87 83 07 58
John Siddall Financial Services Ltd, www.siddalls.net, tel: 01329 288 641, fax: 01329 281 157, jenny@johnsiddalls.co.uk
Pat Bellis, patbellis@wanadoo.fr

Wine contacts and makers
Charles & Ruth Simpson, tel: +33 (0) 4 67 39 07 54, crsimpson@sainte-rose.com, www.sainte-rose.com
Ruth de Latude, www.baronnie-de-bourgade.com (Ruth now does wine courses as well)
Jean-Claude Mas,

www.paulmas.com
Helen Genevier and Julie Statham,
www.picwines.co.uk,
info@picwines.co.uk, tel: +33 (0) 4
99 62 09 27
Gregory Guida, Saint Martin de la
Garrigue,
www.stmartingarrigue.com

Miscellaneous
Alistair Norman, www.upright-
tours.co.uk
Helen Goossens
merton@dircon.co.uk
Stephanie Godwin (dog breeder),
tel/fax: +33 (0) 2 43 03 20 94, god-
winsj-aron@netcourrier.com
www.parsonrussellterrier.com
Teddy Hutton and Nicola Russell,
La Maison Verte, www.lamaison-
verte.co.uk, tel: +33 (0) 4 67 24 88
52, fax: +33 (0) 4 67 24 69 98

Schools
A list of International Schools in
France and contact details (with
thanks to www.frenchentree.com)

Bordeaux International School
53 rue de Laseppe, 33000,
Bordeaux, France
Tel: +33 (0) 5 57 87 02 11
bis@bordeaux-school.com
www.bordeaux-school.com

CIV International School of Sophia
Antipolis
BP 097, 06902, Sophia Antipolis,
France
Tel: +33 (0) 4 92 96 52 24
secretary@civissa.org
www.civissa.org

Mougins School
615 Avenue Dr Maurice Donat,
Font de l'Orme, BP 401 Cedex,
06250, Mougins, France
Tel: +33 (0) 4 93 90 15 47
information@mougins-school.com
www.mougins-school.com

British School of Paris
38 Quai de l'Ecluse, 78290, Croissy-
sur-Seine, France
Tel: +33 (0) 1 34 80 45 94
bspprincipal@wanadoo.fr
www.ecis.org/bsp

College International De
Fontainebleau
Anglophone Section, 48 rue Guerin,
77300, Fontainebleau, France
Tel: +33 (0) 1 64 22 11 77
admin@anglophonesection-
fontainebleau.com
www.anglophonesection-
fontainebleau.com

Ecole Active Bilingue Jeannine
Manuel—Ecole Internationale de
Lille Métropole
418 bis rue Albert Bailly, 59700,
Marcq-en-Baroeul, France
Tel: +33 (0) 3 20 65 90 50
v.leroy@eabjm.com

Ecole Bilingue Greenfield
14 rue da la Mairie, 69660,
Collonges-au-Mont-d'Or, France
Tel: +33 (0) 4 72 27 87 80
greenfield@wanadoo.fr
www.greenfield.fr

Cité Scolaire Internationale Lyon
Section Anglophone, 2 Place de
Montréal, 69361, Lyon, Cedex 07,

France
Tel: +33 (0) 4 78 69 60 06
donnamp@wanadoo.fr
www2.ac-lyon.fr/etab/lycees/lyc-
69/csi/accueil.html

The American School of Lyon
80 chemin du Grand Roule, 69110
Ste Foy les Lyon, Lyon, France
Tel: +33 (0) 4 78 50 44 00
info@tasol.org
www.tasol.org

International School of Bearn
Rue des Fougeres, Quartier
Berlanne, 64160, Morlaas, France
Tel: +33 (0) 6 12 56 68 67
isbearn@wanadoo.fr
site.voila.fr/isbearn

The International School of Nice
15 Avenue Claude Debussy, 06200,
Nice, France
Tel: +33 (0) 4 93 21 04 00
dorothy.foster@cote-azur.cci.fr

American School of Paris
41 rue Pasteur, 92210, Saint Cloud,
France
Tel: +33 (0) 1 41 12 82 82
mcalon@asparis.org
www.asparis.org

Ecole Active Bilingue
Boulevard Malesherbes 117, 75008,
Paris, France
Tel: +33 (0) 1 45 00 11 57
infovh@eab.fr
www.eab.fr

Ecole Active Bilingue Jeannine
Manuel
70 rue du Théâtre, 75015, Paris,

France
Tel: +33 (0) 1 44 37 00 80
reception@eabjm.com
www.eabjm.com

Eurécole
5 rue de Lübeck, 75116, Paris,
France
Tel: +33 (0) 1 40 70 12 81
direction@eurecole.com
www.eurecole.com

International School of Paris
6 rue Beethoven, 75016, Paris,
France
Tel: +33 (0) 1 42 24 09 54
info@isparis.edu
www.isparis.edu

Lycée de Sevres, International
Sections
7 rue Lecocq, 92310, Sevres, France
Tel: +33 (0) 1 46 23 96 35
association.sis@wanadoo.fr
www.sis-sevres.net

Marymount School
72 bd de la Saussaye, 92200, Neuilly
sur Seine, France
Tel: +33 (0) 1 46 24 10 51
school@ecole-marymount.fr
www.ecole-marymount.fr

United Nations Nursery School
40 rue Pierre Guerin, 75016, Paris,
France
Tel: +33 (0)1 45 27 20 24
unns@noos.fr
www.unns.net
Lycée International of St Germain-
en-Laye (American Section)
Rue du Fer a Cheval BP 5230,
78175, St Germain-en-Laye, France

Tel: +33 (0) 1 34 51 74 85
american.intl@wanadoo.fr
www.lycee-intl-american.org

Strasbourg International School
Château de Pourtales, 161 rue
Mélanie, Robertsau, 67000,
Strasbourg, France
Tel: +33 (0) 3 88 31 50 77
info@strasbourgis.org
www.strasbourgis.org

International School of Toulouse
S.A.
Route de Pibrac, 31770, Colomiers,
France
Tel: +33 (0) 5 62 74 26 74
ist@intst.net
www.intst.net